COMPULSION AND RESTITUTION

THE STAIR SOCIETY

COMPULSION AND RESTITUTION

A historical and comparative study of the treatment of compulsion in Scottish private law with particular emphasis on its relevance to the law of restitution or unjustified enrichment

JACQUES ETIENNE DU PLESSIS

EDINBURGH
THE STAIR SOCIETY
2004

Published by The Stair Society

First published 2004

ISBN 1 872517 17 X

British Library Cataloguing-in-Publication Data

A catalogue record for this book is available from the British Library

Typeset in Goudy by Waverley Typesetters, Galashiels
Printed and bound in Great Britain by The Bath Press

Contents

Chapter 4

COMPULSION IN MODERN SCOTS LAW

Chapter 5

COMPULSION IN ROMAN-DUTCH, SOUTH AFRICAN, AND GERMAN LAW

Chapter 6

AN EVALUATION OF THE TREATMENT OF COMPULSION IN MODERN SCOTS LAW

Chapter 7

COMPULSION AND THE TAXONOMY OF THE SCOTS LAW OF UNJUSTIFIED ENRICHMENT

Table of Cases

Scotland

England

South Africa

Sri Lanka

United States of America

Germany

List of Abbreviations

§	Section of the BGB
A	South African Law Reports, Appellate Division (1947–1996)
ADA	Acta Dominorum Auditorum in Civil Causes and Complaints (1466–1494)
APS	Acts of the Parliaments of Scotland (1124–1707)
ADC	Acts of the Lords of Council
AS	Act of Sederunt (Sc)
AC	Law reports, Appeal Cases (Eng)
AD	Appellate Division Reports (1910–1946) (South African)
Afr	Africanus
AJ	Acting Judge
AJA	Acting Judge of Appeal
All ER	All England Law Reports
App Cas	Law Reports Appeal Cases, House of Lords
BGB	Bürgerliches Gesetzbuch (German Civil Code)
BGH	Bundesgerichtshof (German Federal Court)
BGHZ	Entscheidungen des Bundesgerichtshofs in Zivilsachen (Decisions of the German Federal Court in civil matters)
Burr	Burrow's King's Bench Reports
C	Codex Iustinianus; South African Law Reports, Cape Provincial Division (1947–)
CT	Cape Times Reports (1891–1910) (Cape Supreme Court)
CA	Court of Appeals (Eng)
Call	Callistratus
Cels	Celsus
Ch	Law Reports, Chancery Division (Eng)
CILSA	*The Comparative and International Law Journal of Southern Africa*
CJ	Chief Justice
CLJ	Cambridge Law Journal
CLP	Current Legal Problems
CPD	Cape Provincial Division Reports (1910–1946) (South African)
CT	Codex Theodosianus
D	Digest of Justinian
ed	editor, edition
EDL	Easter District Local Division Reports (1910–1946) (South African)
EdinLR	*Edinburgh Law Review*
Exch	Exchequer Reports (Eng)
F	Fraser, Session Cases (Sc)
FC	Faculty Collection
fn	footnote
Gai	Gaius
Guthrie	Guthrie's Sheriff Court Cases (Scot)
HM	Her/His Majesty('s)
H & N	Hurlstone & Norman's Exchequer Reports (Eng)

HL	House of Lords
Inst	Institutes of Justinian
ICR	Industrial Cases Reports
J	Judge
JA	Judge of Appeal
JC	Justiciary Cases
JLS	*Journal of the Law Society of Scotland*
JP	Judge President
JR	*Juridical Review*
KB	Law Reports, King's Bench Division (Eng)
LR	Law Reports (Eng)
Lloyd's Rep	Lloyd's List Law Reports (Eng)
LQR	*The Law Quarterly Review*
LMCLQ	*Lloyd's Maritime and Commercial Law Quarterly*
M	Macpherson's Session Cases (Sc)
MLR	The Modern Law Review
Mod	Modestinus
Mor	Morison's Dictionary of Decisions in the Court of Session 1540–1808
Mor Sup	Morison's Dictionary of Court of Session Decisions 1620–1768
M & G	Manning and Granger's English Common Pleas Reports
M & W	Meeson & Welsby's Exchequer Reports (1836–1847; Eng)
MR	Master of the Rolls
N	South African Law Reports, Natal Provincial Division (1947–)
n	note
NLR	Natal Law Reports (1867–1932) (South African)
OJLS	*Oxford Journal of Legal Studies*
OR	Official Reports (Transvaal, 1894–1898) (South African)
Pap	Papinianus
Paton	Paton's Appeal Cases, (Scot)
Paul	Paulus
Paul Sent	Pauli Sententiae
PC	Judicial Committee of the Privy Council
Pomp	Pomponius
QB	Law Reports, Queen's Bench Division (Eng)
R	Rettie's Session Cases (Sc); South African Law Reports, Rhodesia
RGZ	Entscheidungen des Reichtsgerichts in Zivilsachen
RLR	*Restitution Law Review*
Robert App	Robertson's Scotch Appeal Cases (Sc)
S	Shaw, Session Cases (Sc)
SA	South African Law Reports (1947–)
SALJ	*South African Law Journal*
SC	Session Cases (Sc); Cape Supreme Court Reports (1880–1910)
Sc	Scottish/Scots
SCCR	Scottish Criminal Case Reports
SCLR	Scottish Civil Law Reports
Sh Ct Rep	Sheriff Court Reports 1885–1963 (Sc)
SJZ	*Süddeutsche Juristenzeitung*
SLPQ	*Scottish Law and Practice Quarterly*
SLR	Scottish Law Reporter
SLT	Scots Law Times

SLT (News)	Scots Law Times—News
SLT (Notes)	Scots Law Times—Notes
SLT (Land Ct)	Scots Law Times—Land Court
SLT (Sh Ct)	Scots Law Times—Sheriff Court Reports
SME	*The Laws of Scotland: Stair Memorial Encyclopaedia*
T	South African Law Reports, Transvaal Provincial Division (1947–)
TLR	Times Law Reports
TR	Durnford & East's Term Reports (Eng)
Taunt	Taunton's Common Pleas reports (1808–1819)
THRHR	*Tydskrif vir Hedendaagse Romeins-Hollandse Reg* (South African)
TPD	Transvaal Provincial Division Reports (1910–1946) (South African)
TS	Transvaal Supreme Court Reports (1902–1909)
TSAR	*Tydskrif vir die Suid-Afrikaanse Reg* (South African)
Tulane LR	*Tulane Law Review*
Ulp	Ulpianus
W	South African Law Reports, Witwatersrand Local Division (1947–)
W & S	Wilson & Shaw's Appeal Cases House of Lords (Scot)
WLD	Witwatersrand Local Division Reports (1910–1946) (South African)
WLR	Weekly law reports (Eng)
ZEuP	*Zeitschrift für Europäisches Privatrecht*
ZSS (RA)	*Zeitschrift der Savigny-Stiftung für Rechtsgeschichte (Romanistische Abteilung)*

Preface

This thesis was presented for the degree of Doctor of Philosophy at the University of Aberdeen in 1997. A number of notable developments relating to its main arguments have taken place in the mean time. I am grateful for the opportunity to deal with these matters briefly in this preface.

In 1997 the three Rs of restitution, repetition and recompense were still dominant features of the Scottish enrichment landscape.[1] In the thesis it was argued that this was an unsatisfactory division, especially in the light of its problematic historical development.[2] However, now that the House of Lords has placed its seal of approval on regarding the redressing of the unjustified enrichment as the ultimate aim of these remedies,[3] and the Court of Session has held that they essentially only relate to different ways in which enrichment could arise,[4] the significance of the three Rs has been reduced drastically. Scots law is now much freer than before to adopt approaches and divisions that describe positively what events or circumstances give rise to the enrichment liability. This suggests a heightened relevance of attempts to provide such descriptions. Hopefully this is also true of the attempts in this thesis to delineate more clearly the boundaries between various constructs—more specifically the *condictiones*—that deal with enrichment arising from compulsion.[5] In this way, greater meaning could then be given to the key elements of enrichment liability, and especially the "absence of a legal ground" requirement.[6]

A further notable development, apart from that of the movement away from the three Rs in Scots law, relates to the unjust factors approach to enrichment liability. According to this approach, compulsion is regarded as one of a variety of 'unjust factors' that trigger a restitutionary response. In the thesis it was pointed out that cracks were appearing in the facade of the unjust factors approach, since there were indications that English courts decided certain cases in a way more compatible with the notion of the absence of a legal ground than with an analysis which makes use of unjust factors.[7] Recently, in a courageous and far-reaching re-assessment of the

---

1 See para 7.2.3.i below.

2 See especially ch 7; further see R Evans-Jones and P Hellwege, "Some observations on the taxonomy of unjustified enrichment in Scots law" (1998) 2 *EdinLR* 180.

3 *Dollar Land (Cumbernauld) Ltd v CIN Properties Ltd* 1998 SC 90 (HL) (per Lord Hope of Craighead); also see his earlier decision in *Morgan Guaranty Trust Company of New York v Lothian Regional Council* 1995 SC 151.

4 *Shilliday v Smith* 1998 SC 725 (per Lord Rodger of Earlsferry).

5 See 7.3.1.ii(b), 7.3.2. In *Shilliday v Smith* 1998 SC 725 the "labelling" function of the *condictiones* was recognised (see 727D–F; 728D); however, the extent to which reference to the *condictiones* in the case reflects a preference for a modern civilian style of approach to enrichment liability is disputed (the various interpretations are set out in part 4.2 of J E du Plessis, "Towards a rational structure of liability for unjustified enrichment: Thoughts from two mixed jurisdictions", which is to be published in the proceedings of the 29th Biennial Conference on Comparative Law, hosted by the German Association for Comparative Law in Dresden on 17 September 2003).

6 Lord Hope of Craighead has explicitly stated in *Dollar Land* that enrichment should lack a legal ground (at 98H–I). On the centrality of this notion in structuring enrichment liability, further see the paper referred to in note 5 above.

7 See 7.2.3.ii below (esp text to note 138).

state of the common law of restitution or unjust enrichment, Professor Peter Birks has acknowledged that the swaps cases[8] are best explained by a short "no basis" approach, rather than by trying to massage unjust factors to reach a similar result.[9] In particular, it is significant that he has recognised that after the swaps cases there was "all along nothing special" about *Woolwich Equitable Building Society v Inland Revenue Commissioners*.[10] As argued in the thesis,[11] it was simply a payment made to discharge a non-existent debt. It can therefore easily be accommodated under an "absence of basis" approach.[12]

The third development relates to the manner in which the law of unjustified enrichment could be developed. Both in Scotland and South Africa, the highest courts recently have displayed a marked awareness of the need for a more principled development of the law of unjustified enrichment. In the South African context this has been reflected by the willingness expressed by the Supreme Court of Appeal in *McCarthy Retail Ltd v Shortdistance Carriers CC*[13] to recognise a general enrichment action judicially if an appropriate case arises. In the Scottish context, cases like *Dollar Land (Cumbernauld) Ltd v CIN Properties Ltd*[14] and *Shilliday v Smith*[15] have, as the Scottish Law Commission put it, "restructured the law of unjustified enrichment".[16] These developments indicate what can be achieved by progressive, but historically sensitive, judicial reform. While some may still believe that the law is so unsettled that major legislative reform is required, the path of incremental judicial development now seems much more attractive. But a considerable amount of work still needs to be done to make the best of these new opportunities—especially by academic lawyers.[17] No doubt in these, as in many other matters, the valuable dialogue that exists between mixed legal systems will continue to grow.

Apart from these general remarks, it can be mentioned that some of the themes in the thesis have also been dealt with in more recent publications. These are:

- J E du Plessis, "Force and Fear", in K Reid and R Zimmermann (eds), *A History of Private Law in Scotland* (Oxford, 2000), ch 4, which essentially is a summary of the historical part of the thesis;

---

8 See *Kleinwort Benson Ltd v Lincoln CC* [1999] 2 AC 349 (HL).

9 *Unjust Enrichment* (2003), 98.

10 1993 AC 70 (HL).

11 See 6.3.3, 7.2.4.ii below (esp text to notes 138–142).

12 *Unjust Enrichment*, 119. The fact that it is not necessary to resort to compulsion as an unjust factor does not mean that it is irrelevant when dealing with enrichment claims—here it is of interest that, as the thesis indicates in the civil law context, Birks recognised that in the common law context compulsion could influence the application of a defence (see the remarks in *Unjust Enrichment*, 217 on the relevance of pressure in applying the defence of illegality, and compare them to the text to note 274 under 7.3.2.ii below; on the relevance of compulsion in reclaiming with the *condictio indebiti*, see esp 7.4.3.i below and part 4.2 in the paper referred to at note 5 above, which contains a more detailed analysis of the exact conditions under which recovery of undue payments should be barred, as well of the instruments that could be used towards this purpose.

13 2001 (3) SA 482 (A) at paras [8] to [11].

14 1998 SC 90 (HL).

15 1998 SC 725.

16 Report on Unjustified Enrichment, Error of Law and Public Authority Receipts and Disbursements (Scot Law Com No 169, 1999), para 5.15.

17 For a notable recent exposition of the Scots law of unjustified enrichment, which clearly reflects the movement away from the three R taxonomy, see H L MacQueen, "Unjustified Enrichment", in C Ashton et al, *Fundamentals of Scots Law* (2003), ch 8; the adoption of comparable structures has been advocated by Niall Whitty. See further also Robin Evans-Jones, *Unjustified Enrichment Volume 1: Enrichment by Deliberate Conferral: Condictio* (2003).

- J du Plessis, "Fraud, duress and unjustified enrichment: a civil law perspective" in D Johnston and R Zimmermann (eds), *Unjustified Enrichment—Key Issues in Comparative Perspective* (Cambridge, 2002) 194, which compares modern approaches to the effect of duress and fraud, with particular emphasis on the significance of the due/not due distinction;
- J E du Plessis and R Zimmermann, "The Relevance of Reverence; Undue Influence Civilian Style" 10 *Maastricht Journal* 4 (2003) 1–34, which provides a historical overview of *metus reverentialis* and its relationship to undue influence; and
- J du Plessis and W W McBryde, *Defects of Consent*, in K Reid, D Visser and R Zimmermann (eds), *Mixed Legal Systems in Comparative Perspective: Property and Obligations in Scotland and South Africa* (forthcoming, Oxford University Press, 2004) 117–142, which inter alia deals with the consequences of force and fear or duress in these mixed legal systems; part 7 of the article highlights the need for further analysis of the voidness/voidability distinction.[18]

Dr Ernest Metzger also kindly has included the chapter on compulsion in Roman law in the Roman Law Resources website (http://www,iuscivile.com/). A further publication that may be of particular interest to the Scottish legal historian is an analysis of the well-known force and fear case of *Earl of Orkney v Vinfra*[19] by Professor Angelo Forte, which is due to appear in a forthcoming Miscellany publication from the Stair Society.

In the acknowledgements to the thesis I thanked the following institutions and people, and I would like to make use of this opportunity to do so again:

- The Rotary Foundation, C B Davidson Fund, Harry Crossley Fund and Centre for Science Development, for their financial support;
- Mr Denis Daun, who acted as Rotary counsellor, for his encouragement and hospitality during my stay in Aberdeen;
- The law librarians of the Universities of Aberdeen, Stellenbosch, Cape Town and Regensburg, for their assistance in obtaining research material;
- Professor Niall R Whitty, Professor Reinhard Zimmermann, Professor Gerhard Lubbe, Dr Martin Bauer and Mr David Sellar, for valuable advice;

and especially,

- Professor Robin Evans-Jones, who supervised the thesis, for his unfailing interest, encouragement and guidance.

Finally, I am indebted to Myra Craven for her assistance in editing the thesis for purposes of publication.

Jacques du Plessis
Stellenbosch, September 2004

---

18 See 6.3.3.i below.

19 (1606) Mor 16481. See 3.2.1.i, note 22 below.

Chapter 1

Introduction

Freedom of action, one of the most basic legal values, is violated when a person is subjected to compulsion.[1] It is therefore essential that the law should not only provide deterrents against compulsion, but also provide victims with appropriate relief. However, a distinction needs to be drawn between compulsion which justifies providing relief, and compulsion which simply should be accepted as a feature of daily life.[2] The problem of determining where the line between these categories should be drawn has for centuries been the subject of legal analysis. Its solution has not been made easier by the constant shifts in the views of society: what earlier was regarded as an idle or subtle threat, not worthy of any notice, could later on be regarded as an unacceptable practice, which needs to be counteracted. In modern times, this is particularly true about certain threats of economic harm. But it is not only difficult to determine what forms of compulsion are unacceptable. Once this has been established, the question remains as to what the most appropriate form of relief would be. Where the wrongdoer is guilty of criminal conduct, he should of course be punished in accordance with criminal law, but this may not be sufficient. Where the victim either obligated himself towards the wrongdoer, or transferred something to him, the victim may require further relief—especially from private law in the form of a declaration that a compelled act is invalid, or an order that what was obtained under compulsion should be returned. It can then be a matter of some difficulty to determine which forms of compulsion give rise to these remedies and what the appropriate basis and measure of the relief should be.

This thesis deals with the treatment of compulsion in Scottish private law, and particularly the law of "restitution" or unjustified enrichment.[3] Its primary focus will be on the two problems identified above, namely to determine to what extent compulsion can either be the ground for certain private law remedies, or at least influence their availability, and also to determine the exact nature of such relief. These problems will then be dealt with in the context of Scottish private law in

---

1 See e.g. Ulp D 50.17.116 pr ("nothing is as opposed to consent as force and fear"; F C von Savigny, *System des heutigen Römischen Rechts* (1840) vol 3, 99 ("force is the opposite of freedom"). On the question whether compelled acts should be regarded as voluntary, see 2.1, 3.3.1.i(a) and 6.3.1.iii below (especially the discussion of Paul D 4.2.21.5). The influence of compulsion has interested philosophers through the ages (cf Aristotle, *Nicomachean Ethics*, III 1; T Hobbes, *Leviathan* (1651), ch 14; for more recent philosophical perspectives cf M Philips, "Are Coerced Agreements Involuntary?" (1984) 3 *Law and Philosophy* 133; A Wertheimer, *Coercion* (1987), 3 et sqq; T Honoré, "A Theory of Coercion" (1990) 10 *OJLS* 94;).

2 See P Birks, *An Introduction to the Law of Restitution* (1985, revised 1989), 173 et sq ("[t]he law should not yield unthinkingly to the instinct in favour of relief for compulsion"; it should be noted, though, that he uses the word compulsion in a broad sense—see 7.3.1.i below).

3 It is therefore not concerned with the relevance of compulsion to criminal and criminal procedural law, where certain forms of compulsion can amount to crimes, give rise to defences (such as coercion or necessity), or affect the validity of confessions and witness statements.

general, but particular attention will be paid to relief in the form of remedies based on unjustified enrichment aimed at the recovery[4] of compelled transfers. The reason for this emphasis is that there is currently great uncertainty as to the basis on which Scots law provides relief in cases of unjustified enrichment. In essence, there are two main approaches to the subject, and Scots law faces a choice between taking either, or a combination of them, as its guiding force. The first approach, which developed in the context of the English Common Law, requires proof of an "unjust factor" to obtain recovery. It looks at an enrichment claim from the standpoint of the claimant, and asks whether he can advance any "unjust factor" which entitles him to recovery. The second approach, that of the Civil Law, bases recovery on the notion of retention without legal ground. This approach looks at an enrichment claim from the standpoint of the recipient, and asks on what basis he is entitled to retain what he received. Here the mere fact that a transfer is not due in principle renders its retention unjustified. The debate as to which of these approaches, or variations of them, are most suited to modern Scots law has only begun, but there has already been considerable discussion of the precise cause of action represented by the *condictio indebiti,* which traditionally has been regarded as a remedy for the recovery of undue transfers made in error as to liability. Views on the essential features of this remedy differ drastically: to the proponents of the unjust factors approach, it is primarily concerned with the recovery of transfers made in error, which is regarded as one such an "unjust factor". Others again, who support a civilian approach, stress the fact that where a transfer is in any event not due, it is already retained without legal ground, and in principle should be recoverable on that basis alone. Compulsion is susceptible to similar analysis. It could either be regarded as an "unjust factor", and therefore the basis for an enrichment remedy, or it could be regarded merely as a factor which is incidental to the recovery of a transfer which, if it is not due in any event, is held without legal ground. Unfortunately, unlike the transfer made in error as to liability, the transfer made in compulsion has thus far not received the attention it deserves. This is regrettable if one takes into account the number of transactions and acts of fulfillment or payment which take place daily under pain of the threat of some form of harm. It is then submitted that a process of evaluation, similar to that of the transfer made in error, is required to determine the relevance of compulsion within the broader context of the Scots law of unjustified enrichment.

For the purposes of this book, compulsion will be defined as the improper application of harm or threats thereof in order to induce a person into an act or omission. Although the term "compulsion" is occasionally referred to in Scottish private law, it is not a concept of particular technical significance, and the choice of this definition is primarily motivated by the need to remain as faithful as possible to the basic sense in which it is used in Scots law, namely as a description of "force and fear" and related cases.[5] This means that it covers a spectrum of cases ranging from

---

4 The word "recovery" will be used throughout in the sense of the regaining or redressing of enrichment, and not necessarily the physical recovery of a specific object.

5 Cf Recovery of Benefits Conferred under Error of law (Scot Law Com DP No 95, 1993), vol 2, 201 et sqq; Stair, *Institutions*, 1.9.8; Bankton, *Institute,* 1.10.50. "Compulsion" is therefore regarded as distinct from terms such as "duress" (which is mainly used in English law to describe an area of law related to compulsion in the form of "force and fear" in Scots law), "coercion" (which is popular in American law and can cover duress and undue influence, but excludes inequality of bargaining power: cf Wertheimer, *Coercion*, 3 et sqq; Honoré, "A Theory of Coercion" (1990) 10 *OJLS* 94), and "extortion" (which in Scots law has been used synonymously with force and fear, but also encompasses a broader category of obtaining an advantage from another, most notably through improperly obtaining consent (cf 6.21.i below)).

serious compulsion in the form of actual and threatened physical harm, which was symptomatic of the turbulent social conditions which characterised early Scottish history, to milder cases of compulsion, which are more relevant in modern times. Examples of the latter are threats to breach a contract, withhold goods, terminate provision of a service, or possibly even implied threats inherent in ultra vires demands by public authorities. In Scots law, the rules which deal with compulsion in the sense defined above are scattered over the legal landscape, but are mainly to be found in cases dealing with claims for reduction on grounds of force and fear, and claims for restitution, repetition, or simply "recovery", based on the unjustified enrichment of the recipient at the expense of the person subjected to compulsion. In this context reference is occasionally made to remedies referred to as *condictiones* (of which the *condictio indebiti* referred to above is a prominent example), which are then "represented" by actions of restitution and repetition. Unfortunately many of the rules relating to compulsion are unclear and the subject of considerable dispute, not least of which are the rules relating to the *condictiones*. As far as force and fear is concerned, it is disputed whether the basis of relief is the "overbearing" of a person's will, or rather inducing a decision of will through improper methods. It also has to be determined whether the victim really should display "constancy" or resoluteness, and whether there is sufficient accommodation of compulsion through threats of economic harm. The effect of force and fear is also disputed: it has to be resolved whether it gives rise to voidness or voidability, and whether transfers obtained as a consequence of force and fear are recoverable with remedies based on contract or unjustified enrichment. As far as the law relating to cases of compulsion which cannot be brought home under force and fear is concerned, uncertainty prevails as to whether claims for repetition or restitution should be awarded, and if so, which of the *condictiones* these claims would represent. In this regard, reference has been made to the *condictio indebiti*, the *condictio ob turpem vel iniustam causam*, which is based on the immorality or unlawfulness of the receipt of the compelled transfer, and the *condictio sine causa specialis*, which is a residual remedy.

It is submitted that a lot of the uncertainty and controversy as to the content and effect of the remedies in Scots law dealing with compulsion can be ascribed to a lack of appreciation of their background, and that this can be overcome by placing them in their proper historical and comparative setting.[6] In the first three chapters, the foundations of the modern law will be examined, and particular emphasis will be placed on its Roman or civilian foundations (especially the rules relating to *vis et metus* and the *condictiones*). Thereafter, the reception of these rules in medieval law will be dealt with, as well as their subsequent development at the hands of the courts and the Institutional writers. This will be followed by an examination of developments during the nineteenth and twentieth century, most notably the influence of the Common Law, which contributed to the "mixed" character of modern Scots law. With a view towards evaluating the existing law, the focus will then turn to related rules in comparable systems, most notably South African law, which shares the civilian foundations, but also bears the imprint of Common Law influence, and German law, which represents a continuation of the civilian tradition. Against this background, the final two chapters will evaluate the existing law: in the

---

6 In the words of Lord Kames, "When we enter upon the municipal law of any country in its present state we resemble a traveler, who crossing the Delta, loses his way among the numberless branches of the Egyptian river. But when we begin at the source and follow the current of law . . . all its relations and dependencies are traced with no greater difficulty, than are the many streams into which that magnificent river is divided before it is lost in the sea" (*Historical Law Tracts* (1758), vol 1, ix–x).

penultimate chapter the focus will be more on the content and effect of compulsion (especially through force and fear) within the context of the law of contract, while the final chapter will concentrate on the law of unjustified enrichment. Various approaches to this area of law will then be analysed in terms of their treatment of the recoverability of compelled transfers, and certain proposals will be made as to the most suitable model for Scots law.

Chapter 2

Compulsion in Roman law

2.1 INTRODUCTION[1]

Ancient Roman law was formal in the sense that it preferred at times not to look behind the external manifestations of a legal act in order to determine its validity.[2] The significance of this approach for compelled acts was later encapsulated in a famous phrase by Paulus:

> If I have entered upon an inheritance whilst compelled by fear, I believe that I become heir, because, although I would have declined if I had a free choice, when compelled I still had the will to do it. (Si metu coactus adii hereditatem, puto me heredem effici, quia quamvis si liberum esset noluissem, tamen coactus volui).[3]

Thus, the mere fact that an heir was "compelled by fear" did not imply that he could dispute the validity of his formal decision to accept the inheritance. He exercised his will in making a choice and was bound by it. As Paulus would say, "voluntas coacta tamen voluntas est". It was only in the case of agreements such as *emptio venditio* and *locatio conductio*, which were enforced by *bonae fidei* actions, that the judge had authority to provide relief. He could take anything which relates to good faith into account when he made his judgment, and here the presence of *metus* or duress was obviously relevant. A person attempting to enforce an agreement concluded under compulsion could be defeated by an *exceptio metus*, which was inherent in *bonae fidei iudicia*.[4] Agreements such as the *stipulatio*, on the other hand, were not enforced by *bonae fidei* actions, but by actions which came to be termed *stricti iuris*. Here the judge's hands were tied: he was only able to take into account that which was provided for in the *formula*, and if nothing could be said about *metus*, he was powerless to provide relief.[5] Reform was needed, and the ideal vehicle for such reform

---

1 Cf, generally, Von Lübtow, *Der Ediktstitel "Quod metus causa gestum erit"*; Hartkamp, *Der Zwang im römischen Privatrecht*; Schulz, "Die Lehre vom erzwungenen Rechtsgeschäft im antiken römischen Recht" (1922) 43 *ZSS (RA)* 171; Schulz, *Classical Roman Law*, 600 et sqq; Levy, "Zur nachklassischen in integrum restitutio" (1951) 68 *ZSS (RA)* 360 at 398; Kupisch, *In integrum restitutio und vindicatio utilis bei Eigentumsübertragungen im klassischen römischen Recht*, 123 *passim*; Kaser, "Zur in integrum restitutio, besonders wegen metus und dolus" (1977) 94 *ZSS (RA)* 101 at 123, Kaser, *Das römische Privatrecht I*, 227, 242. For an introductory overview see Zimmermann, *The Law of Obligations*, 651 et sqq.

2 Cf Kaser, *Das römische Privatrecht I*, 227, 242; Buckland, *A Text-book of Roman Law from Augustus to Justinian*, 416.

3 Paul D 4.2.21.5. For a detailed analysis of this text, which deals with the possibility that it could have been interpolated, cf Hartkamp, *Der Zwang im römischen Privatrecht*, 84 et sqq.

4 Cf Kaser, *Das römische Privatrecht I*, 244, 488; Nicholas, *An Introduction to Roman law*, 176. If the defendant proved fraud or duress he could also reduce the damages awarded to the plaintiff without wholly absolving the defendant (cf Pap D 19.1.41; Thomas, *Textbook of Roman Law*, 228).

5 Cf Kaser, *Das römische Privatrecht I*, 245, note 31; Thomas, *Textbook of Roman Law*, 228; Nicholas, *An Introduction to Roman Law*, 163, 176; Buckland, *A Text-book of Roman Law from Augustus to Justinian*, 416 et sq, 679 et sqq.

was the praetor. In this chapter the focus primarily will be on the way in which the praetor reformed the civil law by providing the *actio quod metus causa* and *in integrum restitutio* (*propter metum*) to the victim of compulsion. Attention will also be paid to certain other forms of relief to which the victim was entitled, namely remedies of property law and a particular *stricti iuris* action of the law of obligations called the *condictio*. In examining these developments certain problem areas will be identified, and it will also be sought to become familiar with certain basic concepts which relate to the law of *metus* in its later stages of development.

2.2 COMPULSION AND THE REMEDIES BASED ON *METUS*

2.2.1 *The* formula Octaviana

The first reform aimed at remedying the inability of the *ius civile* to provide adequate relief on grounds of *metus* was the inclusion of the *formula Octaviana* in the praetor's Edict at about 71 BC.[6] Unfortunately, not much is known about this *formula*. Two texts of Cicero indicate that it dealt with "auferre per vim aut metum" or "auferre per vim et metum",[7] but these records are somewhat cryptic and inconsistent. A major problem with the Ciceronian texts is the absence of a clear indication of the factual basis of relief. By this the methods used by the wrongdoer and the effect thereof on the victim are meant. It is therefore not surprising that a diversity of interpretations exists as to what these texts are supposed to mean. According to Carlo Alberto Maschi a distinction should be drawn between *vis* and *metus* as two separate grounds for relief: he uses a distinction which was developed in medieval law, namely between *vis absoluta* and *vis compulsiva*.[8] Maschi then defines the word *vis* in the formula as *vis absoluta*, i.e. physical, bodily force which completely excludes any exercise of will by the victim. Robbery is supposed to involve such violence. *Metus*, one the other hand, is defined as fear caused by *vis compulsiva*, i.e. through the "bending" of the will of the victim.[9] Threats are a source of such fear. According

---

6 Cf Hartkamp, *Der Zwang im römischen Privatrecht*, 191 et sq, 245 et sqq; Von Lübtow, *Der Ediktstitel "Quod metus causa gestum erit"*, 126 et sqq. On the social conditions at the time which may have prompted this measure, cf Zimmermann, *The Law of Obligations*, 651 et sqq. According to Kelly, moral philosophical considerations reflected in Aristotelian and Stoic teaching on will and intention underlay the introduction of this measure (*A Short History of Western Legal Theory* (1992), 53).

7 The two texts are *In Verr* II 3.65.152 and *ad Quint fratr* 1.1.7.21. The latter text indicates that the formula was aimed at assisting the recovery of illicit takings from Sulla's supporters (cf Von Lübtow, *Der Ediktstitel "Quod metus causa gestum erit"*, 127) and its generality makes it arguable that even in early Roman law, collective persecution was covered by the *metus* remedies (cf ch 5 note 183, ch 7 note 231 below).

8 On this distinction see Hartkamp, *Der Zwang im römischen Privatrecht*, 3 et sqq, who refers to Azo, *Summa in C 2,19 (20) de his quae vi metusve causa gesta sunt, § in primis* (Papiae, 1506; Torino, 1966), 38; *Glossa ordinaria*, gl *vi atroci ad D 4.2.1*, gl *non videor* and *per vim ad D 4.2.9 pr.*; Baldus de Ubaldis, *Commentarius super Decretalibus*, in c. *quae causa*, X, *de his quae vi metusve causa fiunt* notes 6–7 (1551), f 171rb.

9 See C A Maschi, *Il diritto romano I. la prospettiva storica della giurisprudenza classica*, 2nd ed (1966), 641 et sq, 647 et sqq, 651 et sqq (references obtained from Hartkamp, *Der Zwang im römischen Privatrecht*, 4 et sqq; Ebert, "*Vi metusve causa*" (1969) 86 *ZSS (RA)* 403 at 404 and Kupisch, *In integrum restitutio und vindicatio utilis bei Eigentumsübertragungen im klassischen römischen Recht*, 193 et sqq). This view was initially followed by Schulz, "Die Lehre vom erzwungenen Rechtsgeschäft im antiken römischen Recht" (1922) 43 *ZSS (RA)* 171, but subsequently rejected in his *Classical Roman Law*, 601.

to Maschi, it is only when specific measures were taken against robbery, namely the *actio vi bonorum raptorum*[10] (contained in an Edict of Lucellus dating from 76 BC), that the formula Octaviana no longer needed to be applied in cases of *vis absoluta* and was restricted to the "active" part of *vis compulsiva*, with *metus* forming the "passive" part. In other words, the concepts *vis* and *metus* now formed a sort of hendiadys: when combined they expressed the notion of compulsion through threats, with *vis* being the ("active") act of threatening, and *metus* the ("passive") effect on the victim.[11] This view that *vis* and *metus* formed a hendiadys, has also been proposed by many other authors, most notably Schulz,[12] but with a crucial difference: they are not in agreement with Maschi's view that the word *vis* in the *formula Octaviana* initially only applied to *vis absoluta*. According to them the hendiadys of *vis* and *metus* did not develop after the action against robbery was recognised. It was already present in the *formula Octaviana*. Thus, the formula never applied to *vis absoluta*, but only to *vis compulsiva*; or, as Schulz puts it, "fear caused by threat".[13] Ebert also supports the view that the *formula Octaviana* did not apply to *vis absoluta*, but bases this view on entirely different reasons.[14] He rejects the view that the words *vis* and *metus* form a hendiadys: according to him, these words rather deal with two ways of "bending" the will of a victim, namely through *vis*,[15] which is defined as physical violence causing fear, and through *metus*, which relates to threats of future harm. However, this view has been subjected to criticism,[16] and at present, it seems doubtful whether a clear answer can be found. The Ciceronian texts alone give very little guidance: the word *auferre* could mean "to rob" or "to take by force", as well as "acquire as the fruits of some act".[17] It could therefore be used in the context of *vis absoluta* (inasmuch as it encompasses robbery) as well as *vis compulsiva*. Use of both the expressions *vis et metus* and *vis aut metus* is further confusing: if only *vis et metus* were used, there would be much more force in the argument that they should be interpreted as a hendiadys. The words could then be read together, and an interpretation of *vis* as a reference to *vis absoluta* would be untenable since it would render the reference to *metus* superfluous.[18] After all, in cases of *vis absoluta* it is irrelevant whether or not the victim experienced fear. Use of the expression *vis aut metus* again indicates

---

10 Other important measures were the *leges repetundarum*, which were specifically aimed against magistrates who enriched themselves by extorting bribes. Cf Von Lübtow, *Der Ediktstitel "Quod metus causa gestum erit"*, 81 et sq, 129 et sqq; Hartkamp, *Der Zwang im römischen Privatrecht*, 251 et sqq; Berger, *Encyclopedic Dictionary of Roman Law*, s v *Repetundae*.

11 See Maschi, *Il diritto romano I. la prospettiva storica della giurisprudenza classica*, 641 et sqq (references obtained from Ebert, "*Vi metusve causa*" (1969) 86 *ZSS (RA)* 403 at 404 and Kupisch, *In integrum restitutio und vindicatio utilis bei Eigentumsübertragungen im klassischen römischen Recht*, 193 et sqq).

12 Schulz, *Classical Roman Law*, 601 sq; Hartkamp, *Der Zwang im römischen Privatrecht*, 5 et sqq, 16. Cf Kupisch, *In integrum restitutio und vindicatio utilis bei Eigentumsübertragungen im klassischen römischen Recht*, 194, note 312.

13 Schulz, *Classical Roman Law*, 601.

14 Ebert, "*Vi metusve causa*" (1969) 86 *ZSS (RA)* 403 at 407.

15 *Vis compulsiva* is then supposed to be restricted to *vis* defined in this way (Ebert, "*Vi metusve causa*" (1969) 86 *ZSS (RA)* 403 at 405 et sqq, 408, 414). As Hartkamp points out, such usage of the term *vis compulsiva* is at variance with existing usage, which defines it as psychological compulsion irrespective of the method employed (*Der Zwang im römischen Privatrecht*, 13 note 5).

16 Cf Kupisch, *In integrum restitutio und vindicatio utilis bei Eigentumsübertragungen im klassischen römischen Recht*, 193 et sqq; on the distinction cf also Hartkamp, *Der Zwang im römischen Privatrecht*, 4 et sq.

17 Von Lübtow, *Der Ediktstitel "Quod metus causa gestum erit"*, 127 et sq; Hartkamp, *Der Zwang im römischen Privatrecht*, 249.

18 Cf Hartkamp, *Der Zwang im römischen Privatrecht*, 249.

that two different concepts could have been intended, and that a hendiadys does not exist. This again provides support for the views of Maschi and Ebert, albeit that they differ as to the exact meaning of *vis*.

It is not only the field of application of the *formula Octaviana* which is heavily disputed: the exact nature of the relief it gave rise to is also unclear. From the words *reddere cogebantur* contained in one of Cicero's texts,[19] it can be deduced that the *formula* was aimed at obtaining some form of restitution, but this is about as far as one can take it. Apparently a penal remedy, aimed at obtaining damages in fourfold, was available to pressurise the recipient into providing restitution.[20] But whether one could only proceed against the wrongdoer, or also against a third party recipient, is unclear.[21]

2.2.2 *Hadrian's* Edictum perpetuum

Two centuries after the adoption of the *formula Octaviana*, an important provision on *metus*, which is recorded in Ulp D 4.2.1, was included in the *Edictum perpetuum* of Hadrian.[22] It is the most important Roman legal text on *metus* and reads as follows: "The praetor says: 'What is done through fear I will not uphold'" ("Ait praetor: 'Quod metus causa gestum erit, ratum non habebo'").[23]

It is apparent that there has been a movement away from the expression *vis et metus*, found in the *formula Octaviana*, to simply *metus*. Ulpian provides the explanation that the reference to force (*vis*) was later dropped because "anything which is done by unmitigated force may be held to be done through fear too".[24] This indicates that the Edict did not encompass *vis absoluta*, but only *vis compulsiva*. In fact, if it encompassed *vis absoluta*, the contraction to *metus* would have been highly unlikely.[25] It should be obvious, however, that it could never have been intended that the Edict applied whenever someone experienced any sort of fear.[26] Where the fear is not caused by wrongful means, but flows from threatened force of legal proceedings,[27] or is "rightfully applied by a magistrate in pursuance of an established law",[28] no relief would be provided. Neither would there be relief if a person brought force to bear on a debtor in order to obtain

---

19 *Ad Quint fratr* 1.1.7.21.

20 Von Lübtow, *Der Ediktstitel "Quod metus causa gestum erit"*, 128; Hartkamp, *Der Zwang im römischen Privatrecht*, 249; Schulz, "Die Lehre vom erzwungenen Rechtsgeschäft im antiken römischen Recht (1922) 43 *ZSS (RA)* 171 at 218; also see Kupisch, *In integrum restitutio und vindicatio utilis bei Eigentumsübertragungen im klassischen römischen Recht*, 158 et sqq.

21 Cf especially Hartkamp, *Der Zwang im römischen Privatrecht*, 253 et sqq, who supports the idea of a claim against third parties, but also discusses the contrary view.

22 Cf Schulz, *Classical Roman Law*, 601 et sq; Hartkamp, *Der Zwang im römischen Privatrecht*, 193.

23 Lenel reconstructed the *formula* as follows: "Si paret metus causa A^mA^m fundum q.d.a. N^oN^o mancipio dedisse q.d.r.a. neque plus quam annus est cum experiundi potestas fuit neque ea res arbitrio iudicis restituetur, q.e.r. erit, tantae pecuniae quadruplum iudex N^mN^m A^oA^o c.s.n.p.a" (*Das Edictum perpetuum*, 2nd ed (1927), 112).

24 Ulp D 4.2.1 ("... quodcumque vi atroci fit, id metu quoque fieri videtur").

25 Cf Hartkamp, *Der Zwang im römischen Privatrecht*, 7. According to him, Maschi regards the expression "... quodcumque vi atroci fit, id metu quoque fieri videtur" as interpolated "weil sie nicht in seine Theorie passen".

26 Maier, *Prätorische Bereicherungsklagen*, 95.

27 Cf C 8.37.9.1 (Diocl et Max), C 2.19.10 (Diocl et Max).

28 Ulp D 4.2.3.1 ("Sed vim accipimus atrocem et eam, quae adversus bonos mores fiat, non eam quam magistratus recte intulit; scilicet, iure licito et iure honoris quem sustinet"). Cf Hartkamp, *Der Zwang im römischen Privatrecht*, 21 et sqq.

payment.[29] Fear was also not understood simply to mean any apprehension whatever, but rather "fear of some evil of exceptional severity" (*maioris malitatis*).[30] It should further not have been the fear felt by a weak-minded man, but rather that fear which might reasonably have an effect upon a man of the most resolute character (a *homo constantissimus*).[31] It did not cover *metus reverentialis*, which is the fear or profound reverence which a son, for example, could feel for his father, and which would induce the son to act in a certain way.[32] Many examples are mentioned of the application of this Edict: these deal with fear of personal harm, such as death,[33] harm to physical integrity and loss of freedom,[34] and possibily also fear of harm of an economic nature.[35] Threats of harm to family are also covered.[36]

Thus far the focus was on the relationship between *vis* and *metus*, and the meaning of *metus*. The question now arises as to what exactly was meant by the expression *quod metus causa gestum erit*. Various possibilities exist.[37] Georg H Maier argues that it means "what has been done with the purpose of causing fear". The conduct instilling fear would therefore be the object of the Edict.[38] This interpretation draws its strength from the view that *metus* is a delict: the focus is on the wrongfulness of the conduct, and not on the emotional state of the victim. However, as Kunkel indicates, this interpretation does not fit in well with the words *ratum non habebo*, which could surely only pertain to the act of the victim and not to the act of the wrongdoer.[39] The conventional approach is then that the Edict applies to the act which the victim concluded out of fear (*metus causa*).[40] However, this approach only really explains why the victim has a claim against the wrongdoer; its fails to explain why third party recipients could also be liable under the Edict. Kupisch's alternative approach overcomes this problem by interpreting *metus causa* "as a consequence of fear", rather than the conventional

---

29 This did not exclude relief by other means. In certain cases of self-help the *lex Julia de vi privata* could impose criminal liability (cf Mod D 48.7.8; Kaser, *Das römische Privatrecht I*, 222; Hartkamp, *Der Zwang im römischen Privatrecht*, 43 et sq, 158 et sqq). Furthermore, through the *decretum divi Marci* a creditor who engaged in self-help could also be punished by the loss of his claim (Call D 4.2.13; cf Kaser, *Das römische Privatrecht I*, 222, and on the post-classical law, *Das römische Privatrecht II*, 41). Incidentally, its fate in Scots law is dealt with in *Stuarts v Whitefoord and the Duke of Hamilton* (1677) Mor 16489. Cf ch 3 note 112 below.

30 Ulp D 4.2.5; also see Ulp D 4.2.23.3.

31 Gai D 4.2.6 ("Metum autem non vani hominis, sed qui merito et in homine constantissimo cadat"). Cf Hartkamp, *Der Zwang im römischen Privatrecht*, 27 et sqq; Zimmermann, *The Law of Obligations*, 653 et sq.

32 Cf Cels D 23.2.22; Hartkamp, *Der Zwang im römischen Privatrecht*, 18, note 1; Von Savigny, *System des heutigen römischen Rechts*, vol 3, 102 note c).

33 Cf Ulp D 4.2.3.1; Ulp D 4.2.7; Paul D 4.2.8; Ulp D 4.6.3.

34 Cf e.g. Paul D 4.2.2 (fear of an attack which cannot be repelled); Paul D 4.2.8.2 (fear of sexual assault); Paul D 4.2.4 and Paul 4.2.8.1 (fear of slavery); Ulp D 4.2.7; Paul D 4.2.22 (fear of imprisonment); Ulp D 4.2.7.1; Ulp D 4.2.23.1 (fear of being brought in chains); Ulp D 4.2.23.2 (an athelete's fear of being confined, thus preventing him from entering into contests).

35 Cf Hartkamp, *Der Zwang im römischen Privatrecht*, 40 et sq. But cf also C 4.13; Dawson, "Economic Duress and the Fair Exchange in French and German law" (1937) 3 *TulaneLR* 35 at 347.

36 Cf Paul D 4.2.8.3; Hartkamp, *Der Zwang im römischen Privatrecht*, 42.

37 For a general overview, see Zimmermann, *The Law of Obligations*, 654.

38 Maier, *Prätorische Bereicherungsklagen*, 96 et sqq.

39 Kunkel, *Römisches Privatrecht*, 261, note 5; Hartkamp, *Der Zwang im römischen Privatrecht*, 55 note 16; Kaser, "Zur in integrum restitutio, besonders wegen metus und dolus" (1977) 94 *ZSS (RA)* 101 at 123.

40 Cf Hartkamp, *Der Zwang im römischen Privatrecht*, 55; Zimmermann, *The Law of Obligations*, 654.

"out of fear".[41] Thus, if a third party who had nothing to do with the extortion receives something as a consequence thereof, he could still fall under the Edict.[42] In this way, the focus of the Edict is constantly on the restitution of what has been obtained, and has to be returned, rather than on the punishment of wrongs.[43]

It is against this background that the remedies the Edict gave rise to—the consequences of *ratum non habebo*—can be examined. Again, academic opinion is divided.[44] Conventional thought,[45] based on the work of Schulz,[46] maintains that classical Roman law provided three separate remedies in cases of *metus*, namely the *exceptio metus, in integrum restitutio* (*propter metum*), and the *actio quod metus causa*. These remedies will now be dealt with in turn.

i. The *exceptio metus*

It has already been shown that the *exceptio metus* was inherent in *bonae fidei iudicia*. The judge could therefore simply refuse to enforce such agreements if they were concluded under *metus*. For plaintiffs not fortunate enough to obtain the relief on this basis, the praetor also provided an *exceptio metus*.[47] The remedy was generally available against the wrongdoer as well as third parties.[48] Incidentally, it will be indicated below how a *condictio* could possibly be provided if a transfer was made by a victim who was not aware that he had this *exceptio* at his disposal.[49]

ii. In integrum restitutio

It has been indicated above that the civil law at times was unable to provide satisfactory relief in cases of *metus*. To overcome this problem, the Edict empowered the praetor to provide *in integrum restitutio* (*propter metum*).[50] The remedy entailed that the praetor ensured a return to the former legal state by way of the annulment of an existing legal state. The victim was therefore entitled to be placed in the position

---

41 Kupisch, *In integrum restitutio und vindicatio utilis bei Eigentumsübertragungen im klassischen römischen Recht*, 146 et sq.

42 Cf Kaser, "Zur in integrum restitutio, besonders wegen metus und dolus" (1977) 94 *ZSS (RA)* 101 at 123 ("Der Prätor will jeglichen im Gefolge einer Furchterregung gemachten Erwerb entkräften oder wieder rückgängig machen"); Zimmermann, *The Law of Obligations*, 654.

43 Cf Kupisch, *In integrum restitutio und vindicatio utilis bei Eigentumsübertragungen im klassischen römischen Recht*, 148.

44 On the difficulties surrounding the interpretation of the text in general, cf Ankum, "Eine neue Interpretation von Ulpian Dig. 4.2.9.5–6 über die Abhilfen gegen *metus*" in *Festschrift für Heinz Hübner*, 3.

45 Hartkamp, *Der Zwang im römischen Privatrecht*, 189 et sqq; Jolowicz, *Historical Introduction to the Study of Roman Law*, 292; Lee, *The Elements of Roman Law with a Translation of the Institutes of Justinian*, 352; Thomas, *Textbook of Roman Law*, 373 et sqq; Buckland, *A Text-book of Roman Law from Augustus to Justinian*, 593 et sqq; Honsell, Mayer-Maly and Selb, *Römisches Recht*, 126, note 72, 375 note 12; Kaser, *Das römische Privatrecht I*, 244 et sqq.

46 See his *Classical Roman Law*, 600 et sqq and "Die Lehre vom erzwungenen Rechtsgeschäft im antiken römischen Recht" (1922) 43 *ZSS (RA)* 171 et sqq.

47 Cf Ulp D 44.4.4.33. Its exact relationship with the *actio quod metus causa* is not clear (see Zimmermann, *The Law of Obligations*, 658).

48 Ulp D 44.4.4.33. Cf Schulz, *Classical Roman Law*, 603.

49 See 2.3.2.i below.

50 Cf the general wording of Ulp D 4.2.1; Schulz, *Classical Roman Law*, 603; Kaser, *Das römische Privatrecht I*, 244 note 20; *Das römische Zivilprozessrecht*, 330 et sqq; Zimmermann, *The Law of Obligations*, 656. The remedy has been described as "the most striking exercise of his *imperium* by the praetor" (Thomas, *Textbook of Roman Law*, 113).

he would have been if there was no compulsion.[51] The exact scope of the relief varied in accordance with the facts of each case, e.g. whether a right of action was lost, an obligation was undertaken, or an object was transferred.[52]

iii. The actio quod metus causa

According to conventional thought, in addition to *in integrum restitutio*, the Edict also provided the separate remedy of the *actio quod metus causa*.[53] If instituted within one year after something was obtained through *metus*, the *actio quod metus causa* could be used to claim four times the damages[54] suffered as a result of the *metus*. If instituted after one year, only simple damages could be claimed. However, since it was an *actio arbitraria*, the defender was allowed to escape this fourfold liability by returning that which was obtained through *metus*.[55] If the pursuer himself obtained something under the transaction, he could not retain it as a windfall, but had to give it back too.[56]

Because the *actio quod metus causa* awarded damages *in quadruplum*, many regard it as mainly a penal action for damages. However, the action was also *in rem scripta*, i.e. not only available against the wrongdoer, but against anyone (also bona fide third parties) who acquired something as the consequence of *metus*.[57] It is rather unusual for a penal action to allow a defender to escape liability for damages by returning that which was obtained through *metus*. This characteristic is treated as important by those who reject the conventional approach, and believe that in classical law the *actio quod metus causa* was not a remedy separate from *in integrum restitutio*, but an instrument aimed at achieving *in integrum restitutio*.[58] The argument

---

51 Kaser, *Das römische Privatrecht I*, 244; Kupisch, *In integrum restitutio und vindicatio utilis bei Eigentumsübertragungen im klassischen römischen Recht*, 3 et sqq; Kunkel, *Römisches Privatrecht*, 381.

52 Thomas, *Textbook of Roman Law*, 113.

53 Cf generally Zimmermann, *The Law of Obligations*, 656, and especially note 43 and authorities quoted there.

54 Cf Ulp D 4.2.14.1; Kaser, *Das römische Privatrecht I*, 244. The claim for damages did not only include the value of what was obtained, but also its fruits (cf Ulp D 4.2.12; Ulp D 4.2.14.7, Paul D 4.2.21.2), lost profits (cf Thomas, *Textbook of Roman Law*, 374; Ulp D 4.2.12) and accidental loss (Ulp D 4.2.12, Ulp D 4.2.14.11; C 2.19.1; Hartkamp, *Der Zwang im römischen Privatrecht*, 221, 227).

55 Cf Ulp D 4.2.14.1; Kaser, *Das römische Zivilprozessrecht*, 257 note 9.

56 Cf Kaser, "Zur in integrum restitutio, besonders wegen metus und dolus" (1977) 94 *ZSS (RA)* 101 at 135 et sqq; cf also Kaser, *Das römische Zivilprozessrecht*, 330; Hartkamp, *Der Zwang im römischen Privatrecht*, 232 et sqq.

57 Cf Maier, *Prätorische Bereicherungsklagen*, 110 et sqq; Hartkamp, *Der Zwang im römischen Privatrecht*, 201 et sqq (esp 203 nn 13, 14); Kaser, *Das römische Privatrecht II*, 90 note 46, *Das römische Privatrecht I*, 244 note 25; *contra* Beseler, *Beiträge zur Kritik der römischen Rechtsquellen*, vol I, 74; Von Lübtow, *Der Ediktstitel "Quod metus causa gestum erit"*, 183 et sqq; Schulz, *Classical Roman Law*, 601. A *mala fide* third party was equated with the wrongdoer (Hartkamp, *Der Zwang im römischen Privatrecht*, 201 note 1). A *bona fide* third party was sometimes treated differently (cf Hartkamp, *Der Zwang im römischen Privatrechtt* 190 et sq, 219 et sqq). He was only liable for loss after *litis contestatio* which could be ascribed to *dolus* on his side (cf Ulp D 4.2.14.5, Maier, *Prätorische Bereicherungsklagen*, 134 et sqq; Hartkamp, *Der Zwang im römischen Privatrecht*, 222 et sqq, 242). Hartkamp discusses the possibility that sometimes *cautiones* had to be given that the third party would return the goods if he found it again (cf Ulp D 4.2.14.11). It is not clear whether a bona fide third party who purchased something which was obtained as a consequence of fear could refuse restitution unless his purchase price was repaid (cf Maier, *Prätorische Bereicherungsklagen*, 145 et sqq; Hartkamp, *Der Zwang im römischen Privatrecht*, 231 et sqq, 243).

58 Cf generally Kupisch, *In integrum restitutio und vindicatio utilis bei Eigentumsübertragungen im klassischen römischen Recht*, 123 *passim*; Kaser, "Zur in integrum restitutio, besonders wegen metus und dolus" (1977) 94 *ZSS (RA)* 101 at 108 *passim*.

is that the purpose of fourfold damages was to provide an incentive for the person who had the goods to return them. Only if he persisted in refusing to give the goods back, should he be punished.[59] Such an analysis certainly fits in well with the *actio arbitraria* nature of the *actio quod metus causa*. The rule that the judge could only condemn for a sum of money did not function properly when the victim wanted what he was entitled to as a matter of right and not (merely) a sum of money. The *actio arbitraria* then provided the judge a way around this problem by allowing him to determine that a monetary amount would be payable if the defendant did not act in a certain way. In the context of *metus*, the *actio quod metus causa* could then be used to effect restitution. This approach also draws much of its persuasive power from the argument that if the *actio quod metus causa* was purely a penal remedy, it is highly questionable why a third party who merely received the goods obtained through *metus*, and not the wrongdoer, would be exposed to the *actio*. It further solves the problem which the conventional approach has in explaining the odd overlapping relationship between the *actio quod metus causa* and *in integrum restitutio*.[60]

In post-classical law the distinction between the *ius civile* and *ius honorarium* was removed, and because the roles of the judge, who granted civilian relief, and the praetor, who granted relief according to the *ius honorarium*, were merged, a single remedy could be granted for all cases of *metus*. Whether it was due to a Justinianic integration (*Verschmelzung*),[61] or purely a continuation of the classical position does not matter: post-classical law did not treat the *actio quod metus causa* and *in integrum restitutio* as distinct remedies.[62] A person who was compelled to enter into a transaction could claim back that which the recipient obtained,[63] as well as threefold damages if restitution did not take place.[64] The actio was *in rem*

59 Cf Zimmermann, *The Law of Obligations*, 656 et sq; Visser, "Rethinking Unjustified Enrichment: A Perspective of the Competition between Contractual and Enrichment Remedies" 1992 *AJ* 203 at 220.

60 Cf Kaser, "Zur in integrum restitutio, besonders wegen metus und dolus" (1977) 94 *ZSS (RA)* 101 at 104 et sqq, 109 et sqq, esp 116; Zimmermann, *The Law of Obligations*, 656 sq; but cf Ankum, "Eine neue Interpretation von Ulpian Dig. 4.2.9.5–6 über die Abhilfen gegen *metus*" in *Festschrift für Heinz Hübner*, 4 note 5 and Gunter Wesener's review of Kupisch's *In integrum restitutio und vindicatio utilis bei Eigentumsübertragungen im klassischen römischen Recht* in (1976) 44 *Tijdschrift voor Rechtsgeschiedenis* 169.

61 Cf Schulz, "Die Lehre vom erzwungenen Rechtsgeschäft im antiken römischen Recht (1922) 43 *ZSS (RA)* 171 at 229 et sqq; Von Lübtow, *Der Ediktstitel "Quod metus causa gestum erit"*, 218; Hartkamp, *Der Zwang im römischen Privatrecht*, 201 et sq. It is not clear where exactly in Ulp D 4.2.9 the discussion of *in integrum restitutio* is supposed to stop, and that of the *actio quod metus causa* is supposed to start. Traditionally it has been placed between Ulp D 4.2.9.6 and 7 (cf Hartkamp, *Der Zwang im römischen Privatrecht*, 190 et sqq), but according to Ankum it should be placed between Ulp D 4.2.9.4 and 5 ("Eine neue Interpretation von Ulpian Dig. 4.2.9.5–6 über die Abhilfen gegen *metus*" in *Festschrift für Heinz Hübner*, 3).

62 Cf Kaser, *Das römische Privatrecht II*, 90 note 47; Levy, "Zur nachklassischen in integrum restitutio" (1951) 68 *ZSS (RA)* 360 at 398 et sqq (esp 405); Hartkamp, *Der Zwang im römischen Privatrecht*, 173 et sqq. *In integrum restitutio*, in its *propter metum* form, actually seems to have disappeared during the time of Constantine. On the process of amalgamation which characterised the post-classical law in general, see Schulz, *Classical Roman law*, 457 et sq. Another feature was the grouping together of certain delicts, such as *furtum*, *rapina*, *damnum iniuria datum* and *iniuria*. However, *metus*, like *dolus*, was not included in the list, although it subsequently came to be termed a "praetorian delict" (see Nicholas, *An Introduction to Roman law*, 210 sq; Thomas, *Textbook of Roman law*, 373 et sq).

63 He could also rely on the agreement: cf Hartkamp, *Der Zwang im römischen Privatrecht*, 50 et sq, referring to C 2.19.4 (Gord 239) and C 2.19.2 (Alex 226).

64 Kaser, *Das römische Privatrecht II*, 90; *Das römische Zivilprozessrecht*, 471. Cf Ulp D 4.2.14.10. Also cf Ulp D 4.2.9.6; Ulp D 4.2.14.1; Ulp D 4.2.14.3; Ulp D 4.2.14.7. On *restitutio*, cf in general Ulp D 4.2.3; Paul D 4.2.8; Ulp D 4.2.9.7; and Ulp D 4.2.12 (regarding the measure of restitution).

scripta,[65] and, as in classical law, the *exceptio metus* was available to ward off claims based on transactions where *metus* was present.[66]

iv. Excursus: Voidness or voidability?

At this stage it is appropriate to pause and to consider briefly the effect of the praetorian law on the validity of transactions concluded under compulsion. At least two options present themselves, namely voidness or voidability (i.e. validity until such time as the victim obtained relief). It is difficult to determine which of these alternatives is preferable, for Roman law did not draw an explicit distinction between voidness and voidability.[67] In these times it was practically unimportant whether one regarded such agreements as void or voidable. The distinction (like that between *vis absoluta* and *vis compulsiva*) is of post-Roman origin. It seems unwise to attempt to force such structuring concepts onto Roman law.[68] The important point is that the victim of compulsion could attack the transaction and claim restitution.[69]

2.3 COMPULSION AND THE *CONDICTIONES*

Thus far the focus has been almost exclusively on the praetorian remedies of the *actio quod metus causa*, *in integrum restitutio* and the *exceptio metus*. However, it was not only the law relating to *metus* which could provide relief to victims of compulsion: mention has already been made of legislative reform through the *leges repetundarum*,[70] the *lex Julia de vi privata*, the *decretum divi Marci*[71] and the Edict of Lucellus against robbery (the *actio vi bonorum raptorum*),[72] as well as the relief the *ius civile* provided where *negotia bonae fidei* were concerned.[73] The attention will now turn to the *condictio*[74]—a remarkable *stricti iuris* action which, like the praetorian remedies, could be used to obtain restitution in cases of compulsion.

---

65 Schulz, *Classical Roman Law*, 604 et sq; cf Ulp D 4.2.9.3 and Ulp 4.2.9.8.

66 Kaser, *Das römische Privatrecht II*, 90; cf Ulp D 4.2.9.3.

67 Cf Kaser, *Das römische Privatrecht I*, 246 et sqq; Kaser, *Das römische Privatrecht II*, 90 note 48 and Zimmermann, *The Law of Obligations*, 678 et sqq, but cf Schulz, *Classical Roman Law*, 602. Paulus regarded compelled transactions are valid in principle (D 4.2.21.5) whereas Ulpian stated that "nothing is so contrary to consent ... as force or fear" (D 50.17.116: "Nihil consensui tam contrarium est, qui ac bonae fidei iudicia sustinet, quam vis atque metus: quem comprobare contra bonos mores est"). This again indicates that compelled transactions were void. In the age between classical and Justinianic law, compelled transactions generally were regarded as void (Levy, "Zur nachklassischen in integrum restitutio" (1951) 68 *ZSS (RA)* 360 at 398 et sqq, esp 404 et sqq). Cf Paul Sent 1.7.10; CT 15.14.8, according to which one of the exceptions to a list of valid transactions concluded between *tyranni* are those *dolo metuve caruerunt*, but again there is support for the contrary position (cf Hartkamp, *Der Zwang im römischen Privatrecht*, 173 note 3, Levy, "Zur nachklassischen in integrum restitutio" (1951) 68 *ZSS (RA)* 360 at 408 note 195).

68 Von Lübtow, *Der Ediktstitel "Quod metus causa gestum erit"*, 73; Kaser, "Zur in integrum restitutio, besonders wegen metus und dolus" (1977) 94 *ZSS (RA)* 101 at 107 et sq.

69 Cf Levy, "Zur nachklassischen in integrum restitutio" (1951) 68 *ZSS (RA)* 360 at 408.

70 Cf note 10 above.

71 Cf note 29 above.

72 Cf text to note 10 above.

73 Cf section 2.1 above.

74 On the *condictiones*, see Kaser, *Das römische Privatrecht I*, 592 et sqq; Kaser, *Das römische Privatrecht II*, 421 et sqq; Zimmermann, *The Law of Obligations*, 834 et sqq; Liebs, "The History of the Roman *Condictio* up to Justinian" in *Essays for Tony Honoré* 163 esp notes 1, 2 and authorities quoted there; J von Koschembahr-Lyskowski, *Die Condictio als Bereicherungsklage im klassischen römischen Recht I* (1903) vol 2 (1907); R von Mayr, *Die Condictio des römischen Privatrechtes* (1900); Von Lübtow, *Beiträge zur Lehre von der Condictio nach römischem und geltendem Recht*; Schwarz, *Die Grundlage der Condictio im klassischen römischen Recht*; Schulz, *Classical Roman Law*, 610 et sqq.

2.3.1 *Classical law*

In early classical procedure, a *legis actio per condictionem* could be used to recover a specific object (*certa res*) or sum of money (*certa pecunia*): in essence, this process entailed that the victim could give notice (*condicere*) before a magistrate that a matter would be referred for trial before a judge.[75] The defendant could avert this process by settlement or by submitting to the claim. The appeal of this procedure throughout its various stages of development lay in its abstract nature: without stating the basis for recovery or *causa debendi*, the pursuer could use the *condictio* to obtain recovery of a *certum* in a variety of circumstances.[76] It is therefore not surprising that the *condictio* came to be applied in certain non-contractual cases of what nowadays would be termed unjustified enrichment.[77] In classical law the basis of relief by way of the *condictio* in such cases was the absence of a *causa retinendi*, i.e. the fact that a person held something of another without being entitled thereto.[78] It is then said that in such cases two requirements had to be met for a successful claim with the *condictio*.[79] First, with a few notable exceptions,[80] there had to be some act of conferment—a transfer or *datio* whereby ownership was acquired.[81] In this regard it has been argued that the *datio* had to be supported by its own *causa dandi*,[82] which in this context indicates

75 Cf G 4.18; Liebs, "The History of the Roman *Condictio* up to Justinian" in *Essays for Tony Honoré*, 163 at 164; Zimmermann, *The Law of Obligations*, 835.

76 G 4.176. However, as Liebs points out, since *sponsio* or *stipulatio* were in any event the only ground for making the claim (in early law), "that peculiarity seems not to have been very remarkable originally" ("The History of the Roman *Condictio* up to Justinian" in *Essays for Tony Honoré*, 163 at 165 note 9).

77 See Zimmermann, *The Law of Obligations*, 836 et sqq.

78 Cf Schwarz, *Die Grundlage der Condictio im klassischen römischen Recht*, 212 et sqq; Kaser, *Das römische Privatrecht* I, 595; Visser, *Die rol van dwaling by die condictio indebiti*, 3 note 9.

79 Kaser, *Das römische Privatrecht* I, 592 et sqq.

80 For a discussion of the exceptions, most notably theft (the *condictio furtiva*) and similar situations which involved taking, such as driving an owner off his land (a *condictio* '*ex iniusta causa*'), see Liebs, "The History of the Roman *Condictio* up to Justinian" in *Essays for Tony Honoré*, 163 at 169 et sqq.

81 Kaser, *Das römische Privatrecht* I, 594; Von Lübtow, *Beiträge zur Lehre von der Condictio nach römischem und geltendem Recht*, 146; Evans-Jones, "From 'undue transfer' to 'retention without a legal basis'" in Evans-Jones (ed), *The Civil Law Tradition in Scotland*, 213 at 219; Honoré, "*Condictio* and payment" 1958 *AJ* 135. It is not clear whether a valid *datio* required a *negotium* between the parties. In Jul D 12.6.33 it is stated that "If I build on your site and you possess the house, there is no room for a *condictio* because there has been no dealing (*nullum negotium*) between us. For one who pays what is not owed does go through a kind of transaction (*aliquid negotii*) by the act of paying. But when an owner takes possession on his own of a building, placed there by another, he enters no transaction." According to Kaser this indicates that the *datio* required a *negotium contractum gestum*, i.e. an acceptable form of co-operation between the parties aimed at reaching a particular legal outcome (cf *Das römische Privatrecht* I, 594). According to Schwarz the *negotium* requirement would not be met where there was a delict (*Die Grundlage der Condictio im klassischen römischen Recht*, 11 et sq). For criticism of the *negotium* requirement, see Liebs, "The History of the Roman *Condictio* up to Justinian", in *Essays for Tony Honoré*, 163 at 172, esp note 63, where it is indicated that a *condictio* could arise from consumption, *accessio*, *commixtio* or *confusio* (also cf Zimmermann, *The Law of Obligations*, 854). On the demise of the *negotium* requirement in Roman Dutch law, cf De Vos, *Verrykingsaanspreeklikheid in die Suid-Afrikaanse reg*, 75 et sqq. This was only in regard to the *condictio sine causa specialis* (i.e. not in regard to the *condictiones indebiti*, *ob turpem vel iniustam causam* and *causa data causa non secuta*, which are dealt with below).

82 Cf Schwarz, *Die Grundlage der Condictio im klassischen römischen Recht*, 191 et sqq, 219 et sqq; Visser, *Die rol van dwaling by die condictio indebiti*, 6 et sq, 11 et sq. On the requirement of a *iusta causa traditionis* in the specific case of a *datio* in the form of *traditio*, see section 2.4 below.

with what purpose the *datio* was made, e.g. to pay a debt.[83] Second, the purpose for which the *datio* was made had to fail.[84] This failure of the purpose meant that what had been received was retained *sine causa*, and that the *condictio* was available to recover it. The following are examples of such a failure of purpose:

(a) Where a person erroneously[85] made a *datio* with the purpose of paying a debt (*solvendi causa*), while the debt was in fact not due (*indebitum*).[86] It seems as if in classical law the *error* requirement essentially entailed that the claimant should prove that he made an undue transfer, which would then give rise to a presumption that it was made in error. The defendant could rebut this presumption by proving that the transfer was made in the knowledge that it was not due.[87]

(b) Due to the fragmented and restricted nature of the Roman law of contracts,[88] a *datio* could also be made in the absence of a valid contract, but in the expectation that the recipient would do something (a *datio ob rem*). If the expected outcome did not ensue, the purpose likewise failed. An exception to the latter case is where the expected outcome did ensue, but the acceptance of the *datio* was morally offensive (a *datio ob turpem rem* or *ob turpem causam*),[89] or illegal (a *datio ob injustam causam*).[90] Recovery was then possible, unless the transferor was also tainted by turpitude.[91]

---

83 Schwarz, *Die Grundlage der Condictio im klassischen römischen Recht*, 229 sq; cf Visser, *Die rol van dwaling by die condictio indebiti*, 11; Visser, "Die Grondslag van die condictio indebiti" (1988) 51 *THRHR* 491 at 495.

84 Schwarz, *Die Grundlage der Condictio im klassischen römischen Recht*, 212 et sqq. Also cf Kaser, *Das römische Privatrecht I*, 595 et sq. He seems to differ from Schwarz by referring to the purpose of the transferor, rather than the agreed upon purpose of the parties. For a more careful approach, cf Visser, *Die rol van dwaling by die condictio indebiti*, 16 et sq. According to him it seems "possible to conclude" that the basis of the *condictio* in classical law was retention of a performance without legal ground. He also states that there is the "strong possibility" that the law regarded cases where the agreed purpose of the performance failed as cases of unjustified retention.

85 On the error requirement in classical law cf, generally, Kaser, *Das römische Privatrecht I*, 596, note 36 and authorities quoted there; Zimmermann, *The Law of Obligations*, 849 et sqq; Visser, *Die rol van dwaling by die condictio indebiti*, 22 et sqq.

86 Kaser, *Das römische Privatrecht I*, 596.

87 Cf Schwarz, *Die Grundlage der Condictio im klassischen römischen Recht*, 96 et sqq, 294 et sqq; Zimmermann, *The Law of Obligations*, 850. The extreme views of Beseler and Solazzi, i.e. that the state of mind of the transferor did not matter at all, and that he could claim with a *condictio* even if he knew no debt was due, seem at variance with the texts (cf G 3.91, Ulp D 12.6.1.1, Paul D 50.17.53; cf Kaser, *Das römische Privatrecht I*, 596 note 36; Zimmermann, *The Law of Obligations*, 849 note 102; Visser, *Die rol van dwaling by die condictio indebiti*, 26 et sq). As to the implication of knowledge on the side of the recipient that the transfer is not due, see Visser, *Die rol van dwaling by die condictio indebiti*, 22; Schwarz, *Die Grundlage der Condictio im klassischen römischen Recht* 297. The possibility cannot be discounted that the wrongdoer could be exposed to a *condictio furtiva*, since receipt of a transfer in the knowledge that it is not due can amount to *furtum*.

88 Cf Zimmermann, *The Law of Obligations*, 843.

89 Kaser, *Das römische Privatrecht I*, 597 et sq; cf Schwarz, *Die Grundlage der Condictio im klassischen römischen Recht*, 169 et sqq.

90 The few texts which deal with the *condictio* where it fulfils this function are Gai D 24.1.6 (transfers contrary to the prohibition of donations between spouses), Ulp D 12.7.1.3 and Ulp D 12.5.6 (broader but vague, with controversial roots in the *condictio furtiva*). Cf Schwarz, *Die Grundlage der Condictio im klassischen römischen Recht*, 274 et sqq; Kaser, *Das römische Privatrecht I*, 598 note 49.

91 Cf text to note 120 below.

The meaning of the transfer *ob turpem rem* or *ob turpem causam* needs to be examined more closely. In essence, it involved cases where the recipient could be condemned with *infamia*,[92] where he acted contrary to certain imperial legislation protecting the *boni mores*, and where he violated rules of practice regarding the integrity of family life.[93] One example of compulsion which lead to *infamia* was that of a person who held goods in deposit for another, and then demanded money for its return. This was quite contrary to his duty of trust.[94]

2.3.2 *Post-classical law*

In post-classical law, the "single" *condictio* disappeared, and was replaced by specific *condictiones*, each with their own field of application. However, in contrast to the classical *condictio*, these *condictiones* displayed a unity of purpose by being more clearly linked to the notion of natural justice, equity or good faith that no person should enrich himself at the expense of another.[95] In fact, there are indications that all the *condictiones* could be grouped together under a "general" *condictio sine causa*.[96] Again, as in classical law, the measure of recovery was determined by what had been obtained without legal ground, and not merely by the amount of enrichment remaining at the commencement of legal proceedings.[97] Two of these specific *condictiones*, namely the *condictio ob turpem vel iniustam causam* and the *condictio indebiti* are of some relevance to cases of compulsion and need to be examined more closely.

i. *The* condictio indebiti

It will be recalled that in classical times the *condictio* could be used to recover a *datio* which was made with the purpose of paying a debt (*solvendi causa*), which was in fact not due (an *indebitum*). Some uncertainty exists as to whether the *condictio*, when fulfilling this function, could be used in classical law to recover a transfer made under

92 Cf Schwarz, *Die Grundlage der Condictio im klassischen römischen Recht*, 169 et sqq, 172 et sqq; Kaser, "Rechtswidrigkeit und Sittenwidrigkeit im klassischen römischen Recht" (1940) 60 *ZSS (RA)* 95 at 112 et sqq).

93 On the meaning of *dare ob rem turpem*, cf Kaser, "Rechtswidrigkeit und Sittenwidrigkeit im klassischen römischen Recht" (1940) 60 *ZSS (RA)* 95; Schwarz, *Die Grundlage der Condictio im klassischen römischen Recht* 169 et sqq.

94 Cf Paul D 12.5.2.1; Kaser, "Rechtswidrigkeit und Sittenwidrigkeit im klassischen römischen Recht" (1940) 60 *ZSS (RA)* 95 at 116. Other examples are *sacrilegium facere* (Ulp D 12.5.2pr), *furtum* (Ulp D 12.5.2pr, Ulp D 12.5.4.1), *homicidium* (Ulp D 12.5.2pr), *iudicem corrumpere* (Ulp D 12.5.2.2), *iniuria* (Ulp D 12.5.4.2), *calumnia* (Paul D 12.6.65, Ulp D 3.6.5.1), *stuprum* (Ulp D 12.5.4pr), *concussio* (C 4.7.3), *meretricium* (Ulp D 12.5.4.3) and *incestum* (Pap D 12.7.5pr). Cf Schwarz, *Die Grundlage der Condictio im klassischen römischen Recht*, 169 et sqq, 172 et sqq; Kaser, "Rechtswidrigkeit und Sittenwidrigkeit im klassischen römischen Recht" (1940) 60 *ZSS (RA)* 95 at 112 et sqq).

95 Cf Pomp D 12.6.14: "For it is by nature fair (*natura aequum est*) that nobody should enrich himself at the expense of another". Also cf Pomp. D 50.17.206; Von Lübtow, *Beiträge zur Lehre von der Condictio nach römischem und geltendem Recht*, 21; Kaser, *Das römische Privatrecht II*, 421 et sq.

96 On the *condictio sine causa generalis*, see Zimmermann, *The Law of Obligations*, 856 et sq. According to Schwarz, "... die causa sei für die Byzantiner dasjenige, was die Leistung oder das Versprechen objektiv, innerlich rechtfertigt, sein Fehlen ruft die condictio auf den Plan; und zwar meinten sie: Entweder ist es gar nicht da, von Anfang an, oder es fällt später fort, oder man erwartet es, aber es trifft nicht ein. Das ergibt sich als byzantinische Lehre aus D 12,7,1,2 und eod. 4. Klarer kann man den Gedanken nicht wiedergeben; denn er ist nicht klar gedacht" (*Die Grundlage der Condictio im klassischen römischen Recht*, 209 et sqq). On the relationship between this notion and the concept of *retinere sine causa* in classical law, cf Visser, *Die rol van dwaling by die condictio indebiti*, 17 et sqq.

97 Kaser, *Das römische Privatrecht II*, 425.

an extorted stipulation. A number of considerations indicate that this may not have been the case. First, the victim would have to prove that the transfer was not due. But according to civil law he had a problem: a stipulation willed under compulsion was nonetheless willed ("voluntas coacta tamen voluntas est"). As Schwarz states: "he who peforms *ex stipulatione*, performs something which is due under civil law".[98] It is only under praetorian law, which recognised the remedies on grounds of *metus*, that one could talk of an *indebitum*. Second, it would have to be assumed that the victim made the transfer with the purpose of paying a debt (*solvendi causa*). This assumption does not hold if the purpose is viewed subjectively: the victim's intention is rather that the compulsion should come to an end. It is only by using a broad, objective interpretation that one could argue that the purpose of the transfer is to discharge a debt. And third, on the assumption that the debt could be regarded as not being due under praetorian law, it would still have to be proved that payment was not made in the knowledge (*scientia*) that it was undue (*indebitum*).[99]

The prima facie conclusion is therefore that recovery with the *condictio* would not be possible. It has been suggested that the victim might have found a way to circumvent this problem.[100] The possibility exists that the victim could have been ignorant of the fact that he could defend himself with the praetorian remedy of an *exceptio metus causa*. If the victim did not know the defence was available, it cannot be said that he knowingly transferred an *indebitum*. Consequently, the victim of an extorted stipulation might have been able to claim with the *condictio* in classical law.[101]

In the more fragmented post-classical law the recovery of an *indebitum* became the domain of a specific *condictio*, namely the *condictio indebiti*. However, it is clear that in post-classical law this *condictio* was not used to provide relief where a transfer was made under an extorted agreement. It was not only the fact that Justinian made error[102] a "positive" requirement for claiming with the *condictio indebiti* which militated against such a development.[103] To Justinian the receipt of such transfers were tainted with turpitude. It will now be indicated how he made his new *condictio ob turpem vel iniustam causam* available for the recovery of such transfers.

ii. The condictio ob turpem vel iniustam causam

Whereas classical law inter alia provided the *condictio* if a transfer was made *ob turpem* or *iniustam causam*, the Digest accommodated these cases in a single title dealing with the *condictio ob turpem vel iniustam causam*.[104] Transfers *ob turpem rem* (or *causam*)

---

98 Schwarz, *Die Grundlage der Condictio im klassischen römischen Recht*, 297.

99 Schwarz, *Die Grundlage der Condictio im klassischen römischen Recht*, 294 et sqq.

100 Schwarz, *Die Grundlage der Condictio im klassischen römischen Recht*, 294 et sqq.

101 Cf Schwarz, *Die Grundlage der Condictio im klassischen römischen Recht*, 297 et sq.

102 Error should not be construed too narrowly, since payments made in doubt whether a debt was due could still be recovered. Cf Liebs, "The History of the Roman *Condictio* up to Justinian" in *Essays for Tony Honoré*, 163 at 178.

103 Cf Zimmermann, *The Law of Obligations*, 850 et sq; Evans-Jones, "From 'undue transfer' to 'retention without a legal basis'" in Evans-Jones (ed), *The Civil Law Tradition in Scotland*, 213 at 220 et sqq. Justinian further qualified the type of error which would be acceptable for claiming with this *condictio*. In general errors of law excluded recovery, and errors of fact did not (cf Zimmermann, *The Law of Obligations*, 850 et sq; on the classical roots, see Visser, *Die rol van dwaling by die condictio indebiti*, 31 et sqq).

104 D 12.5. Where the transfer was made for an honest purpose (*ob honestam causam*), no recovery was possible (cf Paul D 12.5.1.1, Ulp D 12.5.4). Whether it in fact comprised two separate *condictiones* or one is not clear. Cf generally Glück, *Pandecten*, vol 12 ad D 12.5, 50 et sqq; De Vos, *Verrykingsaanspreeklikheid in die Suid-Afrikaanse reg*, 20 et sqq.

have been discussed above and what has been said there need not be repeated here. Transfers *ob iniustam causam* are dealt with briefly in D 12.5.6,[105] which states that: "Sabinus always said that the early jurists were right in holding that the *condictio* would go for anything in someone's hands on an unlawful basis" ("Perpetuo Sabinus probavit veterum opinionem existimantium id, quod ex iniusta causa apud aliquem sit, posse condici"). Apparently, the *condictio ob iniustam causam* was included in the title due to Theodosian reform, whereby the (mere) infringement of a statutory prohibition gave rise to invalidity. This stands in contrast to classical law, which only regarded serious breaches of statutory prohibition as tainted by turpitude, and, hence, granted the *condictio ob turpem causam*.[106]

Digest title 12.5 lists various examples where the *condictio ob turpem vel iniustam causam* applied. A number of these deal with compulsion. First, as has been alluded to above, this *condictio* applied in the case of the (by now degenerate)[107] *stipulatio* extorted by *vis*.[108] Pomp. D 12.5.7 reads as follows: "It is agreed that money exacted under a stipulation itself extorted by force is recoverable" ("Ex ea stipulatione, quae per vim extorta esset, si exacta esset pecunia, repetitionem esse constat"). Although this text seems acceptable if one purely focuses on the turpitudinous conduct of the wrongdoer in accepting the payment, it is in fact problematic. After all, the *condictio ob turpem vel iniustam causam* was a subcategory or modality of the *condictio causa data causa non secuta*. It was used to recover a transfer aimed at obtaining a counterperformance (a *datio ob rem*) where the acceptance of the performance was tainted with turpitude.[109] It did not apply to a transfer aimed at fulfilling a debt (a *datio solvendi causa*). Insofar as the victim's payment on ground of the compelled stipulation is aimed at fulfilling a debt, it is not a *datio ob rem*, but a *datio solvendi causa*. The implication is then that the *condictio indebiti* would be a more appropriate remedy. However, as indicated above, the *condictio indebiti* was now subject to the error requirement, which excludes this possibility.

The second category of examples contained in D 12.5 deal with the situation where someone receives a transfer to do what he is obliged to do in any event. These cases are not expressly link to the notion of *vis* (or *metus*) like D 12.5.7, but still clearly deal with compulsion: each case involves an implicit wrongful threat. The texts are the following. Paul D 12.5.2.1 deals with the situation where "I pay you so that you give me back something deposited with you, a document for instance" ("Si tibi dedero, ut rem mihi reddas depositam apud te vel ut instrumentum redderes"). The implication is clear: unless I pay you, you will not return the document. As indicated above, this was already regarded as a transfer *ob turpem causam* in classical law, since *infamia* attached to the party who asked for the payment to return the object.[110] According to D 12.5.9 pr, this *condictio* is also available "if I lend you clothes for use and then pay you a price to get them back" ("si vestimenta utenda tibi commodavero, deinde pretium, ut reciperem, dedissem"). Initially this case did

105 But also cf Ulp D 12.7.1.3.

106 Zimmermann, *The Law of Obligations*, 846 note 77; Liebs, "The History of the Roman *Condictio* up to Justinian" in *Essays for Tony Honoré*, 163 at 175 et sq.

107 Cf Nicholas, *An Introduction to Roman Law*, 194; Kaser, *Das römische Privatrecht II*, 377; Schulz, *Classical Roman Law*, 476.

108 But cf Evans-Jones, "From 'undue transfer' to 'retention without a legal basis' (the *condictio indebiti* and the *condictio ob turpem vel iniustam causam*)", in Evans-Jones (ed), *The Civil Law Tradition in Scotland*, 213 at 220.

109 Zimmermann, *The Law of Obligations*, 841 et sqq.

110 Cf Kaser, "Rechtswidrigkeit und Sittenwidrigkeit im klassischen römischen Recht", 60 (1940) ZSS (RA) 95, 116.

not involve *infamia* and was not regarded as a *datio ob rem turpem*. The compilers, however, seem to have viewed it differently.[111] The last of these examples is D 12.5.9.1, which deals with the situation where a payment was made to receive something which was in any event owed under a will or *stipulation*.[112]

The final category of cases of compulsion dealt with in D 12.5 concerns the situation where a transfer is made so that someone does not commit a crime. In a certain sense, this is the converse of the former category: it is not a question of a person being obliged to do something, but rather being obliged *not* do something, such as not to commit murder, theft or sacrilege.[113] The above cases of compulsion should be distinguished from cases rather amounting to bribery. Here the claim is normally excluded in any event: after all, both the parties are tainted by the turpitude. Notable examples are where a judge is paid to pronounce in someone's favour,[114] where an adulterer buys his way out,[115] and where a runaway slave pays to prevent disclosure of his whereabouts or his crimes.[116] As far as the measure of recovery is concerned, the recipient was exposed to a claim aimed at recovery of the object (or its value), and its fruits or accessions,[117] but not interest.[118] Recovery was excluded in cases of *turpitudo solius dantis*, i.e. where only the pursuer was tainted with turpitude,[119] and in cases where the *in pari delicto* or *in pari turpitudine* rules applied, i.e. where both the claimant and the recipient were tainted with turpitude.[120] Recovery was obviously allowed in cases of *turpitudo solius accipientis*, i.e. where the turpitude was only on the side of the recipient.[121]

2.3.3 *The relationship between the* condictiones *and the* metus *remedies*

This overview of the treatment of the *condictiones* can be concluded by some brief remarks on their relationship with the *metus* remedies. Classical lawyers were notorious for not creating new remedies if it was at all possible to use existing ones.[122] There are indications in D 12.5.7 that a *condictio* could be used to recover

111 Schwarz, *Die Grundlage der Condictio im klassischen römischen Recht*, 174.

112 It should be noted though that this *condictio* was "residual" in nature. If a payment was made, but this payment was undue because there had to be release in terms of the law of hire, sale or mandate, then actions from those areas of the law were available. Cf Paul D 12.5.9.1.

113 Ulp D 12.5.2.1.

114 Ulp D 12.5.2.2.

115 Ulp D 12.5.4.

116 Ulp D 12.5.4; 12.5.5 (on which see Daube, "Turpitude in Digest 12.5.5" in *Studies in Roman Law in Memory of A Arthur Schiller* 33, especially in regard to the question whether the text concerns a *condictio furtiva*). The situation referred to above should be distinguished from the situation where A gives B something in order that B should supply information as to A's runaway slave or as to a thief of A's goods (Ulp. D 12.5.4.4). As Daube puts it "To want a remuneration for helping the master of a fugitive or one who has suffered a theft is not by itself dishonourable, at least not to a legally relevant degree. Detectives and slave-catchers live on it" ("Turpitude in Digest 12.5.5" in *Studies in Roman Law in Memory of A Arthur Schiller*, 33).

117 Glück, *Pandecten*, vol 12 ad D 12.5, 64; De Vos, *Verrykingsaanspreeklikheid in die Suid-Afrikaanse reg*, 22; Paul D 12.6.15 pr; Paul D 2.6.65.5; Paul D 12.4.7.1 and Paul D 12.4.12 are applied analogously.

118 Glück, *Pandecten*, vol 12 ad D 12.5, 64, De Vos, *Verrykingsaanspreeklikheid in die Suid-Afrikaanse reg*, 22 note 16, relying on C 4.7.4.

119 For example, payments to a prostitute (Paul D 12.5.4.3; cf the discussion in Zimmermann, *The Law of Obligations*, 847 et sq, esp note 91).

120 Cf Ulp D 12.5.2.2; Ulp D 12.5.4; Paul D 12.5.3; Paul D 12.5.8; Ulp D 50.17.154; C 4.7.2. For a discussion, see Zimmermann, *The Law of Obligations*, 846 et sqq.

121 Paul D 12.5.1.2; Ulp D 12.5.4.2; Glück, *Pandecten*, vol 12 ad D 12.5, 61.

122 Cf Von Lübtow, *Der Ediktstitel "Quod metus causa gestum erit"*, 304.

extorted transfers (albeit to a limited extent). So why were the praetorian *metus* remedies created, and the *condictio* not developed further?[123] A number of reasons present themselves. First, the *condictio* initially applied to a very limited category of transactions.[124] Second, the *condictio* was in any event excluded where there was *scientia* or knowledge that a transfer was not due. It is only after the *metus* remedies were introduced that the victim could possibly avail himself of the rather artificial argument that he was ignorant of the *exceptio metus*.[125] Third, the *condictio* could in any event not provide relief against third parties, particularly where a claim was made against the heir of a person who obtained goods on grounds of compulsion. The *condictio* was not aimed at restoring to a previous position (*restituere oportere*), but at *dare facere oportere*, which was not something one would expect a judge to grant in the light of the general protection afforded to heirs.[126] However, probably the most important explanation is the limited scope of the *metus* remedies—the strict standards of fortitude created room for a remedy which could be applied in less serious cases of compulsion. Through an analysis based on turpitude, the *condictio* could be made available.[127] But from a post-classical perspective, the fact that there may have been an overlap in fields of application is not really significant: the recognition of D 12.5.7 in addition to the praetorian action contained in D 4.2 was fully in line with the Byzantine practice to duplicate remedies.[128]

2.4 COMPULSION AND REMEDIES OF PROPERTY LAW

Implicit in a lot of what has been discussed above is the assumption that the person who acquired something as a consequence of *metus*, or some other form of compulsion, became owner thereof. The question was then whether this position could be reversed by granting a praetorian remedy based on *metus*[129] or a *condictio*. The overview of the Roman law of compulsion, can now be completed by more closely examining the effect of compulsion on the transfer of ownership.

In classical Roman law, certain modes of derivative acquisition of ownership[130] such as the more ancient and formal *mancipatio* and *in iure cessio* were abstract. In

123 Cf Von Koschembahr-Lyskowski, *Die Condictio als Bereicherungsklage im klassischen römischen Recht*, vol II (1907), 6. Von Lübtow does not believe that Pomp D 12.5.7 is of classical origin (*Der Ediktstitel "Quod metus causa gestum erit"*, 314).

124 Pomp D 12.5.7 only applies to the *stipulatio*.

125 Cf text to note 100 above.

126 Levy, *Privatstrafe und Schadensersatz im klassischen römischen Recht*, 92 et sq; Von Lübtow, *Der Ediktstitel "Quod metus causa gestum erit"*, 304 et sq.

127 J Kohler, *Lehrbuch des Bürgerlichen Rechts* (1906), vol 1, 518 et sqq; Von Savigny, *System des heutigen römischen Rechts*, vol 3, 107 note (r). Cf J P Dawson, "Economic Duress and the Fair Exchange in French and German Law" (1937) 11 *TulaneLR* 345 at 347 et sq.

128 Von Lübtow, *Der Ediktstitel "Quod metus causa gestum erit"*, 315 et sq ("Die Byzantiner liebten es, nach dem Grundsatz: 'doppelt hält besser' dem Kläger Rechtsmittel in Hülle und Fülle zur Verfügung zu stellen").

129 On the distinction between obtaining an order that the wrongdoer should restore, and obtaining automatic restitution of ownership, cf Kupisch, *In integrum restitutio und vindicatio utilis bei Eigentumsübertragungen im klassischen römischen Recht*, 1 et sqq.

130 On the different modes of acquisition and the distinction between quiritary and bonitary ownership in Roman law, see Kaser, *Das römische Privatrecht I*, 400 et sqq; Schulz, *Classical Roman law*, 338 ET sq; Nicholas, *An Introduction to Roman Law*, 66 et sqq, 116 et sqq; Thomas, *Textbook of Roman law*, 136 et sqq; Honsell, Mayer-Maly and Selb, *Römisches Recht*, 156 et sqq; Ankum and Pool, "*Rem in bonis meis esse* and *rem in bonis meam esse*—Traces of the Development of Roman Double Ownership" in *Essays for Barry Nicholas*, 5.

other words, it was not required that acquisition should be supported by a *causa*, such as payment in terms of a valid agreement.[131] However, this was apparently not the case with *traditio*, which was a more informal mode of acquisition. Here the dominant view is that in classical law the transfer of ownership had to be supported by a *iusta causa traditionis*, such as a valid agreement of sale.[132] Apparently payment or *solutio* was regarded as a valid *causa* in itself: a transfer made with a view towards payment of a debt was therefore regarded as validly supported by a *causa*, even if the debt turned out to be undue.[133] How did all of this fit in the law relating to compulsion? As far as *metus* is concerned, there are indications that where ownership was transferred under compulsion, the praetor provided a rescissory action in the form of an *actio in rem* on the model of the *rei vindicatio*.[134] This remedy apparently was available as an alternative to the *actio quod metus causa*.[135] The wrongdoer's acquisition of rights of (quiritary)[136] ownership could then be thwarted by the *actio in rem*. In the case of the compelled *mancipatio*, the victim apparently had a choice between the rescissory *rei vindicatio* and the *actio quod metus causa*.[137] In the case of the compelled *traditio*, the position is more complicated. If the *traditio* was compelled, but the underlying *causa*, such as an agreement of sale, was valid, the relief did not lie with the *actiones in rem* or *quod metus causa*, but rather with the *lex Julia de vi privata*.[138] However, if the underlying agreement was extorted as well, the validity of the *causa* and the validity of the transfer became questionable. In classical law,

---

131 Cf Kaser, *Das römische Privatrecht* I, 416 et sqq; Zimmermann, *The Law of Obligations*, 271 et sq, 841 et sq. On the general requirements for a *datio* (of which *traditio* is an instance), cf text to notes 81 et sqq above.

132 Cf Kaser, *Das römische Privatrecht* I, 416 et sqq; Kaser, "Zur in integrum restitutio, besonders wegen metus und dolus" (1977) 94 *ZSS (RA)* 101 at 123, 138 et sqq; Zimmermann, *The Law of Obligations*, 271 et sq, 841 et sq. For a critical assessment see D F Pugsley, "Was *iusta causa* necessary for *traditio* in Roman law?" (1974) 37 *THRHR* 13; Gordon, "The Importance of the *iusta causa* of *traditio*", in *Essays for Barry Nicholas*, 123; Evans-Jones and MacCormack, "*Iusta causa traditionis*" in *Essays for Barry Nicholas* 99.

133 Cf Kaser, *Das römische Privatrecht* I, 416 et sqq; Kaser, "Zur in integrum restitutio, besonders wegen metus und dolus" (1977) *ZSS* 101 at 138 et sqq.

134 Kupisch, *In integrum restitutio und vindicatio utilis bei Eigentumsübertragungen im klassischen römischen Recht*, 134 et sqq; Kaser, "Zur in integrum restitutio, besonders wegen metus und dolus" (1977) 94 *ZSS* 101 at 138 et sqq; Zimmermann, *The Law of Obligations*, 656 note 46.

135 In Ulp D 4.2.9.6 it is stated that "... although we think that an action *in rem* is to be granted because the property belongs to the person (*quia res in bonis eius est*) on whom force has been brought to bear, it is still said, not without reason, that if anyone should bring an action for fourfold, the action *in rem* ceases; and the reverse is also true". But cf Von Lübtow, *Der Ediktstitel "Quod metus causa gestum erit"*, 120 et sqq, 255 et sq. He states that it is the Edict's consequence of "ratum non habebo" which provides the victim with a "fictional *rei vindicatio*" and so restores his ownership. The action seems to be regarded as *part* of the relief provided by the *actio quod metus causa*, rather than a separate remedy.

136 Although the wrongdoer obtained quiritary ownership, it is possible that the victim may still have retained bonitary ownership. On the possibility that the victim may still have retained rights of bonitary ownership, see Hartkamp, *Der Zwang im römischen Privatrecht*, 127 et sqq; Kupisch, *In integrum restitutio und vindicatio utilis bei Eigentumsübertragungen im klassischen römischen Recht*, 222 et sqq.

137 Cf Hartkamp, *Der Zwang im römischen Privatrecht*, 127 et sqq on the validity of the compelled *mancipatio*.

138 Cf Ulp D 4.2.12.2; Hartkamp, *Der Zwang im römischen Privatrecht*, 166 et sq. On the position if the underlying agreement of sale was extorted, but not the *traditio*, see C 2.19.4. Hartkamp argues that this is indicative of a confirmation of the transfer, and an abandonment of the praetorian remedies (*Der Zwang im römischen Privatrecht*, 50 et sq).

this may very well have meant that ownership did not pass.[139] In post-classical law, where *traditio* became the dominant mode of derivative acquisition, the position could have been similar, but this is by no means clear.[140]

When one briefly moves on to the effect of compulsion on the validity of transfers in the context of the *condictio*, the picture is more simple. It has been indicated above that in post-classical law the *condictio ob turpem vel iniustam causam* could be used to recover certain transfers made under compulsion, most notably where a person used actual threats (*vis*), or implied threats (e.g. by stating that he will not do something he is supposed to do, unless the victim does something in turn). The question as to whether this compulsion was sufficiently serious to affect the transfer of ownership is not hard to answer. In these cases there was no concurrence between the *condictio* and remedies of property law such as the *rei vindicatio*. Even though a transfer made under an extorted stipulation could be regarded as having been tainted with turpitude, the turpitude did not prevent the passage of ownership.[141]

2.5 CONCLUSIONS

1. Early Roman private law was not well adapted to provide relief to victims of compulsion: it was only in certain cases that a judge could provide relief by relying on considerations of good faith. Given the tumultuous social and political conditions in Republican Rome, it was up to the praetor to remedy this deficiency. The first reform was contained in a *formula Octaviana*, of which the exact contents is unclear. Apparently, it was aimed at enabling recovery of what had been taken, or what was given under force and (or) fear (*per vim et (aut) metum*). At the time, the *actio vi bonorum raptorum* was also introduced, which was a specific action against robbery. Further legislative relief was provided in the form of a *lex Julia de vi privata*, which imposed criminal punishment in cases of self-help, and the *leges repetundarum*, which were specifically aimed against magistrates who enriched themselves by extorting bribes. *The decretum divi Marci* punished a creditor with the loss of his claim if he engaged in self-help, regardless of whether a debt was due.
2. From a modern perspective, the most important Roman remedy against compulsion is to be found in the *Edictum perpetuum* of Hadrian. According to the Edict, the praetor would not uphold what is done as a consequence of fear ("quod metus causa gestum erit, ratum non habebo"). The Edict did not encompass physical bodily force which completely excludes any decision of will of the victim (in medieval terms, *vis absoluta*), but rather compulsion through "bending" the will of the victim ("mental" fear or *vis compulsiva*). It

139 Hartkamp, *Der Zwang im römischen Privatrecht*, 178 et sq.

140 Ulp D 4.2.9.6 indicates that ownership does not pass, but see Hartkamp, *Der Zwang im römischen Privatrecht*, 178 et sq; Von Lübtow, *Der Ediktstitel "Quod metus causa gestum erit"*, 13; and generally Kaser, *Das römische Privatrecht II*, 282 et sqq.

141 Cf Liebs, "The History of the Roman *Condictio* up to Justinian" in *Essays for Tony Honoré*, 163 at 174; Zimmermann, *Law of Obligations*, 845 note 74. Ownership also passed with the transfer of money (Kaser, "Das Geld im römischen Sachenrecht" (1961) 29 *Tijdschrift voor Rechtsgeschiedenis* 220).

was also required that the fear had to be caused by wrongful means, and had to be serious enough to move a *homo constantissimus*. The meaning of the words *ratum non habebo* in the Edict is unclear, but it seems as if the following relief was provided. If the victim was faced with a claim of enforcement he could ward it off with the *exceptio metus*. If he had already made a compelled transfer and wanted restitution, he could institute the *actio quod metus causa*. It is disputed whether this remedy, which exposed the wrongdoer to a penalty of fourfold damages if he did not provide restitution, was aimed at obtaining *in integrum restitutio* (*propter metum*), or whether *in integrum restitutio* was a separate remedy.

3. Under certain circumstances, compulsion could also give rise to a *condictio*—a remedy aimed at recovery of a specific amount or object. In classical law the *condictio* could apparently be used to recover a transfer made in fulfillment of a compelled stipulation. In Justinianic law, which was characterised by a fragmentation of the *condictio*, it was the *condictio ob turpem vel iniustam causam* which was singled out for the fulfillment of this function. This *condictio* was aimed at the recovery of a transfer which was made for a future purpose which succeeded, but whose retention was unacceptable because it was tainted by turpitude. Examples of cases of compulsion where the *condictio ob turpem vel iniustam causam* was used towards this end are where a transfer was made to a person so that he would do what he was supposed to do in any event, such as to return goods which were deposited with him or loaned to him, or to refrain from committing a crime. In this limited context, through recourse to notions of turpitude, the *condictio ob turpem vel iniustam causam* could be applied in cases of compulsion not covered by the praetorian *metus* remedies. The *condictio indebiti* was particularly suited for the recovery of transfers made in order to pay a debt (*solvendi causa*), but which failed, because no debt was due. It was apparently not used in cases where undue transfers were obtained by compulsion. This can be ascribed to the prominence of the error requirement in post-classical law.

4. Compulsion could further give rise to remedies of property law, most notably a rescissory action in the form of an *actio in rem*.

Chapter 3

Compulsion in medieval until nineteenth-century Scots law

3.1 INTRODUCTION

The borders of Scotland were only formed around the turn of the first millennium AD: laws which previously existed in this region are virtually unknown and no longer of any practical significance.[1] It is only after the accession of David I to the throne of Scotland in 1124, when feudal structures were set up through Anglo-Saxon and Norman influence, that a legal system began to develop: Roman law, via canon law, then came to form part of Scots law. Part of this Roman legacy was the law of *metus* and the *condictiones*. Using this reception as a point of departure, the development of various rules of Scottish private law relating to compulsion between the thirteenth and nineteenth centuries will now be traced.[2] A useful point of departure for such an investigation is *Regiam Majestatem*, which is probably the most important legal document of these early times. Its origins are obscure, but it seems to date from the late thirteenth to early fourteenth centuries.[3] Thereafter, the focus will be on the *Practicks*, which were legal compilations based on the "*Auld Laws*" (partly reflected in *Regiam Majestatem*), statutes and decisions. These works emanated from a period of legal reform[4] which commenced with the conversion in 1532 of the temporary court, the Session, into a permanent central court, the College of Justice. The most

---

1 On the historical background to pre-sixteenth century Scots law, cf generally Walker, *The Scottish Legal System*, 77–105; Walker, *A Legal History of Scotland*, vol 1; H L MacQueen, "Mixture or Muddle? Teaching and Research in Scots Legal History" 1997 *ZEuP* 369.

2 On the significance of remedies against compulsion in early Scots law, cf McBryde, *Void, Voidable, Illegal and Unenforceable Contracts in Scots law*, 33; Memorandum on Defective Consent And Consequential Matters (Scot Law Com Memo No 42, 1978), vol 2, para 3.105.

3 Cf A Harding, "Regiam Majestatem amongst medieval law books" 1984 *JR* 97 and Walker, *A Legal History of Scotland*, vol 1, 114 et sqq for an overview of the various views on the origins of this work. For detailed examinations of its content and influences, cf J Buchanan, "The MSS. of Regiam Majestatem" (1937) 49 *JR* 155; H G Richardson, "Roman law in the Regiam Majestatem" 1955 *JR* 155; P Stein, "The Source of the Romano-canonical part of the Regiam Majestatem" (1969) 48 *Scottish Historical Review* 107; A A M Duncan, "Regiam Majestatem: A Reconsideration" 1961 *JR* 199. According to Lord Cooper, this document "represented the chief part of the legal salvage from the wreck of the 14th century" (*Regiam Majestatem and Quoniam Attachiamenta*, ed. and transl. by Lord Cooper, 2). To him it is then supposed to date from the beginnings of the Dark Ages, which is depicted as a period of continuous political strife between Scotland and England lasting from the death of Robert the Bruce in 1329 until the sixteenth century (Lord Cooper, *The Dark Age of Scottish Legal History 1350–1650*, Glasgow University Publications, no XCII (1952); cf also G C H Paton, "The Dark Age", in *An Introduction to Scottish Legal History* 18 et sqq). For criticism of this view, cf inter alia Walker, *A Legal History of Scotland*, vol 2, 758 et sq; H L MacQueen, "Mixture or Muddle? Teaching and Research in Scots Legal History" 1997 *ZEuP* 369 at 378 et sq.

4 Cf J Irvine Smith, "The Transition to the Modern Law", in Paton, *An Introduction to Scottish Legal History*, 25.

notable authors of *Practicks* were Sir James Balfour of Pittendreich (1525–83),[5] and Sir Thomas Hope of Craighall (1580–1646). Their works became the forerunners of the later law reports and Institutional writings.[6] Attention will also be paid to the canon law of force and fear, especially in the context of the law of marriage.

3.2 THE EARLY RECORDS: THE THIRTEENTH TO SEVENTEENTH CENTURY

3.2.1 *The law of "fear and dread"*

Under the heading "*Quot modis quis potest contradicere factum proprium*", Supplement no 25 to *Regiam Majestatem* deals with three "circumstances in which a man may gainsay his own deed".[7] The first and third circumstances are, respectively, minority and insanity. It is then stated that

> if a person should be in prison or in chains or in the hands of robbers, he is not bound by acts done by him under force and fear capable of overcoming a resolute man (... si sit in carcere vel in vinculis vel in manibus raptorum, factum suum non tenet propter vim et metum possunt cadere in virum constantem).[8]

It can hardly be disputed that this passage is Roman in origin:[9] concepts such as *vis et metus* and the *vir constans* are familiar to anyone who has read the Digest title on *metus*.[10] But before the reception and development of these Roman concepts and related rules are dealt with, it is necessary to reflect briefly on an aspect of the text which is not in conformance with Roman law, namely a possibly different basis for relief. The passage clearly links together minority, *vis et metus* and insanity as cases where "a man may gainsay his own deed". This indicates that the basis for relief in cases of *vis et metus* is the influence on a person's mental ability or capacity to form his will. It will be recalled that D.4.1 (*de in integrum restitutionibus*) groups together a much wider variety of cases when a person may not be bound to his deeds (these include error, *vis et metus*, fraud, minority and absence). The reason for the difference in approach is not clear. Unlike the greater part of *Regiam Majestatem*,

---

5 His *Practicks* was completed in 1579, and has been described as the most important Scottish legal document between *Regiam Majestatem* and Stair's *Institutions* of 1681. Cf Balfour, *Practicks*, vol 1, xxxix. Balfour had a long and chequered legal career which culminated in his appointment as Lord President of the Court of Session in 1567.

6 On the *Practicks*, cf in general H McKechnie "Practicks, 1469–1700", in *An Introductory Survey of the Sources and Literature of Scots Law*, 26 et sqq.

7 *Regiam Majestatem and Quoniam Attachiamenta*, Supplement, No 25 (Stair Society volume at 299).

8 *Regiam Majestatem and Quoniam Attachiamenta*, Supplement, No 25. Unfortunately Sir John Skene (1543?–1616) does not offer anything on *vis et metus* or restitution in his *De Verborum Significatione*, an exposition of "termes and difficill wordes" used in certain legal texts, most notably *Regiam Majestatem*. The 1597 Edinburgh edition was consulted.

9 In general, *Regiam Majestatem* seems to have been strongly influenced by English law, and in particular by Ranulph de Glanvill's *De Legibus et Consuetudinibus Angliae* of 1187 (cf P Stein, "The Source of the Romano-canonical part of the Regiam Majestatem" (1969) 48 *Scottish Historical Review* 107; Walker, *A Legal History of Scotland*, vol 1, 108). This prompted later Scottish legal authors, and particularly such a renowned institutional authority as Stair, to deny that it was of any significance to Scots law at all (cf G D G Hall, *The treatise on the laws and customs of the realm of England commonly called Glanvill* (1965), lx; Walker, *The Scottish Legal System*, 91 et sq).

10 D 4.2.

the passage quoted above is not drawn from Glanvill's *De Legibus et Consuetinibus Regni Angliae*. Although this indicates that the origin of the passage might lie in another source, with stronger civilian roots, none of the most likely texts contain such a grouping.[11] However, irrespective of its origin, the impact of the passage was limited. It does appear in the *Practicks*,[12] which indicates that "fear and dread" was regarded as a factor which affects the capacity to consent,[13] but this conclusion is only warranted if the focus is solely on the immediate context in which it is discussed. Unlike *Regiam Majestatem*, the *Practicks* also deal with fraud under the heading of *restitutio in integrum*,[14] which indicates that the basis for relief may in fact have been broader: a victim of fraud, or a person operating under error for that matter, does not experience any defect in mental ability or capacity: the problem is much rather the way in which his consent has been obtained. It is therefore arguable that the authors of the *Practicks* did not share *Regiam Majestatem*'s rather narrow approach to the basis for relief in cases of *vis et metus*, but rather opted for an approach more closely linked to the Digest. In fact, case law not contained in the *Practicks* indicate that *in integrum restitutio* could also be provided in cases of extortion through *laesio enormis*. This clearly shows that it is not merely the procedural defect in obtaining consent, but also the substantive unfairness which gave rise to this remedy.[15]

i. The content of "fear and dread": the **vir constans** *and* **justus metus**

The early law does not define *vis et metus* or "fear and dread": it rather lists factual circumstances in which it would be found to exist. Thus, Supplement no 25 to *Regiam*

---

11 Azo deals with "*de his que vi metusve causa gesta sunt*", but there is no parallel text grouping together minority, *vis et metus* and insanity (*Summa Codicis 2 19(20)*, (Papiae, 1506, Torino, 1906), 38). The same can be said of Goffredus: cf his *Summa super titulis decretalium* (Lyon, 1519; Aalen, 1968), 68 et sq.

12 In Balfour's *Practicks*, under the heading *Restitutio in integrum*, it is stated that a person could "gainsay or cum aganis his awin deid" if he is "of les age" (a minor), "lunatique, wod and furious" (insane) and that "Gif he be in prisoun, in bandis, in the handis and powar of reiffaris (*robbers*), or in his enemeis, nothing done by him may hurt or prejudge him; because he is understuid to do the samin be just feir or dredour, quhilk may fall in ane constant man" (*Practicks*, 45.1). Likewise, under the heading *De Restitutione in integrum*, the *Practicks* of Hope list three cases where "a man may be restored against his own deid". These are deeds done "in minoritie", where he was "mentis inops" and deeds done "... whill he wes in prisone, in bands, or in the hands of his enemeies (ex capite metus) ... Quhatsomever a man does for just fear quhilk may fall in virum constantem may be reduced aither be the doer, or his airs, against the receaver or his airs—such as bands maid for saiftie of a man's owen life, or of his wyfe or children etc." (*Practicks*, VI.38.26).

13 According to Professor W W McBryde the category which today would be classified under force and fear "was treated as though it were a species of temporary incapacity, being linked to those who were of "les age" and lunatique, wod and furious" (*Void, Voidable, Illegal and Unenforceable Contracts in Scots law*, 6).

14 See Balfour, *Practicks*, 45.13; Hope, *Practicks*, VI.38.26. It is not clear why Balfour did not mention fraud as one of the cases where a man may gainsay his own deed in the main heading. He probably did not want to change the *Regiam Majestatem* text. It hardly seems probable that he believed that fraud was subsumed under fear and dread. Even though a concurrence of the remedies on grounds of *metus* and *dolus* was possible in Roman law, there is virtual unanimity that the rules regarding *metus* and *dolus* were never unified (See L van Huyssteen, *Onbehoorlike Beïnvloeding en Misbruik van Omstandighede*, 23 et sqq). Balfour's *Practicks* also contain a completely separate title on "fraudfull and doubill alienations" (Balfour, *Practicks*, 37), but this only deals with fraud in the form of double alienations.

15 Cf the 1231 case of *Abbey of Dunfermline v Richard of Balweri, Registerum de Dunfermelyn* (1842), 223 and the 1234 case of *Bishop of Dunblane v Abbey of Lindores, Chartulary of Lindores*, Scottish History Society (1903), no 50 (quoted in Stein, *The Character and Influence of the Roman Civil Law*, 292).

Majestatem indicates that relief would be provided in certain severe cases of physical compulsion, namely where a person acts while being held in some form of physical captivity, and while experiencing fear which would move a "constant man".[16] These requirements are echoed by Balfour and Hope,[17] who refer to a person being held in prison, in "bands" and in the hands of his enemies and robbers, and who also refer to the "constant man" requirement. These examples apparently include physical harm in the form of *vis absoluta*,[18] but leave it somewhat unclear as to which forms of *vis compulsiva* are covered as well. The scope might have been broader than the texts reveal. First, it was not required that the person subjected to threats necessarily had to be in physical captivity.[19] Second, fear for the safety and preservation of the lives of friends and family was also actionable: the person acting out of fear therefore did not necessarily have to fear harm to himself.[20] And finally, there are some indications that "reverential fear", or *metus reverentialis* could also be actionable.[21] It is tempting

16 A similar approach is also followed in the first recorded case on compulsion in Scots law, namely *Lady Torrs v Lyoun of Logy* (1483) A D A 128*, 145*. The Lyoun of Logy alleged that he was compelled and constrained to make a "letter of tak" (lease) to Lady Torrs, since at the time he was not "at liberty and freedom but in festinans and ward" (imprisoned). The court then demanded that he should prove that he was "compelled and constrained by dread and awe which might fall in a constant person", and "by what compulsion he was compelled to make the said letter" (of tak, or lease). Cf also *King and Gray v Hamilton of Preston* (1532/33) A D C et S 119; *Hamilton v Abbot of Culross* (1494) A D A 202; A P S 11, 205. In the latter case it was alleged that the Convent of Culross was compelled and "coakkit" to make an assedation or assignation to Hamilton and his spouse. Apparently the abbot ("apte"?) of the convent was imprisoned until the assedation was granted. In referring to these cases, Professor McBryde states that "[a]s befits Scottish history, force and fear is a ground for reduction at an early date" (*Void, Voidable, Illegal and Unenforceable Contracts in Scots Law*, 35; *The Law of Contract in Scotland*, 250).

17 Balfour, *Practicks*, 45.XV., 45.XVI; cf also Hope, *Practicks*, VI.38.26.

18 On this concept, see 2.2.1 above. Canon law sources indicate that the distinction was known in medieval Scots law: see 3.2.3 below. From a legal perspective it is a pity that Mary, Queen of Scots, never pursued her claim that she was forced to resign the crown. It might have become one of the most famous cases of *vis absoluta* in legal history. But perhaps the factual basis for such a claim was rather weak. The Rev James Mackenzie comments as follows: "About a month after she entered prison in Lochleven, the Queen signed a deed of abdication in favour of her infant son. Lindsay of the long sword, says the foolish story, laid his heavy, mailed grasp on her slender lily-white hand, and compelled her to sign. Queens, though pinched black and blue, do not sign away a crown. Mary signed her abdication because she knew that the evidence of her crime had come to light, and that if she did not abdicate she could be brought to a public trial. She signed on the same day another deed, appointing the Earl of Moray Regent of the Kingdom during her child's minority" (*The History of Scotland* (1897), 390). Cf also Walker, *A Legal History of Scotland*, vol 3, 84; Sir William Fraser, *Memorials of the Earls of Haddington* (1989), 268 et sqq.

19 Cf Balfour, *Practicks*, 45.VII., 45.XVI. Balfour refers to the case of *The Earl of Morton v The Queen* (cf also Hope, *Practicks*, VI.38.26–27; Spotiswoode, *Practicks*, 205 et sq; Sinclair, *Practicks*, cases 315 and 541; Stair, *Institutions*, 1.9.8.). King James V apparently threatened the Earl of Morton that he would be imprisoned if he did not resign his lands and title to him. After the King's death, the Earl instituted legal proceedings against (inter alia) the Queen, as the King's successor. Even though the Earl was apparently not physically held captive, the court decided that the Earl's fear and dread of his life was sufficient to move a constant man. Reference is also made to *The Laird of Dundas contra the Laird of Cragiehall*, 24 July 1553 (Balfour, *Practicks*, 45.XVI).

20 Balfour, *Practicks*, 45.XV.

21 In *A v B* (1612) Mor 16481 and *Marishall v Marishall* (1623) Mor 16482 certain acts were held to be invalid because they were done *super capite metus reverentialis* and *ob reverentiam maritalem*, but both these reports are quite sparse, and do not state what caused this reverence. In *Hepburn v Nasmyth* (1613) Mor 16482 it was held that a wife's claim of *metus reverentialis* would not be successful unless she had claimed "*verum et expressum metum* by relevant circumstances and deeds". Apparently, one way of ensuring that a wife could not escape form her past actions was by obtaining her consent before a judge while her husband was not present. In the *Jus Feudale* of Sir Thomas

to identify principles which underlie all these examples of compulsion. On its own, the *vir constans* requirement obviously could not fulfil such a function. Relief cannot be provided merely because a person experienced fear which would move a *vir constans*: such an approach would undermine acceptable forms of compulsion such as diligence. However, here it becomes significant that the *Practicks* (unlike *Regiam Majestatem*) also state that the fear or dread had to be *just*.[22] One explanation of this term is that it simply means "fear which would move a constant man", but such an interpretation seems somewhat unnecessary and tautologous. An alternative explanation is that "just fear" is fear which has been instilled by unjust means.[23] This would then stand in contrast to justly inspired fear, such as fear arising from threatened or actual diligence,[24] which could take the form of personal imprisonment,[25] and the poinding[26] or inhibition[27] of property.

Craig of Riccarton (1538–1608) it is stated that "anciently", consent to such an alienation had to be given before a judge. In the absence of the husband, "[i]n our own day it is enough if she subscribes the deed in the presence of witnesses. But it is always possible that she may at some later date be successful in proving that her husband induced her to subscribe by force and fear (*se ad subscribendum coactam vi & metu probare poterit*). According to him "the safest plan is therefore to obtain her consent judicially, outwith the husband's presence" (*Jus Feudale*, 1.15.20).

22 Balfour, *Practicks*, 45.XIII, 45.XIV, 45.XV, 45.XVI, 45.XVII; Hope, *Practicks*, VI.38.26. This requirement is also mentioned in *Earl of Orkney v Vinfra* (1606) Mor 16481. Here it was averred that the Earl of Orkney threatened with "execrable oaths to bereave this Vinfra of his life, and stick him presently through the head with his whinger" (a short stabbing sword) if he did not sign a certain contract. The Earl's defence was that these were only boisterous words, which could not be thought just fear, and that Vinfra previously offered to contract upon the same conditions in a letter. It was then held that the existence of fear was "relevant", but that the letter would first have to be produced before Vinfra would be granted relief. Apparently the court believed that the letter would indicate whether Vinfra acted under fear of his life, or whether he simply wanted to escape from a contract which he would have assented to in any event.

23 From a civilian perspective, cf the later analyses in Voet, *Commentarius ad Pandectas*, 4.2.10 and Pothier, *Traité des obligations*, note 26.

24 This term describes various processes by which a creditor, in aid of recovery of his debt, attached the property or person of his debtor. An early text on diligence is ch 49 of *Quoniam Attachiamenta*, dealing with the brieve of distress for debt (Stair Society edition, 344). However, even in the fourteenth century the general principle was that if a free man found enough cautioners, he should not be imprisoned "on the complaint of another" (*pro querela alicuius*); cf ch 39 of *Quoniam Attachiamenta* (335). On the earlier law against self-help, cf W M Gloag, "The Limits of the Right of Self-redress" (1917) 29 *JR* 124.

25 Civil imprisonment as a form of diligence arose in the ecclesiastical courts, which had jurisdiction over various contracts and obligations. These courts could invoke the Royal authority to enforce their decrees, which meant that a person disregarding the decree to pay his debt would be regarded as a rebel and a caption for his arrest would be issued. This practice also came to be adopted in the civil courts (D Maxwell, "Diligence" in *An Introduction to Scottish Legal History* 229 at 235 et sqq). A part of this process was to denounce the debtor in public as a rebel with three blasts of a horn, a practice which came to be called "horning" (cf Balfour, *Practicks*, 158; Hope, *Practicks*, VI.27.1).

26 Poinding proceeded after the debtor was charged to pay the debt at a certain date and then failed to do so. According to Balfour, if it was proven that someone owed a debt, he had fifteen days to pay, failing which the judge would "cause his Officiar to poind, distreinzie and comprise his movabill gudis and gear" (Balfour, *Practicks*, 119). At first the creditor could simply seize the goods of a debtor to obtain payment, but later on it became necessary to obtain a brieve of distress. In the sixteenth century these brieves were replaced by "letters of horning and poinding", a practice which was continued up to the nineteenth century. Cf Maxwell, "Diligence" in *An Introduction to Scottish Legal History*, 229 at 232 et sqq; Balfour, *Practicks*, 98.

27 Inhibition entailed prohibiting a debtor to alienate his lands to the prejudice of an (inhibiting) creditor (cf Maxwell, "Diligence" in *An Introduction to Scottish Legal History*, 229 at 231; J Irvine Smith, "The Transition to the Modern Law 1532–1660", in *An Introduction to Scots Legal History*, 25 at 33 et sq). Since 1581 it became necessary to register inhibitions. Cf Hope, *Practicks*, II.15.6.

ii. The nature of the relief: "gainsay your deed" and in integrum restitutio

Regiam Majestatem is not as specific as the Digest in describing the nature of the relief in cases of compulsion: all it states is that a person may "gainsay his own deed" (*contradicere factum proprium*), and that such a deed is invalid. Nothing is said about the nature of the remedy, e.g. whether it is penal, whether it is available against third parties, and whether there are any preconditions for restitution. It can only be surmised that a person will "gainsay his own deed" when he refuses performance in terms of a compelled agreement, or when he claims return or restitution of transfers made under compulsion. The *Practicks*, on the other hand, sketch a more detailed picture. First, despite statements that compelled acts were of "nane avail, force nor effect", the victim apparently could choose whether he wanted to enforce the extorted act or seek relief: it is stated that he could seek restitution *at his own pleasure*.[28] This indicates that the effect of compulsion was to render legal acts voidable, rather than void. That certain acts were regarded as voidable in Balfour's time is apparent from the rules allowing ratification of things done by minors.[29] Second, where it has been established that the validity of the victim's act was affected by compulsion, he was provided with relief in the form of *restitutio in integrum*,[30] which essentially entailed that the victim had to be put in the position he would have been in if the compelled act never took place.[31] It should be noted though that obtaining *restitutio in integrum* or simply "restitution"[32] did not only entail the physical "restitution" or "repetition"[33] of transfers of property or things, such as making infeftments,[34] and disposing of or alienating lands, goods or gear. It also entailed a challenge to the validity of a discharge[35] or renunciation, or of obligations and contracts.[36] The victim

---

28 Balfour, *Practicks*, 45.XIII.

29 Cf Balfour, *Practicks*, 45.VIII.

30 See e.g. Balfour, *Practicks*, 45.XV; Hope, *Practicks*, VI.38. Sir Robert Spotiswoode (1596–1646) follows a somewhat different approach in his *Practicks* (which dealt with the law between 1541–1637): unlike Balfour and Hope, he only regards reduction as a remedy in cases of *metus*. *Restitutio in integrum* is dealt with in the context of minority (Spotiswoode, *Practicks*, 301) and (somewhat indirectly) fraud. In the rubric on *dolus et fraus* it is stated that a person who is deceived should be restored *in integrum*, and that a deed "proceeded from fraud should be reduced and decrn'd null" (Spotiswoode, *Practicks*, 81). This statement is based on Balfour, *Practicks*, 45.XVIII.

31 According to the case of *The Lord Flemyng v The Lord Drummelzear* a person should be restored *in integrum* "like as the samin had never bene maid nor obtenit" (Balfour, *Practicks*, 45.XV; cf also *Earl of Morton v Lochleven*; *Earl of Morton v the Queen* (1543) Mor 16479). In the context of reductions *ex causa metus*, Hope clearly states the pursuer should "in the sumonds mak offer of the pryce he gott for doeing the deed, wtherwayes the lybell is not relevant" (Hope, *Practicks*, VI.38.27). But cf Balfour, *Practicks*, 45.XII; Spotiswoode, *Practicks*, 301: although it is stated that a minor seeking restitution should restore and offer that which has reclaimed, the same requirement is not mentioned in the context of compulsion.

32 It is not always clear what is meant by providing "restitution". It does not seem to have had a technical meaning, for in some places it is simply used as the noun formed from the infinitive "to restore". In the context of loan, to restore would mean to give back that which has been transferred, but could also mean giving back its just price and value (Balfour, *Practicks*, 53.I).

33 "Repetition" was awarded in a case involving the recovery of money: cf *Love v Downie* (1586) Mor 16480, which is not discussed in the *Practicks*.

34 Cf Balfour, *Practicks*, 35. "Infeftment" is the investing of a new owner with the right in or legal possession of land or heritage (cf *The Scottish National Dictionary*, s.v. "infeftment").

35 Balfour, *Practicks*, 45.XIII. Cf also Balfour, *Practicks*, 32.X; *Craig v Mowat* (1555) Mor 16480. It seems to be used in the sense of a release from an obligation.

36 Although there was no general form of contract in Balfour's time, the title apparently applied in the same way to all contracts (cf Balfour, *Practicks*, vol 1, xlvi (introduction by P G B McNeill)). Balfour deals with various forms of contract individually, e.g. borrowing and lending (Balfour, *Practicks*, 49), "assedation" (lease—Balfour, *Practicks*, 56) and buying and selling (Balfour, *Practicks*, 57).

could then ask for reduction,[37] or restitution by way of "action" or "exception".[38] Hope, rather confusingly,[39] deals with reduction under two separate subtitles in his title on reduction ("*De Actionibus Rescissoriis*"):[40] he first discusses fear and dread in a subtitle on *restitutio in integrum*,[41] but then also deals with it under a separate subtitle on "reductions *ex capite metus*". The reason for this separation, which is reminiscent of the Roman distinction between the *actio quod metus causa* and *in integrum restitutio*, is not clear: both subtitles deal with reduction, and the content of the subtitle on "reduction *ex capite metus*" fits in as well with the title on *restitutio in integrum*.[42]

Finally, relief could also be obtained against third parties,[43] even if they were bona fide. The basis of this liability is not clear, but it seems to be the enrichment of the third party, rather than ownership, or delict. For example, the Queen, as the King's successor could be made answerable since it would be "absurd and contrary to reason that a minor should be enriched through just fear" ("... quia absurdum est, et contra rationem, quod minor ex justo metu ... fieret locupletior").[44] An obvious reason why the latter ground would not have been appropriate for a claim based on delict is that the Queen did not commit any wrong herself.

3.2.2 *Compulsion and the* condictiones

In the previous chapter it was indicated that in Roman, law the *condictiones*, and more specifically a *condictio ob turpem vel iniustam causam*, provided some relief in cases where something was obtained through compulsion. None of this is apparent in early Scots law, which, in fact, barely contains traces of the recognition of the *condictiones*. For example, there are isolated references in the Melrose Charter of 1280 to renunciations of, inter alia, the *condictio ex lege*, *condictio sine causa*, and *condictio*

Assignations and contracts which were not "onerous or lucrative" (apparently without cause—cf the marginal note) were not valid (Balfour, *Practicks*, 39.I). McNeill indicates that in Balfour's time the word obligation meant a written bond of the law by which a man is bound by reason of any debt or contract (Balfour, *Practicks*, vol 1, xlv, cf Balfour, *Practicks*, 32.I).

37 Cf *The Earl of Morton v The Queen* (1543) Mor 16479, where a reduction of the resignations was granted, and the Earl was "reponed ... in the same estate" before he resigned his title and lands.

38 Balfour, *Practicks*, 45.XIII, Hope, *Practicks*, VI.38.27; *Tenants of Cockburnspath v Lord Home* (1543) Mor 2724; *Forbes v Tenants* (1591) Mor 2724; but cf *Oliphant v Bochti* (1554) Mor 2724. On exceptions in general, cf Balfour, *Practicks*, 88.I.

39 Hope, *Practicks*, vol 1, xiii (introduction by P G B McNeill).

40 Hope, *Practicks*, VI.38.

41 The subtitle *de restitutione in integrum* contains familiar list of cases where a man may "gainsay his own deed", namely if he was a minor, mentally insane (*mentis inops*) or acting *ex capite metus* (Hope, *Practicks*, VI.38.26).

42 In fact, the same case (*Earl of Morton v The Queen* (1543) Mor 16479) is discussed in both titles.

43 Reduction would also be available against a person in whose favour an agreement was concluded or transfer was made, and who is in possession of the property (Balfour, *Practicks*, 45.XIV). Spotiswoode's *Practicks* refers to a case decided after Balfour finished his *Practicks*, namely *Taffie v Fleming*, of 18 July 1632. Although the reports differ somewhat, this is probably the same case reported in Morison's Dictionary as *Cassie v Fleming*, of 27 June 1632. From Spotiswoode's *Practicks* and Morison's Dictionary it transpires that a husband physically assaulted and threatened his wife to agree to the alienation of certain rights over lands to a third party, who apparently had no knowledge of the way in which the husband obtained his wife's consent. If the King compelled someone to act through just fear and dread, that person would not be able to claim *reduction* during the King's lifetime, but only during that of his successor (*Earl of Morton v The Queen* (1543) Mor 16479).

44 *Earl of Morton v The Queen* (1543) Mor 16479; cf Balfour, *Practicks*, 45.XVI.

iniusta causa, while Hope created a heading "*de actione indebiti*",[45] in his *Practicks*. Unfortunately, the heading contains no entry. Although the Roman maxim against unjustified enrichment, *naturaliter aequum est neminem debere cum alterius iactura locupletari*, was referred to as early as 1269,[46] there are no indications that it was linked to the *condictiones*.[47] Neither *Regiam Majestatem* nor Balfour's *Practicks* deal with the *condictiones*. As far as transfers *ob turpem causam* specifically are concerned, not much of value can be found either. *Regiam Majestatem* contains a passage on "valid and invalid pacts" (*de pactis utilibus et inutilibus*), which deals with "pacts" by minors, insane persons, unassisted wives, and pacts which are impossible or disgraceful or relate to a disgraceful thing,[48] but it does not refer to compulsion.[49] Balfour and Hope's *Practicks* contain similar passages,[50] but again provide no indication that compelled pactions are to be regarded as "filthie" or "unhonest". Neither do they state what remedy should be used to reclaim transfers flowing from such pactions.

3.2.3 *Canon Law*[51]

Thus far, the focus has been on authorities and cases dealing with the Civil Law. It should be kept in mind, though, that in pre-reformation Scotland, Canon Law was also an important body of law, not only because it created the framework of government of the Roman Catholic Church, but also because it regulated important aspects of the lives of its members, such as legitimacy, succession and marriage.[52] It is especially the Canon Law of marriage (one of the seven sacraments), which is of present concern. The validity of marriage was something which was largely, if not exclusively, within the jurisdiction of the ecclesiastical courts.[53] Here the basic principle was that whereas the conclusion of marriage should be a simple matter of consent, its dissolution should be difficult.[54] Canon Law drew strongly on its

45 Hope, *Practicks*, VI.13.8.

46 The reference is contained in a record of a dispute between Kelso Abbey and Melrose Abbey (*Lib de Calchou* (Bannatyne Club ed, 1846), no 179, referred to in Stein, *The Character and Influence of the Roman Civil Law*, 292).

47 The Melrose Charter of 1280 is recorded in *Liber S Marie de Melros* (Bannatyne Club ed, 1837), I 288 (cf Stein, *The Character and Influence of the Roman Civil Law*, 292).

48 "[P]actum turpe vel rei turpis et impossibilis de jure et de facto" (Book 1, ch 30 (98 et sq)).

49 *Regiam Majestatem*, Book 1, ch 30, line 10 states that "[i]tem pactum turpe vel rei turpis ... nullam obligationem inducit" ("again a disgraceful pact, or one which relates to a disgraceful thing ... creates no binding obligation").

50 Balfour, *Practicks*, 48.I, III; Hope, *Practicks*, II.1 (of Contracts), para 14; Hope, *Practicks*, II.2 (*De Pactis*) para 2 (which is based on the *Regiam Majestatem* paragraph mentioned above); Hope, *Practicks*, II.3 (*De Obligationibus*) paras 36 and 38.

51 Cf, generally, The Rt Rev Mgr J D Scanlan, "Husband and Wife—Pre-reformation canon law of marriage of the officials' courts", in *An Introduction to Scottish Legal History*, 69; D Baird Smith, "Canon Law", in *An Introductory Survey of the Sources and Literature of Scots Law*, 183; O F Robinson, "Canon law and marriage", 1984 *JR* 22; Walker, *The Scottish legal System*, 42 et sqq; 87 et sqq; 155; Walker, *A Legal History of Scotland*, vol 1, 321 et sqq; P Fraser, *Treatise on Husband and Wife according to the Law of Scotland*, 2nd ed (1876), vol 1, 1–12, 19–41.

52 Baird Smith, "Canon Law", in *An Introductory Survey of the Sources and Literature of Scots Law*, 183 at 185.

53 Cf Scanlan, "Husband and Wife—Pre-reformation canon law of marriage of the officials' courts", in *An Introduction to Scottish Legal History*, 69 at 71; Robinson, Canon law and marriage", 1984 *JR* 22, 24; The Rt Rev Mgr J C Barry (ed), *William Hay's Lectures on Marriage*, Stair Society vol 24 (Edinburgh, 1967), xxxv.

54 Cf Scanlan, "Husband and Wife—Pre-reformation canon law of marriage of the officials' courts", in *An Introduction to Scottish Legal History*, 69; Walker, *A Legal History of Scotland*, vol 1, 321.

Roman roots in applying a stringent test to determine whether a marriage should be dissolved due to force and fear: the effect of the force and fear had to be such as would move a constant wife (or husband): "vis et metus qui possunt cadere in constantem mulierem".[55] The case law of the early sixteenth century dealing with actions for divorce, or rather dissolution, contain dramatic allegations of women being dragged off by armed men and their accomplices, and then being compelled to enter into holy matrimony.[56] The relief granted would be that the marriage would be annulled and the parties be restored *in integrum*.[57]

In addition to the case law, a significant source of the relevant Canon Law is the *Lectures on Marriage* by the then vice-principal of the University of Aberdeen, William Hay. It provides a detailed exposition of the Canon Law of the early sixteenth century in regard to the effect of force and fear on the validity of marriages. A particularly valuable feature of Hay's work is that he compares Canon Law with Civil Law as well as with related works on philosophy. For example, he indicates that what the lawyers term "fear" (*metus*), the theologians or Canon lawyers call "conditional compulsion" (*coactio conditionata*), and the philosophers "mixed violence" (*violentum mixtum*).[58] These forms of compulsion must then be distinguished from what the philosophers call "violence pure and simple" (*violentum simpliciter*), i.e. when a man is absolutely forced (*absolute cogitur*), when someone takes his hand and strikes another with it in spite of his resisting with all his might. On the other hand, in the case of "mixed violence" the victim "consents here and now to avoid a greater evil". Hay then distinguishes between two forms of such "mixed violence" or, to use the civilian term, *metus conditionatus*. The first form involves *metus* or fear which is light and groundless (*levis et vanis*), and which does not affect the validity of a marriage. This stands in contrast to fear which is grave and well-founded (*metus gravis et probabilis*).[59] This is called "just fear, which would affect a strong-minded man or woman".[60] It gives rise to nullity, and as in the case law, it is stated that the parties should be restored *in integrum*. Hay also recounts various forms of fear which would move a constant man: these are death, ruin, extreme bodily harm, disinheritance, slavery, rape "or any other grave or appalling outrage".[61] From Hays' account one can deduce that the Canon Law of *coactio conditionata* drew heavily on the Roman law of *vis et metus*, as developed by the Glossators,

---

55 Cf Scanlan, "Husband and Wife—Pre-reformation canon law of marriage of the officials' courts", in *An Introduction to Scottish Legal History*, 69 at 76 et sqq, as well as the following cases contained in Cosmo Innes (ed), *Liber Officialis Sancti Andree*, Abbotsford Club edition (1845): *Creichtone v Heiring* (case no 6, 1515–1516), *Wardlaw v Perdowy* (case no 20, 1516–1520), *Boyis v Mortoune* (case no 35, 1522), and *Fortoun v Cokburne* (case no 40, 1523).

56 Cf *Wardlaw v Perdowy* (*Liber Officialis Sancti Andree* case no 20, 1516–1520), *Boyis v Mortoune* (*Liber Officialis Sancti Andree* case no 35, 1522), and *Fortoun v Cokburne* (*Liber Officialis Sancti Andree* case no 40, 1523).

57 Cf *Wardlaw v Perdowy* (*Liber Officialis Sancti Andree* case no 20, 1516–1520), *Boyis v Mortoune* (*Liber Officialis Sancti Andree* case no 35, 1522).

58 Barry (ed), *William Hay's Lectures on Marriage*, Stair Society vol 24, 83. Barry translates *violentum mixtum* as "modified" violence, but this somewhat obscures the contrast between simple violence (which only involves force) and mixed violence (which involves force and fear).

59 Cf D 4.2.5.

60 "[Q]ui dicitur metus iustus qui potest cadere in constantem virum similiter in constantam mulierem" (Barry (ed), *William Hay's Lectures on Marriage*, Stair Society vol 24, 85). Cf D 4.2.6.

61 Barry (ed), *William Hay's Lectures on Marriage*, Stair Society vol 24, 85. Cf also Zimmermann, *The Law of Obligations*, 659. On the possibility that canon law could also have provided relief in cases of duress of goods, cf Dawson, "Economic Duress and the Fair Exchange in French and German law" (1937) 3 *TulaneLR* 345 at 348 note 7.

and received in Scotland. All the basic principles are in place: the distinction between *vis absoluta* and *vis compulsiva*, the essential features of *vis compulsiva*, and in particular the importance of displaying firmness and of only acting out of *justus metus*. Unfortunately for Hay, the Canon Law he so ably expounded was not to be applied as such for much longer. On 24 August 1560, a mere twenty-five years after his *Lectures* were completed, the Scottish Parliament declared that:

> The bischope of Rome hais na Jurisdictioun nor autoritie within this realme in tymes cuming ... and that na bischop nor uther prelat of this realme use ony Jurisdictioun in tymes to cum be the said bischop of Romeis autoritie.[62]

The effect of this declaration was, in essence, that the jurisdiction of the ecclesiastical courts, and in particular the application, *eo nomine*, of the Canon Law of the annulment of marriages on grounds of force and fear was transferred to the civil courts.[63] However, although these matters were no longer to be decided expressly in terms of Canon Law, its influence remained. This is no doubt due to the fact that Canon Law and Civil Law shared Roman roots.[64]

3.3 THE ERA OF THE INSTITUTIONAL WRITERS: THE SEVENTEENTH TO NINETEENTH CENTURIES

The seventeenth century was of decisive importance for Scots law: it was the beginning of a movement away from legal compilation, reflected by the *Practicks*, to an age of greater legal analysis.[65] The time for such a change was ripe. On the continent, systematic treatises on Civil Law started to appear, such as Hugo de Groot's famous work *De jure belli ac pacis*, in 1631. What was needed now was a Scots lawyer of sufficient vision and authority to elevate the law of his country from the casuistic morass of the *Practicks*. In 1661 Charles II, newly invested king after the restoration of the monarchy following the Cromwellian revolution, appointed the forty-two year-old James Dalrymple (1619–1695), ennobled as the first Viscount Stair, as a judge in the Court of Session. By all accounts, the decision to appoint Stair was a good one. Indeed, it has been said that "the revolutionary change between the work of Hope, whose *Practicks* show the law as it was in the early 1630s, and Stair, whose *The Institutions of the Law of Scotland* were published in 1681, is inexplicable other than by the sheer genius of Stair".[66] One area which Stair influenced remarkably was the law on force and fear, and in this section his views will receive particular attention. Stair was followed by other authors, who, like him, used an "Institutional" framework. Sir George Mackenzie (1636?–1691), authored the *Institutions of the Law of Scotland*, which differs significantly in structure from Stair's much more famous *Institutions* of the same time by adhering more strongly to the structure of Justinian's *Institutes*. Mackenzie's book was not an academic treatise, but rather a *vade-mecum*,

---

62 A P S, ii, 534–535; cf S Ollivant, *The Court of the Official in Pre-reformation Scotland* (1982), 1.

63 Fraser, *Treatise on Husband and Wife according to the Law of Scotland*, 12 et sqq.

64 Cf Stair, *Institutions* 1.4.1, 1.4.6, 1.9.8. On the modern law, cf E M Clive, *The Law of Husband and Wife in Scotland*, 3rd ed (1992), 89 sqq; J M Thomson, *Family Law in Scotland*, 3rd ed (1996), 34 et sq.

65 Cf, generally, Walker, *A Legal History of Scotland*, vol 4, 1 et sq, 7 et sqq.

66 J Irvine Smith, "The Transition to the Modern Law 1532–1660", in *An Introduction to Scottish Legal History*, 25. It has also been said of Hope that he was "the son of Balfour, but not at all the father of Stair" (Hope, *Practicks*, vol I, xv, (introduction by P G B McNeill)).

which set out basic principles.[67] Although it was rather limited in its scope, it was influential in acting as the basis for the major work of John Erskine (1695–1768), titled *An Institute of the Law of Scotland in Four Books in the order of Sir George Mackenzie's Institutions of that Law*". Erskine employs the general structural plan of the *Institutes* of Justinian, which was also the plan of Mackenzie.[68] Another influential writer is Andrew McDouall, Lord Bankton (1685–1760), author of *An Institute of the Laws of Scotland in Civil Rights.* The last of the institutional works were the *Principles of the Law of Scotland, for the use of the Students in the University of Edinburgh* and the *Commentaries on the Law of Scotland and on the Principles of Mercantile Jurisprudence* by George Joseph Bell (1770–1843). Bell succeeded David Hume (1757–1838), the namesake and nephew of the famous philosopher and historian, in the Chair of Scots Law at Edinburgh in 1822. Even though he does not enjoy the status of institutional writer, Hume made notable contributions to Scots law. Henry Home, Lord Kames (1696–1782), also cannot be ignored.

In this overview, the focus first will be on the law relating to compulsion in the form of "force or fear",[69] "force and fear",[70] extortion,[71] compulsion *ex vi majori*,[72] constraint,[73] or concussion,[74] which are various names by which the law of "vis et metus" or "fear and dread" now became known. For the sake of continuity, all these forms of compulsion will be referred to as cases of "force and fear".[75] Thereafter, the emphasis will be on the significance of compulsion to other areas of law, and in particular the law relating to the *condictiones*.

3.3.1 *The law of force and fear*

Following the pattern of the previous section, the basis or reasons for providing relief in cases of force and fear will be identified first. Thereafter, the contents of force and fear will be examined, with particular emphasis on certain standard manifestations thereof. Finally, the focus will be on the effect of force and fear and its place in the law of contract, delict and unjustified enrichment.

i. The basis for relief

It will be recalled that the *Practicks* did not only (like *Regiam Majestatem*) deal with "fear and dread" in the context of insanity and minority, but also in the context of fraud. This, to a certain extent, indicates that the authors of the *Practicks* did not necessarily regard a defective ability to provide consent as the basis for relief in cases of fear and dread. In the works of the institutional writers, two contrasting approaches are followed.

---

67 Cf Walker, *The Scottish Jurists*, 165.

68 Cf Erskine's introductory words to the first title in Book III: "The general method proposed to be observed in this Institute was, to treat, first of Persons, 2dly, of Things or Rights; and 3dly, of Actions." Having dealt with persons, and heritable rights, in the first two books, he turned to "Moveable rights . . ., the doctrine of which depends chiefly on obligations".

69 Stair, *Institutions*, 1.7.7, 1.9.8, 1.17.2.

70 Bell, *Principles*, para 12.

71 Stair, *Institutions*, 1.9.8; Bankton, *Institute*, 1.10.50.

72 Stair, *Institutions*, 4.40.26.

73 Stair, *Institutions*, 4.40.26; Bell, *Commentaries*, 314.

74 In *Grey v Earl of Lauderdale* (1688) Mor 16501 and *Earl of Lauderdale v Earl of Aberdeen* (1685) Mor 16497, 16498 there are references to concussion. It is stated there that "concussion . . . differs nothing from *metus*, but that the last is done by a private person and the first by one in power and authority".

75 "Extortion" has to be avoided because Erskine, rather confusingly, uses it in the completely different sense of fraud and circumvention (cf Erskine, *Institute*, 4.1.27). Cf 158.

(a) *Coactus volui, tamen volui*

The first approach, that of Stair and Bankton, rejects the notion that force and fear affects the ability to provide consent. According to Stair, contracts must be deeds of the rational appetite or will,[76] and "[d]eeds or obligations extorted are in their own nature, and in equity efficacious because they have truly the consent or act of the will, by which rights are constitute".[77] In support of this view Stair refers to D 4.2.21.5, which contains Paulus's *coactus volui* principle. It should be noted, though, that Stair obviously did not mean that all extorted acts "have truly the consent or act of the will". It will be recalled that in medieval times a distinction was drawn between *vis absoluta* and *vis compulsiva*,[78] and that in the former case, the will plays no part in the act. It is in this context that one has to view Stair's definition of extortion as "... the act of *force*, or other means of fear, whereby a person is compelled to do that which of their proper inclination they would not have done".[79] Stair obviously did not intend that "force" should encompass *vis absoluta*: in such a case there is no consent and the *coactus volui* principle is inapplicable.[80] Bankton makes the point more clearly. After defining extortion as "[t]he compelling one, by the impression or fear of some considerable evil or mischief, to a deed, which otherwise he would not do",[81] he states that

> [t]he Force here is not *absolute*, but *conditional*, in case such a thing [the compelled deed] is not done, and therefore the fear occasioned by it does not exclude all consent. The person put in fear chuses the least of two evils, rather than to part with his right, than suffer pain, or the like grievance threatened; and, as the law expresses it, *Quamvis, si liberum esset, noluisset, tamen coactus voluit*.[82]

The question is now on what basis relief can be provided to the victim if there was no lack of "consent or act of the will". Here Stair breaks new ground in Scots law by placing force and fear in a title on reparation,[83] thereby indicating that it is a delict.[84] This characterisation of force and fear as a delict is not supported by contemporaneous case law, and it is clearly a novel approach in Scots law.[85] It is somewhat improbable

---

76 Cf Stair, *Institutions*, 1.10 ("obligations conventional").

77 Stair, *Institutions*, 1.9.8 (own italics).

78 On this distinction cf 2.2.1, 3.2.1.i above; Hartkamp, *Der Zwang im römischen Privatrecht*, 3 et sqq and sources quoted there. It has been indicated in the chapter on Roman law that the distinction is not of Roman origin (but cf Memorandum on Defective Consent And Consequential Matters (Scot Law Com Memo No 42, 1978) vol 2, para 3.104).

79 Stair, *Institutions*, 1.9.8.

80 Cf Memorandum on Defective Consent And Consequential Matters (Scot Law Com Memo No 42, 1978), vol 2, para 3.105.

81 Bankton, *Institute*, 1.10.50.

82 Bankton, *Institute*, 1.10.50 (own emphasis). For a similar distinction between absolute and conditional fear, cf J Voet, *Commentarius ad Pandectas*, 4.2.1.

83 Cf Stair, *Institutions*, 1.9.8. The title deals with obligations of "reparation, where of delinquence and damages thence arising". According to Stair "[t]he obligation of delinquence ..., is that whereunto injury or malefice doth oblige, as the meritorious cause thereof".

84 Stair, *Institutions*, 1.9.6. References to force and fear in the titles on transaction (Stair, *Institutions*, 1.17.2) and exception (Stair, *Institutions*, 4.40.25) are dealt with below. Bankton follows Stair and discusses "extortion", in a title on "Reparation arising from crimes" (Bankton, *Institute*, 1.10.5). In this title Bankton only deals with the delictual, and not criminal aspects of certain forms of conduct. According to Walker, Bankton "fails adequately to distinguish crimes or public wrongs from delicts or private wrongs" inasmuch as "any damage thereby accrues to the party aggrieved, cognoscible in civil courts of justice" (*The Scottish Jurists*, 198).

85 Cf Birks, "Restitution: A View of the Scots Law" 1985 *CLP* 57 at 70.

that these views were of Stair's own conception,[86] which prompts a search of their historical origins. In this regard it is significant that Stair's writings were not only strongly influenced by Roman law, but also by the works of natural lawyers, most notably Hugo de Groot, and also Spanish Scholastics such as Molina.[87] They, in turn, were influenced by the works of Aristotle and St Thomas of Aquinas. Both Aristotle[88] and St Thomas of Aquinas,[89] like Paulus, thought that what has been willed under compulsion was nevertheless still willed. Because it was obviously unacceptable that the victim should be denied relief even though he "consented", they had to find some basis for providing such relief. The basis they identified was that extortion amounted to an "injustice" or "injury".[90] This idea was followed by Molina,[91] and De Groot.[92] As Gordley put it, "duress was now regarded as a tort or delict to be remedied by allowing the victim to escape from his promise".[93]

(b) Force and fear as a factor excluding consent

Erskine and Bell differ markedly from Stair and Bankton in their conception of the basis of relief in cases of force and fear. In his brief treatment of the topic in book III, which partly deal with contracts and obligations, Erskine states that

> Consent is also excluded by violence, or even by the menace of violence; L. 116, *de reg. jur.*; for violence, whether used or barely threatened, is a necessity laid on a man to act contrary to his will; L. 1, *quod. met. caus.*[D. 4.2.1.]; so that it is only in appearance—in form of words—that a person forced or menaced gives his consent; his will hath truly no part in the contract.[94]

In his treatment of obligations and contracts,[95] Bell also characterises force and fear or "constraint" as one of the factors which exclude consent.[96] This difference in approach has important implications for the choice of a remedy. Although the question of remedies will be dealt with below, it should be obvious at this stage that once it is accepted that there is deficient consent in cases of force and fear, it is not necessary (like Bankton or Stair) to regard it as a delinquency or delict[97] in order to overcome the "problem" that the victim is still bound under the contract.

---

86 Indeed, he has been described as "essentially a conservative theorist of the law, constitutionalism, and order, who put together an eclectic synthesis of ideas held by previous thinkers from nations other than his own. In few, if any, respects can he be regarded as an innovator boldly treading new ground" (Walker (ed), *Stair Tercentenary Studies*, 88).

87 Cf Walker (ed), *Stair Tercentenary Studies*, 70, 87 et sqq; Walker, *The Scottish Jurists*, 129; W M Gordon, "Stair, Grotius and the Sources of Stair's Institutions" in J A Ankum, J E Spruit and F B J Wubbe (eds), *Satura Roberto Feenstra Oblata* (1985), 571. Gordon also points out the influence of Vinnius and Gudelinus.

88 Aristotle, *Nicomachean Ethics*, Book III, 110a.

89 Thomas Aquinas, *Summa Theologica*, I–II, q 6,a 6, ad 1.

90 Cf J Gordley, "Natural Law Origins of the Common Law of Contract", in Barton (ed), *Towards a General Law of Contract*, 397 et sqq, who refers to Thomas Aquinas *Summa theologica* II–II, q 89, a 7, ad 3.

91 L Molina, *De Iustitia et iure tractatus* disp 352. Cf Gordley, "Natural Law Origins of the Common Law of Contract", in Barton (ed), *Towards a General Law of Contract*, 398.

92 Cf H Grotius, *De jure belli ac pacis*, 2.11.7.2.

93 Cf Gordley, "Natural Law Origins of the Common Law of Contract", in Barton (ed), *Towards a General Law of Contract*, 398 et sqq.

94 Erskine, *Institute*, 3.1.16.

95 Bell, *Principles* ch 1, (3 et sqq); Bell, *Commentaries*, 312 et sqq.

96 According to him, "[wh]ere one is compelled into a contract, there is no effectual consent, though ostensibly there is the form of it ..." (*Commentaries*, 314). He also states that error and compulsion are "both totally subversive of consent" (*Commentaries*, 316).

97 Erskine deals with delinquency in *Institute*, 3.1.12, but does not refer to force and fear.

ii. The content of force and fear

A salient feature of the treatment of force and fear in the works of the institutional writers is the extent to which they still rely on the Roman law of *metus*. Stair introduces his whole section on extortion with a discussion of the requirements of the *actio quod metus causa*, noting that the Edict was not competent upon every force and fear, but that it had to be unlawful,[98] and "such as might befall a constant man".[99] He then lists a variety of familiar examples of actionable fear, and concludes by stating that "our customs go much along with the course of the civil law in this, but so as not bound thereby ...".[100] The question is now to what extent Scots law built upon this Roman basis. These developments can be analysed with regard to the following key aspects of the law of force and fear.

First, even though the institutional writers require that the victim had to experience fear which would move a constant man or *vir constans*[101] and not "vain or foolish fear",[102] there are indications that Scots law began operating with less severity than Roman law.[103] With the exception of Erskine,[104] all the institutional writers recognise that the circumstances of each case have to be considered and that certain more vulnerable or "weak" persons, such as "the physically weak, wives, and those weak and infirm of judgment or courage" deserve special protection.[105] According to Bell, if the *effect* of applying force and fear to such persons would be the same as overpowering violence on a firmer mind, nullity would follow.[106] This indicates that the test for fear is in fact subjective, and not objective, as the *vir constans* test seems to imply.

Second, it is at times required that the victim had to yield to *justus metus*.[107] As in earlier law, the meaning of this term is unclear. In certain contexts it does not seem to mean anything other than that the victim had to display the resoluteness of the *vir constans*. As Stair puts it: "that may be a just fear to a woman that will not be to

---

98 Cf D 4.2.3.1.

99 Cf D 4.2.6–4.2.9.

100 Stair, *Institutions*, 1.9.8. Cf Walker, *A Legal History of Scotland*, vol 4, 697.

101 Stair, *Institutions*, 1.9.8; Bankton, *Institute*, 1.10.51; Erskine, *Institute*, 4.1.26; Bell, *Principles*, para 12; Bell, *Commentaries*, 314 et sqq.

102 Cf Stair, *Institutions*, 1.9.8; Bell *Principles*, par 12; Erskine, *Institute*, 3.1.16; 4.1.26.

103 This development was in line with other systems in the *ius commune*: cf J P Dawson, "Economic Duress and the Fair Exchange in French and German law" (1937) 3 *TulaneLR* 345 at 348.

104 Erskine does not recognise that in the application of the *vir constans* test one has to take the circumstances of each individual case into consideration. He also states that reduction would not be "competent upon reverential fear arising from the authority of husbands, parents, magistrates", but does not mention that in cases where such relationships of authority are present it will be easier to establish force and fear (Erskine, *Institute*, 4.1.26).

105 Cf Stair, *Institutions*, 1.9.8, where it is indicated that it would be easier to prove extortion in these cases, and *Institutions*, 4.40.25, where it is stated that "it is not any other fear that gives this exception, but such fear *quae cadit in virum constantem*, as it is commonly described, but too narrowly". Cf also Bankton, *Institute*, 1.10.51; Bell *Principles*, para 12; *Commentaries*, 314 et sqq; *Cassie v Fleming* (1632) Mor 10279. It is only in the discussion of transaction or settlement of legal disputes by agreement that Stair seems to follow a more strict approach: for a transaction to be rescinded on ground of extortion it had to be proven that there was fear of *imminent* harm (Stair, *Institutions*, 1.17.2).

106 *Principles*, para 12; cf Bell, *Commentaries*, 314 et sqq The approach of Bell resembles that of the French author Rebuffe, who maintained that the level of required constancy varied with the constancy of the victim: extraordinary constancy should be expected from an extraordinary constant person, and so forth (cf Dawson, "Economic Duress and the Fair Exchange in French and German law" (1937) 3 *TulaneLR* 345 at 349 note 12).

107 Cf Stair, *Institutions*, 4.40.25 et sqq; *Earl of Lauderdale v Earl of Aberdeen* (1685) Mor 16497 at 16498.

a man".[108] However, Stair also states that "... positive law doth justly annul such consents as are obtained by just fear; just on the part of the sufferer, but unjust on the part of the actor".[109] Although the phrase "unjust on the part of the actor" is rather cryptic, it is arguable that Stair is requiring that it has to be unjust for the actor to rely on something done under such fear. This could indicate that Stair had in mind that the actor should not use unjust or unlawful means to instill the fear. He does, after all, refer with apparent approval to the Roman requirement that the force and fear had to be unlawful.[110] Furthermore, he states that "legal execution, though by force, affords not the exception of *justus metus*, if it be not upon a capital cause".[111] Thus, if lawful means of compulsion are used, or more generally, if compulsion is used in a lawful way, there would be no *justus metus*. Unfortunately, none of the institutional writers deal with this requirement in detail.

Third, whereas the Roman law of *vis et metus* was apparently not applicable where payment of a due debt was obtained through compulsion (the remedy was rather relief under the *decretum divi Marci*), there are indications that the Scots law of force and fear could also be used towards this end.[112]

Fourth, there is a broadening of the examples of actionable force and fear. It will be recalled that in Roman times fear of personal harm, such as death, harm to physical integrity and loss of freedom, and possibly also fear of harm to one's reputation[113] and property[114] was actionable, and that threats of harm to the family were also covered.[115] The institutional writers by and large recognise these cases,[116] but they also note that the law had broadened to include certain other cases as

108 Stair, *Institutions*, 4.40.25.

109 Stair, *Institutions*, 4.40.25.

110 Stair, *Institutions*, 1.9.8.

111 Stair, *Institutions*, 4.40.27.

112 Cf *Wiseman v Logie* (1700) Mor 16505. Earlier indications are that even though the extortion would be criminal, no relief would be provided in civil law if a debt was due (cf Mackenzie, *The Laws and Customes of Scotland in Matters Criminal*, 326 et sq; *Stuarts v Whitefoord and The Duke of Hamilton* (1677) Mor 16489). In the latter case the defenders averred that the victim was in any event obliged to "dispone" his lands by a prior minute. The effect of the extortion was therefore only that the defenders received what was due to them in any case. Although the fact that there was "no damage" was "most relevant" to some of the Lords, the extortion was not proven and the Lords did not decide the merits of this argument. However, it was stated that "[b]y the civil law, there were divers remedies competent to those who had been forced to do any deed: viz. a civil action *ex edicto praetoris*, and a criminal action *ex lege julia*; and a penal remedy *ex decreto Divi Marci*, that a creditor by force, extorting what is truly due, *amittit ius crediti*: And our reductions *ex capite metus* are but civil actions, as that *ex edicto*: And the said other remedies being penal, by the municipal law of the Romans, cannot be introduced by the Lords of Session being civil Judges, without an act of Parliament" (1677) Mor 16489 at 16493.

113 Stair states that the Edict covered infamy or disgrace, but this has not been conclusively established. In support of this view he relies on D 4.2.8.2, which in fact deals with fear of *stuprum* or sexual assault.

114 Cf Hartkamp, *Der Zwang im römischen Privatrecht*, 40 et sq.

115 Cf D 4.2.8.3; Hartkamp, *Der Zwang im römischen Privatrecht*, 42.

116 On fear of personal physical harm, cf Stair, *Institutions*, 1.9.8; Bankton, *Institute*, 1.10.51; Bell, *Principles*, para 12. On fear of harm to property, cf Bankton, *Institute*, 1.10.51; Stair, *Institutions*, 1.9.8, 1.17.2; Bell, *Principles*, para 12; *Wiseman v Logie* (1700) Mor 16505. In this case, Wiseman, the Procurator-fiscal to the northern Justiciary, went with some Highlanders and dragoons, and illegally destroyed some of the property of the Logies, elder and younger, of Boddom. This was apparently done in order to obtain payment of a fine owed by the younger Boddom. "Old Boddom" then tried "to prevent any further destruction", and inter alia granted Wiseman a bill of 560 merks in return for discharging young Boddom from liability. When payment on the bill was claimed, the Logies of Boddom raised the defence that the bill was "null being extorted by force or fear". The court then held that the action was "unwarrantable" and reduced the bill "Old Boddom" gave to Wiseman.

well. In the rest of this section, these developments will be examined in greater detail. Particular attention will be paid to reverential fear (*metus reverentialis*), fear of persons in authority ("men in power'), fear of harm to third parties, the use of diligence or the process of law (*vis legalis*) and threats of accusation.

(a) Battered wives

The "battered wife syndrome of the propertied classes"[117] was a matter of particular concern to the institutional writers and the courts. Where a wife was subjected to threats of physical harm, she was obviously entitled to relief.[118] However, it was more difficult to determine whether she could obtain relief if she merely acted out of awe or "reverence" of her husband, even if he was a vicious man or *vir ferox*: the mere allegation of such fear could obviously not be sufficient.[119] This problem was apparently overcome by the presumption of compulsion where a transaction was extremely prejudicial to the wife.[120]

(b) Men in power

It is not only in its treatment of reverential fear of husbands, but also in its treatment of threats from "men in power" or persons in high authority that Scots law expanded the scope of force and fear. If a "man in power" used threats of physical harm[121] relief is obviously warranted. However, in the absence of such threats, it is difficult to establish whether relief should be provided. Again, the solution was apparently to work with a presumption of fear where a person in great power used "a mean of concussion".[122]

(c) Harm to others

As in Roman times, it is acknowledged that fear of harm to family is actionable.[123] There are, however, indications that even persons not related to the one who is to

---

117 Cf Memorandum on Defective Consent And Consequential Matters (Scot Law Com Memo No 42, 1978), 114.

118 Cf *Cassie v Fleming* (1632) Mor 10279.

119 Cf Stair, *Institutions*, 1.9.8; Bankton, *Institute*, 1.10.51; Erskine, *Institute*, 4.1.26; *Murray v Jaffrey* (1674); *Hepburn v Nasmyth* (1613) Mor 6069, 16482; *Johnston v Provost Napier* (1708) Mor 16511. Twenty-four years after she had granted Provost Napier a disposition of some shops in Glasgow, Johnston attempted to have the disposition set aside on the grounds that she was taken by her husband to a tavern at five o'clock at night, and detained there until twelve. According to her a deed was then obtained from her "by concussion, frowns, and undue importunities and solicitations." The defence was raised that marital reverence was no ground for restitution. The court decided in favour of the provost: apparently there was no proof of threats or actual violence, while the length of time she waited before instituting action was considerably long.

120 Stair, *Institutions*, 1.9.8; *Marishall v Marishall* (1623) Mor 16482.

121 Cf *Earl of Morton v The Queen* (1543) Mor 16479.

122 Bankton, *Institute*, 1.10.51. Cf *Lord and Lady Gray v Earl of Lauderdale* (1688) Mor 16501. In this case the Earl (at the time a Lord of Session) apparently obtained certain papers from Lord and Lady Grey through the exercise of his influence as "a man of power". A transaction was then concluded whereby the Earl gave Lord and Lady Grey an insignificant amount in exchange for the papers. Although it is not clear how this influence was exercised (it seems to have been through threats regarding the validity of their title to their lands), the court regarded it as serious enough to have the transaction reduced "to discourage great men from oppressing when in power" (at 16502). Cf also *Earl Lauderdale v Earl Aberdeen* (1692) Mor Supp vol 88, which dealt with threats by the King.

123 Cf Bell, *Principles*, para 12. In *M'Intosh v Farquharson and Spalding* (1671) Mor 16486, Farquharson and some others took M'Intosh "violently out of his house, and carried him to the mountains of Glenlee, and there detained him, and menaced him ...". It was held that sons who concluded an agreement in order to obtain the release of their father from private captivity could have it set aside since they were "moved out of duty and natural affection".

be harmed could claim relief. Bankton, for example, indicates that where someone advances money or grants a bond to an extorter in order to obtain the release of a third party, the person who advanced the money has a claim against the extorter as well as the third party.[124] It is not required that a special relationship has to exist between the person who extorted the money and the third party.

(d) Diligence

It has been indicated above that early Scots law recognised various methods of lawful compulsion such as personal imprisonment and the poinding or inhibition of property. During the era of the institutional writers these methods of "legal force" or *vis legalis*[125] were also recognised, but there are signs of a development towards more compassion with the position of the debtor, particularly where he is held in "caption". For example, the debtor was not bound when he was "taken caption, being sick and unable to travel without hazard of life", and then granted a bond or right to prevent further harm".[126] Relief was apparently also provided if physical circumstances made it very difficult for the person under fear to dispute liability legally. [127] Furthermore, although the mere fact that a bond was granted or payment was made while a debtor was in caption or threatened with caption did not affect its validity,[128] the existence of a dispute as to the validity of the debt and the absence of a transaction or homologation could be the basis for relief.[129] In this regard the fact

124 *Institute*, 1.10.58. Cf also Stair, *Institutions*, 1.9.8; Erskine, *Institute*, 4.1.26. According to Erskine the claim against the extorter would only be allowed if there is no recourse against the third party. As an example he mentions that people who paid the rebels in the 1745 rebellion not to plunder the effects of the boroughs or villages, could later recover payment from the corporations of these boroughs or villages.

125 Stair, *Institutions*, 4.40.27; Erskine, *Institute*, 4.1.26; Bankton, *Institute*, 1.10.60 ("Legal force is not relevant to reduce any deed; for it is a maxim, that *Juris executio non habet injuriam* [cf D. 47.10.13.1]. The execution of the law can import no wrong; hence it is called *Vis legalis*"); Bell, *Commentaries*, 315. Obviously, where the diligence was itself unlawful, *vis legalis* would not be present (cf *Dundas v Hardie* (1700) Mor 16506, which concerned illegal poinding).

126 Stair, *Institutions*, 1.9.8; Bankton, *Institute*, 1.10.60; *Mair v Stewart of Shambelly* (1667) Mor 16484. Mair's case concerned a rather over-zealous minister who obtained a decreet against his parishioners to pay for the reparation of the manse, and then threatened Stewart, one of his parishioners, that he would be imprisoned if he did not grant a bond of £80. Stewart was "sick and unable to travel without hazard of life" and granted the bond. The bond was then reduced.

127 Cf *Burnet v Ewen* (1680) Mor 16494; *Lutwidge v Murray* Mor Supp vol IV, 652. Here an Englishman, Thomas Lutwidge, sold some tobacco to the Murrays in Scotland. Because they were afraid that Lutwidge might sell the tobacco to someone else, and they wanted him to pay the "Scots duty" (presumably on the tobacco), they obtained a decreet from the Sheriff of Dumfries in order to arrest him "until he found caution." Against this decreet Lutwidge, inter alia, raised the defence that his appearance was "by force of arrestement and concussion being brought *obtorto collo*." This expression is of Roman origin: if a defender would not voluntarily appear in judgment the only remedy left to the pursuer was to drag him by open force to the court, *obtorto collo*—literally "by the throat" (cf Erskine, *Institute*, 4.4.83; John Trayner, *Latin Maxims and Phrases*, s v *obtorto collo*). The court then found that this case was "stronger than ... *Burnet v Ewing*" and granted judgment in favour of Lutwidge.

128 Erskine, *Institute*, 4.1.26; Bankton, *Institute*, 1.10.60; *Thomson v Moubry and Alexander* (1675) Mor 12370. Cf also *Wishart v Arthur* (1671) Mor 9978; *Baillie v Menzies* (1711) Mor 9990. In *Ker v Edgar* (1698) Mor 16503 it was held that "*metus carceris*, by a legal execution, which could have been prevented, or liberty obtained by suspension, was no *justus metus*". A similar decision was made shortly thereafter in *Rutherford v Murray* (1698) Mor 16502. Here the court emphasised that "many securities are the product of legal diligence, and ought not on that head singly to be quarrelled or reversed".

129 Cf Bankton, *Institute*, 1.10.60; *Rue v Houston* (1668) Mor 16484; *Ker v Edgar* (1698) Mor 16503.

that the debtor paid a reduced amount could indicate that the payment was in fact made pursuant to a transaction, and that it was valid.[130] However, relief would be provided if the victim promised or gave more than was initially regarded as due.[131] A third party was also granted reduction of a bill given in order to obtain goods of a debtor which were illegally poinded by his creditor.[132]

(e) Accusation of criminal conduct

An accusation of criminal conduct could lead to fear of imprisonment or even execution. Could it then amount to force and fear if such fear is instilled by groundless accusations? The Institutional writers are not entirely consistent on this question. Erskine believes relief should be granted, but deals with the situation as one where a transfer is granted for a purpose tainted by turpitude, and not as one of force and fear.[133] Bell, on the other hand, entertains the possibility that such a situation could amount to a case of force and fear or "constraint", but is somewhat equivocal, because he also doubts whether a *vir constans* should be shaken by such threats.[134] If one moves on to the case law, it becomes apparent that Erskine's analysis based on turpitude is in fact unnecessary, and that Bell's fears of a lack of constancy are not necessarily justified. In a case concerning baseless charges of forgery which could lead to capital punishment, reduction on grounds of force and fear was allowed. It is therefore apparent that the law of force and fear is in fact broad enough to accommodate these cases without recourse to notions of turpitude.[135]

iii. The effect of force and fear

In view of the uncertainty as to the nature of relief in Roman law, as well as early Scots law, it is not surprising that the relevant law in the era of the Institutional writers also displays a remarkable lack of consistency. It will be recalled that the general approach in the *Practicks* was that the victim of fear and dread would be provided with *restitutio in integrum* or, simply "restitution". This entailed the specific "restitution" or "repetition" of transfers, or the reduction of deeds. However, during

130 Cf *Rue v Houston* (1668) Mor 16484; *Grant of Dalahaple v Major Alexander Anderson* (1706) Mor 16509; *Burnet v Ewen* (1680) Mor 16494.

131 Cf Erskine, *Institute*, 4.1.26; Bell, *Commentaries*, 315; Bankton, *Institute*, 1.10.60 ("... if, under the colour of legal execution, one is forced to grant an extraneous deed that has no concern with the debt in question ... deeds granted by the person so treated will be reducible on that head, since oppression under colour of law, is the worst"). Bankton also refers to magistrates and judges who use their authority to extort certain things by threats, or to compel persons to unfair bargains. They were then held liable to restitution and punishment on grounds of extortion. Cf also *Murray v Spalding of Assintilly* (1672) Mor 16487 (demand for payment of a penalty); *Heriot v Bird* (1681) Mor 16496 (demand of additional security for rent "for years to come"); *Nisbet v Steward* (1708) Mor 16512; *Arrat v Wilson* 1718, Robert. App, 234; *Foreman v Sheriff* (1791) Mor 16515 (claim for more than damage caused by cattle); but cf *Fraser v Black and Knox* December 13, 1810 F C.

132 Cf *Henderson v Buddo* (1782) Mor 14349.

133 Erskine, *Institute*, 3.1.10 ("If, for instance, one accused of a crime should give money to another that that other might not bear false witness against him, he may recover the sum so given by a *condictio ob turpem causam*").

134 *Commentaries*, 315.

135 In *Canison v Marshall* 1764, 6 Paton 759, the Canisons threatened that they would cause Marshall's mother and father to be hanged for forgery if they did not grant a deed in favour of the Canisons. The deed contained a disposition of an estate to which Marshall, as his mother's heir, would have become entitled. Marshall then brought an action of reduction of the deed *ex capite vis et metus*, based on these "unjust and arbitrary threatenings." On appeal to the House of Lords the reduction in favour of Marshall on grounds of force and fear was upheld. The judgment did not consider whether the deed was granted with an illegal or immoral purpose.

the era of the Institutional writers there was a movement away from regarding "restitution" as the appropriate remedy in cases of force and fear. It will be recalled that Stair and Bankton did not regard compelled acts as lacking in consent, and consequently favoured a delictual remedy of reparation. As will be indicated below, other writers did not agree with this approach. In this section the focus primarily will be on these different approaches, and then on the extent to which these approaches had an impact on development of the law. Thereafter attention will be paid to certain other aspects of relief on grounds of force and fear. The most notable of these are whether force and fear gave rise to voidness or voidability and whether relief could be obtained against third parties.

(a) Force and fear as a delinquency or delict

Even though Stair and Bankton, like the authors of the *Practicks*, created titles on "restitution", they do not refer to force and fear. In fact, in his title on "Restitution", Stair expressly states that "things which are attained by force or fear ... have their original from delinquence and come not under this consideration".[136] An obligation of "reparation" (of damages) arises from a delinquence or delict, and it is therefore in their titles on "reparation" that Stair and Bankton deal with force and fear.[137] But what does providing "reparation" then entail? According to Stair,

> [r]eparation is either by restitution of the same thing, in the same case, that it would have been in if it had remained with the owner, and this is most exact; or, where that cannot be, by giving the like value, or that which is nearest to make up the damage, according to the desire of the damnified.[138]

Thus, the obligation of "reparation" does not necessarily have to sound in money: it could also entail the return or "restitution" of an extorted object. Furthermore, in the case of extorted deeds or agreements, the obligation to provide "reparation" apparently only arises once it has been determined that their validity has been affected by force and fear. In other words, these deeds first have to be reduced. Bankton clearly states that a person who is compelled to sell something must, "upon the contract being rescinded, *restore* the price".[139] The references to restitution and reduction in the works of Bankton and Stair lead one to doubt whether it was really of any practical significance to state that force and fear gives rise to an obligation of reparation. In any event, if one turns to the case law, it is quite apparent that throughout the era of the Institutional writers the courts did not display any enthusiasm for the theory that force and fear is a delict: generally speaking, the victim would institute an action for reduction of a disposition, deed, bill or bond,[140] rather than a claim for damages or

136 Stair, *Institutions*, 1.7.8.

137 Stair, *Institutions*, 1.9.2; Bankton, *Institute*, 1.10.50.

138 Stair, *Institutions*, 1.9.4.

139 He further states that deeds concluded under extortion " ... were rescinded by the action *Quod metus causa* among the Romans, (and) they are set aside with us, by an action of reduction on that head by the court of session, whereby the party lesed is relieved, and the offender subjected to damages" (Bankton, *Institute*, 1.10.50).

140 The following cases dealt with reduction on grounds of *metus*: *A v B* (1612) Mor 16481; *Hepburn v Nasmyth* (1613) Mor 6069, 16482 (reduction of an alienation of life-rent lands); *Cassie v Fleming* (1632) Mor 10279 (reduction of wadset [morgage] of lands); *Grant v Balvaird*; *Agnes Grant v* —— (1642) Mor 16483 (reduction of a disposition of a tenement); *Mair v Stuart of Shambelly* (1667) Mor 16484; *M'Intosh v Farquharson and Spalding* (1671) Mor 16486; *Burnet v Ewen* (1680) Mor 16494; *Heriot v Bird* (1681) Mor 16496 (reduction of a bond and disposition of corn and moveables in security for payment of arrear rental); *Barclay v Barclay* (1674) Mor 16488 (reduction

reparation. Where the victim transferred money, there were claims for repetition or restoring the sum.[141] In certain instances, reduction apparently had to precede a claim for repetition.[142] In these cases the underlying purpose behind providing relief (still) seems to have been that the parties should be "reponed" or restored *in integrum*: the victim could not only have a disposition annulled or reclaim a transfer, but he also had to return what he received from the wrongdoer.[143] Although this approach could at times have had the same effect as providing the remedy of "reparation" (especially if the wrongdoer did not provide anything to the victim), the courts simply did not view the remedies on grounds of force and fear in this light.

(b) Force and fear as a ground for reduction

The views of Mackenzie, Erskine, Bell and Hume conform more to the sources. The basic approach is laid down by Mackenzie. Unlike Stair, who focused on the various *rights* the law gives rise to, Mackenzie (like Justinian) focused on the *objects* of the law, namely persons, rights and actions. In his book on actions, i.e. rights of "prosecuting in judgment what is due to us", Mackenzie then identifies the action of "rescission", and one of its subcategories, the action of "reduction": it is through these actions that "we pursue Rights to be declared null and to be reduced".[144] One type of reduction is *reductio ex capite vivis et metus*.[145] This scheme of arrangement is strongly reminiscent of Hope's *Practicks*, with the notable exception that Mackenzie does not acknowledge that in addition to "reduction *ex capite metus*", *restitutio in*

---

of a disposition of an estate); *Stuarts v Whitefoord and The Duke of Hamilton* (1677) Mor 16489; *Hay v Cumming* (1706) Mor 16506; *Johnston v Napier* (1708) Mor 16511 (reduction of disposition of lands); *Earl Lauderdale and Lord Haltoun v Earl Aberdeen* January 123, 1692, Harcarse 154; M Supp vol 88 (reduction of decree and bonds of corroboration); *Wiseman v Logie* (1700) Mor 16505; *Foreman v Sheriff* (1791) Mor 16515; *Henderson v Buddo* (1782) Mor 14349 (reduction of a bill); *Grant of Dalahaple v Major Alexander Anderson* (1706) Mor 16509 (reduction of a bond of corroboration); *Nisbet v Steward* (1708) Mor 16512 (reduction of the discharge of a decree); *Arrat v Wilson* (1718) Robert App 234 (reduction of a discharge and renunciation of trust); *Canison v Marshall* 1764, 6 Paton 759 (reduction of certain deeds).

141 Cf *Love v Downie* (1586) Mor 16480; *Jack v Fiddes* (1661) Mor 2923 (repetition was "sustain[ed]" in a case where a bond was extorted—presumably there was a payment in terms of the bond); *Alexander v Hamilton* 1694 Fount 186 (the defender was "decerned ... to restore the said sum"); *Canison v Marshall* 1764, 6 Paton 759 (the pursuer claimed reduction of a deed, as well as "repetition" of 100 guineas).

142 Cf Stair, *Institutions*, 4.40.27.

143 Cf *Stuarts v Whitefoord and The Duke of Hamilton* (1677) Mor 16489 at 16493 (which states that "all restitutions should repone both parties in integrum"); *Nisbet v Stewart* (1708) Mor 16512 (which indicates that "reponing" the victim also entails that if the victim suffered losses which resulted in benefits by third parties, these losses also had to be made good by the wrongdoer). In *Grey v Earl of Lauderdale* (1688) Mor 16501 reduction was granted of an "oppressed" transaction whereby land was sold for much less than the market value. The "sellers" were then reponed to the lands, upon their repaying the purchase price. However, the Court "shunned to insert the harsh term of concussion, and so did not decern [the purchaser] in restitution of the surplus rents more than the annual-rent of the price paid, though, upon the principles of concussion, one who makes such a transaction can never be *bona fide possessor*" (at 16502). It would therefore seem that in serious cases of compulsion, such as concussion, the measure of what had to be restored was higher, and that a claim of reduction could be supplemented by an award of restitution for lost profits.

144 Mackenzie, *Institutions of the Law of Scotland*, 349.

145 The others are reduction *ex capite inhibitionis* ("whereby we pursue rights to be declared null as granted after inhibition is raised by us"), *ex capite interdictionis* ("if granted after interdictions are raised by us" and reduction *ex capite fraudis* ("if the right were elicit from us by circumvention") (Mackenzie, *Institutions of the Law of Scotland*, 351).

integrum could also be brought home under the rescissory actions.[146] Apparently, Mackenzie regarded *restitutio in integrum* as superfluous: if an action for reduction *ex capite metus* could be used to restore the victim *in integrum*, there seems to be no real need for a seperate remedy called *restitutio in integrum*. Erskine follows Mackenzie: he also does not regard force and fear as a delict,[147] but rather as a ground for obtaining the rescissory[148] action of (simple) reduction of "deeds or writings".[149] Likewise, Hume regards force and fear as a ground for reduction of "deeds and writings",[150] and Bell only refers to the reduction of contracts.[151] Unfortunately, none of these authors shed much light on the way in which relief should be provided where the victim did nor grant a "deed or writing", but transferred property or money under compulsion. For example, in the context of claims against third parties, Bell merely mentions that the victim has "a remedy".[152]

(c) Voidness or voidability?

Acts compelled by *vis absoluta* can only be void, since there is no act to avoid. The more difficult question is to determine the effect of *vis compulsiva*. Unfortunately the views of the Institutional writers are not a model of clarity or consistency.[153] It will be recalled that Stair regarded extorted deeds and obligations as "in their own nature and by equity efficacious because they have truly the consent or act of the will". These views are then followed by a statement that "such deeds and obligations as are by force and fear are made utterly void".[154] This statement should be treated with circumspection. Although it indicates that he favoured voidness as the consequence of force and fear,[155] there are other statements which are more in conformance with the consequence of voidability. The aforementioned statement is made in the context of reduction and annulment, which is more consistent with initial validity than with absolute nullity,[156] and it is also difficult to see how a transaction could be "utterly void", if it was capable of being "elided by a judicial ratification of the deed upon oath".[157] If something is utterly void, there is nothing to ratify. At best, a new

146 Hope, *Practicks*, VI.38.26.

147 Erskine, *Institute*, 3.1.12. Incidentally, as far as the measure of damages is concerned, Erskine states that "[w]here the party injured can be restored precisely to his former state, that method ought to be followed, both as the most natural and the completest reparation ... But where, through the extinction or deterioration of the subject that method of reparation cannot be affected, the value of damage in money must be ascertained by the judge".

148 Rescissory actions were established for the "voiding of deeds, services, decrees, or other writings, or of illegal acts done by any body-corporate or society of men, *ex.gr.* the election of magistrates or other public officers" (Erskine, *Institute*, 4.1.18).

149 Erskine, *Institute*, 4.1.18, 4.11.25. These actions could be requested on various grounds (inter alia inhibition, minority, fraud and circumvention). Cf Erskine, *Institute*, 4.1.25.

150 Hume, *Lectures*, vol 6, 61.

151 Bell, *Commentaries*, 314 et sq.

152 Bell, *Commentaries*, 315.

153 Cf generally McBryde, *Void, Voidable, Illegal and Unenforceable Contracts in Scots law*, 35 et sqq, 168 et sqq; *The Law of Contract in Scotland*, 254, 621; Memorandum on Defective Consent And Consequential Matters (Scot Law Com Memo No 42, 1978), vol 1, para 14; vol 2, para 2.10.

154 Stair, *Institutions*, 1.9.8.

155 McBryde, *Void, Voidable, Illegal and Unenforceable Contracts in Scots law*, 35; McBryde, *The Law of Contract in Scotland*, 254.

156 Cf Memorandum on Defective Consent And Consequential Matters (Scot Law Com Memo No 42, 1978), vol 2, para 3.105; Erskine, *Institute*, 3.1.16.

157 Cf Stair, *Institutions*, 1.9.8; 1.17.14. In *Grant v Balvaird*; *Agnes Grant against* —— (1642) Mor 16483 it was held that judicial ratification prevented a claim of reduction *ex capite metus*.

agreement should be drawn up. Bankton's general exposition of the distinction is clearer. He is the first Scottish writer to draw a distinction between extorted deeds which are intrinsically null,[158] and voidable deeds.[159] For example, if a marriage is concluded because of extortion, it would be difficult to acknowledge that it "existed", and then have it set aside later on. But these seem to be rather extreme cases. The general impression is that the effect of force and fear is to render acts reducible or voidable. Bankton also specifically recognises the possibility that extorted deeds can be ratified—a conclusion inconsistent with nullity.[160] Probably the most clear voice in favour of nullity is Bell, who states that "force and fear annul engagement".[161] However, he also recognises that the party subjected to the compulsion is entitled to "a reduction declaring the contract to be 'utterly void".[162] This indicates that reduction is a prerequisite for declaring a contract "utterly void"'.[163] A similar approach is also followed in the case law: although it is at times stated that the effect of force and fear is to render certain acts "null",[164] the general approach is that there first has to be reduction.[165]

At this stage it may be asked whether it is of any real significance to distinguish between voidness and voidability as possible effects of force and fear. If the victim wants relief, is he not going to claim it? And if he does not claim relief, will the act for all practical intents and purposes not be valid? The answer is that the distinction between voidness and voidability is significant in at least one context, and that is to determine the rights of third parties.

(d) Indirect enrichment

There are essentially two ways in which a third party can benefit from compulsion: he can either obtain something directly from the victim, or he can obtain it from another person (usually the wrongdoer) who in turn has obtained it from the victim. During the era of the Institutional writers, Scots law generally provided the victim with relief in both these cases,[166] even if the third party was bona

158 Cf Bankton, *Institute*, 1.10.57.

159 Cf Bankton, *Institute*, 1.10.58.

160 In Bankton, *Institute*, 1.10.61 it is stated that when a party ratifies a deed, "the action upon the head of force is excluded". Of course, this subsequent ratification must not have been the consequence of extortion either. Bankton refers to Voet, *Commentarius ad Pandectas* 4.2.16. Here Voet states that "[n]otwithstanding a justifiable fear things done in fear keep their fullest stability when after a space of time a person has ratified them in free will and without constraint" (tr Gane (1955), 623).

161 Bell, *Principles*, para 12.

162 Bell, *Commentaries*, 314.

163 Memorandum on Defective Consent And Consequential Matters (Scot Law Com Memo No 42, 1978), vol 2, para 3.107.

164 Cf *Craig v Mowat* (1555) Mor 16480 (a discharge is "null be way of exception"); *Stuarts v Whitefoord and The Duke of Hamilton* (1677) Mor 16489 (force "doth anul the disposition"); *Heriot v Bird* (1681) Mor 16496 ("the disposition ... and the obligation ... were null"); *Dundas v Hardie* (1700) Mor 16506 (a bond is regarded as "null").

165 See 3.3.1.iii(a) above, esp note 140.

166 On direct acquistion from the victim, cf Bankton, *Institute*, 1.10.58; *Tenants of Winton v Bakers of Canongate and Leith* (1748) Mor 16514; *Nisbet v Stewart* (1708) Mor 16512. The case of *Tenants of Winton v Bakers of Canongate and Leith* dealt with a threat by some rebels against the tenants of Winton to induce them to transfer their "victual-rent" (apparently wheat) to the bakers of Canongate and Leith. The idea was that biscuits could be made of it for their army, and that they could obtain some money for it. When the tenants reclaimed the price of the "victuals" from the bakers, the latter's defence was that they had to receive the victual-rent because the orders of the rebels were all under the pain of military execution. The court held that the bakers were liable for

fide.[167] This indicates that the effect of force and fear was that of voidness. However, the above exposition is subject to the possible exception that bona fide third parties who acquired legal rights in heritage and corporeal moveables for value were protected from a claim by the victim.[168] This again is indicative of a consequence of voidability. However, it is doubtful whether even these third parties would have been protected where something was acquired as the consequence of *vis absoluta*. The force is then a *vitium reale* or *labes realis*—a fatal or "radical" defect which prevents the transfer of ownership.[169] All in all, one is therefore left to conclude that the treatment of third parties during the Institutional era does not provide unequivocal support for regarding the consequence of force and fear as voidness and not voidability.

(e) Exception

In the Institutional era it was not deemed necessary for the victim to challenge the validity of his actions by way of a claim for reduction: he could raise an exception[170] as a defence to a claim of enforcement—"a defence which did not object to the libel, but assumed the competency and relevancy of the action, and met the substance and merits of the action".[171] The meaning of the concept "exception" has changed somewhat in modern law,[172] but for present purposes it need not be dealt with in further detail. As far as the circumstances under which exception would be available are concerned, they generally seem to be the same as those which would give rise to a claim of reduction.[173]

---

what they received from the tenants while the compulsion subsisted, but not thereafter. In the *Nisbet* case, Stewart obtained a decree against some of Nisbet's tenants for stealing shipwrecked goods. Nisbet then obtained a discharge of this decree through extortion. According to Stewart, it would not be sufficient for Nisbet to simply offer to "repone" him (Stewart) by giving back the discharge, since the tenants had already obtained a *jus quaesitum* (*tertio?*), i.e. they were benefited by the discharge as third parties. It was then held that giving back the discharge alone was not sufficient, and that Nisbet would have to obtain a renunciation from the tenants, a somewhat unlikely occurrence. If not, he would be personally liable. On acquisition from the wrongdoer, cf *Earl of Morton v Lochleven* (1543) Mor 16479.

167 Cf *Cassie v Fleming* (1632) Mor 16482; Bell, *Commentaries*, 315 ("the effect of compulsion as invalidating consent will not be limited to him who is the party to the contract, but a remedy will be given also against those who profit by the unlawful act"). The passage is reminiscent of the view that in Roman law relief would be provided to a person who acquires something as the consequence of force and fear.

168 Bankton, *Institute*, 1.10.59; cf Memorandum on Defective Consent And Consequential Matters (Scot Law Com Memo No 42, 1978), vol 2, para 3.107. According to *Willocks v Callender and Wilson* (1776) Mor 1519, bills of exchange extorted by concussion are no exception and are invalid in the hands of onerous endorsees. Cf also *Wrightman v Graham* (1787) Mor 1521. But cf 4.2.2. i below on legislative reform.

169 Cf Memorandum on Defective Consent And Consequential Matters (Scot Law Com Memo No 42, 1978), vol 2, para 3.107. On *vitium reale*, cf SME, vol 18 (1993), paras 614, 615. In this respect *vis absoluta* resembles robbery: according to Stair, "fear and fraud have much the same effects, as to singular successors, except in the case of robbery, which as well as theft, is *vitium reale* in moveables" (Stair, *Institutions*, 4.40.28). Cf also Stair, *Institutions*, 4.40.21, where theft and violence are regarded as "*labes reales*, following the subject to all successors otherwise there would be the greatest encouragement to theft and robbery".

170 Cf Stair, *Institutions*, 4.40.25–28; Bankton, *Institute*, 1.8.26–27; Erskine, *Institute*, 3.1.5, and also *Craig v Mowat* (1555) Mor 16480; *Earl of Orkney v Vinfra* (1606) Mor 16481.

171 *Dickson v Murray* (1866) 4 M 797 at 799. Cf Walker, *The Law of Civil Remedies in Scotland*, 140.

172 Cf Walker, *The Law of Civil Remedies in Scotland*, 140.

173 E.g., compare Stair, *Institutions*, 1.9.8 and 4.40.25–28.

3.3.2 *Compulsion and the* condictiones

In contrast to early Scots law, which bears little traces of the reception of the *condictiones*, seventeenth-century case law and legal writings clearly indicate that the *condictiones*, and the *condictio indebiti* in particular, were familiar to Scottish legal practice. However, it is not really in their own name that the *condictiones* became known: throughout the Institutional era they are closely linked to the notion of "restitution". In their various titles on "restitution",[174] the Institutional writers deal with a variety of remedies which nowadays would be regarded as relating to property law or the law of unjustified enrichment, and it is their treatment of the *condictiones* which are presently of concern. As in the chapter on Roman law, particular attention will be paid to the recovery of undue transfers, as well as transfers of which the receipt was tainted by turpitude.

i. Compulsion and undue transfers: the condictio indebiti

During the Institutional era the courts generally awarded the remedy of reduction in cases of force and fear. The reason is obvious: the fruits of extortion were usually written documents which either recorded an obligation to make a transfer (e.g. a bond), or created, established or recorded a transfer (e.g. a bill).[175] Where no such document was provided and the victim was required actually to pay a sum of money, an action of repetition was awarded.[176] In the case of *Jack v Fiddes*,[177] which dealt with a claim of repetition (presumably of payments made under a bond granted by Jack while being incarcerated), the defence was raised that the payment was due, or made under a civil obligation. As the defence put it, "there could be no *indictio* [sic] *indebiti*, where there was *obligatio naturalis* or *civilis* pending".[178] The court was not moved by this defence, and allowed the claim of repetition, apparently on the ground that the initial judgment which held Jack liable for payment was not pronounced by a competent court. This case has subsequently been recorded in Morison's Dictionary under the rubric "*condictio indebiti*". The marginal note also states "*condictio indebiti* sustained". Although this is not expressly borne out by the record, it is at least arguable that the case may have been decided on the basis that a payment of money extorted through compulsion in the form of force and fear can be recovered with a *condictio indebiti*. The question now arises whether such an approach was in line with the Institutional writers' conception of the *condictio indebiti* at the time. Their views will be examined briefly.[179]

Stair deals with undue transfers in his title on the obligation of restitution—that "obediential"[180] obligation "whereby that which is another's coming into our power without his purpose to gift it to us, and yet without our fault, ought to be restored".[181] The obligation to restore *indebite solutum* then arises "when any party through error delivereth or payeth what he supposeth due, or belongeth to another; if thereafter

---

174 Cf Stair, *Institutions*, 1.7.1; Bankton, *Institute*, 1.8; Erskine, *Institute*, 3.1.10; Bell, *Principles*, para 525 et sqq.

175 See text to note 140 above.

176 See text to note 141 above.

177 (1661) Mor 2923.

178 (1661) Mor 2923 at 2924.

179 Cf, generally, R Evans-Jones, "Some reflections on the *condictio indebiti* in a mixed legal system" (1993) 110 *SALJ* 759 at 763 et sqq; R Evans-Jones, "From 'undue transfer' to 'retention without a legal basis' (the *condictio indebiti* and the *condictio ob turpem vel iniustam causam*)", in R Evans-Jones (ed), *The Civil Law Tradition in Scotland*, 213.

180 Stair, *Institutions*, 1.3.2–4.

181 Stair, *Institutions*, 1.7.1.

it appears that it was not due to that other, he who receiveth it is obliged to restore, and yet not by paction or contract".[182] The centrality of the notion that the payment must be undue is obvious,[183] in fact so much so that Stair lists a number of exceptions, when undue transfers do not have to be restored.[184] The question now arises whether the fact that an undue transfer was made under force and fear gives rise to an obligation of restitution, based on the *condictio indebiti*. Although Stair states that if a transaction is brought about by force there has to be "restitution",[185] the answer is in fact in the negative: providing the delictual remedy of reparation could entail making restitution,[186] and the reference to "restitution" is presumably made in this context. Furthermore, insofar as error is a requirement of the *condictio indebiti*, the pursuer is unable to meet it.

Bankton generally follows the approach of Stair. He also deals with the *condictio indebiti* in a title on the obligation of restitution, that natural obligation when one man's goods happen, without his consent, to come into another's possession.[187] According to Bankton, "When one, thro' error, delivers or makes payment of what was not due, but which he believed to be due, he has re-payment, termed in the civil law *condictio indebiti*".[188] Again, the return of the undue payment is central.[189] It is further recognised that "when one knowingly pays, or delivers what is not due, he is understood to gift it, by the rule of law, *Cujus per errorem dati repetitio est, ejus consulto dati donatio est*; and consequently the same is not to be refunded".[190] Apparently, the error requirement is construed here in terms of the lack of knowledge that a debt is due. A person who has such knowledge is then presumed (understood) to make a donation. This point is made more clearly by Erskine. According to him, *indebiti solutio* is the "payment to one of a debt not truly due to him".[191] However, if the payer knew that the payment was not due, he cannot recover it, since he is "presumed to intend to present".[192] The *condictio indebiti* is therefore primarily based on the fact that an undue payment has been made,[193] and error is not regarded as an essential feature. However, error comes to

182 Stair, *Institutions*, 1.7.9. Nothing in the title suggests that the claim for the return of *indebitum solutum* is restricted to money: in fact the reference to the words "delivereth or payeth" (Stair, *Institutions*, 1.7.9) suggests that a claim for restitution could arise in respect of both corporeal property and money.

183 Cf Evans-Jones, "From 'undue transfer' to 'retention without a legal basis' (the *condictio indebiti* and the *condictio ob turpem vel iniustam causam*)", in Evans-Jones (ed), *The Civil Law Tradition in Scotland*, 213 at 233; R Evans-Jones and P Hellwege, "Swaps, Error of Law and Unjustified Enrichment" (1995) 1 *SLPQ* 1 at 8.

184 These are if the creditor received what was due to him, though not due by the person who made the payment, and when there was doubt as to liability followed by a transaction or settlement of a dispute (Stair, *Institutions*, 1.7.9).

185 Stair, *Institutions*, 1.7.9.

186 Stair, *Institutions*, 1.7.7.

187 Bankton, *Institute*, 1.8.

188 Bankton, *Institute*, 1.8.23.

189 Bankton, *Institute*, 1.8.24. Bankton also refers to the absence of a "just cause" supporting the payment.

190 Bankton, *Institute*, 1.8.31.

191 Erskine, *Institute*, 3.3.54.

192 Erskine, *Institute*, 3.3.54.

193 Cf Evans-Jones, "From 'undue transfer' to 'retention without a legal basis' (the *condictio indebiti* and the *condictio ob turpem vel iniustam causam*)", in Evans-Jones (ed), *The Civil Law Tradition in Scotland*, 213 at 229 et sq, 233; Evans-Jones and Hellwege, "Swaps, Error of Law and Unjustified Enrichment" (1995) 1 *SLPQ* 1 at 8.

the fore again in Bell's *Principles*. Under the heading restitution (later repetition)[194] it is stated that

> Whatever has been delivered or paid on an erroneous conception of duty or obligation, may be recovered on the ground of equity ... The action by which, in Roman law, this was effected, was called *Condictio Indebiti*; and the term has been adopted by us.[195]

Although error has a more central place, one again finds the rule that a payment made in full knowledge that no debt or obligation exits, is held to be a donation, and cannot be recovered.[196] Finally, Hume defines the *condictio indebiti* as "That action which lies for the recovery of money that has been unduly paid—paid under the erroneous belief of a debt being due to the party who receives the money".[197] He also stresses the importance and centrality of the notion of the undue transfer: "To make way for this claim, it seems to be necessary that the payment have been absolutely and utterly *indebitum*, not due to that party, by any even natural bond of obligation".[198] In addition, the payment had to be "made out of error—under a mistaken impression of a necessity to pay".[199] Error is then strictly construed to exclude payments in doubt which amount to a "bargain or transaction".[200]

The purpose of these detailed quotations from the Institutional and related writings is to indicate clearly what was regarded as the essential features of the *condictio indebiti*. First, there can be no doubt that it was solely concerned with the recovery of transfers that were not due. Such transfers could take the form of the delivery of (presumably) moveables or the payment of money. Second, the state of mind in which the undue payment was made influenced its recoverability. The general view is that it had to be made in the erroneous belief that it was due, when it was in fact not due. However, Erskine merely states that the payer should not have known that it was not due. Such a person is then presumed to have intended to make a donation.

If one now returns to *Jack v Fiddes*,[201] and the general question whether a payment extorted through compulsion in the form of force and fear can be recovered with a *condictio indebiti*, it can be accepted that the requirement of an undue transfer generally presents no problem.[202] The difficulty arises with the required state of mind of the payer. Insofar as error is a positive requirement of the *condictio indebiti*, i.e. something the pursuer has to prove in order to succeed with the claim, this remedy is inappropriate in cases of compulsion. A person who is compelled to make an undue transfer generally does not believe that it is due. But even if error is not regarded a positive requirement, and it is rather up to the defender to prove knowledge that no debt is due, the *condictio indebiti* still seems inappropriate. The victim would generally know that no debt is due. Finally, there are difficulties associated with regarding

194 The change occurs in the fifth edition of 1860, which was posthumously revised by Patrick Shaw. See 7.2.2.iv below.

195 Bell, *Principles*, 531. Cf also Bell, *Principles*, 526 ("The law gives an action of restitution against one in possession of the property or goods of another without his consent; or who has, in consequence of error, received payment of money not legally due to him")

196 Bell, *Principles*, 533.

197 *Lectures*, vol 3, 172.

198 *Lectures*, vol 3, 172.

199 *Lectures*, vol 3, 174.

200 *Lectures*, vol 3, 174.

201 (1661) Mor 2923.

202 On the position in modern law see generally 4.3.1 below.

a transfer compelled through force and fear as a "payment". If the intention to discharge a debt or obligation is an essential feature of a payment, it can be argued that the victim of compulsion does not make a payment. His intention could be to avoid the threatened harm, rather than to discharge a debt. All in all, it can be concluded that according to the Institutional writers, the *condictio indebiti* cannot be regarded as a suitable remedy for the recovery of an undue payment extorted through compulsion in the form of force and fear.

ii. Compulsion and transfers ob turpem causam[203]

Most Institutional writers (like the Romans) distinguish between a transfer made in order to pay a debt (*solvendi causa*), and a transfer made in the expectation that the recipient would do, or refrain from doing something (*ob rem*).[204] They regard a transfer which is given for a morally offensive or illegal "cause"[205] (a transfer *ob turpem causam* or *injustam causam*)[206] as a transfer *ob rem*, and not as a transfer *solvendi causa*.[207] From the discussion of the Roman law of the *condictiones*, it will be recalled that the *condictio ob turpem vel iniustam causam* could be used to obtain restitution in two situations involving compulsion.[208] First, it was applied in cases of *metus*, and second in cases of compulsion which were not serious enough to fall under the scope of the praetorian remedies, but still justified relief. A notable example is the situation where someone receives something to do what he is obliged to do in any event. This division between two forms of compulsion also can be employed conveniently in an analysis of the position in Scots law.

(a) Compulsion in the form of force and fear

In *Grant of Ballinalloch v Leslie*[209] the pursuer claimed that a bond was made *ob turpem causam*, because it followed from a promise extorted *ob metum*, being signed

203 Cf, generally, Evans-Jones and McKenzie, "Towards a profile of the condictio ob turpem vel iniustam causam in Scots law" 1994 *JR* 60 at 61 et sqq; Evans-Jones, "From 'undue transfer' to 'retention without a legal basis' (the *condictio indebiti* and the *condictio ob turpem vel iniustam causam*)", in Evans-Jones (ed), *The Civil Law Tradition in Scotland*, 213 at 220, 243 et sqq; P Simpson, *Die Rückabwicklung von sitten—und rechtswidrigen Rechtsgeschäften im heutigen deutschen und schottischen Recht*.

204 Stair, *Institutions*, 1.7.7; Bankton, *Institute*, 1.8.21; Erskine, *Institute*, 3.1.10.

205 For present purposes the "cause" can be regarded as the purpose for which a thing is given (cf R Evans-Jones, "The Claim to Recover what was Given for a Lawful Purpose outwith Contract that Fails" 1997 *AJ* 139.

206 Although the reference here is only to transfers *ob turpem causam* (cf Erskine, *Institute*, 3.1.10), it should be noted that it is not clear whether Scots law in fact received two *condictiones* (the *condictiones ob turpem causam* and *ob iniustam causam*), or one (the *condictio ob turpem vel iniustam causam*). For example, Stair refers to "things given for an unjust cause, as *ob turpem causam*" (*Institutions*, 1.7.7), which could be interpreted in favour of both approaches (cf Evans-Jones and McKenzie, "Towards a profile of the condictio ob turpem vel iniustam causam in Scots law", 1994 *JR* 60 at 61 et sq; Simpson, *Die Rückabwicklung von sitten- und rechtswidrigen Rechtsgeschäften im heutigen deutschen und schottischen Recht*, par V.3.B.i). In *Grant of Ballinalloch v Leslie* (1642) Mor 16483 the words *ob turpem causam* and unjust cause seem to be used interchangeably.

207 Stair, *Institutions*, 1.7.7 et sq; Bankton, *Institute*, 1.8.21 et sq; Erskine, *Institute*, 3.1.10. Cf Simpson, *Die Rückabwicklung von sitten—und rechtswidrigen Rechtsgeschäften im heutigen deutschen und schottischen Recht*, para IV.3.B.

208 Cf the discussion of D 12.5.7 at 2.3.2.ii above, where it is indicated that a *condictio ob turpem vel iniustam causam* would be available where money was exacted under a stipulation which was extorted by force.

209 (1642) Mor 16483.

"under fear of life". Although the idea that an extorted transfer can be regarded as a transfer made *ob turpem causam* was somewhat unusual at the time, it was certainly not new—one only needs to recall D.12.5.7 on the extorted stipulation. In the light of the general availability of a remedy such as reduction, the question arises whether it was at all necessary and even legitimate to regard an extorted bond as something given *ob turpem causam*. Here a considerable divergence in opinion exists among the Institutional writers.[210] At the one end of the spectrum there is Stair's view that force and fear has nothing to do with the obligation of restitution, and the *condictiones* in particular. Although he recognises that, subject to certain qualifications, a duty to return (an obligation of restitution) also arises where something is given for an unjust cause or *ob turpem causam*,[211] he states that "... things which are attained by force or fear, ... have their original from delinquence, and come not under this consideration".[212] The view that force and fear is a delict which gives rise to the obligation of reparation, and not the obligation of restitution, is familiar from the discussion of the basis of relief.[213] It will also be recalled that Bankton's approach resembles that of Stair in that he too recognises that an obligation of restitution arises where "things are given for an unlawful cause"[214] and regards "extortion" as a delict. However, Bankton's division between "restitution" and "reparation" is not as sharp as that of Stair: there are indications that he believed that a transfer extorted by force and fear could be regarded as a transfer *ob turpem causam*. This is apparent from his discussion of extortion through the threat of revealing criminal behaviour. Here he somewhat blurs the borders between restitution and reparation arising from delinquency by relying on Digest titles on the *condictio ob turpem vel iniustam causam*[215] in support of the rule that recovery is excluded where both parties are tainted by turpitude.[216] This is strange, because he also applies this exclusionary rule in its more traditional role of restricting the availability of the *condictio ob turpem vel iniustam causam*.[217] It seems quite out of place in a discussion of relief on grounds of delict. Erskine, on the other hand, does not regard force and fear as a delict, and consequently avoids these difficulties. According to him an obligation of restitution (not reparation) arises when something is given *ob turpem causam*. It must then

210 On the general development of the law relating to the influence of public policy on the validity of contracts, cf McBryde, *The Law of Contract in Scotland*, 574 et sqq. He points out that prior to the eighteenth century, the general approach was that a contract would not be null because of its subject matter (cf Stair, *Institutions*, 1.10.7—"every paction produceth action"), but that the position changed during the eighteenth century towards attacking contracts in a wider variety of cases on the basis that they are *contra bonos mores*.

211 Stair, *Institutions*, 1.7.7. Cf generally Evans-Jones and McKenzie, "Towards a profile of the condictio ob turpem vel iniustam causam in Scots law" 1994 *JR* 60 at 61 et sqq; Evans-Jones, "From 'undue transfer' to 'retention without a legal basis' (the *condictio indebiti* and the *condictio ob turpem vel iniustam causam*)", in Evans-Jones (ed), *The Civil Law Tradition in Scotland*, 213 at 220, 243 et sqq; Simpson, *Die Rückabwicklung von sitten—und rechtswidrigen Rechtsgeschäften im heutigen deutschen und schottischen Recht*.

212 Stair, *Institutions*, 1.7.7.

213 See 3.3.1. i above.

214 Bankton, *Institute*, 1.8.22.

215 D 12.5 (*de condictione ob turpem vel iniustam causam*).

216 Bankton, *Institute*, 1.10.55 ("One who being catched in the commission of a crime, [and] is compelled to give money, or other consideration to prevent discovery, has the benefit of this action for restitution, because for fear of death or other punishment, he gives what otherwise he would not; but, if he voluntarily gave it, there being turpitude in both, the possessor retains what he gets").

217 Bankton, *Institute*, 1.8.22.

> ... be restored if the turpitude was in the receiver, and not in the giver; whether the cause of giving was performed or not: L. 1, § 2. *de cond. ob turp.caus.* If, for instance, one accused of a crime should give money to another that other might not bear false witness against him, he may recover the sum so given by a *condictio ob turpem causam*.[218]

Although this is not expressly stated, it does seem as if Erskine is in fact dealing with a *pactum illicitum* concluded under force and fear: a person accused of a crime may very well fear incarceration or even death, and when he has to pay another not to commit perjury against him, this can be regarded as extortion. One can therefore conclude that Erskine at least indirectly acknowledged that force and fear can give rise to a *condictio ob turpem causam*, or, more generally, an obligation of restitution.

(b) Other forms of compulsion

From the aforegoing, it is apparent that during the Institutional era, the link between "force and fear" and illegality was rather tenuous. The reason is obvious: why should force and fear be regarded as something which gives rise to a transfer *ob turpem causam* if there was no need to do so? Relief was simply provided in the form of reduction, restitution or repetition, and no need existed to delve deeper into the structure of the law of the *condictiones*. The same can of course be said of *metus*, which in Roman law by and large was treated as a ground for relief in its own right. It will be recalled, though, that in Roman times certain forms of compulsion did not give rise to remedies based on *metus*, but were still sufficiently serious to warrant relief. More specifically, the *condictio ob turpem vel iniustam causam* could be used to reclaim a transfer compelled through a refusal to do something which someone is obliged to do in any event. For example, I pay you to make you give me back something deposited with you, like a document, or I lend you clothes for use and then pay you a price to get them back. In these cases there was no need to prove fear of personal harm, such as would shake a *vir constans*. The turpitudinous conduct of the recipient obliged him to render restitution. It will now be examined whether Scots law accommodated these cases in a similar fashion.

In his *Principles of Equity*, Lord Kames[219] discusses the powers of a court of equity to remedy imperfections of the Common Law in cases of pecuniary harm caused by

---

218 Erskine, *Institute*, 3.1.10.

219 Kames was a judge of the Court of Session and a prolific writer on Scots law, as well as on non-legal subjects (see generally, Walker, *The Scottish Jurists*, 220 et sqq; P Stein, *Legal Evolution* (1980), 23 et sqq; W C Lehmann, *Henry Home, Lord Kames, and the Scottish Enlightenment* (1971); I S Ross, *Lord Kames and the Scotland of his Day* (1972). His *Principles of Equity* was first published in 1760 and is a highly original work aimed at the historical as well as comparative study of law, written mainly in the natural law tradition, but also influenced by utilitarianism. The title is rather unusual for a book on Scots law, to which the English distinction between Common Law Courts and Courts of Equity is foreign. But according to Kames, equity and common law is united in one court in Scotland, and the decisions of this court, as a court of equity, should then be guided by two principles, namely justice and utility (*Principles of Equity*, 26). The emphasis was on identifying certain *principles* of law, and not to be concerned with detail. According to Professor Peter Stein, "His (Kames's) aim in all his legal writings was to show that law was not just a 'mass of naked propositions ... rarely connected with either premise or consequences, but rather a rational science comparable to moral philosophy" (*Legal Evolution*, 25). But Kames's attempts to bring law and philosophy together were not always happy. Stein quotes David Hume, who in a letter to Adam Smith wrote: "I am afraid of Kames's *Law Tracts*. A man might as well think of making a fine sauce by a mixture of wormwood and aloes as an agreeable combination by joining metaphysics and Scotch law" (*Legal Evolution*, 29).

someone being "overawed to act knowingly against his interest".[220] He then states the following:[221]

> I promise a man a sum not to rob me. Equity will relieve me, by denying action for payment, and by affording me an action for recalling the money, if paid. The latter action is, in the Roman law, styled, *Condictio ob injustam causam*.[222] To take money for doing what I am bound to do without it, must be extortion: I hold the money *sine justa causa*, and ought, in conscience, to restore it. Thus it is extortion for a tutor to take a sum from his pupil's mother for granting a factory to her.[223] And it was found extortion in a man to take a bond from one whose curator he had been, before he would deliver up the family-writings.[224]

The example of paying a person not to rob one can amount to force and fear, but it is the other examples of taking something "for doing what I am bound to do without it", which are of interest. These are clearly not cases of force and fear: there are no threats of personal harm or even harm to property, and the *vir constans* may very well have refused to comply. On the other hand, these are still cases of unacceptable compulsion: each involves an illegal threat not to do something one is supposed to do. What is of interest, is the fact that it was not sought to extend the notion of force and fear to cover these cases, but rather to deal with them in terms of the turpitude of the transfer. It may be that the reason for this derives from as far back as Roman law: for example, in *Rossie v Her curators*,[225] the pursuer claimed suspension of a bond on the grounds that it was "given *ob instrumenta deposita reddenda*, which is a shameful cause". This is an allusion to D 12.5.2, according to which one of the examples where one could claim back that which has been received for an immoral or illegal purpose,

---

220 Book I, part I, ch I, sec III, art II. For present purposes, his discussion of extortion in the sense Erskine used it, namely "oppression" or taking advantage of someone in need, is not relevant (cf Erskine, *Institute*, 4.1.26; 4.1.27). Kames refers to the extortion of a bridegroom's "dependent situation" by his future father in law (*Principles of Equity*, 50 et sqq), to an agreement concluded with a young heir to have double or treble the sum lent upon the death of his father (*Principles of Equity*, 53 et sqq) and to "hard and oppressive conditions" contained in agreements which debtors conclude with their creditors (*Principles of Equity*, 48 et sqq).

221 *Principles of Equity*, 53.

222 Although Kames refers to this *condictio*, he does not clearly state what the measure of relief in these cases would be. According to him, "[t]o restore the party injured to his former situation, where that method is practicable, will be preferred as the most complete remedy. Thus goods stolen are restored to the owner; and a disposition of land procured by fear, or undue influence, is voided in order that the disponer may be restored to his property". However, where this is not possible, the person injured "must be contened with reparation in money" (*Principles of Equity*, 62).

223 Kames refers to Durie, penult Feb 1639, *Mushet contra Dog*, which is recorded as *Mushet v Dog* (1634) Mor 9456. Mushet, the tutor of his brother's children, obtained a bond of 3000 merks from Dog (their mother) in return for granting her a "factory" (i.e. the office of managing their property—cf *The Scottish National Dictionary*, s v "factor" and "factory"). This, in effect, meant selling his office of tutor to the mother. The court found that the agreement was in the nature of *turpia pacta* (agreements tainted with turpitude). It could only be to the detriment of the children, and the bond was consequently suspended.

224 Kames refers to Nicolson (*turpis causa*), July 24, 1634, *Rossie contra her curators*, which is recorded as *Rossie v Her curators* (1634) Mor 9456. Rossie wanted to marry and needed some "evidents" (i.e. documentary proof of entitlement—cf *The Scottish National Dictionary*, s v "evident") from her curator, but he refused to deliver these "evidents" unless she granted him a bond of 200 merks. She then granted the bond, to which her future husband was cautioner, in favour of her curator. After the marriage, Rossie claimed suspension of the bond.

225 (1634) Mor 9456.

is where something is given in order to obtain the return of a deposit.[226] These cases all involve turpitude: it is not only unlawful but also morally objectionable for a tutor or a curator to make a profit out of his office.[227] However, it can be doubted whether these cases can be used in support of the general proposition that *every* transfer obtained through unlawful compulsion is automatically a transfer *ob turpem causam*. But be that as it may: it is not essential at this stage to examine these matters further. The reason is quite simple: by the nineteenth century, the notion that transfers *ob turpem causam* are recoverable with a *condictio* in any event became largely irrelevant. Just like *restitutio in integrum*, the *condictio ob turpem causam* lost its identity as a ground for relief, and the only aspect of it which survived was the rule that recovery is barred where both parties are tainted by turpitude.[228] In this way it resembles *in integrum restitutio*, which also waned as a substantive remedy but left the rule that recovery is excluded if the claimant is himself unable to provide restitution.

3.3.3 *Compulsion and property law: giving and taking*

In the chapter on Roman law it was indicated that, apart from the praetorian relief, compulsion could at times give rise to remedies based on ownership. In other words, the victim could institute a proprietary or vindicatory claim based on the fact that the wrongdoer or a third party recipient did not acquire ownership of the extorted property, and was liable to return it. The use of the term "restitution" in Scots law to describe the relief granted to such a victim makes it somewhat difficult to determine whether or not such a proprietary remedy was in fact awarded. The fact that Stair states that "... such deeds and obligations as are by force and fear are made utterly void"[229] indicates that he may have thought that force and fear gives rise to a defect in title. This, at least, is the way in which Bell understands him when he states that "[i]t is also a radical defect in his title, that the thing has been stolen, or obtained by violence; or that the transference has been procured by force and fear".[230] Thus, to Bell both "violence" (by which robbery or *vis absoluta* is presumably intended) and "force and fear" are defects in title.[231] Hume also regards "concussion" or "force and fear" as a defect in title, but virtually equates it with *vis absoluta*.[232] However, if the above statement of Stair is re-examined in the context of a discussion of defects in

226 "Si tibi dedero, ut rem mihi redas depositam apud te vel ut instrumentum mihi redderes" (cf *Recovery of Benefits Conferred under Error of Law* (Scot Law Com D P No 95, 1993), vol 2, 213).

227 Cf also *Blair v Gib* (1738) Mor 664. The parties submitted an issue for arbitration and the arbiters then withheld their decision (decree arbitral) unless they were paid a certain amount. Apparently they were not entitled to payment. The one party, in whose favour the decree was made, then paid the arbiters. The other party claimed that the decree should be reduced, because it was obtained by "bribery and compulsion". The court ordered that the money paid to the arbiters be given to charity.

228 Cf Hume, *Lectures*, vol 3, 165 et sqq; Bell, *Principles*, para 35; *Recovery of Benefits Conferred under Error of Law* (Scot Law Com D P No 95, 1993), vol 2, 204.

229 Stair, *Institutions*, 1.9.8. On Stair's views on property in general, cf D L Carey Miller, "Stair's Property: A Romanist System?" 1995 *JR* 70.

230 Bell, *Commentaries*, vol 1, 299.

231 Bell (and Erskine) were not loath to indicate that there was a defect in title. As Professor W M Gordon has indicated, both of them maintained that the *causa* of a delivery "is virtually to be equated with the intention to transfer ownership" (Gordon, "The Importance of the *iusta causa* of *traditio*", in *Essays for Barry Nicholas*, 123 at 125; cf Bell, *Principles*, para 1299; Erskine, *Institute*, 2.1.8).

232 Cf Hume, *Lectures*, vol 4, 235 et sq.

title, a different picture emerges. In a passage which deals with the effect of fraud, Stair states that

> ... in moveables, purchasers are not quarellable upon the fraud of their authors, if they did purchase for an onerous equivalent cause. The reason is, because moveables must have a current course of traffic, and the buyer is not to consider how the seller purchased, unless it were by theft or violence which the law accounts as *labes reales*, following the subject to all successors, otherwise there would be the greatest encouragement to theft and robbery.[233]

Thereafter he turns to "fear" and states that

> Fear and fraud have much the same effects, as to singular successors, except in the case of robbery, which, as well as theft, is *vitium reale* in moveables: and therefore what hath been said of fraud in that point needs not here be repeated.[234]

Thus, it is only robbery which creates a defect in title. "Force and fear", or "extortion" in itself is not such a defect.[235] If robbery then gives rise to such a defect, and force and fear does not, it becomes important to distinguish between their respective fields of application. Here it is quite useful to turn for guidance to the criminal law, and in particular the distinction it draws between the crimes of robbery and extortion. Like Roman law,[236] Scots law drew a distinction between the crimes of extortion and robbery: the essential feature of robbery seems to be that it involves the violent taking of something.[237] The problem is now to determine whether it would be robbery if a person threatens immediate violence unless the victim gives something. In modern terms it could be described as the "money or your life situation". Here Hume warns that by regarding such an action as "giving", one could be taking too technical a view of the matter. In his *Commentaries on the Law of Scotland respecting Crimes* he defines robbery as taking something from another against his will through the use or threat of present violence.[238] But he then also states that

---

233 Stair, *Institutions*, 4.40.21.

234 Stair, *Institutions*, 4.40.28. The editorial comment refers to Stair, *Institutions*, 4.35.19 and 21 but it seems as if a reference to Stair, *Institutions*, 4.40.21 is more appropriate.

235 Cf SME vol 18 (1993), para 615.

236 Incidentally, although Scottish lawyers were clearly aware of the relevant Roman criminal law, there could be no reception as in the case of the private law remedies. According to some of the Lords in *Stuarts v Whitefoord and The Duke of Hamilton* (1677) Mor 16489 one of the "divers remedies" in civil (i.e. Roman) law "competent to those who had been forced to do any deed" was a criminal action *ex lege julia*. However, it was held that since this remedy was "penal, by the municipal law of the Romans, it [could] not be introduced by the Lords of Session being civil judges, without an act of Parliament ((1677) Mor 16489, 16493).

237 On this distinction cf, generally, Mackenzie, *The Laws and Customes of Scotland in Matters Criminal*, 160, 326 et sqq; Bankton, *Institute*, 1.10.4, 1.10.50, 1.0.124. Bankton does not distinguish clearly between criminal law and civil law, but he apparently regards the civil remedy of spuilie as appropriate in cases of robbery. Spuilie is defined as "'the Violent Seizing or unlawful taking possession of goods from another without his consent or order of law, for Lucre's sake' and comprehends both Theft and Robbery, which, in a civil suit for damages, is termed as Spuilie or Spoliation; it for most part occurs by seizing the goods, but it will be likewise inferred by excluding the owner from the possession of them". It is therefore essential for spuilie that there should be a "violent seizing or unlawful taking". Extortion, on the other hand, requires that someone should be compelled to some or other deed (Bankton, *Institute*, 1.10.50). He approved of the immediate taking back of that which has been extorted and regarded this remedy as a "sort of self-defence" (Bankton, *Institute*, 1.10.61).

238 Hume, *Commentaries*, 104 et sqq.

> ... in the construction of what shall be deemed a *taking*, we rather attend to the substance of the case, which is, that the invader has got the thing by means of violence, than to the mode of the immediate act of apprehension. A purse shall therefore be held to be *taken*, though the owner, being intimidated, have with his own hand delivered it on demand. ... It is true, it was argued for Samuel Richards (27 February, 19 and 20 June 1710) that to prevail on a woman, by terror of his threats, to deliver him a little money with her own hands was not robbery, but concussion only. No regard was paid to so strange a defence.[239]

The point is clear: something given under threats of immediate violence can be regarded as taken. Hume therefore succeeds in finding an answer to this grey area which exists between an out-and-out "taking" situation, where something is grabbed by force, and the case where a victim "gives" something under extortion. This insight is valuable since it provides the opportunity to streamline private law and criminal law: it would be unsatisfactory if a person convicted of robbery under criminal law would under private law be exposed to a claim based on force and fear or extortion.[240] The above analysis can also be used to refine the earlier statement that "force and fear" only related to *vis compulsiva*. It requires that the concept of *vis absoluta* should be interpreted more broadly to encompass any situation of forceful taking (such as robbery), as well as the situations of giving under immediate threats of violence; *vis compulsiva*, on the other hand, should be interpreted more restrictively. It would then only be in these narrowed down category of cases of *vis compulsiva* that the recipient would become owner, and be exposed to remedies which are nowadays regarded as based on unjustified enrichment. However, it should be noted that at this stage in its development Scots law did not distinguish clearly between vindicatory remedies, whereby an owner could reclaim his own property, and enrichment-based remedies, whereby he could claim relief where another became owner of his property.[241]

3.4 CONCLUSIONS

The pre-institutional era

1. During the thirteenth until early seventeenth centuries there undoubtedly was a reception of the Roman law of *vis et metus*, which came to be referred to as "fear and dread" and *restitutio in integrum*, which at times was simply referred to as "restitution". Initially, fear and dread was grouped with minority and insanity, which indicates that the basis for relief was the lack of mental ability to act. However, subsequently, and apparently through the influence of the Digest, fear and dread was also dealt with in the context of fraud, which indicates that the fact that consent has not been obtained in a proper way could also have formed the basis for relief.

2. Initially, as in Roman times, the range of conduct which would amount to "fear and dread" was quite narrow: it covered physical threats to a person or people close to him, by a person ostensibly able to execute the threat if it was not immediately complied with. The classical situation is that of a person who is held in captivity. Neither fear caused by the threat of harm to property,

---

239 Hume, *Commentaries*, 105.

240 But cf McBryde, *The Law of Contract in Scotland*, 253.

241 For example, in his title on "restitution", Stair conflates these remedies with little apparent concern for the diversity in their nature. Cf Reid, "Unjustified Enrichment and Property" 1994 *JR* 167.

nor fear merely caused by reverence (*metus reverentialis*) was sufficient. The requirement that the victim had to experience "just fear" is not explained, but it could either be a tautologous reference to the *vir constans* requirement, or an indication that the fear should not be caused by unjust means.

3. The victim of fear and dread could "gainsay his own deed" and obtain *restitutio in integrum*. This apparently encompassed the restitution or repetition of property and money. A claim would lie against the wrongdoer responsible for the fear and dread, as well as his heirs, and even bona fide third parties.

4. There is no evidence that any of the *condictiones* of Roman law were used in order to reclaim that which has been transferred on grounds of fear and dread or *metus*. In fact there is little indication that the *condictiones* were received at all.

5. The medieval canon law dealing with the effect of force and fear on the validity of marriages also strongly reflects the influence of Roman law. Some texts contain sophisticated analyses of different forms of compulsion. In general, a stringent standard was applied for the dissolution of marriages. The relief awarded was that the parties should be restored *in integrum*.

The institutional era

6. In dealing with the institutional era a distinction must be drawn between compulsion in the form of force and fear and compulsion as a factor which played a role in the context of the law of the *condictiones*. As far as force and fear is concerned, the institutional writers followed two different approaches in determining the basis for relief. On the one hand there was the view of Stair and Bankton that force and fear does not affect the consent of the transferor ("*coactus volui, tamen volui*"), but that the victim should be provided relief on the basis that a wrong or delict was committed. On the other hand, there was the approach of Erskine and Bell, who regarded force and fear as a factor excluding consent. Despite these differences in approach, certain core elements of extortion or force and fear can be identified. There had to be fear which compelled people to act in a way they would not otherwise do. The fear generally had to be "such as might befall a constant man", but the standard was applied flexibly. There are indications that fear had to be instilled illegally. Bankton, following the Glossators, distinguished between *vis absoluta*, where there was no consent, and *vis compulsiva*, where there was consent, but obtained through force and fear. Erskine and Bell, on the other hand, maintain that force and fear excluded all consent. Special provision was made for wives' fear of their husbands, and fear instilled by "men in power". The fear did not only have to relate to oneself, but could also be fear of harm to family and others. Significantly, fear of harm to property was also acknowledged, as was fear caused by the withholding of a right. Lawful compulsion did not amount to force and fear. It is not clear what the position was if something due was extorted illegally.

7. As far as the effect of force and fear is concerned, Stair and Bankton, on the one hand, treated it as a delinquence or delict which gave rise to the remedy of reparation. Restitution could form part of the process of reparation. Mackenzie and Erskine, on the other hand, did not treat force and fear as a delinquence or delict, and only mention the rescissory action of reduction.

It was acknowledged that remedies based on extortion could be provided against the wrongdoer as well as third parties, even if they were bona fide. The general opinion was that extorted transactions were void, but closer inspection reveals that distinctions were drawn which indicate that force and fear could give rise to voidness and voidability. The issue of force and fear could be raised by exception.

8. As far as the relevance of compulsion to the law of the restitution (and repetition) is concerned, Stair and Bankton did not support the idea that a *condictio* would be available in cases of compulsion. Erskine, Bell and Hume are less clear on this point, but Kames believed that compulsion could give rise to a *condictio ob injustam causam*. However, it is not clear whether such a *condictio* would be available in all cases of compulsion. The examples he mentions involve agreements which violate offices such as curatorship and tutorage, which indicate that they in any event dealt with illegal transactions.

9. Although it was generally stated that the payer had to be in error in order to claim with the *condictio indebiti* (a remedy used to claim the restitution or repetition of payments which were not due), there is case law which indicates that the *condictio indebiti* may have been awarded in cases of compulsion. This case law is at variance with the view expressed by certain institutional authorities that force and fear is a delict, and that error is a requirement for a claim under the *condictio indebiti*.

10. Although there is support among institutional writers for the view that compulsion in the form of "force and fear" is a *vitium reale* which prevents the transfer of ownership, there is also a contrary view that it is only *vis absoluta* which has this effect. In delineating the borders between these categories it is useful to take guidance from criminal law, which generally regarded robbery as involving a violent "taking" and compulsion as a "giving", but also regards the situation of a giving under threat of immediate violence as robbery. From the perspective of property law, the implication of this distinction is that only *vis absoluta* or robbery amounting to a radical defect or *vitium reale*, prevents the transfer of ownership. *Vis compulsiva* or "force and fear", on the other hand, does not amount to such a defect, but rather gives rise to the obligations of restitution or repetition, which nowadays can be regarded as being based on unjustified enrichment.

Chapter 4

Compulsion in modern Scots Law

4.1 INTRODUCTION

During the nineteenth and twentieth centuries, two factors influenced the relevance and treatment of force and fear and related forms of compulsion in Scottish private law. Not much needs to be said about the first factor of greater political and social stability. Better law enforcement and greater reliance on the legal system obviously diminished the incidence of serious cases of physical compulsion: as Sheriff Dallas put it in *Sutherland v Montrose Fishing Co Ltd*, "[i]n Scotland the days are gone, or have not come yet again, when the pistol and dagger are the common weapons of compulsion".[1] The second factor was the growth in the influence of English law: during the eighteenth century closer contact, especially on the commercial front, gave rise to a greater tendency among Scottish lawyers to borrow from English law.[2] The law relating to compulsion was no exception. It is then partly against the background of these considerations that the modern Scots law relating to compulsion will be examined in this chapter.[3] It will be obvious, though, that the modern law still strongly reflects the influence of the works of the Institutional writers and the case law of the seventeenth to eighteenth centuries, which in turn drew much strength from Roman law. In the treatment of the modern law much of the conceptual apparatus and general framework of the previous chapters will be retained. The focus first will be on the law relating to force and fear, and in particular its impact on the validity and enforceability of contracts. Thereafter the relevance of certain forms of compulsion to the law of restitution or unjustified enrichment (particularly the law of the *condictiones*), property law and the law of delict will be examined.

---

1 (1921) 37 Sh Ct Rep 239 at 245. According to M'laren, the editor of the 1871 edition of Bell's *Commentaries*, "[i]n modern times this (force and fear) is seldom a ground for reduction ... In our older cases there are many strange examples of violence exercised, while the vigilance of public justice was relaxed by rebellion, or the police of Scotland in no state of vigour to restrain the more remote inhabitants" (vol 1, 315 note 1). Cf also *Gelot v Stewart* (1870) 8 M 649 at 653; *Sutherland v Montrose Fishing Co Ltd* (1921) 37 Sh Ct Rep 239.

2 Cf, generally, A Rodger, "Thinking about Scots law" (1996) 1 *EdinLR* 3; McBryde, *The Law of Contract in Scotland*, 7 et sq. This is not to say that nothing was borrowed during the time of the Institutional writers: the concept of "voidability" may very well have been imported from English law (McBryde, *The Law of Contract in Scotland*, 625).

3 The focus will be mainly on case law and the works of twentieth century authors. During the nineteenth century, specialised books on private law were published, but little of substance appeared (cf Walker, *The Scottish Jurists*, 392 et sqq). Works which deal peripherally with force and fear are P Shaw, *A Treatise on the Law of Obligations and Contracts* (1847) (Shaw was Bell's brother-in-law); W J Tayler, *Treatise on the Differences between the Laws of England and Scotland relating to Contracts* (1849), 39; J Lorimer, *A Hand-book of the Law of Scotland*, 4th ed by R Bell (1879), paras 1967, 1069.

4.2 COMPULSION IN THE FORM OF FORCE AND FEAR

4.2.1 *The content of force and fear*

Relief on the ground of force and fear is provided when a person acted under fear or apprehension which was induced through force or other means.[4] The modern law of force and fear therefore has retained the essential elements of fear, or *metus*, and force, or *vis*, which were already identified in Roman law. The difficult question is to determine what types of fear and "force" are sufficiently serious to constitute force and fear. This is of practical significance, since it is required that the proof has to be specific. Mere general statements are insufficient.[5] In the following discussion of the content of force and fear, a distinction will be drawn between the requirements for the nature of the "fear" as well as the "threats" which constitute the "force".

i. The nature of the fear

The general approach in modern Scots law is that the victim will only be provided with relief if he experienced fear which has "overpowered" his will.[6] However, this does not mean that any form of fear which has such an effect would be sufficient to obtain relief. As in Roman law, it is still expected that the victim should display some resoluteness or constancy,[7] although in certain instances it has not been required at

4 Cf *Priestnell v Hutcheson* (1857) 19 D 495. There Lord Deas followed Stair in stating that although force and fear is coupled as one ground of reduction, "the act of force is truly only one means of inducing fear, the true ground of reduction being extortion, through the influence of fear, induced in the various ways ...". In *Love v Marshall* Lord Deas expanded somewhat on the "various ways" in which fear had to be induced, namely "by force, or threats of ill-usage" (1870) 9 M 291 at 295). Cf also *Hunter v Bradford Property Trust Ltd* 1977 SLT 33 at 33 ("[i]n the Law of Scotland the mere existence of fear is not enough. It must be fear induced by force or threats of force which would affect the mind of a reasonable person"); *Trustee Savings Bank v Balloch* 1983 SLT 240 at 241 ("if one party to a contract has been forced to enter into it by fear, whether induced by the other party to the contract or by a third party, the former has not freely and voluntarily given his or her consent and the contract is void"); *Hislop v Dickson Motors (Forres) Ltd* 1978 SLT 73 at 74). Also cf Gloag, *The Law of Contract*, 488; Walker, *The law of contracts and related obligations in Scotland*, 297; Guthrie Smith, *Law of Damages*, 43 (he states that "a party (is not) entitled to say that he was induced to sign a deed or do a particular act in favour of another, from the apprehension that certain injurious consequences would be the result of his refusal").

5 Cf *Priestnell v Hutcheson* (1857) 19 D 495 at 500; *Wolfson v Edelman* 1952 SLT (Sh Ct) 97 at 98; *Cumming v Mackie* 1973 SLT 242 at 246; McBryde, *The Law of Contract in Scotland*, 240.

6 Cf *Russo v Hardy* 1997 GWD 6–246, which follows *Hislop v Dickson Motors (Forres) Ltd* 1978 SLT 73. In the latter case it had to be decided whether force and fear was present when Hislop, a woman, was being confronted on two occasions by men, who were her employers and suspected her of embezzling Dickson Motors' money. In deciding that Hislop was in fact acting under force and fear at one of these occasions, Lord Maxwell made much of the fact that she did not act voluntarily, and that she submitted to pressure "which might in the whole circumstance well have overpowered the mind of a woman of normal firmness finding herself in such a situation". Cf also *Mahmud v Mahmud* 1994 SLT 599 at 602B; *Mahmood v Mahmood* 1993 SLT 589 at 592B.

7 Cf inter alia Gloag, *The Law of Contract*, 488; *Wolfson v Edelman* 1952 SLT 97 at 98; *Hislop v Dickson Motors (Forres) Ltd* 1978 SLT 73 at 75 et sq and, most recently, *Russo v Hardy* 1997 GWD 6–246. The latter case dealt with a son who bullied his mother into agreeing to transfer a share in property to him. Here the court still required constancy, or displaying ordinary firmness.

all.[8] When required, the standard is in any event applied flexibly.[9] Thus, it is easier to prove force and fear when no prior debt is due by the victim,[10] or where no value has been received.[11] Youth, age, infirmity and sex could also give rise to a lesser degree of resoluteness being expected.[12] The fear can also relate to threats of harm to a spouse, parent, child or near relation,[13] but the mere fact that someone acted out of affection or respect is not actionable.[14]

ii. The nature of the threats of harm

It is not only by requiring resoluteness that the overpowered or overborne will requirement is qualified: a number of cases recognise the familiar principle that the threatened action has to be illegal or unwarrantable to found a plea of extortion.[15] This section will deal with specific examples of threats which were regarded as "illegal or unwarrantable" in the modern law. These are threats of personal physical harm, diligence, prosecution, loss of employment, the withholding or detention of property and a residual category of cases of economic harm.

---

8 Cf *Mahmud v Mahmud* 1994 SLT 599, where Lord Prosser stated the following: "I would add that in my opinion it is a question of fact whether, in the particular case and having regard to the particular individual, the reality of consent has been destroyed, and the will has been overborne. The passage cited to me from Walton [*A Handbook of Husband and Wife according to the Law of Scotland*, 3rd ed (1951) 50] states that the rule of the canonists that the degree of force used must be such as might have coerced a person of average strength of will—*virum constantem*—cannot be now a practical guide. Walton goes on to say that if the court is satisfied that one will was unduly dominated by the other, in such a way as to induce an unwilling consent, it will not decline to grant a remedy on the ground that a person of cooler temper and firmer purpose would not in the circumstances have yielded. I regard these observations as sound" (at 601F).

9 Cf *Hislop v Dickson Motors (Forres) Ltd* 1978 SLT 73, where Lord Maxwell held that "it is arguable that when dealing with the particular type of pressure involved in threats and also perhaps when there is actual imprisonment (*Mackintosh v Chalmers* (1883) 11 R 8) the requirement of the overpowering of the mind of reasonable firmness has been somewhat departed from (Bell's *Commentaries*, 7th ed, i, 315) but in other cases in my opinion it is still the law".

10 Cf *Russo v Hardy* 1997 GWD 6-246; Gloag, *The Law of Contract*, 488, referring to Stair, *Institutions*, 1.9.8.

11 Cf *Gelot v Stewart* (1871) 9 M 957 at 958.

12 Cf SME, vol 15 (1997), para 673; McBryde, *The Law of Contract in Scotland*, 250 et sq; Gloag, *The Law of Contract*, 492 ("where a deed has been granted by a married woman and the allegation is that she was induced to grant it in fear of her husband, a case of threats sufficient to induce fear in a woman of ordinary capacity must be made out"). However, this did not mean that the courts would come to the assistance of women that easily (cf *Buchan v Risk* (1834) 12 S 511; *Craig v Paton* (1865) 4 M 192; *Priestnell v Hutcheson* (1857) 19 D 495 at 499). In the latter case a husband (who had been unfortunate in business) was threatened with diligence by the Bank of Scotland. His wife thought this would result in his imprisonment. She then signed a deed in order to prevent the diligence. Later on she approached the court for its reduction. Lord Deas' approach to the case was quite clear: the threats used by the bank were legal, and the consequence of the husband's indebtedness. The wife acted from affection for her husband and not out of fear.

13 Gloag, *The Law of Contract*, 489, especially note 7.

14 Gloag, *The Law of Contract*, 492 note 2; *Priestnell v Hutcheson* (1857) 19 D 495. The scope for relief in cases of *metus reverentialis* is still narrow: cf Guthrie Smith, *Law of Damages*, 42.

15 Cf *Priestnell v Hutcheson* (1857) 19 D 495 at 500; *Mackintosh v Chalmers* (1883) 11 R 8; *Education Authority of Dumfriesshire v Wright* 1926 SLT 217; *Wolfson v Edelman* 1952 SLT (Sh Ct) 97 at 98. In *Hunter v Bradford Property Trust Ltd* 1977 SLT 33, Lord Migdale quotes Pothier, where he states that "The violence which leads to the rescission of a contract should be an unjust violence, adversus bonos mores and the exercise of a legal right can never be allowed as a violence of this description" (*Traité des Obligations*, para 26).

(a) Personal physical harm

Two types of threats of harm need to be distinguished, namely threats of personal violence, which are obviously illegal, and threats of confinement. As can be expected, there are very few recent cases of force and fear through threats of personal violence.[16] As far as threats of confinement are concerned, Gloag refers to two English cases[17] for support of the proposition that threats of confinement in a lunatic asylum could also be sufficient to cause a situation of force and fear. Although there is no similar authority in Scots law, it is submitted that there is no reason in principle why such confinement should be treated differently from illegal confinement in a prison.[18]

(b) Diligence

In the days where imprisonment for debt was still lawful, securities granted for the debt owed by someone in prison were upheld.[19] However, as indicated before, if the diligence was not lawfully exercised, or was lawfully exercised but used to extort assent to an obligation which is separate or independent from the obligation to pay the debt due, relief would be provided.[20] These principles regarding the exercise of diligence still remain valid, but it should be noted that from the end of the nineteenth century the number of reported cases dealing with the abuse of diligence declined. This can be ascribed to the abolition of imprisonment for most types of debts by

---

16 Cf *Gelot v Stewart* (1870) 8 M 649; (1871) 9 M 957. The latter case concerned a situation which, as Lord Neaves put it, reflected "a state of society to which we are not accustomed in our country, and which is altogether peculiar" (at 653). Dr Stewart, who resided in Paraguay, was in disfavour with its President, Marshall Lopez. A certain Madame Lynch, Lopez's mistress, apparently threatened Dr Stewart that she would persuade Lopez to execute him if he did not grant a £4000.00 bill in favour Gelot, to whom she was indebted. Stewart then drew a bill on his brother, Robert (who was resident in Scotland) and made it payable to Gelot. When the bill was not paid, he wrote a letter to his brother urging him to do so. When Stewart returned to Scotland, Gelot tried to obtain payment of the bill and Stewart asked for its reduction. Although the cased is characterised by considerable disputes of fact, it was found that force and fear was present. Cf also *Cumming v Mackie* 1973 SLT 242, which may have dealt with threats of physical violence. Here the defender was a gambler who refused to allow payment of a £500 cheque he gave the pursuer in lieu of gambling debts incurred at the pursuer's gambling club. He averred that he was escorted to the pursuer's office in the club, where the pursuer was abusive and threatening of him, and that he signed under duress "in order that he might leave the ... club, and because of the ... abuse and threats". But, because the averments were not specific enough, the court held that he did not prove his case. According to the court it had to be established that the threats were such as would have affected the mind of a reasonable person, and this had not been done. A more recent case involving fear of physical harm is *Russo v Hardy* 1997 GWD 6–246.

17 He refers to *Biffin v Bignold* (1862) 7 H & N 877 (apparently *Biffin v Bignell*). Here a husband allegedly threatened his wife that unless she consented to live away from him on an allowance of twelve shillings a week, she would be sent to another asylum after being released from the one she was presently in. However, the court found that on the facts there was no duress, for the husband simply told the wife what would probably be the consequences if she returned to him. He also refers to *Cumming v Ince* (1847) 11 QB 112. Here Ince and Hooper were prosecuting a commission of lunacy against their mother, Mrs Cumming. This was dropped after she entered into an arrangement to give certain deeds. At the time she was held in an asylum. It was held that she was acting under constraint, did not agree to the arrangement out of her own free will, and was entitled to the deeds.

18 Cf Bell, *Commentaries*, 315.

19 Cf 3.3.1.ii(d) above.

20 Erskine, *Institute*, 4.1.26. Cf 3.3.1.ii(d) above.

the Debtors (Scotland) Act 1880.[21] Various other changes in legislation followed, so that today civil imprisonment is only available in a highly restricted category of cases.[22] In *M'Intosh v Chalmers*,[23] the last[24] case in Scots law to deal with the unlawful or irregular use of imprisonment as a form of diligence, certain principles were laid down which would therefore still be relevant if this form of diligence is used. These principles can be summarised briefly as follows: when a person in prison under legal diligence grants a bond which is not supported by adequate "consideration",[25] or if his creditor was moved by an "improper motive",[26] such an act would be invalid. On the other hand, when he is in prison under illegal diligence, it would not be possible to conclude a valid transaction.[27] Diligence through threats of recourse to the normal mechanisms for enforcing a claim does not affect the validity of acts concluded under fear of such threats.

21 Cf *Memorandum on Defective Consent And Consequential Matters* (Scot Law Com Memo No 42, 1978) vol 2, 112: McBryde, *Void, Voidable, Illegal and Unenforceable Contracts in Scots law*, 33 et sqq; G Maher and D J Cusine, *The Law and Practice of Diligence* (1990), 237. On the consequences of imprisonment for debt in nineteenth century Scotland, see Anonymous, "Imprisonment for debt in Scotland" (1931) 47 *The Scottish Law Review* 33. A prisoner could try to obtain his release through a disposition *omnium bonorum*—a conveyance to a trustee for behalf of all his creditors, including the one who had imprisoned him, of everything that he had possessed. The court would then usually free him on granting the disposition. A more unusual way of at least obtaining temporary liberty was by seeking refuge in the "Sanctuary", an area in Edinburgh from where he was safe from being arrested and taken to prison again.

22 These are: if a fine imposed for contempt of court is not paid, if there was a breach of an order made under the Court of Session Act 1868, if there was a failure to pay aliment, or if there was a failure to obtemper a decree *ad factum praestandum* (Maher and Cusine, *The Law and Practice of Diligence*, 237).

23 (1883) 11 R 8. The facts are briefly as follows. Two brothers, William and Alexander M'Intosh, were wholesale spirit merchants trading under the name of M'Intosh Brothers. Chalmers, who "concerned himself generally with the affairs of the company", was a friend of Alexander M'Intosh. The two brothers were on very bad terms, and this gave rise to a rather unusual scheme to force William M'Intosh out of the firm. Alexander M'Intosh, Chalmers and John M'Intosh (another brother, who was also a partner in the business) obtained an assignation of a bill owed by the firm. Chalmers then charged William M'Intosh on this assignation, and had him imprisoned. In order to obtain his release, William M'Intosh then signed a dissolution of the firm of M'Intosh Brothers, an agreement to hand over all the assets of the firm to his brother (Alexander), and a letter of indemnity to relieve Chalmers of all liability for damages in respect of his incarceration. Not surprisingly William M'Intosh succeeded in proving that the firm was liable, and that this meant Alexander as well, who was one of the parties who obtained the assignation. It would therefore hardly be acceptable that he be forced to pay part of Alexander's debt to Chalmers. William M'Intosh succeeded in his claim of reduction. Cf also the discussion in Trotter, *The Law of Contract*, 183.

24 The events which gave rise to this case took place during 1880, and therefore before the Debtors (Scotland) Act 1880 (43 & 44 Vict) came into operation on 1 January 1881 (s 1).

25 *M'Intosh v Chalmers* (1883) 11 R 8, 15; cf *Fraser v Black*, December 13, 1810 FC.

26 Cf also Glegg, *A Practical Treatise on the Law of Reparation in Scotland* (1892) 178. According to Glegg, a diligence which is regular "in itself" could be subject to reduction if it is not bona fide used to obtain payment of the amount due. Cf also *Rudman v Jay and Co* 1908 SC 552. Here it was argued that it would be a wrongful use of diligence if a warrant for imprisonment was obtained in the knowledge that the debtor has no possible means of complying with his debt. However, on the facts the court held that it was the intention of the user of the diligence to induce the debtor's friends to intervene and grant a security. The use of the diligence was therefore found to be justifiable.

27 *M'Intosh v Chalmers* (1883) 11 R 8 at 16. A different view is expressed by Lord Rutherfurd Clark, who did not agree that it would be sufficient to prove that the diligence was illegal in order to obtain reduction. However, there is no authority in Scots law for Lord Rutherfurd Clark's proposition, which smacks of the extreme individualism which was prevalent in Britain during the latter half of the nineteenth century. Nevertheless, like the rest of the court, he did hold for the pursuer, but on the basis that the *purpose* for which the diligence was sued was not to recover the debt honestly, but to help Alexander "in his designs against his brother William".

(c) Prosecution

It is a matter of some difficulty to determine whether a threat to report an alleged crime to the police can amount to force and fear. Irrespective of whether a crime was committed or not, agreements to stifle prosecution are generally illegal[28]—in other words, affected by moral turpitude and contrary to public policy.[29] However, the courts are apparently still willing to enforce such agreements if the purpose was only to obtain what was due. In such a case there is apparently no scope for an attack on the validity of the agreement on either the ground that it is illegal, or that it is concluded under force and fear.[30]

(d) Loss of employment

None of the Institutional writers deal with threats of loss of employment as a ground for force and fear, possibly because rights of employment were rather precarious at the time. However, in *Gow v Henry*[31] and *Education Authority of Dumfriesshire v Wright*[32] the courts had the opportunity to consider the possible impact of such

---

28 *Smith & Sons v Buchanan* (1910) 2 SLT 387. The defender agreed to pay £60 in order to prevent criminal prosecution, although it was not, and could not be proven that any crime had been committed. His defence was that the agreement was illegal, since it is "... contrary to public policy that a citizen who believes that a crime has been committed and is minded to give information of it so that the law may take cognisance of it, should trade with the supposed crime for his private benefit and bargain, for money or other consideration, that he will desist from doing what it is his duty to do in the interests of the public". Lord Cullen regarded this principle "as a sound one", and refused to enforce the agreement to pay the £60. He was not influenced by the fact that *in casu* no crime had been committed: "I am unable, however, to see that this alters the legal quality of the bargain as it was intended between the pursuers and the defender. The social duty of reporting cases of crime to the criminal authorities cannot be regarded as limited to cases where one has demonstration of the facts or certainty as to the true legal quality of the facts" (at 388).

29 Cf generally, and for examples, McBryde, *The Law of Contract in Scotland*, 576 et sqq, 586 et sqq, 628 et sq.

30 Cf *Hislop v Dickson Motors (Forres) Ltd* 1978 SLT 73 at 75; Gloag, *The Law of Contract*, 491. In both *Ferrier v Mackenzie* (1899) 1 F 597 and *Lamson Paragon Supply Company v Macphail* 1914 SC 73 the question was left open. In *Ferrier*'s case a promissory note was granted in order to prevent a prosecution of an employee on grounds of embezzlement. A claim of enforcement was met with the defence that the promissory note was signed "under pressure from [the] pursuer, in circumstances constituting a *pactum illicitum*", and that it was void. However, on the facts it was found that no agreement made under threats of criminal proceedings was proven, although there was talk about "Peterhead" (presumably Peterhead prison) after the bill was granted. The court did not express any clear opinion on the illegality of the agreement. Lord Trayner merely stated that it was a "delicate question" whether "an engagement to refrain from criminal prosecution in return for payment of the loss incurred through the alleged crime would amount to a *pactum illicitum*". *Lamson Paragon Supply Company v Macphail* also concerned a claim of embezzlement. After returning from a trip to the West Indies to collect money for the company, Macphail was apparently confronted by its management to explain why he had used the money collected for his own purposes. He then wrote a letter to the managing director, promising to pay the £110 8s 8d he used, and expressing his gratitude to the directors "for their kindness in not prosecuting me". This apparent gratitude did not last long, however, for MacPhail later on denied liability, averring that his necessary expenses exceeded the amount mentioned in the letter, and that he did not owe the company anything. He further alleged that the letter gave rise to an agreement not to prosecute, which was void under Scots and English law. However, on the facts the court found no agreement existed, and that it was therefore not necessary to investigate, in the words of Lord Guthrie, "whether an agreement to refrain from criminal prosecution, in return for payment of money due, amounts to a *pactum illicitum* by the law of Scotland".

31 (1899) 2 F 48.

32 1926 SLT 217.

threats.[33] In *Gow*'s case, Henry was threatened with the loss of his employment unless he entered into a settlement with a third party.[34] The claim did not succeed on the facts, but the case can be regarded as authority for the proposition that such a settlement would have been invalid, if these facts were proved.[35] In *Education Authority of Dumfriesshire v Wright*[36] a claim based on force and fear again failed, but apparently sufficient grounds existed for threats of dismissal. The court held that only illegal or unwarrantable threats give rise to reduction of a contract on grounds of force and fear.

(e) Detention of property

With greater social stability and proper law enforcement, threats of physical harm to property, like threats of personal physical harm, diminished in importance as methods of force and fear. But one could of course also instill fear by detaining or withholding property, rather than by causing or threatening physical harm. This is apparent from Kames's treatment of certain compelled transfers: where a person was induced into making a transfer through threats of refusal to deliver certain documents, it was apparently regarded as recoverable on the basis that the transfer was made *ob turpem causam*. It will be recalled that this was presumably necessary since the law of force and fear was not sufficiently developed to take these cases of compulsion into account. However, there are indications in modern law, where the *condictio ob turpem vel iniustam causam* has virtually disappeared, that such an analysis is unnecessary. For example, in *Sutherland v Montrose Fishing Co Ltd*[37] some trade

---

33 The delictual implications of threats of loss of employment are not considered here. Cf *Hewitt v Edinburgh Lathsplitters' Association* (1906) 14 SLT 489.

34 The pursuer, a "scavenger" at the Cleansing Department in Dundee, claimed £250 damages for injuries sustained by his son, who was run over by a horse and cart belonging to Henry, a carting contractor. He then signed a receipt for £8 in settlement of this claim. Later on he claimed that he signed this receipt because Henry brought to bear upon him the influence of Arthur, the superintendent of the Cleansing Department: Arthur apparently threatened Gow with the loss of his work if he did not settle with Henry.

35 Cf Gloag, *The Law of Contract*, 489. In the court of first instance it was held that it was not proven that Henry was induced to grant the receipt on grounds of "force or fear, compulsion, or illegal pressure of any kind" ((1899) 2 F 48 at 50). However, this finding was overruled on appeal. In a further appeal to the Court of Session it was again held that this was not proven.

36 1926 SLT 217. Wright, a teacher, failed to keep certain registers in accordance with regulations. Because of this the Education Authority then intimated to Wright that unless he resigned or accepted a transferral, they would dismiss him. He believed that they could legally dismiss him, although the mere failure to keep registers in accordance with the regulations was not a sufficient ground for dismissal. Out of fear of losing his employment as well as pension, he then signed a letter in terms of which he promised to resign his office in attaining the age of sixty years, which was to be soon. But on attaining that age, he refused to comply with the contents of the letter, and claimed avoidance of the undertaking it gave rise to. This claim was, inter alia, based on force and fear. But according to the Lord Ordinary (Constable), this was not a case of force and fear, for threats can only give rise to avoidance on ground of force and fear if they are unlawful, "i.e. the action threatened must be illegal or unwarrantable". *In casu*, it was held that the intimation by the Education Authority of an intention to dismiss Wright was not an illegal or unwarrantable act. This seems to be a somewhat strained interpretation of what is illegal or unwarrantable: it is clearly stated that Wright's conduct (the failure to keep the registers properly) did not warrant his dismissal; why should a threat to dismiss him on this ground not be unwarrantable?

37 (1921) 37 Sh Ct Rep 239. Cf also *Mcafee v Gray or Mcafee* Outer House, 6 July 1990 (Lord Cameron of Lochbroom). The Mcafees, partners in the same law firm, were in the process of obtaining a divorce. While Mrs Mcafee was in severe personal distress and need, her husband threatened that he would withhold the authorisation of legal aid payments due to her unless she discharged her rights to claim a certain capital sum from him. The pressure was too much for the

unionists threatened that they would close the dock gates and prevent the departure of the company's fishing boats from a harbour if certain wage claims were not met. If the boats did not sail this would have brought financial harm to the company; these threats were backed up by further threats from the trade unionists that the crews of the ships would leave as well. It was then agreed that the higher wages would be paid. The matter came to court and it was held that the agreement, which inter alia affected Sutherland (a member of the trade union and a crew member) was invalid due to force and fear.[38] In his judgment, Sheriff-Principal M'Clure indicated that the mere fact that someone was not in a state of bodily fear did not preclude recovery.[39] On the facts, the detention of the ships and its consequences were regarded as so serious that it could be said that the employer who agreed to the higher wages was acting under force and fear.[40]

(f) Economic Duress

In modern times the means of compelling people into action may not be as dramatic or violent as those used by the Earl of Orkney[41] or Sir John Whitefoord,[42] but this does not detract from their effectiveness. The skilful use of threats of economic harm is part of modern commercial practice, and, as long as these threats are lawful, no relief would be provided. Unfortunately it is not that easy to determine what makes a threat of economic harm unlawful. Scottish courts thus far have had limited opportunity to consider "economic duress", to use the English term,[43] but the indications at present are that the courts are careful in broadening the scope of force and fear to include these cases. For example, threats of breach of contract are not normally regarded as "illegal or unwarrantable": it seems that if a party threatens breach, he will have to accept the consequences, such as liability for damages, and that the other party should not let these threats induce him into any conduct. In this regard it is submitted that *Hunter v Bradford Property Trust Ltd*[44] afforded the

---

wife, and she agreed. In a subsequent action the wife sought to have this agreement set aside on the grounds that it was not "fair or reasonable" at the time it was entered into (cf the Family Law (Scotland) Act 1985, s 16(1)(b)). These allegations were regarded as serious enough to allow a proof before answer. Although the case did not fall to be dealt with on grounds of force and fear, the underlying principle seems to be that threats of such a nature would be unacceptable.

38 (1921) 37 Sh Ct Rep 239 at 249 et sq per Sheriff-Principal McClure.

39 He relies on *Wiseman v Logie* (1700) Mor 16505.

40 Force and fear is defined in terms of the test used in Erskine, *Institute*, 3.1.16, where it is required that the victim's will "hath truly no part in the contract". Reference is also made to the English case of *Williams v Bayley* 1866 LR 1 HL 200, where it was held that the victim had to act as a "free and voluntary agent". These tests resemble the problematic "overborne will" test, referred to above. For criticism, cf 6.2.1.iii below. An unfortunate aspect of the judgment (at 250 et sq) is the confusion it reflects between force and fear (dealt with in Erskine, *Institute*, 3.1.16) and extortion through taking advantage of another's situation of need (dealt with in Erskine, *Institute*, 4.1.27). This compeletly ignores the question whether the defender created the situation of need or not.

41 Cf *Earl of Orkney v Vinfra* (1606) Mor 16480.

42 Cf *Stuart v Whitefoord and the Duke of Hamilton* (1677) Mor 16488.

43 On the relationship between the English law of "duress of goods" and the Scots law of force and fear, cf McBryde, *The Law of Contract in Scotland*, 252 et sqq.

44 Decided on 22 January 1957; 1977 SLT 33. On appeal to the House of Lords the case was argued on the ground of essential error, and whether the new deed (the one assented to after threats of cancellation of the sale) was gratuitous. Although it cannot be denied that the new deed was one-sided, it is submitted that this should not have been the ground on which the case should have been argued. Rather, it is the way in which their consent was obtained which was so reprehensible. Unfortunately this was not discussed in the House of Lords.

ideal opportunity to recognise that threats of breach of contract, or similar threats could, under certain circumstances, give rise to a situation of force and fear. Here two sisters, the Hunters, were in charge of businesses left to them by their father. They experienced serious financial difficulties, and then entered into an agreement with the defender in terms of which properties belonging to the sisters would be sold by them, and a particular distribution of the profits would be made. The evening before the sale was to take place, one of the defender's directors, Denham, threatened to cancel the sale if the sisters would not agree to changes in the agreement, which would entitle the sisters to a considerably smaller share of the profits than provided for in the agreement. The meeting was long and acrimonious, and lasted into the early hours of the morning, and finally the sisters relented. The issue of force and fear was raised in the Court of Session. Here the Lord Ordinary expressed support for the principle enunciated in *Education Authority of Dumfriesshire v Wright*[45] that the action threatened must be illegal or unwarrantable in order to amount to force and fear, and found that the sisters did in fact act under fear. As far as the threats were concerned, he said that

> ... the threat and the only threat made by Mr Denham was to cancel the roup [sale] fixed for the next day. There was nothing illegal in this. The defenders were, in terms of the first agreement, the persons who were to sell the property. True they were bound to do so as early as possible but the only person required to arrange for the disposal of the property were the defenders. If they decided to cancel the roup fixed for a particular day they were entitled to do so. Mr Denham's threat was accordingly not one of an unjustifiable or unwarrantable act. Such a threat could not form the basis of an action of reduction on the grounds of force and fear.[46]

It is submitted that the court took an unduly narrow view of what the defender proposed to do. This was not merely a question of dates. It is quite clear from the facts as a whole that if the sisters did not agree to the changes of the contract, there would be no sale or roup at all. That relief on the ground of force and fear was not provided in these circumstances can hardly be regarded as satisfactory, especially if *Hunter v Bradford Property Trust Ltd*[47] is contrasted with *Wolfson v Edelman*.[48] The latter case clearly did not involve threats of economic harm which could be described as "illegal or unwarrantable". The pursuer, Wolfson, was a director of Mastercraft (Light Engineering) Ltd, a company which experienced financial difficulties. Wolfson then took certain steps to make arrangements with its creditors. It owed approximately £800 to A & C Edelman (1939) Ltd, of which Edelman, the defender, was the managing director. After Wolfson paid approximately £800 to A & C Edelman, he reclaimed this sum on the ground of extortion through force and fear by (a) threats to have the transactions of Mastercraft (Light Engineering) Ltd examined, (b) threats by Edelman to use all his influence to bring the company into bankruptcy, and (c) threats to hold the company's directors liable for certain disbursements in respect of Wolfson's personal debts. Sheriff-Substitute Dobie was not impressed by these averments, and regarded them as either too vague, or merely lawful and legitimate threats.[49]

This concludes the overview of the nature of the actual or threatened conduct which could induce the type of fear needed to succeed with a claim of force and

---

45 1926 SLT 217.
46 1977 SLT 33 at 34.
47 Decided on 22 January 1957; 1977 SLT 33.
48 1952 SLT 97.
49 1952 SLT 97 at 98.

fear or extortion. The examples examined thus far give some indication of the way in which courts apply the requirement that the threatened action had to be illegal or unwarrantable. However, they merely serve as illustrations of this general requirement and do not form a closed category which defines it.

4.2.2 *The effect of force and fear*

Earlier sources do not really distinguish between the effect of force on fear when reclaiming transfers made in fulfilment of contractual obligations, as opposed to other types of transfers: Balfour's *Practicks*[50] contains a long list of transfers, which encompassed both these categories, whereas Stair's[51] treatment of force and fear as a delict also indicates that he was not solely concerned with its effect on the validity of contracts. This view was followed by Bankton.[52] However, later authors such as Erskine[53] and Bell[54] discuss force and fear in the context of factors excluding consent necessary to constitute an obligation. This lead has by and large been taken in modern law, where the emphasis mainly is on the role of force and fear as ground of reduction of contracts[55] and as a defence against a claim of enforcement. In the following section, the modern law will then be examined mainly in a contractual context. Here three issues are of importance, namely whether force and fear renders a contract void or voidable, how claims for performance of a contract concluded under force and fear can be defended, and how performances which have already been made pursuant to such contracts can be recovered.

i. Voidness or voidability?[56]

The question whether force and fear gives rise to voidness or voidability has still not been resolved in modern Scots law. The difference between these two concepts has been defined as follows: whereas an agreement is void if there is a "fundamental infirmity in its constitution", it is voidable if it is "brought into being by means which the law regards as illegitimate".[57] A void agreement is then "a mere nullity",[58] and reduction of a written contract is therefore unnecessary in

50 Balfour, 45.XIII–XVII.

51 Deeds and obligations are dealt with in Stair, *Institutions*, 1.9.8.

52 Bankton, *Institute*, 1.10.5.

53 Erskine, *Institute*, 3.1.16.

54 Bell, *Commentaries*, vol 1, 315; Bell, *Principles*, para 12.

55 Reduction is the appropriate remedy for having deeds, bills, bonds, and other documents declared invalid. Cf *Wolfson v Edelman* 1952 SLT (Sh Ct) 97 at 98; *Hunter v Bradford Property Trust* 1977 SLT 33; *Priestnell v Hutcheson* (1857) 19 D 495. As to the Court of Session's jurisdiction to award reduction, cf Rule of Court 58. The traditional association of force and fear with the reduction of a contract has rendered uncertain its effect on the recoverability of transfers of property and money which are not intended to fulfil a contractual obligation. In principle, if such a transfer is not due, remedies based on unjustified enrichment should be available. But it is unclear whether "force and fear" is then the ground for relief, or whether such a transfer is recoverable because a legal ground for its retention is in any event absent. This question relates to the fundamental issue whether compulsion is an "unjust factor" in Scots law, and is dealt with at 7.3 below.

56 On voidness and voidability in general, see McBryde, *Void, Voidable, Illegal and Unenforceable Contracts in Scots Law*, esp 165 et sqq; McBryde, *The Law of Contract in Scotland*, 621 et sqq; Honoré, "Degrees of Invalidity" (1958) 75 *SALJ* 32; Van der Merwe and Van Huyssteen, "The force of agreements: valid, void, voidable, unenforceable" (1995) 58 *THRHR* 549.

57 Gloag, *The Law of Contract*, 531.

58 Gloag, *The Law of Contract*, 531; Walker, *The Law of Civil Remedies in Scotland*, 145; Walker, *The Law of Contracts and Related Obligations in Scotland*, 299.

theory, though advisable in practice.[59] Although the issue is not free of doubt it would seem as if a void agreement can be adopted under certain circumstances.[60] A voidable agreement, on the other hand, is valid until reduced by the innocent party.[61] The balance of modern authority then accepts that force and fear gives rise to voidness.[62] This is no doubt in accordance with a fair amount of authority, not least of which Stair.[63] However, there are at least two features of the modern case law which indicate that such an approach is unsatisfactory. First, force and fear does not exclude homologation or ratification.[64] This is inconsistent with an approach which regards the effect as voidness: it is difficult to see how something which is void can be ratified. Second, the possibility that bona fide third parties can acquire something in spite of it being obtained by force and fear can be reconciled more easily with voidability, rather than voidness.[65] In *Stewart Brothers v Kiddie*[66] Lord Trayner made short shrift of a claim that force and fear excluded

---

59 McBryde, *The Law of Contract in Scotland*, 622; Walker, *The Law of Civil Remedies in Scotland*, 145, but cf Walker, *The Law of Delict in Scotland*, 694.

60 Cf McBryde, *Void, Voidable, Illegal and Unenforceable Contracts in Scots Law*, 180.

61 Cf McBryde, *The Law of Contract in Scotland*, 623, 626.

62 Cf Gloag, *The Law of Contract*, 488 (he refers to Stair, *Institutions*, 1.9.8.; Erskine, *Institute*, 3.1.16; Bell, *Principles*, para 12; Bell, *Commentaries*, vol 1, 314); Walker, *The Law of Civil Remedies in Scotland*, 156 (he relies on D 4.2, Stair, *Institutions*, 1.9.8, Erskine, *Institute*, 3.1.6; Bell, *Principles*, para 12); Trotter, *The Law of Contract in Scotland*, 198 (he refers to Stair, *Institutions*, 1.9.8). But cf McBryde, *The Law of Contract in Scotland*, 254 et sqq).

63 Cf Stair, *Institutions*, 1.9.8 ("deed and obligations as are by force and fear, are made utterly void").

64 Cf Gloag, *The Law of Contract*, 488 (" . . . it has been decided, somewhat inconsistently, that partial payment, after the apprehension had ceased, amounted to homologation"). *Thomson v Annandale* (1829) 7 S 305 supports the proposition that partial payment, after the apprehension had ceased, can amount to homologation. In this case the Thomsons accepted a bill of £244 11s in favour of Annandale. Although the bill was payable on December 5, the Thomsons had already paid £80 before this date, "without objection or constraint". They then claimed suspension of the bill on grounds of concussion. This claim was rejected by a Lord Ordinary, "having adverted to the payment of £80 sterling to account of the debt", and the First Division of the Court of Session confirmed this decision. Unfortunately the reported judgment is very short, and does not refer to any authority.

65 Cf Gloag, *The Law of Contract*, 492; Walker, *The Law of Contracts and Related Obligations in Scotland*, 297. For a detailed analysis of indirect enrichment in general, cf N R Whitty, "Indirect enrichment in Scots law" 1994 *JR* 200, 1994 *JR* 239, esp at 258. The position of competing claims of the victim and the general body of creditors upon insolvency of the wrongdoer is complicated. According to the *tantum et tale* doctrine, creditors can only attach the estate of the common debtor "*tantum et tale*", as it stands vested in him (cf G Stewart, Diligence (1898), 128, as quoted in N R Whitty, *Position Paper on Constructive Trusts*, vol 1 (document prepared for a seminar on constructive trusts held on 19 October 1996), 17). According to Whitty, "the doctrine's effect is that the right of a trustee in sequestration, or of an adjudger, poinder or arrester, over the debtor's property is subject to certain types of personal rights vested in personal creditors. These may be referred to as "preferred personal rights" (17). Where a bankrupt has been unjustifiably enriched by fraud, the victim of such fraud has a "preferred personal right". It is submitted that force and fear sufficiently resembles fraud to warrant also providing the victim of force and fear with such a "preferred personal right" (cf Whitty, *Position Paper on Constructive Trusts*, vol 1, 46, 51).

66 (1899) 7 SLT 92. Here Kiddie's paramour, Myles "terrified" her (it is not stated how) into settling a claim for damages she had against Stewart Brothers for injuries sustained by her. Myles and Stewart Brothers were apparently not connected in any way, and it seems that Myles wanted to get hold of a cash payment in lieu of damages as soon as possible. Kiddie later on brought an action for damages for the injuries sustained. The defence was raised that there was a settlement. She then claimed that the settlement should be reduced, inter alia on grounds of force and fear.

bona fide acquisition by third parties: "The defenders are not shown to have known and, in fact, did not know anything of this, and are therefore not affected by it."[67] Such a view is compatible with the approach adopted by the legislature a few years earlier when the Bills of Exchange Act, 1882[68] was amended to protect a bona fide holder in due course.[69] This was a clear indication that it would be necessary to reassess the accepted view that force and fear renders a contractual undertaking void. However, when *Stewart Brothers v Kiddie*[70] came to be reconsidered virtually a century later in *Trustee Savings Bank v Balloch*,[71] the contrary view was taken[72] with little apparent justification.[73] The position therefore is still uncertain.[74]

ii. Force and fear as a defence

Force and fear is not only a ground for a claim of reduction, but can also be pleaded as a defence to a claim of enforcement.[75] It has been shown that Roman law acknowledged the *exceptio metus*, and that force and fear could also be pleaded by way of exception in earlier Scots law. This is also the position in modern law. In *Trustee Savings Bank v Balloch*[76] Lord Cowie clearly stated that the relevant objections to the agreement (i.e. force and fear) "can be stated and maintained by way of exception".[77] It should be noted, though, that use of the term "exception" is not common in modern practice.[78]

---

67 (1899) 7 SLT 92 at 93. Cf also Smith, *A Short Commentary on the Law of Scotland*, 838; *Bradford Property Trust Ltd v Hunter* 1970 SLT 173.

68 45 & 46 Vict. c 61.

69 Cf ss 27(2), 29, 30(2), 32(2), and 38. For the earlier position cf *Willocks v Callender* (1776) Mor 1519 and *Wightman v Graham* (1787) Mor 1521, where the rights of innocent third party endorsees weighed less than that of the grantor of the bill who acted under force and fear. As to the possibility that in Scots law (as in English law) transfers could be "traced" in the hands of third parties, cf Whitty, *Position Paper on Constructive Trusts*, vol 2, 195 et sqq.

70 (1899) 7 SLT 92.

71 1983 SLT 240.

72 Lord Cowie held that "[t]here is undoubtedly judicial support for the view that in a question as to the validity of an agreement between two parties, if one of them has been forced into the agreement by force and fear applied by a third party, that is irrelevant unless the other party was implicated in the force and fear or was cognisant of it" (at 241) In this regard he referred to *Stewart Brothers v Kiddie*. But then, after having regard to *Cassie v Fleming* he stated that "[i]n my opinion, notwithstanding the case of *Stewart Brothers v Kiddie*, the correct view in principle is that if one party to a contract has been forced to enter into it by fear, whether induced by the other party to the contract or by a third party, the former has not freely and voluntarily given his or her consent and the contract is void. In these circumstances it matters not that the other party to the contract was not implicated in the force and fear not [sic—nor?] that he was not aware of its use. This seems to me to be the ratio decidendi of *Cassie v Fleming* and I see no reason to dissent from it" (at 241). Cf also Lord Justice-Clerk Inglis's judgment in *Wardlaw v Mackenzie* (1859) 21 D 940 ("[i]n ordinary circumstances, where force and fear are employed to impetrate a deed, the deed is absolutely null in a question with an innocent third party ..." (at 947). The case concerned fraud, and therefore the passage on force and fear is strictly speaking *obiter*.

73 Gloag certainly did not regard *Cassie v Fleming* as that persuasive and the Inner House has still not decided this issue. But cf the commentary to *Scott v Kelly* 1992 SCLR 646 at 648.

74 Cf Whitty, "Indirect enrichment in Scots law", 1994 *JR* 239 at 258; McBryde, *The Law of Contract in Scotland*, 254 et sq.

75 Gloag, *The Law of Contract*, 488 n 7.

76 1983 SLT 240.

77 1983 SLT 240. But cf the early case of *Dickie v Gutzmer* (1829) 8 S 147, which is oddly at variance with this established position. Gutzmer's father granted a letter of guarantee of his son's debts to Anderson & Co. Later on the son became insolvent, and after being threatened with an illegal diligence, the father, who was bedridden at the time, endorsed a bill to Anderson & Co. After Gutzmer's father's death, Dickie (a trustee of Anderson & Co) tried to obtain payment from

iii. **Restitutio in integrum *and restitution***

It has been shown that *restitutio in integrum* underwent a metamorphosis in Scots law: whereas force and fear initially entitled a person to *restitutio in integrum* or, simply, restitution, it later on became a rule that failure to provide *restitutio in integrum* was a bar to recovery. This is still the position in modern law, which holds that reduction of a voidable agreement is impossible if mutual *restitutio in integrum* cannot be made.[79] Thus, an agreement to take shares cannot be rescinded after the company has gone into liquidation, for the original shares cannot be restored.[80] Apparently, reduction would also not be possible in cases where work was done, where an article has been resold, or where it has been altered.[81] However, it is also acknowledged that complete restitution is in fact never possible since time always lapses between conclusion of the contract and reduction. Furthermore, if an article has only been used or diminished in value without the pursuer being responsible, reduction would not be barred.

So far then as to the voidable agreement. In the case of the void agreement, the position is somewhat uncertain. Obviously the ability to provide *restitutio in integrum* is irrelevant when a person acted under force and fear, and thereafter obtained reduction without rendering or receiving any performance in terms of the extorted agreement. Furthermore, it cannot be a bar to recovery either if he transferred unilaterally: the defender has given nothing which should be restored. However, where both sides made transfers the general rule seems to be that *restitutio in integrum* is not a bar to reduction (insofar as it is necessary in the case of a void agreement).[82] In other words, the victim need not restore the other party to the position he was before the contract was made. He is therefore entitled to recover irrespective of his inability to return the counterperformance he received.[83] This right of recovery is presumably based on unjustified enrichment.[84]

Gutzmer on grounds of the father's endorsement of the bill and a letter the father wrote stating that he intends to pay it. Gutzmer then excepted that the letter and bill were obtained through illegal diligence. In the Inner House it was held by Lord Glenlee that if Gutzmer "... was to bring a reduction of the letter, he might be entitled to ask to go before a Jury; but he cannot do so, when it is objected to by way of exception merely. We must adhere in this action; and the defender may, if he chooses try an action of reduction and repetition, and then he will get to a Jury" (at 149).

78 Cf *Butterworths Glossary*, s v "exception".

79 McBryde, *The Law of Contract in Scotland*, 626 (especially n 65 and authorities quoted there); Walker, *The Law of Civil Remedies in Scotland*, 162 (especially n 64 and authorities quoted there); Gloag and Henderson, *The Law of Scotland*, 67. Other bars to recovery are homologation or ratification (Gloag, *The Law of Contract*, 542; SME, vol 15 (1997), para 673) and unnecessary delay in taking action (SME, vol 15 (1997), para 673).

80 Cf *Holdsworth v City of Glasgow Bank* (1880) 7 R (HL) 53 at 60; *Western Bank v Addie* (1867) 5 M (HL) 80; Gloag, *The Law of Contract*, 539. For critical comments cf *Memorandum on Defective Consent And Consequential Matters* (Scot Law Com Memo No 42, 1978), vol 1, 55 et sqq, vol 2, part iv (152 et sqq).

81 Gloag, *The Law of Contract*, 540.

82 Gloag, *The Law of Contract*, 542. Gloag refers to *Balls v Macdonald* 1909 SLT 310 (which concerned a void assignation); *General Property Investment Co v Matheson's Trustees* (1888) 16 R 282 (which concerned a void purchase by a company of its own shares). Also cf McBryde, *The Law of Contract in Scotland*, 622, Recovery of Benefits Conferred under Error of Law (Scot Law Com D P No 95, 1993), vol 2, 223; McBryde, *Void, Voidable, Illegal and Unenforceable Contracts in Scots law*, 180.

83 Apparently it is only in the case of certain bona fide acquisitions in terms of void agreements that "equitable adjustments" can be made. Cf Gloag, *The Law of Contract*, 531 ("where there is no fraud, and the parties to an agreement which is actually void have acted upon it in reliance on its validity ...").

84 Cf McBryde, *The Law of Contract in Scotland*, 622 et sqq and, less directly, Gloag, *The Law of Contract*, 321, 531. Cf further *Wolfson v Edelman* 1952 SLT (Sh Ct) 97 and *Dickie v Gutzmer* (1829) 8 S 147, which specifically refer to repetition.

4.3 OTHER FORMS OF COMPULSION

Thus far the focus has been on compulsion in the form of force and fear, and particularly on its role as a ground for reduction. However, as in older Scots law, relief nowadays is also provided in certain cases of compulsion which do not fall under the law of force and fear. This section examines these forms of compulsion and their effect. Here it is essential to identify the nature and substantive requirements for relief. Although the labels used in the case law to describe the relief are rather cryptic, it can be accepted that the basis of this relief is the unjustified enrichment of the recipient. Again one encounters the law of the *condictiones*.[85]

4.3.1 *Compulsion and the recovery of undue transfers*

A person who is confronted with a demand for a payment for which he does not regard himself liable would usually deny liability and refuse to make the payment. It would then be up to the person who makes the demand to take the steps he deems necessary to obtain payment. This could take the form of lawful threats of harm, such as diligence. However, where the demand is backed up by unlawful threats of harm, whether explicit or implicit, the victim may very well feel that (in the short term at least) he still has to comply with the demand. As indicated above, recovery is possible if such compulsion was serious enough to amount to force and fear.[86] However, cases exist where payments are made under unlawful compulsion which falls short of force and fear, but which still in some way influences a person's decision to make transfer. In this section it will be examined how modern Scots law deals with two factual situations which involve such compulsion. Both situations concern demands for payments which are not due. The first case is where an excessive demand is made under monopolistic conditions for the fulfilment of an existing duty. The second is the unlawful demand for the payment of tax.

i. Excessive demands under monopolistic conditions

If someone who provides a service charges a price which his customers consider excessive, or unfairly discriminatory in relation to other customers, they cannot force him to lower his price to a level which is considered "fair" or "undiscriminatory". All they can do is take their custom elsewhere. This is the way in which the market system generally operates. However, where a service is provided in a non-competitive environment, the consumer may have no alternative but to pay the excessive charge. To overcome this problem some form of regulation is necessary. One possibility is to regulate the price of such a service through legislation. For example, in nineteenth-century Britain it was deemed necessary to avoid exploitation by railway companies which carried goods by rail. In the twentieth century further attempts were made to prevent the abuse of monopoly power, particularly by the suppliers of electricity. Such statutory enactments then seek to curb the excesses of monopolistic power and protect the consumer.[87] Any demand which falls foul of such a provision would be unlawful and the consumer would not be liable for payment. In practice, the problem existed that the consumer who has not yet established that the demand is unlawful

85 Cf Gloag, *The Law of Contract*, 57.

86 This is apparently possible despite the fact that the payment may have been due: cf *Hislop v Dickson Motors (Forres) Ltd* 1978 SLT 73.

87 Cf Recovery of Benefits Conferred under Error of Law (Scot Law Com D P No 95, 1993), vol 2, 215 et sqq.

would refuse payment at his peril: his refusal to pay could be met with the implied if not express threat that the service would be suspended or terminated. In the face of such compulsion the consumer may have no alternative but to pay, and recover the excessive payment in due course. For example, in *British Oxygen Company, Limited v South of Scotland Electricity Board*,[88] the defender, which supplied electricity to the pursuer, demanded payment in excess of what was permissible under statute. The pursuers then paid the amount demanded, because, as Lord Patrick put it

> [t]his is a case where statute has conferred on a public body a monopoly of the right of supplying a commodity ... (The customer) has no reasonable alternative but to take the supply which is essential to him, pay for it at the rates objected to, and hope to recover from the Board any payments in excess of those warranted by the statute. In such special circumstances I should have thought that principle demanded that excess charges, demanded by and paid to the board, and ultimately held to be unwarranted, should be recoverable by action at law.[89]

On appeal to the House of Lords, Lord Patrick's remarks met with approval.[90] It was found that there was improper compulsion in respect of which the pursuer would be able to recover if it was discriminated against in terms of the charges levied on it, in relation to other users of electricity.[91]

So far then as to factual situations under which excessive payments demanded under monopolistic conditions can be recovered. But not much has been said about the appropriate remedy. This is partly ascribable to procedural considerations. For example, in *British Oxygen Company Ltd v South West Scotland Electricity Board*[92] the relief claimed was a declarator and recovery of the sums "overcharged". However, despite this obscurity, it seems clear that the claim was in fact based on the unjustified enrichment of the defender.[93] It is more problematic to determine which specific remedy based on unjustified enrichment should be awarded. The cases contain a number of references to the *condictio indebiti*. For example, in *Lanarkshire Steel Co Ltd v Caledonian Railway Co*,[94] it was stated that

---

88 1958 SC 53; 1959 SC (HL) 17.

89 1958 SC 53 at 79. In one of the "railway cases" of English law, *Lancashire and Yorkshire Railway Co v Gidlow* (1875) LR, 7 HL 517, Lord Chelmsford formulated the following rule in the context of the action for money had and received: "Now there can be no doubt that where a person pays money which he is not bound to pay, with a full knowledge of the facts, he cannot recover it back in an action for money had and received ... But there has always been an exception made in cases where a party has paid money under compulsion. It has been decided that where a carrier refused to deliver goods until a payment was made by the person to whom the goods belonged, amounting to more than the carrier had a right to charge, the customer might in an action for money had and received recover back the money so paid" (at 527).

90 1959 SC (HL) 17 at 38 et sq.

91 A comparable situation arose in *Lanarkshire Steel Co Ltd v Caledonian Railway Co* (1903) 6 F 47, which dealt with a claim by the pursuer that it paid railway rates under protest and in excess of what was allowed by statute. The implication of its refusal to pay these rates was that the railway company would no longer carry its traffic. According to the pursuer, this would have meant closure of its works (cf 49 et sq). However, on the facts the pursuer did not establish that the payments were in fact illegal, and consequently the defender was entitled to retain the payments. The fact that the charges may have been "unreasonable" was not, in the opinion of the court sufficient to render them recoverable (cf the judgments of the Lord President at 55 et sq and of Lord Kinnear at 61 et sq).

92 1958 SC 53; 1959 SC (HL) 17.

93 Cf Recovery of Benefits Conferred under Error of Law (Scot Law Com D P No 95, 1993), vol 2, 201 et sqq, 206, 210 et sqq, 217; Stewart, *The Law of Restitution in Scotland*, 34.

94 (1903) 6 F 47.

> ... if a trader paid an overcharge, it may be that he could only recover damages, but if payment has been *extorted from him under protest*, I think he can reclaim payment on the ground that the money all along belonged to him, and ought not to have been in the hands of the railway company ... This appears to amount to treating the question as one of *condictio indebiti*, and if this was the true category to which it should be referred, the conclusion at which the Lord Ordinary has arrived might be correct ...[95]

However, on the facts, the *condictio indebiti* could not be awarded, "... as no judgment or decision has been pronounced declaring the rate to be illegal, and the railway company exacted it as a condition of agreeing to accept the goods for carriage, it does not seem to me that the case would be one of the *condictio indebiti*". Also, in *British Oxygen Company Ltd v South West Scotland Electricity Board*[96] the House of Lords approved of the dictum of Wills J in *Great Western Railways Co v Sutton*,[97]

> ... where the learned judge said that he had 'always understood that when a man pays more than he is bound to do by law for the performance of a duty which the law says is owed to him for nothing, or for less than he has paid, there is a compulsion or concussion in respect of which he is entitled to recover the excess by *condictio indebiti*, or action for money had and received'.[98]

This reference indicates that that the House of Lords did not regard the *condictio indebiti* as an inappropriate remedy in these circumstances. However, it was also stated that "[t]he claim does not fit well into the *condictio indebiti*, in respect that money was not paid under the mistaken belief that it was due".[99] Recent case law on the *condictio indebiti* also indicates that it is too closely associated with the notion that the undue transfer has to be made in error to render it applicable to cases where undue transfers are made under some element of compulsion, rather than in error. For example, in the landmark decision of *Morgan Guarantee Trust Company of New York v Lothian Regional Council*,[100] Lord President Hope held that "... the *condictio indebiti* is available for the recovery of money paid or property transferred under an obligation which is void but was erroneously thought to be valid".[101] It should be clear that the *condictio indebiti* thus understood comprises two elements, namely a transfer under a void obligation, i.e. a transfer which is not due, and the error on the side of the transferor that the transfer was due. Although it is no longer required that the error has to be excusable,[102] equitable considerations can

---

95 (1903) 6 F 47 at 58, also see 54 (own emphasis).

96 1958 SC 53; 1959 SC (HL) 17.

97 (1869) LR, 4 HL 217 at 249.

98 1959 SC (HL) 17 at 48. Cf *Maskell v Horner* [1915] 3 KB 106 at 119.

99 1958 SC 53; 1959 SC (HL) 17. However, it was also (rather confusingly) held that "we are in a very special tract of country" expressing approval of the dictum of Willes J, quoted above, which refers to the *condictio indebiti*.

100 1995 SCLR 225.

101 1995 SCLR 225 at 229. The *condictio indebiti* is generally dealt with in Gloag, *The Law of Contract*, 57, 60; Walker, *Principles of Scottish Private Law*, vol 2, 507; Smith, *A Short Commentary on the law of Scotland*, 626; Walker, *The Law of Contracts and Related Obligations in Scotland*, 584; McBryde, *The Law of Contract in Scotland*, 204.

102 The general requirement that the error must be excusable has been abolished in *Morgan Guaranty Trust Company of New York v Lothian Regional Council* 1995 SCLR 225. A distinction used to be drawn between errors of law and fact. As a general rule errors of fact were treated as excusable, while errors of law were not (cf *Taylor v Wilson's Trustees* 1975 SC 146; *Peter Walker & Sons (Edinburgh) Ltd v Leith Glazing Company Ltd* 1980 SLT (Sh Ct) 104). The distinction used to be foreign to Scots law, but in two Scottish cases decided at the beginning of the nineteenth century,

bar recovery.[103] In modern Scots law, as in the times of the Institutional writers, the content of the error requirement is uncertain: it could entail that the transferor actually must have thought a debt was due when it was not,[104] or it could also be said that he should not have known that no debt is due.[105] In the latter case, payments in doubt as to whether they are due should then also be recoverable.[106] But whichever way the error requirement may be understood, it is clear that a person who makes a transfer under compulsion generally is not in error, but knows no debt is due. It is exactly because of this state of mind that he is unwilling to pay and has to be subjected to compulsion. Therefore, insofar as error is an essential feature of the *condictio indebiti* it cannot be regarded as a suitable remedy for the recovery of compelled undue transfers in modern Scots law. Whether this position is satisfactory will be considered further on.[107]

ii. Ultra vires demands for the payment of tax

Thus far the emphasis has been on compulsion in the form of threats of refusal to provide a service while enjoying monopoly power and being under a duty to do so. The picture is different when someone is confronted by the essentially confiscatory demand for payment of tax. Here no duty exists on the revenue: it is simply exercising a statutory power to demand payment and upon failure to comply with such a demand the taxpayer is exposed to a battery of remedies aimed at enforcement. These include additional interest and penalties.[108] It is doubtful, however, whether the mere existence of an implied threat of the negative consequences which attach to non-payment of tax in any way affects the recoverability of illegally exacted tax

---

the House of Lords deviated from this traditional approach. In *obiter dicta* in *Sinclair v Wilson & McLellan* (1830) 4 W & S 398 and *Dixons v Monklands Canal Co* (1831) 5 W & S 448, Lord Brougham expressed support for the English view that any error of law should exclude the claim for repayment, and also required that the error be avoidable. These *obiter dicta* formed the basis of the modern development of the Scots law on error of law and excusability. A distinction was then drawn between an error as to a general law (such as an Act of Parliament), which barred repayment, and an error as to a private contract or disposition, which was regarded as equivalent to an error of fact (cf *Aitken and others v Robert Baird and Company* (1877) 4 R 1005; *Glasgow Corporation v Lord Advocate* 1959 SC 203; *British Hydro-Carbon Chemicals Limited and British Transport Commissioners (Petitioners)* 1961 SLT 280). However, this distinction was not rigidly adhered to (cf *M'Nair v Arrol* 1952 SLT (Sh Ct) 41, where recovery with the *condictio indebiti* was allowed even though there was an error as to the interpretation of a statute). The distinction was criticised in *Taylor v Wilson's Trustees* 1975 SC 146 and *Glasgow Corporation v Lord Advocate* 1959 SC 203.

103 Cf *Morgan Guaranty Trust Company of New York v Lothian Regional Council* 1995 SCLR 225.

104 Cf *Morgan Guaranty Trust Company of New York v Lothian Regional Council* 1995 SCLR 225.

105 According to Gloag "[i]t is a general rule that if a man chooses to make a payment in the knowledge that it is not due, he cannot recover it" (*The Law of Contract*, 63). Cf *MacIntyre v Murray and Muir* (1915) 31 Sh Ct Rep 49 at 51 et sq; *Dalmellington Iron Company v Glasgow & South-Western Railway Company* (1889) 16 R 523 at 534.

106 Cf *Balfour v Smith & Logan* (1877) 4 R 544; J E du Plessis and H Wicke, "Woolwich Equitable v IRC and the condictio indebiti in Scots law" 1993 SLT (News) 303. In Judicial Abolition of the Error of Law Rule and its Aftermath (Scot Law Com D P No 99, 1996) this interpretation is disputed (at para 4.27) but it should be noted that if the payer in that case really was assured that the sum was due, it is hard to explain why he made another inquiry shortly after paying.

107 At 7.3.2.i below.

108 For an overview of the taxation process cf C Whitehouse, *Revenue Law—Principles and Practice*, 14th ed (1996), 13 et sqq.

payments.[109] This is illustrated by the case of *Glasgow Corporation v Lord Advocate*[110] which concerned the charge of a purchase tax. The Corporation had its own printing and stationery department which manufactured and supplied stationery for the use of its various departments. In 1951 the Commissioners of Customs and Excise charged the Corporation purchase tax on such goods manufactured by the Corporation. The Corporation then paid the tax although it unsuccessfully represented to the Commissioner and the Secretary of State for Scotland that it was exempted from paying the tax. The dispute ended in litigation, in which the Corporation (inter alia) claimed repayment of the tax on the basis that it was illegally exacted. Lord Sorn, however, made short shrift of this argument. According to him,

> ... since we now know that these payments were not due, it was suggested that they stood in the position of money illegally exacted. But in the present case there is nothing unconstitutional about what happened ... this is not a case of resisting an unwarranted exaction, but a case of trying to recover money, and the two things are not the same. The real question is whether money paid under a mistake in law can be recovered under the *condictio indebiti*.[111]

The matter was then dealt with in terms of the "doctrine of *condictio indebiti*", which "gives a right to recover from another money paid under the mistaken belief that it was due".[112] Although the payment was regarded as undue and made in the erroneous belief that it was due, the claim fell foul of the rule that recovery is denied if the error is one of law. This rule has recently been abolished,[113] and it seems clear that nowadays the *condictio indebiti* would be awarded in such a case, just as it was awarded in *Bell v Thomson*, an earlier case which concerned an error of fact.[114]

109 It is settled that the mere threat of legal process itself does not affect the recoverability of payments. Cf *MacIntyre v Murray & Muir* (1915) 31 Sh Ct Rep 49 at 51 ("[i]t is well established that money paid under stress of legal process cannot be recovered"). In Trotter's section on "*indebito solutio*" in a short chapter on quasi-contract in his *The Law of Contract in Scotland* it is also stated that "no action lies for the repayment of money paid under compulsion of legal process, for *interest reipublicae ut sit finis litium* (it is for the interest of the state that there should be an end of lawsuits)" (555). The basis for his statement that an action does not lie is an eighteenth century English case, *Marriot v Hampton* (1797) 7 TR 269. Marriot bought goods from Hampton, paid for it and obtained a receipt from Hampton. Later on, even though it had been paid, Hampton brought an action for payment against Marriot. Marriot unfortunately had lost the receipt and had to pay Hampton again. When Marriot finally found the receipt he wanted to reclaim the second, undue payment. This claim was refused. Even though the court was of the opinion that such famous authority as *Moses v Macferlan* (1760) 2 Burr 1009 supported the plaintiff, it gave more weight to the policy consideration that "there must be an end to litigation, otherwise there would be no security for any person".

110 1959 SC 203.

111 1959 SC 203 at 242.

112 1959 SC 203 at 231 (per Lord President Clyde; also see the judgment of Lord Sorn at 242).

113 *Morgan Guaranty Trust Company of New York v Lothian Regional Council* 1995 SCLR 225.

114 (1867) & M 64. The case dealt with an illegal demand by the Police Commissioners for payment of certain levies. It was held that the demand for the levies, although unwarranted, did not amount to compulsion. However, because the pursuer made an error of fact, recovery was in principle possible (cf 67, 69). On the facts, the money sought to be reclaimed unfortunately was already spent. The relevance of the latter finding is doubtful. In *Magistrates of Dunbar v Kelly* (1829) 8 S 128 it was held that there was no statutory or customary legal rule which warranted certain imposts being levied by the royal burgh of Dunbar. Consequently, an action of repetition was granted to Kelly and others in respect of payments made by them to the royal burgh. The defences that the impost was levied bona fide, and that its fruits had already been expended in the public improvement of the burgh (129), and that it was "by the bona fides protected from repetition", were not upheld.

But what would the position be if there was no error at all? Would the element of compulsion inherent in a demand for payment of tax then affect recovery? Here the case of *Agnew v Ferguson*[115] is of interest. Agnew leased collieries from Ferguson and regularly owed him royalties in terms of the lease. Ferguson was of course liable to pay tax on the royalty income: as the court put it, the income tax was "a burden on the landlord" (Ferguson), and not the lessee (Agnew).[116] However, apparently for purposes of convenience, the Revenue authorities regularly collected the tax directly from Agnew, who then had a statutory right to deduct these tax payments from the royalties due to Ferguson. The problem in the present case was that, as a matter of established practice with his previous landlords, Agnew had not availed himself of this right to claim a deduction, but paid over the full royalties to the landlord in the expectation that the tax payments would be refunded to him. Agnew therefore paid royalties to Ferguson knowing full well that a part thereof (the amount he could have deducted) was not due to Ferguson. When Ferguson refused to refund Agnew, Agnew claimed repayment of these undue amounts. Despite the absence of error, it was held that Agnew was entitled to recovery. According to the Lord Justice Clerk,

> . . . I am not able to hold that if the pursuer, being compelled to do something by statute, paid the tax due, and for which the landlord is responsible, he loses all right to its return if he does not deduct it from his next payment. The right to deduct payment is a privilege conferred upon him for his advantage, which is of the nature of a lien; but I cannot see that he having made payment, under compulsion, of what is due by the other party, cannot recover from that other as due to him what he has so advanced, although he has not deducted it from a sum due by him to his landlord . . .[117]

Significantly, although the matter did not concern a payment made in error, the court held that, "this is a simple case of *condictio indebiti*—money paid which was not due—and which the receiver of that money has no title, moral or legal, to retain.[118] It is therefore apparent that the compulsion inherent in a demand for payment by the Revenue authorities is relevant to a claim based on payment of tax which is due by another. The appropriate remedy is then the *condictio indebiti*. The question is of course whether similar relief would be provided if the taxpayer seeks to reclaim an overpayment directly from the revenue. This question has not been conclusively decided in the modern law, and it will dealt with when the modern law is evaluated further on in the context of the landmark decision of the House of Lords in *Woolwich Building Society (formerly Woolwich Equitable Building Society) v Inland Revenue Commissioners*.[119]

iii. The effect of a reservation

It has been indicated above that outwith the law of force and fear it is possible to reclaim certain illegally exacted payments. To round off this discussion, it has to be pointed out that where a person makes a payment which he believes is not due, he can ensure its recoverability by making such a payment subject to an express reservation.[120]

---

115 (1903) 5 F 879. Cf especially the *dicta* at 883.
116 (1903) 5 F 879.
117 (1903) 5 F 879 at 882 et sq.
118 (1903) 5 F 879 at 884.
119 [1992] 3 WLR 367; [1993] 1 AC 70 (CA and HL). Cf 6.3.3 below.
120 Cf *British Railways Board v Glasgow Corporation* 1976 SC 224 at 232 et sq; Gloag, *The Law of Contract*, 63.

Apparently, a "mere protest" is insufficient.[121] Obviously, if such a reservation gives rise to an express or implied agreement that the payment should be returned if it turns out to be undue, it can be recovered with a contractual claim. In the absence of such an agreement, a so-called definite reservation would still enable the payer to reclaim under the *condictio indebiti* despite the fact that payment had not been made in error.[122]

4.3.2 *Compulsion and the recovery of transfers tainted by turpitude*

In contrast to earlier law, there is no authority in modern Scots law for the proposition that compelled transfers can be regarded as transfers *ob turpem causam*.[123] However, this does not mean that compulsion cannot play a role in determining whether relief should be provided when a transfer was made pursuant to an illegal agreement. Here the general rule is that recovery is excluded if both parties are tainted by turpitude.[124] It is only if the one party can be regarded as less tainted by turpitude

---

121 Cf Gloag, *The Law of Contract*, 63; *Balfour-Melville v Duncan* (1903) 41 SLR 149 where the pursuer made certain undue payments "under protest and under reservation of his right to claim repayment of the sums overpaid . . .". This was regarded as insufficient to allow him to reclaim with the *condictio indebiti*, or to entitle him to repetition. In the words of Lord Kinnear: "To recover overpayments under (the *condictio indebiti*) . . . it is necessary that the pursuer should show that they were made in error or ignorance, and in such circumstances as will entitle him to be relieved against his own mistake. But if all that he can allege is that he paid a debt in full, when he might have insisted, if he had thought fit, upon making a certain deduction, and if it appears on his own showing that he did so in full knowledge of his legal rights, and of the facts bearing upon his liability, I see no ground in law on which he should be entitled to recover" (at 152). Gloag's statement that in the absence of a definite reservation, "[a] mere protest will be sufficient if the party claiming the payment had the power to inflict some immediate disadvantage in the event of a refusal, reflects English law, not Scots law. He refers to *Maskell v Horner* [1915] 3 KB 106 (where market duties were paid on a threat of seizure of goods) and to *Brocklebank v The King* [1925] 1 KB 52 (where the shipping controller, whose permit was necessary for the sale of a ship, demanded and received a payment for which there was no legal justification).

122 *British Railways Board v Glasgow Corporation* 1976 SC 224 at 232 et sq. In earlier cases such as *Glasgow Corporation v Glasgow Tramways Co Ltd* (1897) 24 R 628 and *Lanarkshire Steel Co v Caledonian Railway Co* (1903) 6 F 47, the relevance of the *condictio indebiti* was not as clearly recognised. In *Glasgow Corporation v Glasgow Tramways Co* a company made certain payments to a corporation, but neglected to deduct certain amounts from these payments. Later on the company tried to obtain payment of the amounts they could have deducted. The Court of Session granted the claim, partly on the grounds that "the right of relief was asserted, never withdrawn, and on more occasions than one expressly mentioned as being reserved" (at 638). It was not clearly stated that the case dealt with a *condictio indebiti* (there is only an oblique reference on 636; cf *British Railways Board v Glasgow Corporation* 1976 SC 224 at 232 et sq). The decision was reversed on appeal to the House of Lords ((1898) 25 R (HL) 77), but on the grounds that the Tramways contractually agreed that they would pay the amounts which they now claim the Corporation was liable to pay. The statements as to the effect of the reservation therefore remain unaffected. In *Lanarkshire Steel Co v Caledonian Railway Co* (1903) 6 F 47 recovery was excluded because legislation relating to railways was interpreted so as to allow certain "unreasonable", but not "illegal", charges to be retained. The payments were therefore not regarded as due. According to Lord M'Donald in *British Railways Board v Glasgow Corporation* 1976 SC 224, "It appears from the judgment of Lord Kinross at 58 that if the increases had in fact been illegal the sums could have been recovered under the *condictio*, presumably by virtue of an express reservation, which was made at the time of the payment" (at 233).

123 But cf Recovery of Benefits Conferred under Error of Law (Scot Law Com D P No 95, 1993), vol 2, 201 et sqq; Gloag and Henderson, *The Law of Scotland*, 434. For an analysis of these views, cf 7.3.1.ii(b), 7.3.2.ii below.

124 Cf Gloag, *The Law of Contract*, 585; Walker, *The Law of Contracts and Related Obligations in Scotland*, 161 et sq; SME, vol 15 (1997), para 764.

than the other[125] that some remedy based on unjustified enrichment is awarded.[126] Compulsion can then play an important role in indicating that the parties to an illegal agreement are not equally tainted by turpitude.[127]

An important field of application of this principle is the situation where a creditor compels a debtor to grant him a preference upon insolvency. In essence, a voluntary disposition or payments made by a debtor to a creditor within certain periods before insolvency are void.[128] Such void dispositions or payments can then be reclaimed with a statutory remedy.[129] However, there is no such remedy where a creditor compels a debtor to give him a secret preference in order to concur in a composition. In support of the view that compulsion affects the relative turpitude of the parties, Gloag refers to *Arrol v Montgomery*[130] and *Macfarlane v Nicoll*.[131] In *Arrol*'s case the court rejected the creditor's defence, based on the maxim *in turpi causa melior est conditio possidentis*, that the debtor could not recover his payment because of its turpitude. The "extortion"[132] showed that the creditor was less tainted with turpitude and that recovery should not be barred. The creditor was then held liable in repetition.

In *Macfarlane*'s case the situation was somewhat more complicated. The Clyde Galvanizing Company experienced financial difficulties, and wanted to offer

125 The exclusionary rules are encapsulated in sayings such as *in turpi causa melior est conditio possidentis* (cf *Cuthbertson v Lowes* (1870) 8 M 1073 at 1075) and *in pari delicto potior est conditio possidentis* (for examples, cf generally McBryde, *The Law of Contract in Scotland*, 612 et sqq).

126 Cf Gloag, *The Law of Contract*, 587; McBryde, *The Law of Contract in Scotland*, 612, 629, 632; *Macfarlane v Nicoll* (1864) 3 M 237 (especially 247), where repetition based on the *condictio indebiti* was awarded. Although the remedy involves illegality, it is not described as a *condictio ob turpem vel iniustam causam*. In modern Scots law it seems as though the latter *condictio* has virtually disappeared (cf Recovery of Benefits Conferred under Error of Law (Scot Law Com D P No 95, 1993), vol 2, 205, where it is mentioned that the survival of the *condictio ob turpem causam* is only clearly recognised in "Repetition", by J Cowan QC in *Encyclopaedia of the Laws of Scotland*, vol 12, para 1183; the latter reference is further made in the context of English authority: cf Evans-Jones, "From 'undue transfer' to 'retention without a legal basis' (the *condictio indebiti* and *condictio ob turpem vel iniustam causam*)" in Evans-Jones (ed), *The Civil Law Tradition in Scotland*, 213 at 243 n 117). More recently, in Gloag and Henderson, *The Law of Scotland*, it has been argued that the *condictio ob turpem (vel iniustam) causam* should be the basis of recovery of certain compelled transfers (474). However, there is no modern recorded Scottish case in which the existence of this *condictio* has been recognised (e.g., it is excluded from Lord Cullen's list of *condictiones* in *Morgan Guaranty Trust Company of New York v Lothian Regional Council* 1995 SCLR 225 at 247). On the position in South African law cf 5.3.3.i below.

127 Cf Gloag, *The Law of Contract*, 587 ("[w]hen the parties to an illegal transaction are not *in pari delicto*, the one who is less blameworthy may found upon the illegality. This rule applies when one party has been in a position enabling him to compel the other to concur in the illegal act").

128 On the statutory provisions regulating reclaiming such dispositions, cf Gloag and Henderson, *The Law of Scotland*, 1043 et sqq. Cf also *Bob Gray (Access) Ltd v T M Standard Scaffolding* (Sh Ct) 1987 SCLR 720; *Walkraft Paint Co Ltd v Lovelock* 1964 SLT 103; *T v L* 1970 SLT 243; McBryde, *Bankruptcy*, 152 et sq. Undue preferences are generally challengeable under s 36 of the Companies Act 1985.

129 On these provisions see the previous footnote. The courts have examined the influence of compulsion on dispositions in order to determine what constitutes a "voluntary" disposition or payment in terms of the abovementioned provisions. However, since the primary concern here is the common law of unjustified enrichment, the cases dealing with the statutory remedy will not be analysed in detail. Cf, generally, *Nordic Travel Ltd v Scotprint Ltd* 1980 SLT 189 at 193; *Darven v Logan* (1861) 1 Guthrie 85.

130 (1826) 4 S 499.

131 (1864) 3 M 237.

132 *Arrol v Montgomery* (1826) 4 S 499 at 501. Cf *Stair Memorial Encyclopaedia*, vol 15, para 763 n 4.

its creditors a composition. One of its most important creditors, Nicoll, then publicly indicated that he would agree to the composition, but in private told the representatives or partners of the company that he would only do this if they granted him some bonds representing the difference between the debt due to him, and the amount he would be entitled to according to the disposition. On the same day that Nicoll granted a discharge, the company granted him post-dated bills to the value of this difference. Approximately three years later, the estates of the company and its partners were sequestrated, and Macfarlane was appointed as trustee. He then claimed reduction of these bills and repetition of the sums paid. The basis for these claims was the fact that the bills were obtained extortionately and in violation of the composition contract. The defences were raised that the trustee represented frauds (the partners), and that the payment was made in full knowledge that defences could be raised against their validity. In other words, the payment was made voluntarily. In the Inner House, Lord Deas then held that the preferences were illegal.[133] However, this did not mean automatic invalidity. According to Lord Deas, it was necessary to distinguish between various categories of bills granted. It was then held that payment could not be demanded of the bill which had not yet been paid, since this would constitute an undue preference to Nicoll.[134] This amounts to an application of the principle of *ex turpi causa non oritur actio*: the court will not give effect to an illegal agreement. However, it was also held that Nicoll was liable to repay the value of a bill which was subsequently made over to a third party (Mills), since payment of such a bill could not be resisted.[135] Finally, it was held that the payments of the bill made directly to Nicoll were voluntary and not recoverable.

For a proper appreciation of this case it is important to distinguish between the various types of compulsion present in the case. First, there was compulsion at the time of the signing of the discharge and the granting of the bills. The presence of such compulsion prima facie indicates that the parties are not equally "blameworthy" (as Gloag would put it) and that the *in pari delicto* principle should be relaxed so as to enable recovery of a transfer made pursuant to the agreement.[136] Second, since the third party endorsees of the bills could enforce their claim for payment, such lawful compulsion could not be resisted. However, this was not the case when payments were made directly to Nicoll. The relevance of compulsion to the application of the *in pari delicto* principle in the present case can then be summarised as follows. The presence of compulsion in the formation of an illegal contract does not automatically give rise to relaxation of the *in pari delicto* principle. It has to be established whether performance under such a contract could also be resisted. Here the initial granting of the bills could not be resisted, but subsequent claims for payment by Nicoll could. Recovery of such payments should therefore not be allowed. It is only the claim for

---

133 (1864) 3 M 237 at 243 et sq ("if it be a condition of a particular creditor's accession to the compromise contract, that he is to get preference bills, that is illegal; and under ordinary circumstances such a transaction is liable to be set aside").

134 (1864) 3 M 237 at 244.

135 According to Lord Deas, "Our own law and practice I take to be, that if a bill granted as a preference in this way is paid through concussion, as we express it, the money may be recovered back. But concussion, I think, means, with us, when it is paid to a party who is in such a position that he can legally and effectually compel payment ...; and if he can compel the payment, and the payment is made to him, our law and practice will hold that to be concussion, and that the money may be recovered back" ((1864) 3 M 237 at 244 et sq).

136 Cf *Smith v Cuff* (1817) 6 M & S 160; Burrows, *The Law of Restitution*, 187 for an interesting common law perspective.

enforcement by a third party endorsee which could not be resisted: here the *in pari delicto* principle should be relaxed, and a right to recovery should arise.

4.3.3 *Compulsion and the measure of recovery*

In an action of repetition based on the *condictio indebiti* the defender may raise the defence of loss of enrichment,[137] or more specifically "bona fide consumption".[138] However, this defence can fail where the recipient of money compelled the payment.[139] Where a payment is made in error, the pursuer may claim payment of interest (presumably from the date of payment) if the money is wrongfully withheld,[140] or if there was an implied or actual agreement to pay such interest if the capital is not due.[141] There is no reason why the retention of a compelled payment should not likewise be regarded as a case of wrongful withholding, giving rise to a claim for interest accruing from the date of the payment.[142]

4.4 COMPULSION AS A DELICT

It will be recalled that Stair and Bankton treat force and fear or extortion purely as a delict—mainly on the basis that what is willed under compulsion is nonetheless

137 Cf *Royal Bank of Scotland plc v Watt* 1991 SC 48, 1991 SLT 138; *Credit Lyonnais v George Stevenson and Co Ltd* (1901) 9 SLT 93; *Stair Memorial Encyclopaedia*, vol 15, para 30; Recovery of Benefits Conferred under Error of Law (Scot Law Com D P No 95, 1993), vol 2, 77 et sqq.

138 Cf *Hunter v Hunter's Trustees* (1893) 21 R 949. Here a widow was erroneously paid more than she was entitled to under her husband's will. It was held that she was not liable to repay the overpayments. The court relied on the "equitable rule or principle of property received and consumed in good faith" (at 953). No claim of repetition could then be granted (at 955). Cf also *Bell v Thomson* (1867) 6 M 64; Recovery of Benefits Conferred under Error of Law (Scot Law Com D P No 95, 1993), vol 2, 142 et sqq. In *Darling's Trustees v Darling's Trustee* 1909 SC 445 it was held that the "doctrine of bona fide *percepta et consumpta*" only relates to fruits, and that loss of enrichment could not be claimed in regard to the capital (at 451). Cf also *Carmichael v Caledonian Railway Company* (1870) 8 M (HL) 119. This restriction has been criticised (cf Recovery of Benefits Conferred under Error of Law (Scot Law Com D P No 95, 1993), vol 2, 147 et sqq, 150 et sq). Apparently the Crown is not entitled to rely on this defence in certain cases (cf Recovery of Ultra Vires Public Authority Receipts and Disbursements (Scot Law Com D P No 100, 1996), 27 et sqq, 32).

139 Cf Recovery of Ultra Vires Public Authority Receipts and Disbursements (Scot Law Com D P No 100, 1996), 27 et sqq, where it is indicated that the defence of bona fide consumption may not be available where the Crown used an improper form of compulsion. Cf *Unigate Foods Ltd v Scottish Milk Marketing Board* 1975 SC (HL) 75 at 90 and *Magistrates of Dunbar v Kelly* (1829) 8 S 128.

140 Cf Recovery of Ultra Vires Public Authority Receipts and Disbursements (Scot Law Com D P No 100, 1996), 47, which deals with the conflict of authority on whether interest runs from the date of payment.

141 According to Lord President Normand in *Haddon's Executrix v Scottish Milk Marketing Board* 1938 SC 168, "[a] party may receive money in good faith, believing it to be his own, from a party who thinks that he is bound to tender it, and in that case there may be good reason for the recipient saying 'I got payment from you on your offer of payment and am not to be held answerable for the use of the money when it was in my possession'. But here the party making the payment says 'I am not due you this money; I pay only under compulsion of diligence. I intend to have it back from you, and I am going to litigate the matter for that purpose'. Surely a party in such circumstances must repay with interest, and the fact that the party is a public board makes not the slightest difference" (at 172). The court found that there was an agreement to repay. Cf also *Glasgow Gaslight Co v Barony Parish of Glasgow* (1868) 6 M 406 at 413 et sq.

142 Cf Recovery of Ultra Vires Public Authority Receipts and Disbursements (Scot Law Com D P No 100, 1996), 48 n 111.

willed. In modern Scots law the position is somewhat different. Compulsion in the form of force and fear is mainly dealt with in the context of the law of contract, and more specifically, is regarded as a factor affecting the validity of contracts. There is no modern case law which deals with force and fear, or any other form of compulsion examined thus far for that matter, as a delict.[143] Neither do the textbooks display much enthusiasm for doing so either.[144] Walker notes that force and fear in the form of *metus* had a delictual character in Roman law, and that there are Institutional authorities who referred to it as a delict. But from his discussion it is obvious that in modern law this delictual dimension of force and fear is of minor importance, and that it rather gives rise to "the quasi-contractual obligation of restitution, the equitable action of reduction and other remedies to prevent one party enjoying an advantage over another obtained by force".[145] However, this does not mean that a delictual claim cannot lie. Such a claim would be particularly apposite where there was loss of enrichment, or loss was suffered which is not covered by contractual or enrichment based remedies. The measure of damages generally is so much compensation as would put the victim in the position he would have been in if the delict had not been committed.[146] It therefore excludes "exemplary damages"[147] (reminiscent of the award *in quadruplum* of Roman times), but includes "special damages" (to use the English terminology), such as loss of the use of an object.[148] A factor which of course limits the applicability of the remedy of damages is that fault on the part of the defender is a general condition of liability *ex delicto*.[149] Where a bona fide third party has obtained something as the consequence of extortion, there would be no fault on his side, and consequently no delictual remedy could be brought against him. However, this should not leave the wrongdoer scot-free. In the absence of any unjustified enrichment on his side (e.g. if he gives the extorted object to a third party) the delictual remedy of damages might well be the only remedy with which one could claim from him. This remedy would be particularly relevant if the third party disappears or becomes insolvent. Entitlement to contractual remedies such as reduction should therefore not necessarily exclude a claim in delict.[150]

143 Cf Walker, *The Law of Delict in Scotland*, 693 et sqq. In his *Introduction to the Scots Law of Delict* (1989), W J Stewart only deals with extortion incidentally in a discussion of the English case of *Rookes v Barnard* ([1964] AC 1129). This case involved illegal threats by workmen to strike if a worker who left a union was not removed. Stewart calls this case "clear authority for a delict of intimidation".

144 In the first Scottish law book to deal exclusively with delict, Guthrie Smith's *Law of Damages*, force and fear is still specifically dealt with as a delict (42 et sq).

145 Walker, *The Law of Delict in Scotland*, 694. He also warns earlier on in his work that delictual claims must be distinguished from *quasi ex contractu* claims for restitution (vol 1, 15).

146 Walker, *The Law of Delict in Scotland*, 461. Although it has been stated that the purpose of a delictual claim is to restore the parties "*in integrum*", such terminology is confusing in the context of a delictual claim (cf Walker, *The Law of Civil Remedies in Scotland*, 808; from a South African perspective cf *Davidson v Bonafede* 1981 (2) SA 501 (C)). It is particularly confusing in the light of the fact that this term is also used as a condition for attacking the validity of contracts (cf 4.2.2.iii above).

147 Walker, *The Law of Civil Remedies in Scotland*, 815.

148 Walker, *The Law of Civil Remedies in Scotland*, 814.

149 Walker, *The Law of Delict in Scotland*, 42.

150 Inasmuch as force and fear resembles fraudulent misrepresentation it can be argued analogously that the victim of force and fear should be able to claim reduction and the accompanying restitution of transfers, as well as damages based on a wrong.

4.5 COMPULSION AND PROPERTY LAW

In examining the effect of compulsion, and force and fear in particular, it thus far has been assumed that the recipient-defender acquired ownership, and that the pursuer's claim for "restitution" or repetition was based on the recipient's unjustified enrichment. Only rarely was it necessary to examine whether remedies of property law, based on the pursuer's ownership, were appropriate. In this concluding section a more general impression will be obtained of the relevance of compulsion to modern property law, and in particular to remedies based on ownership and the loss of possession.

4.5.1 *Transfer of ownership*

According to the Scots law of property, the transfer of ownership is prevented by a *vitium reale* or *labes realis*—a fatal or "radical" defect.[151] Where ownership has not passed, the owner has the remedy of "vindication", which can be regarded as "shorthand for remedies based either on ownership of the property or on the holding of some other real right giving entitlement to possession such as lease". The remedies then sought are usually delivery in the case of moveables and ejection or removing in the case of land.[152] These remedies of "vindicatory restitution"[153] are not based on unjustified enrichment since the claimant states that he has been owner, or holder of the right all along. Unfortunately, there are very few indications in modern law whether compulsion, and particularly "force and fear", amounts to a "radical" defect, giving rise to such remedies. In the discussion of the law during the era of the Institutional writers it was mentioned that the protection which at times was afforded to third parties militated against such an approach, despite the many voices which demanded that anything done under force should be "utterly void". In modern law the matter has still not been resolved: bona fide third parties are not protected if they obtained something as the consequence of robbery[154] or fraud resembling theft[155] but it will be recalled that it is not settled in the case law whether a third party can retain something acquired as a consequence of force and fear.[156] There is, however support for the view that only robbery (and presumably *vis absoluta*), creates a *real vice*.[157] This implication is then that ownership passes in cases of force and fear as well as other forms of compulsion, and that the new owner can retain ownership until such time as it has been indicated that his title can be reduced. It should be noted though that different rules apply to money or negotiable instruments, and that these rules are less favouable for the victim. If money has been taken by theft or violence it can be

151 Cf SME vol 18 (1993), para 614.

152 Reid, "*Unjustified Enrichment and Property Law*" 1994 *JR* 167 at 190 sq.

153 Cf Reid, "*Unjustified Enrichment and Property Law*" 1994 *JR* 167 at 169.

154 Cf Corporeal Moveables – Protection of the Bona Fide Acquirer of Another's Property (Scot Law Com Consultative Memo No 27, 1976), para 18.

155 Cf *Morrisson v Robertson* 1908 SC 332; *Cundy v Lindsay* (1878) 3 A Cas 459; Trotter, *The Law of Contract in Scotland*, 4 et sqq; SME vol 18 (1993), para 617 et sq. In Morrisson's case an error in identity was induced by a middleman's fraud. It was found that no sale took place and that ownership was not transferred: in fact, the third party was regarded as being in the same position as someone who had obtained the goods from a thief (at 337).

156 Cf the discussion of *Stewart Brothers v Kiddie* (1899) 7 SLT 92 and *Trustee Savings Bank v Balloch* 1983 SLT 240 at 4.2.2.i above.

157 According to Professor W M Gordon, "A transfer of property brought about by force and fear is often said to be void and is certainly open to reduction as affected by a vice of consent, but the better view may be that only robbery creates a real vice" (SME vol 18 (1993), para 615).

recovered from the taker but not from any third party who has bona fide acquired it.[158] This seems to indicate that one neither would be able to institute a vindicatory claim *qua* owner, nor a claim based on unjustified enrichment.[159] As far as negotiable instruments are concerned, it has been indicated that in terms of the 1882 Bills of Exchange Act, a holder in due course of a negotiable instrument would be protected in favour of the person claiming relief on grounds of force and fear.[160]

4.5.2 *Loss of possession*

In conclusion it briefly can be mentioned that in modern Scots law possession can be recovered by an action of spuilzie, although it is not referred to by that name in practice. This action is supposed to lie "where a person in lawful possession of goods has been unjustifiably dispossessed".[161] Prima facie, it would seem as if this possessory remedy cannot be applicable to cases of force and fear: for the action of spuilzie to lie there has to be a "*taking away* of moveables",[162] whereas force and fear entails inducing another to *give* something.[163] However, there are indications that this requirement should not be taken too literally: in certain cases where possession of goods has been obtained from the owner through fraud, and the goods then came into the hands of third parties, the return of possession was ordered.[164] It is arguable that third parties who have obtained something which was initially given due to force and fear should be faced with a similar claim for the return of possession.[165]

4.6 CONCLUSIONS

1. The most important rules of modern Scottish private law dealing with compulsion are to be found in the law relating to force and fear as a ground for reduction and the law relating to the return or "repetition" of certain undue transfers. Compulsion is also relevant to the law of delict and property.

---

158 Cf Bell, *Principles*, paras 527-529; D M Walker, *Principles of Scottish Private Law*, vol 2 (1989), 423; "Repetition" by J Cowan QC in *Encyclopaedia of the Laws of Scotland*, vol 12, para 1183.

159 Cf Bell, *Principles*, para 528.

160 45 and 46 Vict c 61, ss 27(2), 29 and 32(2); A G Guest (ed), *Chalmers and Guest on Bills of Exchange, Cheques and Promissory Notes*, 14th ed (1991), 278 et sq; D M Walker, *Principles of Scottish Private Law*, vol 2 (1989), 423 .

161 Walker, *The Law of Delict in Scotland*, 1002; cf also Carey Miller, *Corporeal Moveables in Scots Law*, 219; Stair, *Institutions*, 1.9.17, 4.30.1.

162 Stair, *Institutions*, 1.9.16; cf Erskine, *Institute*, 3.7.16.

163 Cf Reid, "*Unjustified Enrichment and Property Law*" 1994 *JR* 167 at 190.

164 Cf Walker, *The Law of Delict in Scotland*, 1007. He refers to *Hart and Gemmell v Panton & Co* (1861) Guthrie 439 and *Muir Wood & Co v Moore and Kidd* (1876) Guthrie 444. In Hart's case a dealer gave a watch-maker some watches and guard chains to show to third parties. The watch-maker then sold the watches and chains at a low price to a pawnbroker and absconded. The court found that the watches and chains were in fact stolen, that ownership in them remained with the dealer, and that the dealer could reclaim them from the pawnbroker. In *Muir Wood & Co* v *Moore and Kidd*, a certain Geddes hired, or pretended to hire a piano from Muir Wood & Co. He then pledged the piano to Moore and Kidd for a loan of £10. The court then found that the piano was stolen and that Moore and Kidd were bound to return it.

165 It should be noted, though, that the cases referred to above could be regarded as cases of theft. Inasmuch as theft, like robbery, resembles *vis absoluta*, rather than *vis compulsiva*, it is possible that such a claim for the return of possession would only be available where there was *vis absoluta*. Cf also Stair *Institutions*, 1.9.16 ("... things stolen or robbed, though they might be criminally pursued for as theft or robbery, yet they may also civilly be pursued for as spuilzie"); Walker, *The Law of Delict in Scotland*, 1002 ("... conduct amounting criminally to theft would equally support a civil action of spuilzie").

2.1 Compulsion in the form of force and fear is a ground for the reduction of deeds. In order to succeed with a claim of force and fear it has to be proven that a person acted out of fear induced by force or threats of harm. At times it is stated that his will has to be overpowered, but this is qualified by the requirements that the fear has to be reasonable and that the conduct instilling it has to be illegal or unwarrantable.

2.2 It is not clear whether force and fear leads to voidness or voidability. Insofar as force and fear gives rise to voidness, a claim of reduction is strictly speaking not necessary: the contract is *ipso iure* void, and remedies such as "restitution" or "repetition", based on unjustified enrichment, are available. The inability of the victim to provide *restitutio in integrum* is then not a bar to recovery. Insofar as force and fear gives rise to voidability, the appropriate remedy is a claim of reduction. The inability to provide *restitutio in integrum* then is a bar to reduction. The effect of force and fear on the reclaimability of transfers in the hands of third parties is disputed.

3. Compulsion also influences the availability and extent of remedies based on unjustified enrichment.

3.1 Certain compelled undue transfers are recoverable outwith the field of application of the law of force and fear. For example, it is possible to recover excessive transfers demanded under "monopolistic conditions" for the fulfilment of a duty (such as the provision of a service) which the recipient is obliged to fulfil in any event. There are indications that such claims for recovery are in fact based on the *condictio indebiti*. The compulsion inherent in an express or implied threat that the legal process would be used when an ultra vires demand is made for payment of tax apparently is relevant when the recoverability of such a payment has to be determined. The right to recovery may be preserved by way of an express reservation.

3.2 Under certain circumstances a compelled transfer can be regarded as made *ob turpem causam*, or with a base or immoral purpose. According to certain exclusionary principles, a transfer *ob turpem causam* is not recoverable if both parties are tainted by turpitude. However, where one party was compelled, e.g. where a creditor refuses to agree to a compromise unless the debtor grants him a preference, these rules can be relaxed. A right to recovery with an action of repetition, based on unjustified enrichment, would then be available. There are very few indications of the existence of the *condictio ob turpem vel iniustam causam* in modern Scots law.

3.3 In an action of repetition based on the *condictio indebiti* the defender may raise the defence of bona fide consumption, but where the recipient of money compelled payment the defence of bona fide consumption may fail. The pursuer may further be able to claim payment of interest from the date of receipt if there was wrongful withholding of the transfer. This presumably includes retention of a compelled transfer.

4. Compulsion gives rise to a claim in delict which can apparently concur with claims based on contract and unjustified enrichment.

5. There is support for the proposition that compulsion in the form of force and fear can amount to a *vitium reale* which prevents the transfer of ownership. Apparently only *vis absoluta* is sufficiently serious to have this effect, and give rise to "vindicatory restitution". The possessory remedy of spuilzie also does not seem to be applicable to cases of compulsion. The appropriate remedy is rather a claim based on unjustified enrichment.

Chapter 5

Compulsion in Roman-Dutch, South African and German law

5.1 INTRODUCTION

Although legal education in Scotland dates from the times of the founding of the oldest universities in the fifteenth century,[1] there were political, economic and other considerations[2] which forced many aspiring Scottish lawyers to look towards the universities of the Continent—and after the Reformation, of Holland in particular—to provide them with legal education. From the beginning of the sixteenth until the end of the seventeenth centuries, some 1600 Scottish students studied law at Leyden University in Holland.[3] But the Dutch influence did not remain restricted to the provision of legal education. During the important formative years of Scots law in the seventeenth century, the Dutch Institutional writers, or "old authorities", were studied by Scottish legal writers,[4] referred to in legal teaching in Scotland,[5] and cited in Scottish decisions.[6] However, since the eighteenth century the civilian

1 Cf Walker, *A Legal History of Scotland*, vol 2, 281 et sqq. For example, the first Civilist at King's College in Old Aberdeen started teaching at about 1495. The 1514 constitution required law students to read the Institutes of Justinian, and that the course should be the same as at the University of Orleans (L J Macfarlane, *William Elphinstone and the Kingdom of Scotland* (1985), 380).

2 It would seem as if the instruction in Civil Law at the Scottish Universities was insufficient. Cf in general T B Smith, "A Meditation on Scottish Universities and the Civil Law" (1959) 33 *TulaneLR* 621 at 625 et sq. For example, Smith states that by the seventeenth century the appointment of a Civilist at Aberdeen was apparently held "as a source of profit to the incumbent, rather than the students ..." and that "up to 1860, the Civilists in Aberdeen seem to have evaded or delegated their duties" (at 626).

3 Cf J C Garner, "French and Dutch Influences" in *An Introductory Survey of the Sources and Literature of Scots Law* (1936), 226 at 232 et sqq; the speech of Lord Macmillan in *Stewart v London, Midland and Scottish Railway Co* 1943 SC (HL) 19 at 38 et sq. For an explanation of this phenomenon, cf T B Smith, "Scots Law and Roman-Dutch Law—A Shared Tradition" 1961 *JR* 32 at 41 et sqq.

4 Stair, in particular, visited Holland twice, and studied the works of the old authorities. According to A J G Mackay, "he was imbued with their liberal and philosophical spirit which transmuted the letter of the Roman law, and adopted it to the advancing civilisation and extending commerce of the age. Thus the modern European *Ius Gentium* flowed from Holland by a direct channel into the law of Scotland" (*Memoir of Sir James Dalrymple* (1873), 55); cf also Smith, "Scots Law and Roman-Dutch Law—A Shared Tradition" 1961 *JR* 32 at 36; H L MacQueen, "Mixture or Muddle? Teaching and Research in Scottish Legal History" 1997 *ZEuP* 369 at 373.

5 Cf A Grant, *The Story of the University of Edinburgh during its first three hundred years*, vol 2 (1884), 366.

6 Cf Garner, "French and Dutch Influences", in *An Introductory Survey of the Sources and Literature of Scots Law*, 226 at 232. Cf, for example, in the context of force and fear, Bankton, *Institute*, 1.10.61 (reference to Voet, *Commentarius ad Pandectas*, 4.2.16); *Wiseman v Logie* (1700) Mor 16505 (reference to Grotius, *De iure belli ac pacis*, 2.11); *Wightman v Graham* (1787) Mor 1521 (reference to Voet, *Commentarius ad Pandectas*, 4.2.10).

influence started to diminish: stronger political ties with England inevitably lead towards a movement away from Continental European Civil Law towards English Common Law.

This development was roughly paralleled in the Cape of Good Hope, which received Roman-Dutch law as its common law in the seventeenth century, but which was then subsequently strongly influenced by English law. Both the Scottish and South African legal systems are nowadays regarded as mixed legal systems, mixtures of the Common Law and Civil Law families. This similarity of development invites comparison between Scots law of the Institutional era and Roman Dutch law, as well as between modern Scots and South African law. Such comparisons enable an evaluation of different experiences with legal material shared from similar sources. It can help to identify the pitfalls of indiscriminate borrowing, but also the possibilities of careful selection.[7] It should be apparent, though, that the mere fact that a rule has been forged from both systems obviously does not imply that it is inherently superior to anything which the systems from which it has been derived has to offer.[8] It may well be that the existing law could have been developed in terms of its own principles and dogmatic structure, without any need for borrowing or selection.

It is here where it becomes important also to examine systems which provide an indication of how the existing law could be developed without detracting from its integrity by importing and "mixing". An examination of German law would then be particularly useful in developing those areas of Scots law which have still retained some of the richness of its civilian heritage. German private law is (largely) codified in the *Bürgerliches Gesetzbuch* (BGB) of 1900,[9] which was strongly influenced by the nineteenth-century Historical and Pandectist schools, of which the members were formidable students of Roman law. This Code has remained remarkably unaltered for almost a century, and still reflects its compilers' rigorous approach to Civil Law. It therefore stands to reason that when one is faced with problems in areas of Scots law with a civilian dimension, a comparison with the position in German law could be of value. But before the German law is examined, it is first necessary to turn to Roman-Dutch law. After all, it was the Dutch authors who handed over to Germany the torch of legal science which had been lit in Italy, and which then went to France before it reached the Netherlands.[10]

5.2 ROMAN-DUTCH LAW

After centuries of neglect, Roman law again became the object of serious study in Italy at the end of the eleventh century. Gradually its influence spread across Europe, and so the Netherlands, which was once part of the Roman Empire, also came to adopt this Roman *ius commune*.[11] In the seventeenth century significant progress was made: new universities and law faculties were founded, and authors like De Groot

7 Cf N R Whitty, "The civilian tradition and debates on Scots law" 1996 *TSAR* 227, 1996 *TSAR* 442.

8 Cf R Evans-Jones, "Some reflections on the condictio indebiti in a mixed legal system" (1994) 111 *SALJ* 759.

9 It has been said that "in language, method, structure, and concepts the BGB is the child of the deep, exact, and abstract learning of the German Pandectist School with all the advantages and disadvantages which that entails" (Zweigert and Kötz, *Introduction to Comparative Law*, 150).

10 F Wieacker, *Privatrechtgeschichte der Neuzeit*, 2nd ed (1967) 169.

11 Cf De Wet, *Die Ou Skrywers in Perspektief*, 78 et sqq, 99 et sqq, 109 et sqq.

and Voet[12] wrote works of such high merit that this century has come to be termed the golden age of Roman-Dutch jurisprudence.[13] Like the Institutional writers, these authors did not deal with Roman law in its "pure form", but rather Roman law which was integrated with local law and adapted to local needs.

5.2.1 *The content of* metus

Roman-Dutch law remained remarkably faithful to Roman law in its treatment of the content of *metus*.[14] The scope of cases where relief was provided was not broadened significantly, although there are indications of a movement away from a casuistic approach to one of greater abstraction and categorisation. Just as the Glossators and Canonists distinguished between *vis absoluta* and *vis compulsiva* (a division unknown to Roman law)[15] Voet drew a distinction between *vis absoluta*, and conditional force or *vis conditionalis*.[16] The former, according to Voet, excludes all consent—for example if something is taken away with such force that the owner still retains ownership, as in the case of robbery (*vi bonorum raptorum*).[17] Conditional force, or *vis conditionalis*, in turn, does not exclude consent, since actual force is not exerted, but only expected. Since *vis compulsiva* is nothing else than threatened force, it could therefore be equated to Voet's *vis conditionalis*.[18] But a description of *vis compulsiva* as threatened force does not say much about its content as a source of *metus*. Roman-Dutch legal sources still contain the familiar list of threats of harm which can give rise to *metus*. These threats mostly relate to personal physical harm.[19] Grotius, for example, cites the following cases of "vare" (*metus*) or "groote vreeze" (grave fear): fear of "dood" (death), "onteering" (violation),[20] "groote pijn" (severe pain) and "onwettelicke gevanckenisse" (illegal imprisonment).[21] Then again, there were certain types of fear which could never warrant relief. Most Roman-Dutch authors did not regard fear of economic harm as actionable. The only exceptions are Zoesius[22] and Van Leeuwen,[23] who also regarded fear of goods being lost (*metus ammissionis bonorum*) as actionable cases of *metus*. Furthermore, fear of dishonour (*infamia*), annoyance (*vexatio*) or

---

12 Johannes Voet (1647–1713) was professor of law in the University of Leyden. He also lectured to Scottish students, and has been quoted in works on Scots law (cf sources quoted at note 6 above).

13 Cf De Wet, *Die Ou Skrywers in Perspektief*, 125 et sqq.

14 This seems to have been the position in the *ius commune* in general. Cf Zimmermann, *The Law of Obligations*, 658 et sqq.

15 Cf 2.2.1 above.

16 Voet, *Commentarius ad Pandectas*, 4.2.1. The distinction is similar to that in Bankton, *Institute* 1.10.50.

17 On the remedies they give rise to, cf 5.2.2 below.

18 Cf Joubert, *General Principles of the Law of Contract*, 105 n 14.

19 As to the position in the *ius commune* in general, cf Zimmermann, *The Law of Obligations*, 659. He refers to a little mnemonic used for listing the various instances of fear of severe evil (*metus maior malitatis*), namely "excusat carcer, status, mors, verbera, stuprum".

20 Wessels indicates that the word might be used in the broader sense of dishonour (*The Law of Contract in South Africa*, vol 1, para 1883), but it rather seems to bear the narrower meaning of violation or stuprum.

21 *Inleidinge tot de Hollandsche Rechts-geleerdheid*, 3.48.6.

22 Zoesius, *Commentarius ad Digestorum seu Pandectarum*, 4th ed (Lovanii, 1688), 4.2 n 15. Cf also *Union Government (Minister of Finance) v Gowar* 1915 AD 246 at 451 et sq. Joubert describes this as an "isolated opinion" (*General Principles of the Law of Contract*, 106).

23 *Censura Forensis Theoretico-Practica* (Lugduni, 1741), 4.41.9 (cf Wessels, *The Law of Contract in South Africa*, vol 1, para 1175). Van Leeuwen makes these comments in the context of a discussion of the contract of marriage.

reverential fear (*metus reverentialis*)[24] were not generally regarded as sufficient grounds for a successful claim based on *metus*. But these are rather hackneyed lists and do not assist in determining what to do with borderline cases. In this regard it is instructive to examine Voet's views. He also provides a list similar to that of Grotius, but more importantly, states the general requirements that fear (a) has to be inspired in violation of good morals (*contra bonos mores*),[25] and (b) ought to be justifiable in the sense of being grievous enough (*iustum ... id est satis gravem*).[26] These requirements will now be dealt with in turn.

i. *Fear must be inspired illegally or* contra bonos mores[27]

According to Voet, fear has to be inspired in violation of good morals (*contra bonos mores*), and therefore unjustly (*injuste*). If a "just cause" (*justa causa*) was the basis of the inspiration of fear, relief could not be allowed. The requirement is not new—Ulpian mentions it[28]—but Voet does elevate it to greater prominence.[29] He discusses a few examples of such fear, and explicitly mentions that a contract should remain valid and not be rescinded on the ground of fear if the person who entered into it was brought to court by a physical summons of law, or was civilly imprisoned.[30]

ii. *Fear must be justifiable or* iustus

Roman law required that a certain measure of resoluteness should be displayed when faced with threats which instil fear. In Roman-Dutch law this requirement, which was encapsulated in the notion of the *vir constans* or the constant man, was retained.[31] However, it was recognised that some people are more easily made afraid than others, and that the law cannot ignore this difference. Voet mentions that the age, sex and standing of a person must be taken into consideration when assessing the seriousness of his or her fear.[32] It was apparently not sufficient merely to aver that a threat had been made: except in the case of threats of death, it had to be proved that the person who made the threat was in a position to carry it out and intended to do so.[33]

5.2.2 *The effect of* metus

The effect of *vis absoluta* was radical: anything taken away by *vis absoluta* could be recovered from *any* possessor by a direct *vindicatio rei*, "without the invocation of the extraordinary relief of restitution".[34] In other words, since ownership did not pass,

---

24 Cf Voet, *Commentarius ad Pandectas*, 4.2.11, 4.2.12 and 4.2.13. An exceptional case where relief was provided, was when a father influenced his child into making a contract on pain of disinheritance, or something equally as bad. Van Huyssteen indicates that in the South Netherlands the position in practice was not as strict as indicated by the authorities, and that the *actio quod metus causa* was provided in cases where there was exploitation of someone's need (*Onbehoorlike Beïnvloeding en Misbruik van Omstandighede in die Suid-Afrikaanse Verbintenisreg*, 60 et sq, 67; cf Van Leeuwen, *Het Roomsch Hollandsch Recht*, 4.42.4).

25 Voet, *Commentarius ad Pandectas*, 4.2.10.

26 Voet, *Commentarius ad Pandectas*, 4.2.11.

27 Cf in general P J J Olivier, "Onregmatige Vreesaanjaging" (1965) 28 *THRHR* 187 at 190 et sqq.

28 Ulp D 4.2.3.1 (see 2.2.2 below).

29 Cf Joubert, *General Principles of the Law of Contract*, 106.

30 Voet, *Commentarius ad Pandectas*, 4.2.10.

31 Voet, *Commentarius ad Pandectas*, 4.2.11; Van Leeuwen, *Censura Forensis* 4.41.1. But cf Grotius, *De Jure Belli ac Pacis*, 2.11.7.

32 Voet, *Commentarius ad Pandectas*, 4.2.11.

33 Voet, *Commentarius ad Pandectas*, 4.2.13.

34 Voet, *Commentarius ad Pandectas*, 4.2.1.

the victim could use this proprietary remedy to reclaim his property, and did not have to indicate that a duty to provide *restitutio in integrum* existed. Anything done under *vis absoluta* would also be void *ab initio*. The effect of *vis compulsiva* is more difficult to determine, and brings us back to the age old problem of whether *metus* is so serious that it gives rise to (automatic) voidness, or whether what is willed under compulsion is nonetheless willed, and therefore is valid until avoided.

i. Voidness and voidability

Although lip service was paid to Ulpian's view, contained in D 50.17.116, that "nothing is so opposed to consent as force and fear",[35] Roman-Dutch authors preferred Paulus's view that a person whose will is formed in fear has not acted involuntarily, and that his actions are therefore only voidable and not void.[36] This is apparent from Grotius's treatment of natural law,[37] as well as municipal law.[38] However, he also regards it as reasonable that satisfactory remedies should be provided for the victim who is bound to obligations obtained by fear.[39] Grotius therefore in effect recognises that under natural and municipal law *metus* did not automatically give rise to a defect in an obligation, but that the obligation would be valid until a remedy[40] is provided. It is therefore voidable and not void. Voet is much clearer on this issue: according to him, consent is present in acts performed in fear, and therefore they are not *ipso iure* void, but valid until set aside.[41] To this end an action for restitution, based on the Roman *actio quod metus causa*,[42] could be used. He further states that things done in fear may be ratified, be it tacitly or expressly.[43] This again indicates that fear gives rise to voidability and not voidness.[44] Unlike Grotius, Voet does not only refer

35 Voet, *Commentarius ad Pandectas*, 4.2.1.

36 Cf Joubert, *General Principles of the Law of Contract*, 105 n 12.

37 "On the whole I accept the opinion of those who think that the person that makes a promise under the influence of fear is bound by it, if the municipal law, which can annul or diminish an obligation, is not taken into consideration. For in such a case there is a consent, not conditional, as we just now said in regard to the person in error, but absolute" (*De Jure Belli ac Pacis* 2.11.7.2). However, he then adds that "[a]t the same time, this I think, is indubitably true, that if the person to whom the promise is made has inspired a fear, not just but unjust, even though slight [*metum ... non iustum, sed iniustum, quamvis levem*] and the promise has resulted therefrom, he is bound to release the promisor if the latter so wishes, not because the promise was without force [*non quod inefficax fuerit promissio*], but on account of the damage wrongfully caused [*sed ob damnum iniuria datum*]" (*De Jure Belli ac Pacis*, 2.11.7.2).

38 In his *Inleidinge*, Grotius turns to the municipal Roman-Dutch law and also states that obligations which are created due to fear do exist, because a forced will still remains a will ("om dat ghedwongen wille mede een wille is") (*Inleidinge tot de Hollandsche Rechts-geleerdheid*, 3.48.6).

39 *Inleidinge tot de Hollandsche Rechts-geleerdheid*, 3.48.6.

40 Cf 5.2.2.ii below.

41 *Commentarius ad Pandectas*, 4.2.2 ("Cum ergo illis, quae metu gesta, consensus adsit, consequens est, ut regulariter non ipso iure nulla sint, sed subsistant donec rescindantur"). However, Voet notes that there are a few exceptions to this rule: a promise of dowry, or marriage wrung out by fear would be *ipso iure* null (*Commentarius ad Pandectas*, 4.2.15).

42 *Commentarius ad Pandectas*, 4.2.3.

43 *Commentarius ad Pandectas*, 4.2.16.

44 Joubert states that the Roman-Dutch writers in general accepted that a contract induced by threats was not void, but voidable (*General Principles of the Law of Contract*, 105), but that the contrary view was held by Van der Linden (*Koopmans Handboek*, 1.14.2). Van der Linden states that when the consent of a contracting party is extorted by undue violence or fear, the contract is imperfect and invalid. He partly bases his views on De Groot, *Inleidinge tot de Hollandsche Rechts-geleerdheid*, 3.48.6, which does not provide authority, since De Groot only writes of ways in which obligations could be made without force ("krachteloos konnene werden gemaeckt"). This statement is not inconsistent with the view that *metus* leads to voidability.

to the effect of *metus* on the validity of obligations, but also discusses its effect on all acts, be it entering into a contract or making a transfer.[45]

ii. Restitutio in integrum

Having established that *metus* was a ground for relief, it now becomes necessary to determine what remedy could be used towards this purpose. It will be recalled that in Roman law, the relationship between the *actio quod metus causa* and *restitutio in integrum* as forms of praetorian relief is disputed. In Roman-Dutch law there is evidence of an assimilation of these rules: in general, it can be stated that *metus* or "vare" (fear) is a ground for an action of restitution. There are, however, indications that Grotius regarded *metus* as a delict.[46] It should be noted that these views are expressed in the context of a discussion of natural law, and that Grotius does not repeat them when he discusses municipal law.[47] In fact, in his *Inleidinge*, *metus* is dealt with in a title on "herstelling",[48] which can be regarded as the Dutch equivalent of *restitutio in integrum*.[49] Voet also states that in the case of fear an action for restitution (based on the Roman *actio quod metus causa*) is used.[50] It would therefore seem as if in municipal law the "suitable remedy" in cases of *metus* was an action aimed at obtaining *restitutio in integrum*.[51] The purpose of instituting this action is to obtain the setting aside of acts done under *metus*,[52] and to have the parties restored to a "fair position" by the magistrate.[53] Its aim was to "make a matter or cause whole again",[54] "to reset and restore a transaction to its original state",[55] or "to put all things back in their original condition".[56] It did not only entail giving back that which had been received, but also making up for the enjoyment of fruits and use (*weder-geving van vruchten ende ghenoten baten*), as well as compensation for damage (*vergoeding van*

45 Cf *White Brothers v Treasurer-General* 1883, 2 SC 322, where (in a discussion of Voet's views) it is recognised that the want of free consent on the part of the person entering into the contract, or making the payment, lies at the root of the rule which invalidates contracts or payments extorted by force or intimidation (at 350).

46 Cf the discussion of the possible influence on Stair at 3.3.1.i(a) above.

47 Cf 5.2.2.i above.

48 *Inleidinge tot de Hollandsche Rechts-geleerdheid*, 3.48.

49 *Inleidinge tot de Hollandsche Rechts-geleerdheid*, *Registers van Rechstermen*, 346.

50 *Commentarius ad Pandectas*, 4.2.3, 4.1.1 et sq.

51 Voet regards *metus* as "the first cause of restitution" or *prima causa restitutionis* (*Commentarius ad Pandectas*, 4.2.1). Cf also Van der Linden, *Koopmans Handboek*, 1.18.10; Van Leeuwen, *Het Roomsch Hollandsch Recht*, 4.42.

52 Grotius states that its purpose was to make the obligation without effect (*krachteloos*) by a mutual restoring of the positions the parties were in before the obligation was formed (*Inleidinge tot de Hollandsche Rechts-geleerdheid*, 3.48.5).

53 *Commentarius ad Pandectas*, 4.1.1. When Voet discusses *metus* in the next title, he uses the expression "... et suae restituantur aequitati per magistratum" (*Commentarius ad Pandectas*, 4.2.2). It is not clear what is meant by the use of the word *aequitati*, but it could relate to the so-called equitable discretion which the courts had in granting the remedy (cf Voet, *Commentarius ad Pandectas*, 4.1.1; Lambiris, *Orders of Specific Performance and Restitutio in Integrum in South African Law*, 192). It is a moot point whether it was really necessary to approach the courts for relief. In Roman law *bonae fidei* contracts would be *ipso iure* void if concluded because of *metus*. Could it then not be said that in Roman-Dutch law such contracts would be *ipso iure* void as well? Van der Keessel seems to say that theoretically this should be so, but that in practice it would be safer to approach the courts for *restitutio in integrum*. Cf his *Praelectiones iuris hodierni ad Hugonis Grotii introductionem ad iurisprudentiam Hollandicam*, 3.48.6.

54 *Commentarius ad Pandectas*, 4.1.1.

55 *Commentarius ad Pandectas*, 4.1.1. On *restitutio in integrum* in Roman-Dutch law in general, cf Lambiris, *Orders of Specific Performance and Restitutio in Integrum in South African Law*, 191 et sq.

56 *Commentarius ad Pandectas*, 4.1.21.

schade).[57] Unlike Roman law, Roman-Dutch law did not punish someone by ordering him to pay the fourfold if he refused to provide restitution: he would only be ordered to pay the single amount (*in simplum*).[58] The reason is important: by that time the action was not regarded as penal any more, but was directed at the recovery of the property—it was, as Voet puts it, *non poenalis sed rei persecutoria*.[59]

The right to claim restitution was subject to certain limitations. First, there was no restitution[60] if the person who acted under fear sustained no loss. If a creditor privately seized a debtor's goods and so doing took the law into his own hands, he did not lose his right to claim payment. Voet also stated that he could not be forced to repay with the *condictio indebiti* if repayment had taken place.[61] However, this did not mean he would go unpunished: he would have to pay the debtor damages and could also be punished by the judge in accordance with degree of violence used.[62] Second, the person claiming restitution had to give back what he received under the transaction. Thus, if A compelled B to buy his home and B then paid A the price, B had to return the home in order to reclaim the payment.[63]

iii. Indirect enrichment

As in Roman law, the general position in Roman-Dutch law was that an action based on fear could be granted against the person who caused the fear, as well as all possessors of the thing lost through fear, whether they are in good or bad faith.[64]

5.2.3 *Compulsion and the* condictiones *in Roman-Dutch law*

Thus far the focus has been on the role of the action for restitution in providing relief to victims of *metus*. But the examination of Roman law has shown that other

57 *Inleidinge tot de Hollandsche Rechts-geleerdheid*, 3.48.5.

58 Cf Groenewegen, *Tractatus de legibus abrogatis*, ad Codex 2.19(2).4; Van der Keessel, *Praelectiones iuris hodierni*, 3.18.6. There was not only a duty to return the actual thing lost through fear, but also fruits received, consumed and to be received (Voet, *Commentarius ad Pandectas*, 4.2.7).

59 *Commentarius ad Pandectas*, 4.2.18. Cf also *Commentarius ad Pandectas*, 4.2.8, which contains the somewhat confusing expression that judgment is not given for the fourfold nowadays, *sed tantum in id quod interest condemnatio interponi solet* (i.e for damages only). This text is found in the context of the loss of the object sought to be reclaimed. It therefore seems that if the object still existed, restitution would have to be provided. But if it has been lost after judgment (as opposed to being sold or transferred by onerous title) the possessor would have to make good the damage of the claimant (*Commentarius ad Pandectas*, 4.2.8).

60 Gane's translation of "Rescissione opus non est"—which seems to be preferable to the more literal translation "no rescission" (625).

61 *Commentarius ad Pandectas*, 12.6.2. However, Voet adds the reservation that "an action is to be kept in readiness for the debtor who pays, if he in any way has an interest in the exaction not having been made in a fashion which cannot be approved". Unfortunately, he does not state under what circumstances such an "interest" would exist.

62 *Commentarius ad Pandectas*, 4.2.17.

63 *Commentarius ad Pandectas*, 4.2.9.

64 *Commentarius ad Pandectas*, 4.2.4. Cf also Joubert, *General Principles of the Law of Contract*, 109. Van Leeuwen maintains that the action is available against third parties in possession of compelled transfers, "after they have refused to give it up, knowing that it has been taken from us by violence or intimidation ("Datur haec actio omnibus qui metu quid amiserunt, non tantum adversus eum qui ab initio metum intulit, sed etiam adversus omnes, qui rem per vim aut metum nobis ablatam, aut extortam possident, postquam sciente rem nobis vi aut metu ablatam restituere recusaverint", *Censura Forensis* 1.4.41.9, Part I Book IV, 278). Once the victim claims relief from the third party, this knowledge follows automatically, and the conclusion is therefore that it did not matter whether the third party initially received in good faith or not (cf Joubert, *General Principles of the Law of Contract*, 110; De Wet and Van Wyk, *Die Suid-Afrikaanse Kontraktereg en Handelsreg*, 50).

legal instruments could also be used to provide victims of compulsion with relief. For present purposes the most notable of these instruments were the *condictiones*, and it is therefore appropriate also to examine whether they fulfiled a similar purpose in Roman-Dutch law.[65]

i. The condictio ob turpem vel iniustam causam

In his discussion of the Roman-Dutch law of unjustified enrichment, Professor Wouter de Vos observes that although Roman and Roman-Dutch law had different systems of procedure, this did not mean that the traditional enrichment actions known to Roman law underwent any significant changes in their content.[66] However, there were certain changes in the Roman-Dutch law of contract which at least created the potential for a change in the future fields of application of the *condictiones*. It will be recalled that Roman law only recognised a limited number of contracts, and that the *condictio ob turpem vel iniustam causam* was used to reclaim certain transfers which were not made on the basis of these recognised contracts, but in order to elicit a future counterperformance (*ob rem*). It will also be recalled that the *condictio causa data causa non secuta* could not be used to effect recovery of transfers tainted by turpitude (*ob rem turpem*) once the purpose of the parties was in fact effected by performance. However, in Roman-Dutch law the suitability of this scheme was challenged when the principle was accepted that a "mere" agreement is actionable (*ex nudo pacto oritur actio*).[67] This implied that a transfer made pursuant to an immoral or illegal agreement (a *pactum illicitum*) could be regarded as a transfer aimed at discharging an obligation created by such an agreement. Thus, if an agreement was void because of immorality or illegality, the parties should have been able to use the *condictiones indebiti* or *sine causa*[68] to reclaim performance. To retain the *condictio ob turpem vel iniustam causam* as an independent remedy in this context therefore became

---

65 The different fields of application of (real) vindicatory remedies and the *condictiones* in Roman-Dutch law cannot be dealt with here in further detail. Suffice it to say that in general, when a moveable has been delivered *sine causa*, an enrichment action was granted, on the ground that it would no longer be possible to grant a vindicatory remedy (*rei vindicatio*) once ownership had passed (cf Grotius, *Inleidinge tot de Hollandsche Rechts-geleerdheid*, 3.30.18; Voet, *Commentarius ad Pandectas* 12.6.1, 12.6.12; Carey Miller, *The Acquisition and Protection of Ownership*, 126). But this general rule was subject to an exception: fraud could affect the validity of the real agreement by which ownership should pass (cf J E Scholtens, "Justa causa traditionis and contracts induced by fraud" (1957) 74 *SALJ* 280 at 285). No authority dealing specifically with this issue in the context of *metus* could be found, but since it was generally agreed that agreements concluded on grounds of *metus* were voidable, and not void, it would seem as if ownership did indeed pass and that a vindicatory remedy could not be granted. The primary remedy would then be *restitutio in integrum*.

66 De Vos, *Verrykingsaanspreeklikheid in die Suid-Afrikaanse reg*, 61. He observes that the various enrichment actions were still referred to by name, even though this was procedurally no longer required.

67 Cf *Commentarius ad Pandectas*, 2.14.9 (Voet criticised Simon van Leeuwen for not recognising this position in his *Censura Forensis* 1.4.2 n 2). Cf, generally, De Vos, *Verrykingsaanspreeklikheid in die Suid-Afrikaanse reg*, 62 n 1 and authorities cited there; R Feenstra, "Pact and Contract in the Low Countries from the 16th to the 18th century" in Barton (ed), *Towards a General Law of Contract*, 197; R Feenstra, "Klagbarkeit der pacta nuda" in R Feenstra and R Zimmermann (eds), *Das römisch-holländische Recht—Fortschritte des Zivilrechts im 17. und 18. Jahrhundert*, 123 at 143 et sq; R Zimmermann, "Roman-Dutch Jurisprudence and its Contribution to European Private Law" (1992) 66 *TulaneLR* 1685 at 1689 et sqq; Simpson, *Die Rückabwicklung von sitten—und rechtswidrigen Rechtsgeschäften im heutigen deutschen und schottischen Recht*, ch 3.

68 Cf Zimmermann, *The Law of Obligations*, 862 et sq.; and generally Reuter and Martinek, *Ungerechtfertigte Bereicherung*, 175 et sq.

questionable. Furthermore, it will be recalled that in Roman law, the *condictio ob turpem vel iniustam causam* was only applied when recovering a transfer made pursuant to a *stricti iuris* transaction, such as a *stipulatio*.[69] If the transaction was bona fide, the compulsion rendered the transaction ineffective in any event and the judge could, for example, deny enforcement. In Roman-Dutch law this distinction was obsolete. Insofar as all contracts could now be regarded as bona fide, remedies such as the *condictio ob turpem vel iniustam causam* which were linked to *stricti iuris* transactions were no longer necessary to effect recovery of extorted transfers.[70]

However, the Roman-Dutch authors did not readily accept these implications of the rise of *ex nudo pacto oritur actio* and the recognition of the bona fide basis of contracts. They retained the *condictio ob turpem vel iniustam causam*, accompanied by its historical adjunct, the *in pari delicto* or *in pari turpitudine*-rule.[71] There was some debate as to whether the action was simple, or twofold in nature, i.e. whether there was only a *condictio ob turpem vel iniustam causam*, or whether there was a *condictio ob turpem causam* as well as a *condictio ob iniustam causam*. Although the majority opinion seems to be that the distinction was unnecessary[72] (Grotius, for example, only refers to a *condictio* for "all cases where something has been given for an illegal or dishonest cause"),[73] a notable author such as Voet draws a distinction between the *condictio ob turpem causam* and the *condictio ob injustam causam*.[74]

It is then against this background that the applicability of the *condictio ob turpem vel iniustam causam* to cases of compulsion will be examined. Here the following

---

69 This is also recognised by Voet. After saying that the *condictio ob turpem causam* is available where someone has to pay for the return of something which is due to him in any case, Voet states that "In *bonae fidei* transactions, however, what has been given with a view to restoration can also be reclaimed by action on the contract itself, and thus such actions may run together with this action on a base cause, a thing which does not happen in transactions *stricti iuris*" (*Commentarius ad Pandectas*, 12.5.1). Thus, if someone is contractually bound to return something in terms of a *bonae fidei* transaction, he could in any event reclaim that which has been given with a view to restoration. The *condictio ob turpem vel iniustam causam* is then a concurrent, but apparently superfluous remedy.

70 Voet himself acknowledges that, "by the usage of all nations, if not all, at least the more noteworthy, differences which were encouraged by the Roman law between proceedings *bonae fidei* and those *stricti iuris*, have become obsolete and are wont to be little heeded" (*Commentarius ad Pandectas*, 2.4.20; cf also *Commentarius ad Pandectas*, 22.1.11; Groenewegen, *Tractatus de legibus abrogatis*, *ad Inst*. 4.6.28; *contra* Van der Keessel, *Praelectiones*, *ad Inleiding* 3.1.46; *Tuckers Land and Development Corporation v Hovis* 1980 (1) SA (A) at 651 et sq). However, he does not discuss what "action on the contract" could be used for recovery in Roman-Dutch law (cf *Commentarius ad Pandectas*, 12.5.1).

71 On this rule in Roman-Dutch law, cf D P Visser, "Das recht der ungerechtfertigten Bereicherung" in Feenstra and Zimmermann (eds), *Das römisch-holländische Recht—Fortschritte des Zivilrechts im 17. und 18. Jahrhundert*, 369 at 412 et sq.; De Vos, *Verrykingsaanspreeklikheid in die Suid-Afrikaanse reg*, 68. The traditional view is that a relaxation of this rule was not possible. But also see Visser at 413.

72 Cf De Vos, *Verrykingsaanspreeklikheid in die Suid-Afrikaanse reg*, 66 et sqq; Visser "Das recht der ungerechtfertigten Bereicherung" in Feenstra and Zimmermann (eds), *Das römisch-holländische Recht—Fortschritte des Zivilrechts im 17. und 18. Jahrhundert*, 369 at 409.

73 *Inleidinge tot de Hollandsche Rechts-geleerdheid*, 3.30.17 ("alle 't gunt iemand heeft gegeven om een onrechtmatighe ofte andersins oneerlicke zake"). Cf also De Vos, *Verrykingsaanspreeklikheid in die Suid-Afrikaanse reg*, 22. Visser formulates its purpose in Roman-Dutch law somewhat differently, namely to obtain the retransfer of all transfers whose *acceptance* was tainted with turpitude, be it due to a special law or any other reason ("Das recht der ungerechtfertigten Bereicherung" in Feenstra and Zimmermann (eds), *Das römisch-holländische Recht—Fortschritte des Zivilrechts im 17. und 18. Jahrhundert*, 369 at 409).

74 *Commentarius ad Pandectas*, 12.5.1 et sqq.

general divisions can be made of the various ways in which the *condictio ob turpem vel iniustam causam* (whether in its split or unified form), could be used to effect recovery in cases of compulsion. The first two examples can be regarded as belonging to the *condictio ob turpem causam*, which was used to reclaim ("*repetitur*") what has been given on account of an act involving turpitude on the side of the receiver in such a way that the party suing is not tainted by the turpitude.[75] The third example can be regarded as belonging to the *condictio ob iniustam causam*, which was an action by which that is reclaimed which was given, or otherwise found in the hands of another, on a cause which does not involve particular turpitude, but has nevertheless been disapproved of by law.[76] The cause is then not a future one, as in the case of the transfer *ob turpem causam*, but rather a past one.[77]

(a) Transfers made pursuant to threats of harmful delictual or criminal conduct

According to Voet, the *condictio ob turpem causam* was available for the recovery of something transferred due to threats of false accusations, *injuria* or actionable wrong and theft.[78] These situations generally involve threats of harmful delictual or criminal conduct. Due to the relatively restricted scope of the action for restitution based on *metus*, the *condictio ob turpem causam* apparently was regarded as a suitable remedy for relief in these cases of compulsion. However, this does not mean that the action for restitution based on *metus* was excluded whenever compulsion was accompanied by turpitude. According to Voet, this action could be used by the victim, "whether involved in a lawful matter while acting under fear, or spending his time on something unlawful".[79]

(b) Transfers made to ensure performance of a duty

The second group of examples deal with the cases where something has been given

> ... with a view to something being restored or done which ought as a matter of course to be restored or done. I mean, say, something given to a depositary,[80] borrower for use, lessor, seller, mandatary, heir under a last will who is bound as regards a legacy, promisor who is bound under stipulation as regards a thing promised, and such like persons who, in order that they may restore the things deposited, lent for use, leased,

75 *Commentarius ad Pandectas*, 12.5.1 ("Condictio ob turpem causam est actio personalis stricti iuris, qua repetitur quod datum est ob factum continens turpitudinem ex parte accipientis, ita ut condicens turpitudinis expers sit ...").

76 *Commentarius ad Pandectas* 12.5.4 ("... actione scilicet personali, qua repetitur id, quod datum fuit, aut aliter penes alium est ob causam, nullam quidem turpitudinem specialem continentem, sed tamen jure civili improbatam").

77 *Commentarius ad Pandectas*, 12.5.4.

78 *Commentarius ad Pandectas*, 12.5.1. Voet drew the example of the lawsuit from D 3.6.5.1, which falls under a title dealing with vexatious litigants.

79 *Commentarius ad Pandectas*, 4.2.3 ("... sive in re licita versatus fuerit, dum metum patiebatur, sive illicito vacaret negotio"). Cf also Huber, *Heedensdaegse Rechtsgeleertheyt*, 4.32.8. If there was no such intimidation, and a person paid another not to make his shameful conduct known, he would not be able to reclaim (*Commentarius ad Pandectas*, 4.2.3). In this regard, Voet refers to D 12.5.4, which deals with the *condictio ob turpem causam*. However, this does not indicate that he meant the *condictio ob turpem causam* should be made available in this case. His remarks are clearly made in the context of the availability of the action for restitution.

80 These statements are based on D 12.5.2.1 according to which a *condictio* lies "in the case where I pay to make you give me back something deposited with you, a document for instance" ("si tibi dedero, ut rem mihi reddas depositam apud te vel instrumentum mihi redderes").

or found in their hands under cause of mandate, or deliver the things sold, or pay the things bequeathed or promised.[81]

In each of these cases, a person refuses to act unless the victim gives him something while being under no obligation to do so. It should be apparent, though, that some of the examples referred to above fit in rather uncomfortably with the notion of immorality or unlawfulness—can the situation where someone refuses to return a deposit really be regarded as similar to the more conventional cases of turpitude such as betting, holding lotteries, prostitution and the corrupting of officials?[82] To the extent that Voet is reflecting the position in Roman-Dutch law, and not only Roman law, it is apparent that both systems experienced similar problems: *metus* or duress mainly involved threats of physical harm, and the law still had to develop to cover these cases of economic compulsion. As in Roman law, Roman Dutch law therefore found it convenient to emphasise the "immoral" nature of the compelled transfer to justify providing relief in the form of the *condictio ob turpem causam*.

(c) Transfers made under an extorted agreement

The third example which Voet mentions is when something is reclaimed which has been paid on a stipulation extorted by force. The example clearly is taken from Roman law.[83] Insofar as the principle was still applicable to Roman-Dutch law of his time, it indicates a rather unnecessary concurrence between the action for restitution based on *metus* and the *condictio ob (turpem vel) iniustam causam*. However, it may well be that Voet was in fact only referring to the position in Roman law: Groenewegen, for example, indicates that an action for restitution was appropriate and not a *condictio ob turpem vel iniustam causam*.[84]

An interesting question which now arises is whether, given the developments in the law of contract, it was appropriate to apply the *condictio ob (turpem vel) iniustam causam* to the above cases of compulsion. The answer depends on the seriousness of the compulsion and its effect on the transfer as well as any agreement underlying it. Where the compulsion was serious enough to justify relief on grounds of *metus* (category (c)), the *condictio* was for all intents and purposes unnecessary. On the other hand, where the compulsion was not so serious (categories (a) to (b)) another remedy was required. Here the *condictio ob turpem vel iniustam causam* is an attractive remedy insofar as a transfer made to the extorter with the purpose that he would not make false accusations, or that he would return your goods, etc., could be regarded as being made *ob rem*. Such a transfer has as its purpose the avoiding of the threatened harm. But there is an alternative: the transfer could be regarded as a failed transfer made with the purpose of discharging a debt (*solvendi causa*). Here one enters the terrain of the *condictio indebiti*.

ii. The condictio indebiti

In Roman-Dutch law, the *condictio indebiti* could be used to recover an undue transfer or *datio*[85] made in error as to liability.[86] However, some difference of opinion

81 *Commentarius ad Pandectas*, 12.5.1.

82 On these examples, cf Visser "Ungerechtfertigte Bereicherung" in Feenstra and Zimmermann (eds), *Das römisch-holländische Recht—Fortschritte des Zivilrechts im 17. und 18. Jahrhundert*, 369 at 409.

83 Cf D 12.5.7; see 2.3.2 above.

84 Groenewegen, *Tractatus de Legibus Abrogatis*, 12.5.

85 Cf Visser, "Das recht der ungerechtfertigten Bereicherung" in Feenstra and Zimmermann (eds), *Das römisch-holländische Recht—Fortschritte des Zivilrechts im 17. und 18. Jahrhundert*, 369 at 409; De Vos, *Verrykingsaanspreeklikheid in die Suid-Afrikaanse reg*, 23 et sq, 69 et sq; Zimmermann, *The*

existed among the authors as to the relevance of error. To Voet[87] and Vinnius,[88] who regarded the existence of a quasi-contract as the foundation of the *condictio indebiti*, proof of error was essential. To others, such as Grotius, who regarded the idea of enrichment as the foundation of the *condictio indebiti*, error does not seem to have been regarded as essential. It was rather said that recovery of an *indebitum* should be excluded where it looked like someone intended to make a gift.[89] The applicability of the *condictio indebiti* to cases of compulsion, where the transferor clearly knew that a transfer was not due,[90] yet also did not intend to donate, was therefore unclear. The positions can be summarised briefly as follows: (1) The *condictio indebiti* obviously applied to the situation where both parties thought that a debt was due.[91] This included the situation where someone doubted whether he was indebted.[92] (2) If the transferor did not know a debt was not due, but the transferee did, the *condictio indebiti* could also be used. There was also support for the idea that a personal action based on theft—the *condictio furtiva*—could be used.[93] (3) If the transferor knew that no debt was due, but the transferee did not, no *condictio* would be available. The transferor would then be understood to have made a donation.[94] (4) If both knew the debt was not due, it could be assumed that a donation was intended,[95] and that recovery would not be possible. However, such an assumption was obviously not justified in cases of compulsion. For those who regarded error as an essential feature of the *condictio indebiti*, this did not matter. Knowledge excluded error, and alternative remedies such as the action for restitution and the *condictio ob turpem vel iniustam causam* had to do the work. But this should not have presented a problem to others, such as Grotius, who did not regard error as an essential feature of the *condictio indebiti*.

Law of Obligations, 848; T Honoré, "Condictio and Payment" 1958 *AJ* 135; Lotz, "Enrichment" in Joubert (ed), *The Law of South Africa*, vol 9, para 67. Lotz points out that the *condictio indebiti* was not only available in cases of a *datio* in the strict sense of the term; it could cover a *res incorporalis* and perhaps even a *factum*. The burden of proof was on the pursuer (Voet, *Commentarius ad Pandectas*, 12.6.14). There was a presumption in favour of the receiver, "since a payer is not believed to be so very slack as readily to throw away his moneys and to squander them when they are not due".

86 For present purposes it is unnecessary to deal with the debate in Roman-Dutch law as to whether one should distinguish between errors in fact or of law. The majority of authors seemed to believe that no distinction should be made, and that it only needs to be proven that an undue payment was made in error. It was also not required that the error should be excusable, a notable exception being Voet (cf Visser, *Die rol van dwaling by die condictio indebiti*, 323). One of the authors, Arnoldus Vinnius uses an interesting argument to support this opinion: someone who makes a transfer under fear is not barred from claiming simply because he did not know that he could raise an *exceptio quod metus causa*; on the same account, if someone transferred something not due acting under an "other" error of law, he should also be able to reclaim (*Commentarius ad Inst.* 3.28.6; cf Visser, "Ungerechtfertigte Bereicherung" in Feenstra and Zimmermann (eds), *Das römisch-holländische Recht—Fortschritte des Zivilrechts im 17. und 18. Jahrhundert*, 369 at 397).

87 Voet, *Commentarius ad Pandectas*, 44.7.5.

88 Vinnius, *Commentarius ad Inst*, 3.28(27)6.

89 *Inleidinge tot de Hollandsche Rechts-geleerdheid*, 3.30.6; cf Visser, *Die rol van dwaling by die condictio indebiti*, 151.

90 Cf Visser, *Die rol van dwaling by die condictio indebiti*, 323.

91 *Commentarius ad Pandectas*, 12.6.6.

92 *Commentarius ad Pandectas*, 12.6.6 (based on C 4.5.11).

93 *Commentarius ad Pandectas*, 12.6.6.

94 *Commentarius ad Pandectas*, 12.6.6 (based on D 50.17.53; D 12.6.50).

95 *Commentarius ad Pandectas*, 12.6.6.

5.3 SOUTH AFRICAN LAW

Unlike Roman and Roman-Dutch law, modern South African law draws a clear distinction between the content and effect of compulsion in a contractual and non-contractual context. This section first will deal with the content of certain forms of compulsion, and with their effect on the recoverability of transfers made in a contractual setting. Various contractual remedies will be discussed. The focus will then shift to transfers made in a non-contractual context, with particular attention being paid to remedies based on unjustified enrichment.

5.3.1 *The content of* metus *or duress in a contractual context*

It is a general principle of South African contract law that consent should be obtained in a proper manner. Duress (*vis compulsiva*) is then regarded as one of the improper ways of obtaining consent.[96] The content of *vis absoluta*, where there is no consent at all, is by and large the same as in Roman-Dutch law.[97] Here the focus will be on the content of the practically more important phenomenon of duress, which has undergone significant changes in modern South African law. The *locus classicus* is *Broodryk v Smuts NO*.[98] In this case it was stated that proof of the following "elements" is necessary to set aside a contract on the ground of duress.

1. Actual violence or reasonable fear.
2. The fear must be caused by the threat of some considerable evil to the party or his family.
3. It must be the threat of an imminent or inevitable evil.
4. The threat or intimidation must be *contra bonos mores*.
5. The moral pressure used must have caused damage.[99]

Each of these "elements", which are derived from Roman, Roman-Dutch and English law,[100] presents problems. First, it is not clear why a distinction is drawn between "actual violence" and "reasonable fear". If "actual violence" is intended to be *vis absoluta*, it should be dealt with separately: after all, the other "elements" are then irrelevant. If "actual violence" is not intended to be *vis absoluta*, but some less serious form of violence, it is difficult to conceive why it should be contrasted with "reasonable fear": fear caused by such violence should certainly be regarded as reasonable. It is therefore apparent that the first "element" of duress essentially only requires that the fear should be reasonable.[101] Similar problems surround the second and third "elements", which require that the fear should be caused by a

---

96 Cf, generally, Van der Merwe et al, *Contract—General Principles*, 85. Duress is known as "dwang" or "vreesaanjaging" in Afrikaans, and has also been referred to as *vis conditionalis* (cf Wessels, *The Law of Contract in South Africa*, vol 1, para 1166). For an indication of the position of duress in the broader context of voidable contracts, cf G F Lubbe, "Voidable Contracts", in R Zimmermann and D Visser (eds), *Southern Cross—Civil Law and Common Law in South Africa* (1996), 261.

97 Cf 5.2.1 above; Olivier, "Onregmatige Vreesaanjaging" (1965) 28 *THRHR* 187. Relief would also be provided if the victim's will was in fact excluded by the temporary deprivation of contractual capacity (cf *Smith v Smith* 1948 (4) SA 61 (N); Lubbe and Murray, *Contract*, 362).

98 1942 TPD 47.

99 *Broodryk v Smuts NO* 1942 TPD 47 at 51 et sq.

100 Cf Wessels, *The Law of Contract in South Africa*, vol 1, para 1167.

101 Cf the judgment of Corbett J (as he then was) in *Arend v Astra Furnishers (Pty) Ltd* 1974 (1) SA 298 (C).

threat of "considerable" and "imminent or inevitable" evil. The centrality of a threat is obvious,[102] but it is not at all clear why it is required that the fear should be reasonable, *and* that the evil or harm should be "considerable" and "imminent or inevitable". This seems superfluous, for it is difficult to perceive any purpose for asking whether the threatened evil was "considerable", "imminent" or "inevitable" other than to determine whether the fear was reasonable. Thus, it would seem that these qualifications of the threatened harm are unnecessary and that the first three elements in essence only require a threat of harm causing reasonable fear. According to some authors, it should not even be required that the fear be reasonable, for it would be anomalous if the person who causes another to act under duress could claim that such a person should not have been frightened so easily.[103] However, this problem seems to be more academic than real. Even though reasonable fear is still required by the courts, it hardly seems to constitute a serious hurdle in the way of the person claiming fear—in fact, little remained of the once lofty *homo constantissimus* standard.[104] Before moving on to the fourth element of duress, the fifth "element", which requires that the moral pressure must have caused damage, can briefly be dealt with. This element has been criticised as being unnecessary[105] and of little independent practical relevance. The presence of damage rather helps to prove wrongful conduct or the existence of a causal link between the threatened harm and the induced conduct.[106]

Thus far it has been shown that in essence it is only required that there had to be reasonable fear, which was caused by a threat, and that not too much should be made of the requirement of "reasonable fear". The same cannot be said of the fourth "element", namely that the threat had to be *contra bonos mores* or illegal. In determining the illegality of the threat, South African law follows a broader approach than Roman-Dutch law: it is now clearly acknowledged that the threatened harm could be personal[107] as well as proprietal.[108] The concept "duress of goods" is then sometimes used to describe threats directed at someone's property in order to induce him to enter into an agreement.[109] However, initially "duress of goods" did

---

102 Cf e.g. 5.2.1 above.

103 De Wet and Van Wyk, *Kontraktereg en Handelsreg*, 45; Kahn et al, *Contract and Mercantile Law: A Source Book*, 343.

104 *Block v Drogon, Dreier & Co* 1910 WLD 330 serves as an example. Here Block, a bookkeeper at Drogon, Dreier & Co, was threatened by its representatives with prosecution for theft of money if he did not return some notes given to him as salary. He then handed the notes to the representatives, and later reclaimed them. An independent audit revealed that there was no theft. The court found that the impression Block gave was that he was "an ignorant and stupid man" (at 332). Nonetheless, these weaknesses, which must have had a bearing on his lack of resolution in defending himself against the baseless charges, were not held against him, and he was granted relief.

105 Cf Joubert, *General Principles of the Law of Contract*, 109.

106 Cf Lubbe and Murray, *Contract*, 365.

107 The fear of personal harm could be fear of personal physical harm (cf *Freedman v Kruger* 1906 TS 817, which dealt with fear brought about by wrongful arrest and assault), but could also be fear of harm to personal reputation (cf *Steiger v Union Government* (1919) 40 NLR 75—fear of stigma and disgrace attached to dismissal from the civil service—at 81 et sq).

108 Cf De Wet and van Wyk, *Kontraktereg en Handelsreg*, 45. They state that there is no need to distinguish between these two cases, since the important issue is only whether the conduct in question is unlawful.

109 Cf *Hendricks v Barnett* 1975 (1) SA 765 (N). As mentioned before, a distinction must be drawn between "duress of goods" in a contractual and a non-contractual setting. In the latter case the remedies are not contractual, but based on unjustified enrichment. Cf 5.3.3.ii below; Joubert, *General Principles of the law of Contract*, 107; Van der Merwe et al, *Contract—General Principles*, 90.

not affect the validity of a contract. In *White Bros v Treasurer-General*,[110] the Chief Justice of the Cape, Sir Henry de Villiers (as he then was) examined the English and Roman-Dutch authorities and held that the relevant English principles were the same as those of the Civil Law. He concluded that a threat to take or injure property would not amount to duress sufficient to avoid a contract, although such "duress of goods" could be sufficient to allow for a claim to return a payment as long as it was accompanied by some "unequivocal act on the part of the person paying to show that the payment was not a voluntary one".[111] Such an act of protest, however, would not be necessary in cases of "menaces to the person". This remained the position for some years: "duress of goods" accompanied by an act of protest would be sufficient to allow reclaiming a payment which already was known not to be due. It would not be sufficient, though, to avoid a contract and enable recovery of a payment made in terms of such a contract—such a payment would be regarded as due.[112] The position changed almost a century later, when it was accepted in *Hendricks v Barnett*[113] that a contract could also be set aside on the ground of duress of goods or economic duress.[114] However, it was further held that in cases of duress of goods it is necessary to show an *unequivocal protest*.[115] The protest requirement, which formed part of the law relating to the reclaim of undue payments, therefore became a requirement for setting aside a contract. However, more recent authority seems to be moving away from this position.[116] In fact, it seems as if there is no reason to treat duress of goods

110 1883, 2 SC 322.

111 *White Bros v Treasurer-General* 1883, 2 SC 322 at 351. Cf also the judgment of De Villiers CJ in *Benning v Union Government* 1914 AD 420 at 423.

112 Cf *Union Government (Minister of Finance) v Gowar* 1915 AD 416 at 433. For a comparable rule in English law cf *Skeate v Beale* (1841) 11 Ad & E 910.

113 1975 (1) SA 765 (N).

114 The facts of the case are briefly as follows. Barnett used to be the owner of a dairy and racehorse stud farm and Hendricks, an expert horse-breeder, was his manager. Barnett sold his farm, but Hendricks agreed to remain in his employ until the bloodstock was sold by auction. Barnett left the management of the stud farm largely in Hendricks's hands, and needed Hendricks at the auction to help him identify the individual horses to the satisfaction of prospective buyers. He then promised to pay Hendricks a bonus upon termination of his employment, which was to be after the sale. Four days before the auction was to take place, Hendricks threatened to leave Barnett's employment unless Barnett paid him an adequate bonus. Since Barnett knew that without Hendricks's help the auction could not take place, and that he would suffer financial loss, he gave Hendricks two cheques—one due immediately and the other post-dated. After the auction, Barnett stopped payment of the post-dated cheque, upon which Hendricks applied for provisional sentence. Barnett's defence was then that he acted under duress when he agreed to give the cheque. In his judgment, Hoexter J then made the following notable comment: "Where a litigant seeks restitution *metus causa* a distinction must be drawn between the case where the *metus* resides in a threat to his person and the case where the improper pressure is exerted through duress of goods. The distinction relates to the matter of proof rather than to the actual ingredients of the cause of action, but it is an important one" (*Hendricks v Barnett* 1975 (1) SA 765 (N) at 768H–769A).

115 *Hendricks v Barnett* 1975 (1) SA 765 (N) at 769F. Affirmed without further consideration in *Kapp v TC Valuta (Pty) Ltd* 1975 (3) SA 283 (T).

116 Cf *Savvides v Savvides* 1986 (2) SA 325 (TPD). Mr Savvides, who had left his wife and family, stipulated that he would only return to his family after his wife signed a power of attorney nominating him to transfer ownership of the family home, which was registered in her name. She then signed a document to this effect, and later attempted to have it set aside on the ground of duress. It was held that the husband's threats of harm (inter alia financial) which might befall her if he did not return, lead her to act under duress, and that the document should be set aside (331H–I). "Economic duress", as a broader category than "duress of goods", encompassing all illegal threats of economic harm, has not been explicitly recognised.

as a separate category of duress at all. As some writers put it: "Insofar as it (duress of goods) refers to a threat directed at the property of the contractant, it must be treated like a threat directed at any other protected interest."[117]

The overview of the content of the requirement that threats have to be illegal can be concluded by mentioning that an illegal threat is not only a threat of unlawful action, but also arises when a threat of lawful action is made to obtain a result to which the person who exerts the duress is not reasonably entitled under the circumstances. This can be gathered from cases dealing with threats of criminal prosecution.[118] Of course, if such threats give rise to illegal agreements,[119] such as those of compounding, they would in any case be void for illegality.[120] It is not quite clear how these two grounds for relief could co-exist, although they could presumably be pleaded in the alternative. Surely, once it has been established that an agreement is illegal, and that no obligations ever existed, it would be illogical to have regard to the issue of duress, which is only of importance in the context of avoiding already existing obligations.[121] As far as threats of civil proceedings are concerned, it would seem as if such threats are normally regarded as acceptable.[122] The courts have not recently dealt with this issue, but it could well be that they would have to depart from this established position.[123]

Finally, although this element or requirement is not mentioned in *Broodryk v Smuts*, it sometimes is said that fault in the form of *dolus* (intent) or *culpa* (negligence) should be a requirement for relief on grounds of duress.[124] It is submitted that this view, for which there is little authority, stems from a failure to separate the contractual and delictual dimensions of duress.[125] For contractual relief it is only necessary to meet the requirements mentioned above; a claim in delict has to satisfy the requirements of the Aquilian action,[126] namely (a) conduct, (b) wrongfulness, (c) fault, (d) causation and (e) damage.[127]

---

117 Van der Merwe et al, *Contract—General Principles*, 90.

118 Cf Van der Merwe et al, *Contract—General Principles*, 87 et sqq, in particular the discussion of the supposed conflict between various provincial divisions on this issue.

119 See, generally, Lubbe and Murray, *Contract*, 237 et sqq

120 According to Corbett J (as he then was), "... generally speaking a contract induced by the threat of criminal prosecution is unenforceable on the ground of duress and, in certain instances, also on the ground that it involves the compounding of a crime and the stifling of prosecution" (*Arend v Astra Furnishers (Pty) Ltd* 1974 (1) SA 298 (C) at 311); cf J S McLennan, "General Principles of Contract" 1971 *Annual Survey of South African Law*, 106.

121 Cf J R Harker, "The Effect of a Threat of Criminal Prosecution on Contract" (1977) 40 *THRHR* 139 at 145; De Wet and Van Wyk, *Kontraktereg en Handelsreg*, 44.

122 Cf *Houtappel v Kersten* 1940 EDL 221; *Kruger v Sekretaris van Binnelandse Inkomste* 1973 (1) SA 394 (A); *Slater v Haskins* 1914 TPD 264. In the latter case a contract of liquidation of a partnership was induced by a threat to cite someone as co-respondent in divorce proceedings and to claim delictual damages. Nonetheless, the court upheld the validity of the contract.

123 Cf Olivier, "Onregmatige Vreesaanjaging" (1965) 28 *THRHR* 187 at 201.

124 Cf Olivier, "Onregmatige Vreesaanjaging" (1965) 28 *THRHR* 187 at 188.

125 Cf Van der Merwe et al, *Contract—General Principles*, where it is stated that "... the question arises whether proof of fault is at all necessary where the contract is rescinded without a claim for damages. Since the basis of duress as a ground of rescission lies in the inability to express an intention in a free and unfettered manner due to the improper conduct of a co-contractant, one may well ask whether the unlawful expression of a threat should not suffice for rescission of the contract" (89).

126 Cf Olivier, "Onregmatige Vreesaanjaging" (1965) 28 *THRHR* 187 at 207, who states that the wrongfulness would lie in the encroachment on someone's personality rights.

127 Cf N J van der Merwe, "Aspects of the law of Contractual Torts" (1978) 95 *SALJ* 317–328; Van der Merwe and Olivier, *Die Onregmatige daad in die Suid-Afrikaanse reg*, 229 et sqq; Joubert, *General Principles of the Law of Contract*, 106.

5.3.2 *The effect of* metus *or duress in a contractual context*

In a case of *vis absoluta* there is never consent, and therefore no juristic act;[128] consequently contractual remedies such as *restitutio in integrum* cannot be provided.[129] Apparently one would then have to claim with a *rei vindicatio* on the basis that there was no valid real agreement by which ownership passed.[130] But the problem of *vis absoluta* is essentially of academic importance. In the rest of this section the focus will be on the effect of duress (or *vis compulsiva*) on the validity of the contract, and the remedies to which it could give rise.

i. Voidability, rescission and restitutio in integrum

In South African law, a contract concluded under duress is voidable.[131] Someone sued under a contract can raise the defence that it has been concluded under duress.[132] Voidability implies that the contract will continue to exist until the aggrieved party rescinds it.[133] Upon rescission, all obligations and acts of fulfilment cease to be valid. The aggrieved party then has to restore what he has performed and is obliged to return what he received. This restoring of the parties to their original position is usually referred to as *restitutio in integrum*.[134] It does not only relate to returning what has been obtained, but also to paying enough to restore the other party fully to his previous position.[135] In order to obtain the contractual remedy of *restitutio in integrum* it is generally required that one should tender restoration in order to indicate one's own willingness and ability to provide restoration.[136] It would seem as if the measure of the duty to provide full restitution is close[137] to the measure of damages in cases of delict: there the aggrieved party has to be placed in the position he would have been if the delict had not been committed.[138]

ii. Indirect enrichment

The person acting under duress can claim against the person who caused the duress as well as *mala fide* third parties. Although the matter has not yet been decided by the courts, he can presumably also claim against an innocent person with whom he

128 A juristic act is an act intended to have legal consequences. It is not necessarily a lawful act.

129 De Wet and van Wyk, *Kontraktereg en Handelsreg*, 47.

130 Cf Olivier, "Onregmatige Vreesaanjaging" (1965) 28 *THRHR* 187 at 188.

131 *Broodryk v Smuts* 1942 TPD 47; De Wet and Van Wyk, *Kontraktereg en Handelsreg*, 44. Cf Lubbe, "Voidable Contracts", in Zimmermann and Visser, eds, *Southern Cross—Civil Law and Common Law in South Africa*, 261 sqq.

132 Joubert, *General Principles of the law of Contract*, 106; Wessels, *The Law of Contract in South Africa*, vol 1, para 1201 (based on D 44.4.4.33).

133 The court cannot rescind the contract; it can merely confirm that rescission has taken place (cf *Davidson v Bonafede* 1981 (2) SA 501 at 505).

134 Cf Hutchison et al, *Wille's Principles of South African Law*, 446.

135 Van der Merwe et al, *Contract—General Principles*, 101.

136 Cf Lambiris, *Orders of Specific Performance and Restitutio in Integrum in South African Law*, 291 et sqq.

137 But obviously not identical (cf Van der Merwe et al, *Contract—General Principles*, 106). Cf also Lambiris, *Orders of Specific Performance and Restitutio in Integrum in South African Law*, 333 n 60. For example, *restitutio in integrum* does not cover consequential loss.

138 Cf *Davidson v Bonafede* 1981 (2) SA 501 (C), where Marais AJ held that "in the end, it seems to me to be a question of degree as to whether any particular financial adjustment which falls to be made is one which is an integral element in the granting of *restitutio in integrum*, or is one which is collateral to it, and so should form the subject of a distinct claim for damages" (at 511G). On the disputed relationship between *restitutio in integrum* and enrichment remedies, cf De Vos, *Verrykingsaanspreeklikheid in die Suid-Afrikaanse reg*, 158; Visser, "Rethinking Unjustified Enrichment", 1992 *AJ*, 215 et sq.

has concluded an agreement under duress caused by another. Various influential authors concede that this has been the position in Roman and Roman-Dutch law, but criticise it on the grounds that the innocent party (as in the case of fraud) should not be blamed for the conduct of an outsider.[139] It is less clear whether the person acting under duress can also claim against other bona fide third parties. As we have seen, the position in Roman and Roman-Dutch law was that anyone who had obtained something as the consequence of *metus* was liable, but this rule has not yet been affirmed in South African law. Joubert states that "when property has passed out of the hands of the culpable party and is presently in the hands of another, recourse should be had to the actions based on enrichment".[140] Presumably, it would then make no difference if the claim is for money or property. He recognises that there is no general enrichment action in South African law, and suggests that since the *negotium* requirement has fallen away, the *condictio sine causa*[141] may afford a remedy. However, there is no authority on these propositions in South African law.

5.3.3 *Compulsion and the* condictiones

The *condictiones* received from Roman-Dutch law play an important role in the South African law of unjustified enrichment. In general, the *condictiones* are aimed at "the recovery of property in which ownership has been transferred pursuant to a juristic act which was *ab initio* unenforceable or has subsequently become inoperative".[142] For present purposes the *condictio ob turpem vel iniustam causam* and the *condictio indebiti* are relevant.

i. The condictio ob turpem vel iniustam causam

In modern South African law the *condictio ob turpem vel iniustam causam*, as tempered by the *par delictum* rule,[143] is used to reclaim money or property which was paid or delivered pursuant to an illegal agreement.[144] Illegal agreements that are void cannot give rise to any obligations. Since a claim based on duress is only of importance in the context of avoiding already existing obligations, it follows that such a claim is irrelevant when voidness due to illegality has been established. But this does not mean that the presence of compulsion is entirely irrelevant to the recovery of transfers tainted by illegality.[145] In modern South African law the principle of public policy is used to determine whether the *par delictum* rule should be relaxed so as not to bar the *condictio ob turpem vel iniustam causam*.[146]

---

139 Cf De Wet and Van Wyk, *Kontraktereg en Handelsreg*, 44 et sq; supported by Lubbe and Murray, *Contract*, 365; Van der Merwe et al, *Contract—General Principles*, 89; Kahn et al, *Contract and Mercantile Law*, 343; Hutchison et al, *Wille's Principles of South African Law*, 448.

140 Joubert, *General Principles of the law of Contract*, 110 n 76 refers to Mazeaud, *Lecons de Droit Civil* (1962), vol 2. This edition could not be traced, but the subsequent editions provide no authority in support of this proposition.

141 Joubert, *General Principles of the Law of Contract*, 110 n 76.

142 Cf *Pucjlowski v Johnston's Executors* 1946 WLD 1 at 6; Lotz, "Enrichment" in Joubert (ed), *The Law of South Africa*, vol 9, para 65.

143 As indicated before, this rule essentially states that where transferor and transferee are both tainted with turpitude, the law should not intervene and the transfers should remain where they are (cf De Wet and van Wyk, *Kontraktereg en Handelsreg*, 91; Lubbe and Murray, *Contract*, 294).

144 Cf Hutchison et al, *Wille's Principles of South African Law*, 637; Lotz, "Enrichment" in Joubert (ed), *The Law of South Africa*, vol 9, para 70 et sqq.

145 Cf J R Harker, "The Effect of a Threat of Criminal Prosecution on Contract" (1977) 40 *THRHR*, 139 at 145.

146 Cf *Jajbhay v Cassim* 1939 AD 537 at 544.

The fact that a transfer was made under compulsion could then indicate that such a relaxation is required.[147]

ii. *The* condictio indebiti

In modern South African law the *condictio indebiti* is generally used for the recovery of undue payments made in error.[148] However, for almost a century it has been held that the *condictio indebiti* is also available in certain cases of compulsion. By a curious twist of fate, this development cannot be ascribed to a careful broadening of the scope of the *condictio indebiti* based on a re-assessment of its civilian roots (a process which took place in Germany at the end of the century), but rather to a somewhat clumsy effort to inject the English law of duress of goods into South African law. It will be recalled that in *White Brothers v Treasurer-General*[149] De Villiers CJ expressed the view that a threat to take or injure property would not amount to duress sufficient to avoid a *contract*, although such "duress of goods" could be the basis for a claim to return a payment which was accompanied by an unequivocal act showing it was not made voluntarily. After first mentioning that, according to the Dutch authors, it is the lack of free consent "which lies at the heart of the rule which invalidates contracts or payments extorted by force or intimidation",[150] De Villiers CJ then observed that the English law of duress of goods was based on similar considerations. He then "reconciled" the principles of the English case law[151] and the "true principles of civil law" by showing that just as the payment is involuntary in the case of menaces to the person, it is also involuntary in the case of the illegal detention of goods.[152] However, according to him there was one crucial difference: in the case of duress of goods there had to be some unequivocal objection at the time of payment.[153] Such an objection would not be necessary in cases of menaces to the person. An unfortunate aspect of this analysis is that such an objection was not required in English law. The cases De Villiers CJ dealt with simply happened to have involved such objections. The extraordinary result is therefore that in attempting to introduce the English notion of duress of goods into South African law, while remaining faithful to the Roman-Dutch notion of involuntariness, De Villiers CJ "imported" his own invention—the protest requirement.[154] Another problematic aspect of the judgment is that it does not

---

147 Cf Van der Merwe et al, *Contract—General Principles*, 50 n 72; Wessels, *The Law of Contract in South Africa*, vol 1, para 666 et sq.

148 Cf *Union Government v National Bank of South Africa Ltd* 1921 AD 121; *Le Riche v Hamman* 1946 AD 648; *Frame v Palmer* 1950 (3) SA 340 (C). It should be noted though that the "principles underlying the *condictio* are not immutable", and that parties are entitled to an analogous application of the *condictio indebiti* (*Bowman, De Wet and Du Plessis NNO and others v Fidelity Bank Ltd* 1997 (2) SA 35 (A). Cf also *Kommissaris van Binnelandse Inkomste en 'n Ander v Willers en Andere* 1994 (3) SA 283 (A) 333G–H).

149 1883 2 SC 322.

150 *White Brothers v Treasurer-General* 1883 2 SC 322 at 350.

151 He referred to *Parker v Great Western Railway Co* (7 M & G 253) and *Parker v Bristol and Exeter Railway Co* (6 Exch 702).

152 "Involuntary" in this context would then not mean that there is "a total absence of consent", but only that the "consent is forced and not free" (*White Brothers v Treasurer-General* 1883 2 SC 322 at 351).

153 *White Brothers v Treasurer-General* 1883 2 SC 322 at 351 et sq.

154 Cf *Maskell v Horner* [1915] 3 KB 106: "I doubt whether Rowlatt J (in *Brisbane v Dacres* 5 Taunt. 143) intended to find that there must be anything in the shape of an express notice or declaration to the defendant of the plaintiff's intention to keep alive his right to recover. It is clear ... that no express words are necessary and that the circumstances attending the payments and the conduct of the plaintiff when making them may be sufficient indication to the defendant that the payments were not made with the intention of closing the transaction" (per Lord Reading CJ at 119 et sq).

clearly state which remedy of "restitution" could be used for recovery on the ground of "duress of goods".[155] Clarity was brought in *Union Government (Minister of Finance) v Gowar*[156] where De Villiers AJA held that "... where money has been paid under protest the *condictio indebiti* lies".[157] Thus, partly due to the influence of English law, the *condictio indebiti* was extended in South African law to reclaim undue[158] transfers made under compulsion.[159] Subsequently it has been held that in a claim based on duress of goods, proof of a protest indicates the lack of voluntariness of the transfer,[160] but such proof has not uniformly been insisted upon.[161] Of course, if the compulsion has been lawful the plaintiff cannot rely on lack of voluntariness.[162]

155 De Villiers CJ mentions *restitutio in integrum* in the decision, but does not clearly state that this is the appropriate remedy. But cf his judgment in *Benning v Union Government (Minister of Finance)* 1914 AD 420 where *restitutio in integrum* as well as the *condictio indebiti* were mentioned as possible remedies (at 422).

156 1915 AD 426.

157 *Union Government (Minister of Finance) v Gowar* 1915 AD 426 at 444.

158 An undue transfer is a transfer which was "indebite in the widest sense of the word, i.e. there must have been no legal or natural obligation to give it" (Lotz, "Enrichment" in Joubert (ed), *The Law of South Africa*, vol 9, para 67). This is a core feature of the *condictio indebiti*. Cf *Le Riche v Hamman* 1946 AD 648 at 656.

159 Cf *Caterers Ltd v Bell and Anders* 1915 AD 698 at 712; *Gluckman v Jagger & Co* 1929 CPD 44 at 47; *Cranborne Road Council v Derbyshire Estates Ltd* 1967 (1) SA 8 (R); *Miller and Others v Bellville Municipality* 1973 (1) SA 914 (C); *Commissioner for Inland Revenue v First National Industrial Bank Ltd* 1990 (3) SA 641 (A) at 646 et sq.

160 Cf De Vos, *Verrykingsaanspreeklikheid in die Suid-Afrikaanse reg*, 172; *Miller and Others v Bellville Municipality* 1973 (1) SA 914 (C). In the latter case the municipality refused to grant approval of Miller's building plans unless a certain portion of land was surrendered free of charge to it. Miller then transferred the land, but afterwards proved that this condition was illegal. He then sought to reclaim the land, and founded his claim on a *condictio indebiti*. He inter alia averred that this *condictio* should be available due to the pressure exerted by the municipality. The court then found that he could not claim with the *condictio indebiti* since it had not been proven that the payment or transfer was made involuntarily. According to Van Winsen J, "... it was not sufficient proof of the involuntariness that the transfer was effected in response to a demand made *colore officii* as a condition of the exercise by defendant of a statutory duty to consider and, if in order, to pass building plans. If this is the effect of the remarks of Scrutton, LJ in *Brocklebank Ltd v The King* ... then they are in my view not in accordance with our law. The fact that defendant applied pressure to plaintiffs to obtain transfer does not necessarily render involuntary plaintiff's action in yielding to such pressure by transferring the land" (at 921H–922A). In holding that the transfer was not involuntary, the judge referred to the lack of protest, due to ignorance of the true legal position. In essence, proof of a protest was required in establishing lack of voluntariness.

161 Cf *Kruger v Sekretaris van Binnelandse Inkomste* 1971 (4) SA 200 (C), 1973 (1) SA 394 (A). After examining the judgment of De Villiers CJ in *White Brothers v Treasurer-General* 1883 2 SC 322 at 351 Van Winsen J held that he did *not* understand it to mean "... that the only way in which it can be proved that the payment is involuntary is by proof of a protest made at the time of payment ... The law as set out above does not, in my opinion, require as a condition precedent to successful recovery of money paid under pressure that such a protest should have taken place. It is sufficient if from the totality of evidence it appears that the payment was made involuntarily" (*Kruger v Sekretaris van Binnelandse Inkomste* 1973 (1) SA 394 (A) at 398).

162 Cf *Caterers Ltd v Bell and Anders* 1915 AD 698. The defendant firm of attorneys refused to deliver deeds of transfer to the plaintiff unless certain charges were paid. These were then paid with reservation of the right to recover payment. Innes CJ held that it was essential to prove that goods wrongly detained were legally claimable by the plaintiff, which was not proven in this case. Therefore, since there was no illegal threat, there could be no duress of goods (at 705; on lawful threats cf also *Kruger v Sekretaris van Binnelandse Inkomste* 1973 (1) SA 394 (A) at 410; *Goldroad (Pty) Ltd v Fidelity Bank (Pty) Ltd* 1996 (4) SA 1151 (TPD). Not any unlawful threat would suffice though—something of the *vir constans* requirement also applies here. Cf e.g. *Lilienfield & Co v Bourke* 1921 TPD 365, where a lessee was induced into paying certain rates by an illegal threat

Thus far, the emphasis has been on the relevance of a protest in the context of compulsion in the form of duress of goods. However, it is quite possible that a payment could be made under protest or reservation in the absence of such compulsion. This situation especially arises when an undue payment is made pursuant to an *ultra vires* demand for the payment of tax. The question as to whether the *condictio indebiti* is an appropriate remedy in these circumstances was examined in the Appellate Division decision of *Commissioner for Inland Revenue v First National Industrial Bank Ltd.*[163] The facts of the case can be summarised as follows. The Commissioner demanded that a bank should pay stamp duty on a credit card scheme which it administered. At first the bank disputed liability, but later on it made various payments of stamp duty under protest. After failing to recover the payments from the Commissioner, the bank succeeded in obtaining judgment that it was not liable to pay the duty. The capital sum of the duty was then repaid by the Commissioner, but the bank maintained that the Commissioner was also liable to pay interest on the payments, from the date that each payment had been made. The Commissioner disputed the liability to pay interest and the matter came before the Appellate Division. The nature of the claim was pivotal: if it was contractual, interest would run only from the date of judgment, but if it was based on the *condictio indebiti*, interest would run from the date of the demand. In his majority judgment, Nienaber AJA (in response to a submission by counsel for the Commissioner) held that it would be an oversimplification to say that the *condictio indebiti* is only available in cases of mistake, since this *condictio*'s field of application has been extended to cases of duress—i.e. "when a payment (or indeed any performance), although deliberate, perhaps even advised, was nevertheless involuntary because it was effected under pressure and protest".[164] However, it was found that no such duress existed *in casu*, since the payments "though expressed to be under protest, were made voluntarily". There was "no question (in the language of *Gowar*'s case . . . and assuming the doctrine to be thus limited) of goods being detained or of rights being withheld—here, at the best for the Bank, there was the prospect of penalties being imposed".[165] On the facts it was by no means certain that such penalties would be imposed: the Commissioner was empowered to remit penalties; the bank never asked the Commissioner to suspend payment of the duty as long as the liability was disputed; and there were no indications that such a request would have been refused. Even though the demand for paying the duties was illegal, there was not sufficient duress to allow for recovery with the *condictio indebiti*. Having then decided that the

---

to cancel the lease. It was held that although there was a protest, the "duress" under which the payments were made by the plaintiffs "was a phantom of their own minds", and that the payments were made voluntarily (at 371 et sq). On the other hand, *Brakpan Municipality v Androulakis* 1926 TPD 658 dealt with a real danger of a writ being issued to obtain repayment of an invalid order for costs made by a magistrate who thought he sat in a judicial capacity, but was in fact sitting in an administrative capacity. The payments of costs which were then made under protest were held to be recoverable. *Lilienfield & Co v Bourke* was distinguished on the basis that in that case the payments were not made because of the real danger of the writ being issued, but only because of the lessor-payer's ignorance of the law (cf *Commissioner for Inland Revenue v First National Industrial Bank Ltd* 1990 (3) SA 641 (A) at 662 et sq.)

163 1990 (3) SA 641 (A). The case can be regarded as the South African equivalent of *Woolwich Building Society (formerly Woolwich Equitable Building Society) v Inland Revenue Commissioners* [1992] WLR 367; [1993] 1 AC 70 (CA and HL).

164 *Commissioner for Inland Revenue v First National Industrial Bank Ltd* 1990 (3) SA 641 (A) at 646F–647D.

165 *Commissioner for Inland Revenue v First National Industrial Bank Ltd* 1990 (3) SA 641 (A) at 647F–G.

condictio indebiti could not be used for recovery, Nienaber AJA found that a right of recovery could be based on a contract stemming from the fact that payment was expressly made "under protest".[166] The content of the contract is that the transfer should be returned if not due. *Mora* interest could then only run from the date of judgment that the debt was undue, and not earlier.

However, the decision was not unanimous. In a minority judgment, Nicholas AJA held that the true cause of action was in fact the *condictio indebiti*, but based on the consideration that if the other party accepts the payment made under protest, he is taken to have agreed to return it if it turned out to be undue.[167] The alternative contention of counsel, namely that a tacit independent contract was concluded, "independent in the sense that the Bank could sue on it without having to rely on the *condictio indebiti*", was rejected.[168] The minority judgment therefore clearly differs from the majority in distinguishing between two types of "agreement" concluded by the bank and the Commissioner: the one preserves the *condictio indebiti* and the other provides a contractual basis for recovery. This lack of uniformity in approach is regrettable and, it is submitted, indicative of a failure to work out clearly the key features of the *condictio indebiti*. Recourse to implied agreements smacks of fiction, while the identification of "agreements" which "preserve" the *condictio indebiti* is a matter of some subtlety. In the final chapter it will be attempted, from a Scottish perspective, to present these issues on a more satisfactory basis, taking into account the developments in the civilian tradition in general. This section will then be concluded with an overview of the views of some South African academics, who to a certain extent also attempt to analyse the *condictio indebiti* in the context of this tradition.

Excursus: South African academic opinion

South African academic views on the applicability of the *condictio indebiti* in cases of compulsion can be summarised as follows. First, there is the view that error is an essential feature of the *condictio indebiti*. Its availability in cases of compulsion is then unacceptable, since the compelled transferor usually knows no debt is due and can hardly be regarded as making the transfer in error. Wessels, for example, clearly states that in cases of duress of goods, "since the money is not paid under a mistake or under an impression that it was due, a *condictio indebiti* will not lie". According to him, the appropriate remedy in such a case is the *condictio sine causa*.[169] However,

166 *Commissioner for Inland Revenue v First National Industrial Bank Ltd* 1990 (3) SA 641 (A) at 651 et sqq.

167 *Commissioner for Inland Revenue v First National Industrial Bank Ltd* 1990 (3) SA 641 (A) at 658A–C. Cf also *Gluckman v Jagger & Co* 1929 CPD 44 where it was held that the *condictio indebiti* would be available "... whenever a man pays money which is not due if he pays it by mistake or under duress or when it is made a condition of the payment that if it is found not to be due it is to be returned" (at 47). The last phrase ("when it is made a condition of the payment that if it is found not to be due it is to be returned") seems to be taken over from *Lilienfield & Co v Bourke* (1921 TPD 365) where it was used to describe a payment "under protest". Apparently, using the expression "under protest" (as De Villiers AJA did in *Union Government (Minister of Finance) v Gowar* 1915 AD 426) was regarded as too restrictive.

168 *Commissioner for Inland Revenue v First National Industrial Bank Ltd* 1990 (3) SA 641 (A) at 658D. According to Nicholas AJA, "[t]he contract which was made was not independent, but was ancillary or subsidiary to the *condictio indebiti*: it did not create a substantive right but recognised that the bank had the procedural right to seek a *condictio* (or *repetitio*) despite the fact that the *solutio* was being made voluntarily and with knowledge that it was made *indebite*" (at 658H).

169 Wessels, *The Law of Contract in South Africa*, vol 1, para 1182.

this type of approach has been rendered obsolete by more modern case law which clearly states that the *condictio indebiti* is in fact available in these cases. The second approach[170] accommodates this development by regarding compulsion as a substitute for the error, which would normally be required when claiming with the *condictio indebiti*.[171] If this analysis is correct, the position in South African law would be comparable to that in France.[172] A third, alternative, explanation is simply to regard error and compulsion as but two of a variety of factual situations under which the *condictio indebiti* would be awarded in order to recover undue transfers.[173] In a legal historical and legal comparative study of the role of error in the context of the *condictio indebiti*, Visser states that the *condictio indebiti* should be available whenever an undue transfer is retained *sine causa* because its purpose, namely to discharge a debt, has failed. According to him, this purpose should then be viewed "objectively"[174]—in other words it is not necessary that the transferor actually (subjectively) should have had the erroneous belief he was discharging a debt. This explains its application to compelled transfers (made under protest):[175] "objectively" speaking the transfer was supposed to discharge a debt, and if none was due, it failed to perform this function, and the *condictio indebiti* should be available. Van der Walt, on the other hand, regards it as unnecessary to employ an analysis based on the "failure of the purpose of the transfer" at all: he simply requires that there should be a transfer and the absence of an obligation entitling the recipient to keep the transfer.[176] This difference of opinion has parallels in modern German thought, and will be dealt with below.

---

170 Although De Vos prefers the *condictio sine causa specialis*, he acknowledges that this is not the view of the courts (*Verrykingsaanspreeklikheid in die Suid-Afrikaanse reg*, 172). In South African law the *condictio sine causa specialis* covers the falling away of the legal basis of a due transfer, the alienation or consumption of property by a person in possession, and a variety of other cases of *sine causa* retention which do not fall under any of the established *condictiones*. Presumably De Vos intends that the recovery of compelled undue transfers falls under the latter category. On the *condictio sine causa specialis* cf, generally, *Govender v Standard Bank of SA Ltd* 1984 (4) SA 392 (C), Eiselen, *Unjustified Enrichment—A Casebook* (1993), 240 et sqq; Lotz, "Enrichment" in Joubert (ed), *The Law of South Africa*, vol 9, para 75 et sqq.

171 As to the content of the error requirement, it has been indicated that the Roman-Dutch authors were divided on whether a distinction should be drawn between mistakes of law and of fact, and whether it should be required that mistakes should be excusable. Recently, in *Willis Faber Enthoven (Pty) Ltd v Receiver of Revenue and another* 1992 (4) SA 202 (A), the South African Appellate Division had occasion to consider these issues. It was decided that the distinction between mistakes of fact and law is "manifestly unjust in the majority of cases" (223G) and that it should be abolished. But, partly on grounds of a statement by Voet that "ignorance of fact should appear to be neither slack nor studied" (*nec supina nec affectata—Commentarius ad Pandectas* 12.6.7), it was stated that "an *indebitum* paid as result of a mistake of law may be recovered provided that the mistake is found to be excusable in the circumstances of the particular case" (224B–C). Excusability was retained, and Voet won the day.

172 Cf Englard, "Restitution of Benefits conferred without obligation" in *International Encyclopedia of Comparative Law*, vol X, 24 n 183. Under French law, proof of error is required in certain cases of recovery of payments that are not due. In cases of compulsion ("contrainte"), the compulsion is assimilated to error, which seems to be nothing but a fiction. On the general position, cf Jean-Luc Aubert, *Jacques Flour et Jean-Luc Aubert—Les Obligations*, vol 2, 4th ed (1989), 28 et sq.

173 Cf *Commissioner for Inland Revenue v First National Industrial Bank Ltd* 1990 (3) SA 641 (A); Lotz, "Enrichment" in Joubert (ed), *The Law of South Africa*, vol 9, para 67; Joubert, *General Principles of the Law of Contract*, 107.

174 Visser, *Die rol van dwaling by die condictio indebiti*, 218, 226 et sq., 314.

175 Visser may be overemphasising the importance of a protest in these cases (cf 5.3.3.ii above, where it is indicated that the "absence of voluntariness" could arise even if there was no protest).

176 "Die Condictio Indebiti as Verrykingsaksie" (1966) 29 *THRHR* 220 at 222 et sq.

This concludes the overview of modern South African law on the content and effect of compulsion. It should be clear that much of the legal development reflects the common characteristics of Scots and South African law, namely of being uncodified legal systems which are influenced by conflicting traditions. It was shown that the courts used a unique synthesis of Common Law and Civil Law to broaden the spectrum of cases of compulsion sufficiently serious to justify the provision of relief. And it was also shown how the courts have been gradually trying to provide greater clarity as to the appropriate remedy for providing such relief. It should then be apparent that South African law and Scots law have many problems in common. The question now arises whether the mass of casuistry surrounding compulsion can be reduced to certain essential elements. More than a century ago, the compilers of the German civil code had to provide solutions to some of the problems which are similar to the ones identified in Scottish and South African law. We shall now turn to an examination of these solutions.

5.4 GERMAN LAW

5.4.1 *The content of compulsion*

In German law the concept *Drohung* describes the application of psychological pressure through threats. It can be translated roughly as duress.[177] Although duress primarily is regarded as a factor which affects the validity of contracts, one would search in vain for a discussion thereof in the second book of the BGB, which deals with the law of obligations. Since it affects the formation of the will, it is not only relevant to the law of obligations, but also to other branches of private law such as family law and the law of succession. The section dealing with duress therefore has been placed in the first book of the BGB, which contains principles applicable to the whole of private law.[178] Duress can affect the validity of any declaration of will or *Willenserklärung*. The concept of duress therefore has no independent relevance as such in German law: its function is merely to help identify a particular case where the validity of a *Willenserklärung* is affected. Such a *Willenserklärung* is essential for any juristic act or *Rechtsgeschäft* to come into being.[179] Thus, if an invalid *Willenserklärung* was supposed to give rise to the transfer of ownership, the transfer would be invalid, and proprietary remedies would lie. And if the invalid *Willenserklärung* was supposed to create an obligation, it would be invalid, and what was transferred pursuant thereto would be retained without legal ground.[180]

---

177 Compulsion through the application of psychological pressure should be distinguished from abuse of a necessitous condition (cf Zweigert and Kötz (tr Weir), *Introduction to Comparative Law*, 456 et sqq). The historical roots of the latter category lie in the law of *dolus*, and not in the law of *metus*.

178 In § 123 BGB. For the background to this provision see Mugdan (ed), *Die gesammten Materialien zum Bürgerlichen Gesetzbuch für das deutsche Reich* (1899, 1979), vol 1, 465 et sqq (*Motive*, vol 1, 204 et sqq). In references to the *Bürgerliches Gesetzbuch* (BGB), § means "section", para I "first paragraph" and sent 1 "first sentence".

179 Cf Zweigert and Kötz, *Introduction to Comparative Law*, 348 et sqq. The reason why a declaration of will, and not only a juristic act, is affected by § 123 BGB, is that the compilers of the BGB wanted to provide maximum protection to a person acting under duress (*Denkschrift*, in Benno Mugdan (ed), *Die gesammten Materialien zum Bürgerlichen Gesetzbuch für das deutsche Reich* (1899, 1979), 834).

180 Cf, generally, *Medicus, Allgemeiner Teil des BGB*, nn 242 et sqq; 487 et sqq; 726; Brox, *Allgemeiner Teil des Bürgerlichen Gesetzbuchs*, nn 101 et sqq.

The most prominent provision affecting the validity of transactions made under duress is § 123 para I BGB, which provides that someone who has been induced to make a declaration of will through intentional misrepresentation (fraud) or unlawful threats (*Drohung*), may rescind (*anfechten*) the declaration. *Drohung* only comprises *vis compulsiva* or psychological compulsion (*psychischer Zwang*), and not *vis absoluta* or the physical or bodily overpowering of a person.[181] *Drohung* specifically entails that one person deliberately promises another that harm will befall him in future, asserts that he can affect its realisation in order to influence the decision of will of the threatened person, and consequently induces him to enter into a juristic act.[182] The mere exploitation of a situation of distress (*Zwangslage*) does not constitute *Drohung*.[183] No *vir constans* standard is set, as used to be the case in German common law, but if someone has been threatened with a mere trifle it would be extremely difficult to prove that the threat in fact induced the conduct of the threatened person.[184] The threat has to be illegal. This illegality can lie in the threatened conduct (e.g. to assault someone or destroy his property), the desired result (e.g. to assist in fraud), or the relationship between the threatened conduct and desired outcome (e.g. threatening to tell the police that someone committed a crime, in order to obtain payment of his debt).[185] Related BGB provisions are § 138 para I BGB, according to which juristic acts which are contrary to morality are void, and § 138 para II BGB, according to which voidness also attaches to juristic acts whereby one person obtains a disproportionate counterperformance from another through exploitation of the need, lack of experience or judgment, or exceptional pliancy of that person. § 138 para I BGB could be relevant to cases involving compulsion,[186] but it should be borne in mind that the problem of compulsion relates to the way in which a legal transaction was made, and not to its content. Although § 138 para II BGB also deals with the way in which a legal transaction was made, its requirements are very specific and aimed at situations where vulnerability is exploited, but no illegal threat is made. Furthermore, it requires that there should be an obvious disproportionality in performances, which relates to the content of the agreement, and not the way in which it has been concluded.

---

181 Cf BGH DB 75, 2075; Palandt, *Bürgerliches Gesetzbuch*, § 123 n 15; Kramer in *Münchener Kommentar*, Band 1, § 123 n 32; Giesen, *BGB Allgemeiner Teil: Rechtsgeschäftslehre*, 99 et sqq. The reason is obvious: in the case of *vis absoluta* there has been no *Willenserklärung* (Brox, *Allgemeiner Teil des Bürgerlichen Gesetzbuchs*, n 414).

182 Cf BGHZ 2, 287(295), Kramer in *Münchener Kommentar*, § 123 n 33; Brox, *Allgemeiner Teil des Bürgerlichen Gesetzbuchs*, n 414. The typology does not satisfactorily take into account the case of psychological compulsion caused by the present application of force which is not so strong that it amounts to *vis absoluta*. To regard such compulsion as involving threats of *future* harm seems somewhat fanciful.

183 Kramer in *Münchener Kommentar*, § 123 BGB n 33. Although it is possible that a group could be subjected to a collective threat (*Kollektivdrohung*), these situations have traditionally been dealt with in terms of specific legislation rather than on the general level of § 123 BGB (cf, in the context of claims arising from the persecution of Jews in Nazi Germany, BGHZ 10, 340; BAG RzW 59, 502; KG SJZ 47, 257; Palandt, *Bürgerliches Gesetzbuch*, § 123 n 18; Kramer in *Münchener Kommentar*, § 123 BGB n 41).

184 Kramer in *Münchener Kommentar*, § 123 BGB n 34.

185 Brox, *Allgemeiner Teil des Bürgerlichen Gesetzbuchs*, nn 417–420. Kramer in *Münchener Kommentar*, § 123 BGB n 35.

186 Kramer in *Münchener Kommentar*, § 123 BGB n 35.

5.4.2 *The effect of compulsion*

i. Remedies based on unjustified enrichment

German law does not follow a casuistic approach, where specific rules justify recovery, but rather operates with a number of basic requirements.[187] In each claim based on unjustified enrichment it has to be proved that the enrichment has taken place without legal ground, or *sine causa*. Once a declaration of will has been avoided on grounds of duress in terms of § 123 para I BGB, it is void *ab initio* in terms of § 142 para I BGB. Any juristic act of which this declaration of will formed part, would then be invalid as well. If such a juristic act was supposed to act as the legal ground or *causa* of a transfer, that legal ground would be regarded as having never existed, and it would be possible to reclaim the transfer with a claim based on unjustified enrichment. How these remedies are provided will now be considered.

The German law of unjustified enrichment has been codified in §§ 812–822 BGB. Of particular importance is § 812 para I sent 1 BGB, which contains a general enrichment action partly based on the *condictiones* of Roman law. According to this provision, a person who obtains something without legal ground at the expense of another through a transfer of that person or in any other way is liable to return it.[188] The distinction drawn between obtaining something through a transfer (*Leistung*), and obtaining it in any other way is crucial. Since the provision is phrased in very broad terms, it is not surprising that academic writers and the courts have attempted to identify certain standard categories of unjustified enrichment.[189] Nowadays it is generally accepted that the following main categories of enrichment claims exist in German law, namely the enrichment claim based on the failure of the purpose of a transfer (*Leistungskondiktion*), the enrichment claim based on an encroachment (*Eingriffskondiktion*), the enrichment claim based on payment of another's debt (*Rückgriffskondiktion*) and the enrichment claim based on expenses incurred to the advantage of another (*Verwendungskondiktion*).[190] In practice the *Leistungskondiktion* is of particular importance. According to the prevailing view, the *Leistungskondiktion* is available when someone has made a *Leistung*, i.e. intentionally has conferred a benefit on another with a specific purpose in mind,[191] and this purpose then failed for some or other reason. As Reuter and Martinek put it, "in the case of the *Leistungskondiktion* the lack of the legal ground for the *Leistung* lies in the failure of its purpose".[192] However, there is also a minority opinion, which regards the emphasis on the purpose of the transfer as unnecessary. To the supporters of this view, the legal ground for a *Leistung* is simply the relationship of indebtedness it pertains to. A contract of sale, for example, provides such a relationship for a *Leistung* in the form of a payment of the purchase price. The advantage of this approach can briefly be illustrated as follows. If the purchaser in the example mentioned above accidentally pays the purchase price twice, but also happens to owe the seller a

187 Cf König, *Ungerechtfertigte Bereicherung—Tatbestände und Ordnungsprobleme in rechtsvergleichender Sicht*, 75.

188 § 812 para I sent 1 BGB reads: "Wer durch die Leistung eines anderen oder in sonstiger Weise auf dessen Kosten etwas ohne rechtlichen Grund erlangt, ist ihm zu Herausgabe verpflichtet".

189 The most famous attempts are those by W Wilburg, *Die Lehre von der ungerechtfertigten Bereicherung nach österreichischen und deutschem Recht* (1934) and E von Caemmerer, "Bereicherung und unerlaubte Handlung", in *Festschrift für Ernst Rabel*, vol 1 (1954), 333 et sqq.

190 On these various remedies, cf Von Caemmerer, *Gesammelte Schriften*, vol 1, 228 et sqq, 237 et sqq, 241 et sqq, 378 et sqq, 383 et sqq.

191 Cf BGHZ 40, 272 (277); BGHZ 58, 184 (188).

192 Reuter and Martinek, *Ungerechtfertigte Bereicherung*, 125.

separate debt (say, a loan), the seller can then set off the purchaser's enrichment claim based on the second payment against his own claim for payment of the loan (cf § 387 BGB). The second payment would then no longer be retained without legal ground. This consequence cannot be explained with an analysis based on the failure of the purpose of the second payment,[193] and it indicates that such an analysis is in fact unnecessary.

However, for purposes of this overview of the modern law, the focus will have to be on the majority view. Since the *Leistungskondiktion* unites various cases of *sine causa* retention brought about by a transfer, it should not be surprising that German authors have found it convenient to categorise the fields of application of this remedy along the lines of the *condictiones*.[194] According to the prevailing view, the *Leistungskondiktion* in its *condictio indebiti* guise is applied when the purpose of a transfer failed because the intended discharge of a debt free of a defence did not materialise. More specifically, if a declaration of will has been rescinded because of duress (§§ 123 para I, 142 para I BGB), it is then the *condictio indebiti*[195] variety of the *Leistungskondiktion* which is used as enrichment remedy.[196] The absence of an error does not present a problem. Since its application in practice was fraught with uncertainty, sharp procedural manoeuvres and iniquitous dismissals of claims, the compilers of the BGB decided to jettison error,[197] and by all accounts this decision seems to have been a good one: it has not only lead to a dogmatically more satisfactory position, but has also met the demands of practice.[198] It should be noted, though, that by discarding error the compilers did not lose sight of the fact that when it was a requirement of the *condictio indebiti* it prevented reclaiming transfers made in the knowledge that they were not due: After all, it can never be said that

---

193 Cf Canaris, *Lehrbuch des Schuldrechts*, vol 2(2), § 67 III 1. It might seem as if this approach is unable to deal with the *datio ob rem*, which is not supported by an obligation at the time of transfer. However, such a *datio* is still supported by underlying understanding as to the basis on which it is to be held by the recipient. This is sufficient to justify its retention.

194 Cf Medicus, *Bürgerliches Recht*, n 689; Reuter and Martinek, *Ungerechtfertigte Bereicherung*, 125 et sqq; Koppensteiner and Kramer, *Ungerechtfertigte Bereicherung*, 49 et sq.

195 It should be noted that the German legislator did not retain the independent German common law remedies of *restitutio in integrum*, *actio quod metus causa* or *condictio ex iniusta causa*. The reasons for not incorporating a provision dealing with *restitutio in integrum* mainly relate to problems with its application in earlier times, and changed procedural views and institutions (*Motive: Allg. Theil* in Mugdan (ed), *Die gesammten Materialien zum Bürgerlichen Gesetzbuch für das Deutsche Reich*, 566 et sq). It was considered unnecessary because the provisions on unjustified enrichment could perform this role satisfactorily (cf Visser, "Rethinking Unjustified Enrichment" 1992 *AJ* 203 at 215 et sq). The *actio quod metus causa* was likewise dropped because general provisions were adopted on delict and unjustified enrichment, and there was a desire not to burden the code with unnecessary provisions (*Motive: Einzelne unerlaubte Handlungen*, in Mugdan (ed), *Die gesammten Materialien zum Bürgerlichen Gesetzbuch für das Deutsche Reich*, 423). The same was true of the *condictio ex iniusta causa*, which was used in the German common law to reclaim illegally extorted bestowments (cf König, *Ungerechtfertigte Bereicherung- Tatbestände und Ordnungsprobleme in rechtsvergleichender Sicht*, 47).

196 Medicus, *Schuldrecht II (Besonderer Teil)*, § 126 III 2; Koppensteiner and Kramer, *Ungerechtfertigte Bereicherung*, 50. This would also be the case for §§ 134, 138 BGB. Cf Reuter and Martinek, *Ungerechtfertigte Bereicherung*, 129 et sq.; Koppensteiner and Kramer, *Ungerechtfertigte Bereicherung*, 50. Since § 142 para I BGB operates *ex tunc*, the remedy is obviously not the *condictio ob causam finitam* (Reuter and Martinek, *Ungerechtfertigte Bereicherung*, 141).

197 Cf König, *Ungerechtfertigte Bereicherung—Tatbestände und Ordnungsprobleme in rechtsvergleichender Sicht*, 33. Cf also Visser, *Die rol van dwaling by die condictio indebiti*, 257 et sqq

198 Cf König, *Ungerechtfertigte Bereicherung—Tatbestände und Ordnungsprobleme in rechtsvergleichender Sicht*, 33.

someone who had such knowledge paid in error. But this problem was overcome without great difficulty: the function of the error requirement nowadays is fulfiled by § 814 BGB,[199] which states that recovery is not possible if the transferor knew that he was not obliged to transfer.[200] In this way it would be possible to exclude recovery if the transfer was made with the intention to donate, out of sheer generosity, or similar grounds.[201] Of course, the transferor would be entitled to attempt to preserve his right of recovery of an undue transfer by way of a reservation or protest, but since it is not the transferor who has to prove an error, but the recipient who has to prove knowledge on the side of the transferor, such a reservation plays a much less significant role in German law than in systems where proving an error is required.[202] But recognition of the knowledge bar obviously still did not solve the problem of allowing an enrichment claim in cases of compulsion, since the transferor could well know that the debt is not due, and then be barred by § 814 BGB. To surmount this problem, the courts have adopted two approaches. The first, which follows the views of the compilers of the BGB,[203] is simply to grant claims like these in terms of § 812 BGB to the exclusion of § 814 BGB.[204] The basis of the bar is the fact that a person acts contrary to his previous conduct (*venire contra factum proprium*). Where he has not acted freely it can hardly be held against him that he has now created the impression that the recipient is entitled to keep the transfer.[205] All that the transferor has to prove is that no obligation to make the transfer existed. If the recipient raises the defence of § 814 BGB, the transferor then has to prove that he acted under compulsion.[206] In the case where an obligation did exist, i.e a debt was due, but compulsion was used to obtain its discharge, it apparently would be sufficient for the transferor to prove that he was illegally compelled to transfer. The recipient would then have to prove the existence of the obligation and that he was entitled to use self-help.[207] The second approach, which involves the use of § 817 sent 1 BGB, deserves separate treatment, and is discussed in the next section.

---

199 For the historical background, cf König, *Ungerechtfertigte Bereicherung—Tatbestände und Ordnungsprobleme in rechtsvergleichender Sicht*, 41 et sq.

200 According to § 814 BGB it is not possible to reclaim transfers effected in order to fulfil an obligation if the transferor *knew* that he was not bound to do so, or if the transfer was made in compliance with a moral duty, or made for the sake of propriety (cf RGZ 99, 161 (165) and generally, Canaris, *Lehrbuch des Schuldrechts*, vol 2(2) § 68 III a). Normally someone who transfers while doubting whether a debt is due, would not be regarded as knowing that the debt is due, and should be able to reclaim. However, it may be that his claim would be excluded if the recipient could assume in terms of §§ 157, 242 BGB that the transferor intended that the recipient should keep the transfer even if the debt does not exist (König, *Ungerechtfertigte Bereicherung—Tatbestände und Ordnungsprobleme in rechtsvergleichender Sicht*, 39).

201 König, *Ungerechtfertigte Bereicherung—Tatbestände und Ordnungsprobleme in rechtsvergleichender Sicht*, 39.

202 König, *Ungerechtfertigte Bereicherung—Tatbestände und Ordnungsprobleme in rechtsvergleichender Sicht*, 45.

203 *Protokolle*, in Mugdan (ed), *Die gesammten Materialien zum Bürgerlichen Gesetzbuch für das deutsche Reich*, 1561 et sq; *Motive*, in Mugdan (ed), *Die gesammten Materialien zum Bürgerlichen Gesetzbuch für das deutsche Reich*, vol 2, 851.

204 This approach was followed in a case where someone had to pay freight charges that were not due in order to obtain release of his goods. Cf König, *Ungerechtfertigte Bereicherung—Tatbestände und Ordnungsprobleme in rechtsvergleichender Sicht*, 48 et sq.

205 Jauernig (ed), *Bürgerliches Gesetzbuch*, § 814 n 1, 2 d.

206 König, *Ungerechtfertigte Bereicherung—Tatbestände und Ordnungsprobleme in rechtsvergleichender Sicht*, 49.

207 König, *Ungerechtfertigte Bereicherung—Tatbestände und Ordnungsprobleme in rechtsvergleichender Sicht*, 49.

(a) Compulsion, the *condictio ob turpem vel iniustam causam*, and § 817 sent 1 BGB

Thus far the focus has mainly been on the *Leistungskondiktion* as "derived" from § 812 para I BGB. However, for reasons which still are not very clear, the BGB also recognises a type of *Leistungskondiktion* in § 817 sent 1. This provision allows the reclaim of a performance of which the *acceptance* (*Annahme*) violated a statutory provision or morality. One would have thought that the rise of the notion of a general unitary contract based simply on agreement, and not dependent on any specific form, made it questionable to retain the *condictio ob turpem vel iniustam causam.*[208] Nowadays, German law acknowledges the notion of a general unitary contract based simply on agreement, and if a performance is without legal ground, since the underlying transaction was void on grounds of illegality (§§ 134, 138 BGB), such a performance should be reclaimable with the (*condictio indebiti*) *Leistungskondiktion* of § 812 para I BGB.[209]

Does this then leave any field of application for § 817 sent 1 BGB? Some authors believe not,[210] but it has been argued that it does have an independent field of application in the following circumstances. First, § 817 sent 1 BGB would apply to the exclusion of § 812 para I BGB where there is a valid underlying transaction, but the purpose of the transfer was still of such a nature that its acceptance violated statutory provisions or public policy. This possibility is essentially theoretical. It is now accepted that § 134 BGB (which deals with statutory illegality) also applies to the unilateral violation of a statute.[211] This renders the school example where an official requires a benefit to which he is not entitled for the performance of a duty (a violation of § 331 StGB) applicable to both § 817 sent 1 BGB and § 812 par 1 BGB. Other examples deal with the situation where a person demands payment of "hush-money" to avoid prosecution, without compensating any loss.[212] But even here it can be argued that the agreement as to the basis of the payment violates § 138 BGB, and that § 812 par 1 BGB is still available. Alternatively, one may succeed in a claim based on § 123 BGB, which could also give rise to relief in terms of § 812 par 1 BGB. Second, a claim based on § 817 sent 1 BGB would be useful if a claim based on the *condictio indebiti* under § 812 par 1 BGB is excluded by § 814 BGB, which applies when the transferor knew that no debt was due.[213] The argument is based on the assumption that § 814 BGB is restricted to § 812 para I BGB, and does not apply to § 817 sent 1 BGB. However, it has been indicated that one does not need § 817 sent 1 BGB to do the work of allowing a claim even if someone knew he is making an undue transfer; one could just as well restrict § 814 BGB not to cover these cases.[214]

From the above it can therefore be concluded that the *condictio ob turpem vel iniustam causam*, as received in German law through § 817 sent 1 BGB is of little practical significance. By and large its applicability to cases of compulsion is overshadowed by the general action contained in § 812 para I BGB.

---

208 Cf Zimmermann, *The Law of Obligations*, 857 et sqq, 862.

209 Koppensteiner and Kramer, *Ungerechtfertigte Bereicherung*, 61.

210 Cf Honsell, *Die Rückabwicklung sittenwidriger oder verbotener Geschäfte*, 34 et sq; BGHZ 8, 348, 370; Canaris, *Lehrbuch des Schuldrechts*, vol 2(2), § 68 I 6.

211 Canaris, *Lehrbuch des Schuldrechts*, vol 2(2), § 68 I 6; but cf Medicus, *Bürgerliches Recht*, n 694.

212 Lieb in *Münchener Kommentar*, § 817 n 8; Canaris, *Lehrbuch des Schuldrechts*, vol 2(2), § 68 I 6.

213 Medicus, *Bürgerliches Recht*, n 694.

214 Lieb in *Münchener Kommentar*, § 817 n 7. Cf Honsell, *Die Rückabwicklung sittenwidriger oder verbotener Geschäfte*, 33 n 6; T Mayer-Maly, "Rechtsirrtum und Bericherung", in K Kuchine (ed), *Rechtsbewahrung und Rechtsentwicklung—Festschrift für Heinrich Lange* (1970), 294.

(b) The *in pari turpitudine* rule and § 817 sent 2 BGB

According to § 817 sent 2 BGB reclaimability is excluded if the transferor's conduct is also tainted with turpitude.[215] This bar to recovery, or *Kondiktionssperre* applies to claims in terms of § 812 BGB as well as § 817 sent 1 BGB.[216] A convincing group of cases where the transferor's claim would *not* be barred by § 817 sent 2 BGB, are those where there was a violation of law or morality but the transferor was moved by an unlawful demand of the recipient.[217] According to Honsell it is doubtful whether § 817 sent 2 BGB should apply in cases where the conduct of the recipient was morally neutral, even though it should not have been made the object of an agreement in terms of § 138 BGB. Some of the examples he mentions are payments made to an opposing team so that they lose a football match, or to a wife in order to consent to a divorce.[218] The argument is that if a wife accepts the payment, and then does not consent to the divorce, she should not be allowed to retain the payment. He particularly mentions the situations similar to extortion (*erpressungsähnliche Tatbestände*) of *Schweigegeld*. If someone receives payment to keep quiet about something that he just happens to have heard, that money should be reclaimable. There is even a decision allowing repayment where the receiver *threatened* to make certain information known unless he is paid.[219] This would suggest that in cases involving turpitude, compulsion could be relevant to show that § 817 sent 2 should not apply, and that recovery could take place with § 812 BGB or, on the assumption that it has independent relevance, § 817 sent 1 BGB.

(c) Indirect enrichment

Because German law regards *Drohung* as an even more dangerous and reprehensible disturbance than fraud,[220] it draws a distinction between the position of third parties in cases of fraud and duress. Unlike fraud, the effect of duress on a transfer is so strong that it would be possible to institute a claim for recovery even if the threat is not made by the recipient but by a third party.[221] In this regard German law has

---

215 Koppensteiner and Kramer, *Ungerechtfertigte Bereicherung*, 61.

216 Medicus, *Bürgerliches Recht*, n 696.

217 Lieb in *Münchener Kommentar* § 817 n 8; Koppensteiner and Kramer, *Ungerechtfertigte Bereicherung*, 61; Reuter and Martinek, *Ungerechtfertigte Bereicherung*, 181. They all say that § 817 sent 2 BGB should not restrict the operation of § 817 sent 1 BGB when "sich der Leistende aus zu respektierenden Gründe einer sittenwidrigen Forderung des Leistungsempfängers beugt".

218 Honsell, *Die Rückabwicklung sittenwidriger oder verbotener Geschäfte*, 141 et sqq.

219 RG Recht 1908 Nr. 3598. Honsell criticises RGZ 58, 204, where the court denied the claim for recovery of the payment because its purpose was to avoid punishment. The court conceded that it might be possible that the plaintiff's claim would not be barred by § 817 sent 2, but then he must have certain private interests to protect, such as preventing his dependants from the grave consequences of his punishment. Honsell does not find this last argument really persuasive; the purpose of the payment is always the evasion of punishment and one should not ask whether other honourable motives are present (144, n 33).

220 Cf Giesen, *BGB Allgemeiner Teil: Rechtsgeschäftslehre*, 171.

221 BGH NJW 66, 2399; *Palandt—Bürgerliches Gesetzbuch*, § 123 n 18. In the *Denkschrift*, we find the following reason for protecting the victim: practice has shown that threats sometimes lead to benefits being conferred on many people, and that it would be very harsh to expect the victim to prove that third parties were in fact aware of the threats (Mugdan (ed), *Die gesammten Materialien zum Bürgerlichen Gesetzbuch für das Deutsche Reich*, 834; cf also *Protokolle zum Allg. Theile* in Mugdan (ed), *Die gesammten Materialien zum Bürgerlichen Gesetzbuch für das Deutsche Reich*, 723).

held on strongly to its Roman roots.[222] The remedy for claiming against a third party to whom a transfer had been made by the claimant, would presumably be a *Leistungskondiktion*. Depending on the seriousness of the duress, vindicatory remedies could also be available.[223]

ii. Other remedies

Apart from the above-mentioned enrichment-based claims, and (depending on procedural considerations) at times in preference thereto, certain other claims can also be instituted. The claims are based on *culpa in contrahendo*, delict, and on the invalidity of the transfer of ownership (the *Verfügungsgeschäft*). Someone who is entitled to have a declaration of will rescinded through *Anfechtung* can usually obtain cancellation of a contract on grounds of *culpa in contrahendo*.[224] He would also be able to claim damages because of parties' blameworthy conduct during negotiations.[225] The legal basis of this liability is § 249 BGB, which aims at putting the threatened person in the position he would have been in, had someone not influenced his ability to decide freely.[226] If a case of compulsion is covered by the provisions of the criminal code dealing with coercion (§ 240 StGB—*Nötigung*) and extortion (§ 253 StGB—*Erpressung*), it would also be possible to claim delictual damages in terms of § 823 para II BGB, which provides that a person incurs delictual liability if he infringes a statute intended for the protection of others. Furthermore, a delictual claim could be brought under § 826 BGB, which provides that a person who intentionally causes damage to another in a manner contrary to morality is bound to compensate that person for the damage.[227] Damages are measured by comparing the present position of the claimant with the position he would have been in if he had not made the declaration of will.[228] Finally, certain remedies of property law may also be available. In German law it is essential to distinguish between a *Verpflichtungsgeschäft*, i.e. a juristic act (such as a contract of sale) which gives rise to an obligation to make a transfer, and a *Verfügungsgeschäft*, i.e. a juristic act whereby a right (such as ownership) is directly transferred, encumbered, changed or nullified.[229] If a declaration of will is rescinded under § 123 BGB, the validity of both these juristic acts could be affected. Above we have seen that where ownership has passed (i.e. the *Verfügungsgeschäft* was valid), the claimant would have to use remedies based on unjustified enrichment. It remains to be considered what influence compulsion can have on the validity of a

---

222 Zweigert and Kötz point out that this is also the position in civilian systems such as French, Italian, Spanish and Dutch law. English law differs fundamentally, in that actual knowledge on the side of the third party is needed before the person acting under duress can rescind an agreement (*An Introduction to Comparative Law*, 458).

223 Cf 5.4.2.ii below.

224 Jauernig (ed), *Bürgerliches Gesetzbuch*, § 123 n 5; *Palandt—Bürgerliches Gesetzbuch*, § 123 n 27; Giesen, *BGB Allgemeiner Teil: Rechtsgeschäftslehre*, nn 303, 307. But cf Brox, *Allgemeiner Teil des Bürgerlichen Gesetzbuchs*, n 425, 413.

225 On *culpa in contrahendo* in general, cf Larenz, *Lehrbuch des Schuldrechts*, vol 1, § 9 I; F Kessler and E Fine, "*Culpa in contrahendo*, bargaining in good faith, and freedom of contract: a comparative study" (1964) 77 *HarvardLR* 401.

226 On the concurrence between the various claims, cf Giesen, *BGB Allgemeiner Teil: Rechtsgeschäftslehre*, n 307.

227 Cf Giesen, *BGB Allgemeiner Teil: Rechtsgeschäftslehre*, n 303 and Medicus, *Bürgerliches Recht*, n 626; Brox, *Allgemeiner Teil des Bürgerlichen Gesetzbuchs*, n 425. Cf, generally, Canaris, *Lehrbuch des Schuldrechts*, vol 2(2), § 68 I 1 c).

228 Cf Giesen, *BGB Allgemeiner Teil: Rechtsgeschäftslehre*, n 303.

229 Cf for a general, elementary overview Brox, *Allgemeiner Teil des Bürgerlichen Gesetzbuchs*, nn 101 et sqq.

Verfügungsgeschäft. If such a juristic act is void, ownership does not pass, and the owner can then institute a vindicatory claim against the recipient in terms of § 985 BGB, according to which an owner can demand that a possessor return his property.[230] The problem is of course to determine whether someone who has transferred something under compulsion is still owner. The key to this problem lies in § 935 para I BGB,[231] which basically provides that the acquisition of ownership is not possible if something has been stolen from the owner, became missing, or was otherwise lost (*abhanden gekommen*). Since one way in which something can become "lost" is through duress (*Drohung*), the claimant can rely on this paragraph to prove that ownership has not passed, and that the possessor should return his property in terms of § 985 BGB. The problem is that not all cases of duress are regarded as sufficiently serious to affect the validity of a *Verfügungsgeschäft*, and it is difficult to determine where the border lies. According to the *Bundesgerichtshof*,[232] one would have to prove that there was duress through irresistible physical violence or equivalent psychical compulsion. This view has been criticised by Baur, who favours a broader approach to cover all situations of *Drohung*.[233] However, this view has not yet been accepted.

5.6 CONCLUSIONS

Roman-Dutch law

1. Following the Glossators, a distinction was drawn between *vis absoluta*, which excluded any decision of will, and gave rise to vindicatory remedies, and *vis conditionalis* or *vis compulsiva*, which was covered by the law of *metus*. The content of *metus* did not differ notably from Roman law: the requirement of constancy was watered down somewhat, but the scope of recognised cases of illegal threats of harm was still narrow. There is some authority that illegal threats of economic harm could give rise to a claim based on *metus*, but this was not the prevailing view.

2. Generally speaking, anything done under *metus*, such as granting a promise, entering into a contract, or making a transfer, was voidable, not void. An action for restitution based on *metus* could be used to obtain the setting aside of that which was done under *metus*. Someone who refused to provide restitution, was liable to pay the value of what he was supposed to restore. A delictual claim for damages could be instituted in addition to a claim of restitution. Someone who acted under *metus* could apparently ward off a claim with an *exceptio*. It was possible to claim against third parties.

3. In cases of compulsion not amounting to *metus*, such as threats of certain wrongs and of refusal to do something which was one was obliged to do in any event, the *condictio ob turpem vel iniustam causam* could apparently be used to obtain recovery. The *condictio indebiti* was regarded as inappropriate, presumably because it was generally restricted to undue transfers made in error.

---

230 Cf Giesen, *BGB Allgemeiner Teil: Rechtsgeschäftslehre*, n 303; Josef Esser and Hans-Leo Weyers, *Schuldrecht Band II Besonderer Teil* (1991) § 49 III.

231 § 935 para I does not apply to money, bearer instruments, or things sold by public auction (cf § 935 para II BGB).

232 BGHZ 4, 10 (34 et sqq).

233 Baur, *Lehrbuch des Sachenrechts*, § 52 V 2b bb.

South African law

4. South African law received the distinction between *vis absoluta* and *vis compulsiva*, or duress. In a contractual context, the content of duress has been obscured somewhat by case law, but in practice this does not seem to have any serious implications. Although a threat of economic harm in the form of "duress of goods" is recognised as an actionable form of duress, it is required that such duress has to be accompanied by some form of protest. Such a protest is not required in the case of duress through threats of personal physical harm.

5. A contract concluded under duress is voidable, i.e. valid until rescinded. Upon rescission all obligations are terminated and *restitutio in integrum* has to be provided. This entails putting the parties to the contract in the positions they were in before conclusion of the contract. Even if a contract was concluded with an innocent party, it would be voidable if induced by the duress of an outsider. Once it has been determined that a contract is void for illegality, the presence of duress is only relevant in so far as it helps determine the relative turpitude of the parties' conduct, and, consequently, the recoverability of their transfers.

6. In a non-contractual context, it has long been recognised that certain undue transfers obtained under unlawful compulsion can be reclaimed with the *condictio indebiti*. However, then it must be proven that payment was made in protest. Proof of such a protest is then supposed to indicate that the transfer was "involuntary". Some academic opinion as well as judicial decisions are critical of requiring such a protest. The *condictio indebiti* is therefore not restricted to undue transfers made in excusable error as to liability. Academic opinion diverges as to the basis on which the *condictio indebiti* can perform these different functions.

German law

7. The core provision in the German civil code dealing with compulsion is § 123 BGB, which is partly based on the law of *metus* and inter alia determines that a declaration of will induced by an unlawful threat (*Drohung*) can be rescinded. The threat need not necessarily be made by the person receiving the transfer, but could also be made by a third party. If the decision of will of the threatened person is affected, and he is consequently induced to enter into a juristic act, such an act will be voidable. In cases of compulsion, provisions regarding the legality of juristic acts could also be relevant. A juristic act falling foul of these provisions would be void.

8. If a declaration of will has been rescinded under § 123 BGB, any juristic act of which the declaration of will has formed part would be invalid. If such a juristic act was supposed to be the legal ground or *causa* for a transfer, such a transfer would be without legal ground or *sine causa*. Under §§ 812–822 BGB remedies based on unjustified enrichment could then be used to reclaim the transfer.

9. The enrichment remedy appropriate to cases of unlawful threats is the *Leistungskondiktion*, which, according to the prevailing view, bases reclaimability on the failure of the purpose of a transfer. However, according to an alternative approach such an analysis is unnecessary, since it is sufficient

merely to identify the absence of a relationship of indebtedness between the parties.

10. The *condictio indebiti* variation of the *Leistungskondiktion* is applicable when a compelled transfer which is not due fails to discharge an obligation. Recovery is not barred by the rule that a transfer made in the knowledge that it is not due cannot be recovered. The reason for this is that the basis of the knowledge rule is to prevent the transferor from acting contrary to his previous conduct (*venire contra factum proprium*). This reproach cannot be brought upon the victim of compulsion.

11. § 817 sent 1 BGB also acknowledges a *Leistungskondiktion* based on the *condictio ob turpem vel iniustam causam*. Some argue that this is the appropriate provision on which to rely when reclaiming a transfer made under extortion. However, it is doubtful whether this remedy is needed. Of greater importance is § 817 sent 2 BGB, which determines that a transferor would be barred from recovery if he acted with turpitude. This provision is interpreted to apply to all enrichment claims. Proof of compulsion can indicate that this provision should not prevent recovery.

12. Apart from remedies based on unjustified enrichment, unlawful threats could also give rise to remedies based on delict, *culpa in contrahendo*, and the invalidity of transfer of ownership.

Chapter 6

An evaluation of the treatment of compulsion in modern Scots law

6 INTRODUCTION

In the introductory chapter it was indicated that an evaluation of the modern law can benefit from tracing its historical roots and viewing it from a broader comparative perspective. In this chapter it will be sought to give effect to this objective. The emphasis will be on the modern Scots law of contract and unjustified enrichment, which are the main areas of law dealing with the recoverability of compelled transfers. Residual delictual and property law based remedies will only be dealt with incidentally.

Following the established pattern, the emphasis will first be on force and fear, especially within a contractual context. Here a lack of development is manifest: the Scottish Law Commission has stated that "on the whole [it] has not been developed by modern case law and the authorities are redolent of a bygone age",[1] while McKendrick has argued that a new general doctrine of force and fear should be adopted, "to bring the Scots law in this area out of the dark ages".[2] These comments mainly relate to the content of force and fear, and in particular the lack of development in broadening its horizons by explicit recognition of the actionability of a greater variety of threats of economic harm. But the effect of force and fear is also unclear: it still has to be determined whether it gives rise to voidness or voidability of contracts, and whether the remedies are based on contract or unjustified enrichment.

Thereafter the emphasis will be on cases of compulsion which fall outside the perimeters of force and fear. Here again it is apparent that the law is not in a satisfactory state. While it is recognised that certain compelled payments are recoverable, the basic requirements for the claims are not clearly spelled out. It will be indicated that this is merely symptomatic of a much greater underlying problem, namely to determine the basis for unjustified enrichment claims in Scots law in general. This subject will then be dealt with more comprehensively in the final chapter.

6.2 COMPULSION IN THE FORM OF FORCE AND FEAR

6.2.1 *The content of force and fear*

i. What's in a name?: "force and fear", "force or fear" and "extortion"

It is somewhat ironic that more than two millennia after Cicero reflected on the inconsistency of early Roman nomenclature by using both the expressions *vis et metus*

1 Memorandum on Defective Consent And Consequential Matters (Scot Law Com Memo No 42, 1978), vol 2, 119.

2 E McKendrick, "Economic Duress—A Reply" 1985 SLT (News) 277 at 280.

and *vis aut metus*, similar terminological uncertainty characterises modern Scots law.[3] While "force and fear" is generally favoured by the courts as well as some academics,[4] there is also support (as in the times of the Institutional writers) for the use of the expressions "force or fear"[5] and "extortion".[6] It is submitted that this diversity in usage leads to unnecessary confusion and that it is desirable to maintain standard terminology when describing the subject matter of this area of law. But before these labels are evaluated it is necessary to identify the key features of the subject matter they are supposed to cover. From the chapter on the modern law it is clear that it essentially concerns the situation where someone acts out of fear induced by force or other means. Force, whether actual or threatened, is therefore not a primary requirement for a claim, but rather only one way of illegally instilling fear. Since fear caused by threats of other forms of harm, especially economic harm, is increasing in significance, it is quite understandable that the courts generally focus on the fact that the victim acted under fear,[7] and then seek to determine whether unacceptable means were used in instilling the fear. The courts do not distinguish between force on the one hand, and fear on the other as separate grounds for claiming relief.[8] This is an economical approach, followed as early as Roman times,[9] when *vis et (aut) metus* was contracted to *metus*—a term which, incidentally, is still used in modern South African law.[10]

An important implication of placing the emphasis on the fact that someone acted under fear is that *vis absoluta* cannot be regarded as a form of "force and fear".[11] Since *vis absoluta* is purely a case of applying force in a way which excludes any decision of will of the victim, his fear is irrelevant. Another implication is that it makes it critical to determine what method was used to instil fear in the victim, since fear alone is not sufficient. Here it is significant that the method of instilling fear generally involves some form of threat.[12] It should be noted, though, that restricting the unacceptable methods of instilling fear to illegal threats is not entirely satisfactory. Where a person acts out of fear induced by physical force which falls short of *vis absoluta* it is doubtful to state that he acted because he was subjected to illegal threats of (future) harm. It is rather the actual (present) harm

---

3 Cf the discussion of the terminology in *Hislop v Dickson Motors (Forres) Ltd* 1978 SLT 73 at 64; *Priestnell v Hutcheson* (1857) 19 D 495; *Hunter v Bradford Property Trust Ltd* 1977 SLT 33; *Trustee Savings Bank v Balloch* 1983 SLT 240 at 241; *Love v Marshall* (1870) 9 M 291.

4 Cf *Wolfson v Edelman* 1952 SLT (Sh Ct) 97; *Hunter v Bradford Property Trust Ltd* 1977 SLT 33; *Trustee Savings Bank v Balloch* 1983 SLT 240; Gloag, *The Law of Contract*, 488; Walker, *The Law of Contracts and Related Obligations in Scotland*, 296; SME, vol 15 (1997), 439; Woolman, *An Introduction to the Scots law of Contract*, 73.

5 Cf Gloag and Henderson, *The Law of Scotland*, 119; McBryde, *The Law of Contract in Scotland*, 250.

6 Cf *Priestnell v Hutcheson* (1857) 19 D 495 at 499; *Hislop v Dickson Motors (Forres) Ltd* 1978 SLT 73 at 74.

7 Cf 4.2.1 above; *Hislop v Dickson Motors (Forres) Ltd* 1978 SLT 73; *Priestnell v Hutcheson* (1857) 19 D 495; *Hunter v Bradford Property Trust Ltd* 1977 SLT 33; *Trustee Savings Bank v Balloch* 1983 SLT 240 at 241; *Love v Marshall* (1870) 9 M 291.

8 But cf Guthrie Smith, *Law of Damages*, 42 where a distinction is drawn between "force" and "fear". "Force" is then supposed to be physical violence, i.e. violently laying hands on another, while "fear" is supposed to encompass moral violence, i.e. operating on the fears of another by threats of mischief.

9 Cf D 4.2.1; *Priestnell v Hutcheson* (1857) 19 D 495.

10 Cf 5.3 above.

11 Cf also Bankton, *Institute*, 1.10.50; Voet, *Commentarius ad Pandectas*, 4.2.1.

12 Cf Gloag, *The Law of Contract*, 488. On modern German law, where the existence of a wrongful threat (*Drohung*) is a distinct ground for rescinding juristic acts cf § 123 I BGB, 5.4 above.

which causes him to act. For example, where a person who has been abducted and locked up in a cellar signs an agreement to obtain his release, he is acting out of fear induced by present harm, rather than out of fear induced by threats of future harm. Although the focus on the existence of threats takes account of the practically most significant method of inducing fear, such an approach is therefore not comprehensive enough.

It is against the background of these remarks that the labels of "force and fear", "force or fear" and "extortion" will be evaluated. As far as "force and fear" is concerned, this label appears to be somewhat misleading insofar as it suggests that "force", whether actual or threatened, is an essential element for a claim based on "force and fear". However, this problem can be overcome by interpreting force broadly to encompass actual force which does not amount to *vis absoluta*, as well as illegal threats of harm in general. In fact, the expression "force and fear" can then be regarded as a hendiadys, meaning "fear induced by force".[13] A more suitable modern version would be "fear induced by either force, threats of force, or threats of other forms of harm".

Although the expression "force and fear" is generally used in modern law, support has been expressed for use of the term "force or fear". It will be recalled that Stair used this term,[14] and to some this indicates the possibility of separate pleas.[15] Presumably, the argument is that the pursuer could either plead that he acted under "force" or that he acted under "fear". The advantage of this approach is that if "force" is split from "fear", it would be easier to accommodate *vis absoluta*—something which the current approach, which emphasises fear, fails to do. However, the disadvantage is that uncertainty arises as to the position of force which does not amount to *vis absoluta*, but still causes fear (e.g. the incarceration example mentioned above). Are these now cases of "force" or "fear"?[16] Furthermore, the danger of isolating fear from one of its prime causes, namely force or the threat thereof, is increased. As indicated above, the mere fact that someone acted out of fear has never been sufficient to provide the basis of relief. It has to be induced by someone else in an unacceptable way, and here force has always been particularly relevant. It should therefore be apparent that no clearly discernible advantages are to be gained by using the expression "force or fear", rather than "force and fear".

A further term used to describe the situation where someone acts out of fear induced by force or other means is "extortion". This causes some confusion, since the term bears a variety of meanings. For example, to Gloag, like Erskine, "force or fear" relates to threats of an injury by one party and apprehension of it by another, while "extortion" apparently relates to cases where someone exploits the need of another and tries to keep him bound to a contract with inequitable terms.[17] However, other modern authors interpret the relationship between force and fear (or "force or fear") and extortion differently. Their view is that there are various forms of extortion, of which force and fear (or "force or fear") is but one. McBryde, for example, distinguishes between various sets of rules governing situations of extortion, namely

13 Cf *Wolfson v Edelman* 1952 SLT (Sh Ct) 97; *Hunter v Bradford Property Trust Ltd* 1977 SLT 33; *Trustee Savings Bank v Balloch* 1983 SLT 240; Gloag, *The Law of Contract*, 488; Walker, *The Law of Contracts and Related Obligations in Scotland*, 296; SME, vol 15 (1997), 439; Woolman, *An Introduction to the Scots law of Contract*, 73.

14 Stair, *Institutions*, 1.9.8.

15 Gloag and Henderson, *The Law of Scotland*, 119.

16 If so, it would be at variance with Institutional authority: cf Bankton, *Institute*, 1.10.50.

17 Gloag, *The Law of Contract*, 492.

the rules regarding force and fear, enorm lesion, and unfair contract terms.[18] The most recent edition of Gloag and Henderson's *Law of Scotland* follows a similar approach by regarding "force or fear" as one way of extorting consent.[19] According to Walker, extortion (i.e. when someone pays or undertakes to pay a "grossly excessive price") can be the result of fraud, force and fear, facility and circumvention or undue influence.[20] Woolman also distinguishes between the rules of force and fear, which deal with a special case of improper conduct in the bargaining process, namely the use of some form of coercion or unfair pressure, and the possible "general principle" that relief should be provided in cases of extortion.[21] Extortion is then viewed from a broader perspective, in the sense that it covers procedurally improper means of obtaining consent, as well as substantive unfairness or "unconscionability".[22] It should then be obvious that a label which is used in such a broad sense can hardly be regarded as appropriate for also describing the specific situation where someone acts out of fear induced by force or other means.

ii. Vis absoluta

Having established that the law of force and fear essentially deals with *vis compulsiva*, and not *vis absoluta*, it becomes important to determine more exactly where the dividing line between these categories lies. This distinction also has practical implications, which will be dealt with later on: it determines whether remedies based on property law or unjustified enrichment should be available, whether the victim has the choice to uphold the validity of what he has done, and whether transfers are recoverable in the hands of third parties. As far as the definition of *vis absoluta* is concerned, it is obvious that consent is excluded altogether if a person's hand is grabbed and made to trace a signature, so that the victim is a mere instrument of the wrongdoer.[23] This complete absence of volition can also be experienced when a person is put in a hypnotic trance,[24] or temporarily is mentally deprived of the legal capacity to act,[25] or where a person of far inferior strength is threatened with

---

18 *The Law of Contract in Scotland*, 250 et sqq. Cf also W W McBryde, "Extortionate Contracts" (1976) 21 *JLS* 322.

19 Gloag and Henderson, *The Law of Scotland*, 119.

20 *The Law of Contracts and Related Obligations in Scotland*, 311.

21 *An Introduction to the Scots Law of Contract*, 73 et sqq; 78 et sqq.

22 When someone merely acts out of feelings of guilt—of being pressurised by his own conscience, relief would not be provided. Cf, for example, *Anderson v Anderson* 1991 SLT (Sh Ct) 11. Here a husband, on the verge of leaving his wife and moving in with another woman, signed a document in which he donated his money and shares to his wife. He later regretted this, and claimed that this was done under pressure of the wife, and "to mollify her following his departure from the former matrimonial home." It was held that this averment was unsubstantiated, and that he was not pressurised, but "quite happy to do what he did at the time, that he signed for his own peace of mind, feeling guilty about leaving the pursuer to live with another woman and accepting that this departure was 'a bolt from the blue'" (13). The validity of the disposition was upheld.

23 For an analysis of these cases, cf Memorandum on Defective Consent And Consequential Matters (Scot Law Com Memo No 42, 1978), vol 2, 2 et sqq.

24 Cf American Law Institute, Restatement of The Law of Contracts (1932), para 494; Restatement of The Law of Contracts—Second (1981), para 174.

25 Cf the South African case of *Smith v Smith* 1948 (4) SA 61 (N). Here the plaintiff was "assaulted, bullied, threatened, and cajoled" (64) into marrying the defendant. It was found that "the worry she experienced over her proposed marriage to the defendant, together with the improper pressure to which she was subjected almost constantly by her father and the defendant, induced in her a state of *mental incompetence, if not of physical ill-health*, which deprived her of the power either of resisting that pressure further or of freely and properly applying her mind to the question of her consent to the marriage" (own emphasis, at 66).

immediate personal violence to sign a document in ignorance of its true nature.[26] However, there are (extremely marginal) situations where the will is exercised, but so barely that it can hardly be said that it was exercised at all.

Although care should be taken in comparing superficially related institutions in criminal law and private law,[27] it is submitted that the following example taken from the Scots law dealing with the crime of robbery (as opposed to extortion) illustrates this point. In criminal law it would be fatuous to distinguish between the situation where a robber holds a gun to someone's head and takes money from him, and the situation where he says "give me your purse or I shall kill you", and the victim then does so.[28] The latter case is also regarded as one of robbery. Likewise, it is submitted, it should be regarded as an instance of *vis absoluta*.[29] In essence it would have made no difference whether the victim handed over the money or not: the immediacy of the threat and the inevitability of the outcome rendered the exercise of the will practically irrelevant.

iii. Vis compulsiva

Once it is recognised that the exercise of a will could be present in cases of *vis absoluta*, the danger is of course that the borders with *vis compulsiva* become blurred. However, it is submitted that such uncertainty is inevitable. As the *Memorandum on Defective Consent and Consequential Matters* by the Scottish Law Commission states,

> We find it extremely difficult to determine at what point consent may be regarded as altogether excluded—as contrasted with consent most reluctantly extorted ... We accept that in some extremely rare cases *vis absoluta* may exclude completely rational exercise of the will of a declarant. In such situations the ostensible act should be regarded in law as an absolute nullity. We cannot hope to catalogue all the means—psychological, chemical or violent—by which the evil ingenuity of man has in the past or may in the future compel a victim to act involuntarily against his interests. Therefore our provisional conclusion is that it should be left to unfettered judicial decision, based on the evidence of all relevant circumstances, to determine whether the ostensible act of a coerced victim was, on the one hand, in no sense the expression of his will or, on the other, a reluctant declaration of his will secured by extortion.[30]

Unfortunately, as indicated before, a number of recent cases require an overpowering of the will or mind in order to establish force and fear.[31] The application of this test complicates the task of distinguishing between *vis absoluta* and *vis compulsiva* (and, consequently, between cases where the effect is voidness and voidability), since it implies that in both cases there is no consent at all. It is somewhat ironic

---

26 Cf American Law Institute, Restatement of The Law of Contracts, para 494; Restatement of The Law of Contracts—Second, para 174.

27 Cf McBryde, *The Law of Contract in Scotland*, 253.

28 Cf Hume, *Commentaries*, vol 1, 105; 3.3.3 above.

29 As the Memorandum on Defective Consent And Consequential Matters (Scot Law Com Memo No 42, 1978) states, "[t]he existence, or otherwise, of robbery seems to us to constitute in general a sound test for distinguishing between *vis absoluta* and *vis compulsiva* so far as transfers of moveables by coercion are concerned" (vol 2, 4).

30 Memorandum on Defective Consent And Consequential Matters (Scot Law Com Memo No 42, 1978), vol 2, 6 et sq. Cf also American Law Institute, Restatement of The Law of Contracts, para 492 ("As a practical matter it is obvious that there is no absolute demarcation between fear that deprives a person of free will and judgment, and lesser degrees of fear; or at least if there is a difference in kind between varying degrees of fear it is only between an extremity of terror sufficient to destroy every motive except the desire to escape, and lesser degrees").

31 Cf 4.2.1(i) above.

that some of these cases rely on English authority,[32] while English lawyers have also been critical of the test.[33] In fact, the House of Lords has rejected the notion that duress deprives a person of his free choice or overbears his will: in the words of Lord Simon of Glaisdale, "duress again deflects, without destroying the will of one of the contracting parties".[34] Similar sentiments have been expressed by Scots lawyers. Professor McBryde (like Lord Simon of Glaisdale) acknowledges that such a "vitiated consent" test is problematical for "[d]uress does not 'overbear' the will, nor destroy it: it 'deflects' it".[35] Or, as Thompson puts it, the person acting under force and fear's "sentience is unaffected; the duress consists of him performing an action he would not normally choose to perform due to pressure which severely threatens his interests".[36] This is the age-old idea of Paulus, as acknowledged by Stair and other Institutional authorities,[37] which faces one again: what is willed under force is nonetheless willed. In other words, the problem is not that someone did not will something but the *way* in which his will was formed.[38] One must therefore strongly agree with Professor McKendrick that it should cause the Scottish lawyer grave concern that the overborne will theory still appears to form the basis of force and fear.[39] However, it is of course not sufficient to say that force and fear does not relate to the overbearing of a will, but to the improper way in which consent has been obtained. It still has to be determined what makes the obtaining of consent improper. Here it has been argued that one should focus on the reasonableness of the alternatives available to the victim. Such an approach is clearly unsatisfactory, for the test of lack of reasonable alternatives "deflects attention from the fundamental

---

32 In *Mahmood v Mahmood* 1993 SLT 589 Lord Sutherland relied on *Pao On v Lau Yiu Long* [1980] AC 614 in stating that "the ultimate question must be whether there was such coercion of the pursuer's will as to vitiate consent." He was particularly influenced by a passage of Lord Scarman, where it was held that "duress, whatever form it takes, is a coercion of the will so as to vitiate consent". Cf also *Mahmud v Mahmud* 1994 SLT 599, which also referred to the *Pao On* case, as well as to *Hirani v Hirani* (1983) 4 FLR 332.

33 Cf *Lynch v DPP of Northern Ireland* [1975] AC 653. Cf also the criticism of Professor P S Atiyah, *Essays on Contract* (1986), 129. He rejects the theory of the "overborne will" and acknowledges that the coerced promisor still intends to make his promise (130). The presence of duress rather depends on whether the duress was "legitimate", which is not a "neutral" issue.

34 [1975] AC 653 at 695B–C. Although it was a criminal case, these remarks were made in the context of a discussion of the English law of contract. This approach was not followed in some subsequent decisions, most notably the Privy Council decision of *Pao On v Lau Yiu Long* [1980] AC 614.

35 *The Law of Contract in Scotland*, 252. According to him "it is easier to apply the 'overborne will' theory to the involuntary act than it is to the voluntary action under pressure, which is more analogous to the effect produced by fraud or undue influence. Until this difference is recognised, it will be difficult to construct a satisfactory theory of force and fear in Scots law".

36 Thompson, "Economic Duress" 1985 SLT (News) 85 at 88. Cf also Palmer, *The Law of Restitution*, vol 2, 248. In the context of the law in the United States, he mentions that "[t]he emphasis on overcoming the will in cases of duress occasionally leads courts to the erroneous conclusion that the coercion must have deprived the party subjected to it of the capacity of rational action." For a general objection to the view that coerced agreements are "involuntary", cf Philips, "Are coerced agreements involuntary?" 1984 *Law and Philosophy* 133.

37 Stair, *Institutions*, 1.9.8.

38 Cf Guest (ed) *Chitty on Contracts*, vol 1, 401 ("... as long as the doctrine of duress is treated as resting on an absence of consent, or of a voluntary act, it would seem immaterial what has caused the absence of consent, or the act to be involuntary. Duress would be a question of fact, and not of law" and 802 ("Once it is accepted that the basis of duress does not depend on the absence of consent, it follows that it is the nature of the pressure or the threats which becomes all-important").

39 McKendrick, "Economic Duress—A Reply" 1985 SLT (News) 277.

issue which is the behaviour of the party exerting the pressure".[40] The example has been mentioned of someone who has to sell his house during a slump in the property market: he has no reasonable alternative to sell his house, yet no-one would seriously argue that this would mean he sold under force and fear and should therefore be provided with relief. The notion that "inequality of the exchange" could act as an alternative basis for force and fear is also unacceptable, for the obvious reasons that first it does not form part of Scots law,[41] and second it focuses on the substance of what was agreed upon, rather than the way in which the agreement was obtained. An alternative approach, proposed by Professor McKendrick, comprise two tiers: while the role of consent is only to show that the pressure exerted was a *cause* of the victim's action, the more difficult problem is to determine which forms of exerting pressure are so improper that they constitute force and fear. Here he urges one to focus on the threats used in concluding the contract.[42] Certain threats should not be allowed in the course of negotiating contracts "to ensure that people can participate freely in the market place and to seek to achieve an efficient allocation of resources in society".[43] The categories of procedural unfairness should be restricted to threats which are wrongful in themselves, threats which seek to bring about an unlawful goal, and undue influence. McKendrick concludes by stating that if the Scottish courts were to adopt this two-tier approach, they would not only thereby provide "a sound basis for the doctrine of economic duress, but also a general doctrine of duress . . .".[44]

McKendrick's general approach appears to be sound, but it should be refined somewhat to bring it closer into line with the existing Scots law. In the overview of the Scots law it was shown that central to a claim based on force and fear was the question whether *reasonable fear* should be caused or induced by *illegal or unwarrantable threats*.[45] McKendrick's two-tier approach does not fully take this into account in that it fails to deal adequately with the requirement of reasonable fear and does not cover all threats which constitute force and fear,[46] while including

40 McKendrick, "Economic Duress—A Reply" 1985 SLT (News) 277 at 278; cf also McBryde, *The Law of Contract in Scotland*, 253.

41 For an attempt to popularise it England, cf the judgment of Lord Denning in *Lloyds Bank Ltd v Bundy* [1975] QB 326.

42 Cf also Woolman, *An Introduction to the Scots Law of Contract*, 66 ("It is ... not strictly correct to say that one person's will is actually overborne ... Rather he is influenced or pressurised in such a way as to choose one action instead of another. So it is the illegitimacy of the threats which becomes crucial").

43 "Economic Duress—A Reply" 1985 SLT (News) 277 at 279 (referring to A E Leff, "Thomist Unconscionability" 1980 *Canadian Business Law Journal* 424).

44 McKendrick, "Economic Duress—A Reply" 1985 SLT (News) 277 at 280.

45 This scheme of duress is roughly comparable to the one on coercion provided by the American philosopher Wertheimer, although he also regards undue influence as a form of coercion. According to Wertheimer's theory, coercion has two prongs. The first is the *threat*, or proposal prong: A illegally threatens, or proposes to B that if he does not do X, the harmful event Y will happen. Of course A should be able to influence the realisation of this event (Y), otherwise it would be merely a hollow threat. The second prong is the *choice* prong: the person subjected to the threat should have no real choice but to submit to it. This prong could be compared with the requirement that fear should be reasonable. In terms of this analysis, force and fear could be described as a form of coercion. Cf A Wertheimer, *Coercion* (1987). For a critical but mainly positive analysis, cf T Honoré, "A Theory of Coercion" (1990) 10 *OJLS* 94.

46 The illegality of a threat could also lie in the relationship between the threatened conduct and the desired outcome. According to Professor Sir T B Smith, "[m]enaces, if they are to avoid a contract, must not be of something which the person applying pressure has a right to do. Thus if a security is elicited by a threat to take bankruptcy proceedings against a debtor, this cannot

undue influence, which is traditionally distinct from force and fear in Scots law.[47] These elements of force and fear will now be analysed in greater detail.

(a) Reasonable fear

Scots law (like South African law) demands that the fear has to be reasonable.[48] In both systems this requirement can be traced to the *homo constantissimus* standard of Roman law, as watered down to the *vir constans* standard of the *ius commune*. As indicated before, "reasonable fear" is of limited significance in South African law: it receives little recognition in practice and academics have criticised it on the basis that the person who instilled the fear should not be able to raise the defence that the claimant should not have been frightened so easily. The Scottish Law Commission has also expressed the view that the traditional requirement of reasonable constancy is not necessary,[49] and judicial criticism has also been expressed.[50] It is submitted that its only use is to help determine whether a causal link existed between the threat and that which has been done under fear. In other words, it indicates whether the threat induced that which has been done under fear. One could argue that fear of a mere trifle cannot be reasonable, and could therefore not give rise to a situation of force and fear. In the same way one could argue that if someone reacts to the threat of a mere trifle, it is difficult to infer that the threat actually induced him to act. The "reasonable fear" requirement could therefore be regarded as a test for causality. This explanation seems more convincing than one based on exalted standards of fortitude and constancy.[51]

(b) Illegal or unwarrantable threats

The notion that threats have to be illegal or unwarrantable in order to constitute force and fear[52] is certainly not new, and can be traced back to the requirement in

---

be challenged if payment alone is sought. But a threat to take bankruptcy proceedings might invalidate a promise to marry elicited under such pressure" (cf *A Short Commentary on the Law of Scotland* 838; cf 5.4.1 above on the position in German law).

47 On the distinction between force and fear and undue influence, cf 7.3.1. 1 (a) below. It should be recognised, though, that at times the border between undue influence, force and fear and even *vis absoluta* are not clear. Cf *Mahmud v Mahmud* 1994 SLT 599 and *Mahmood v Mahmood* 1993 SLT 589. Both these cases were decided on the basis of force and fear, but given the general nature of the pressure exerted on the victims, it could be argued that they were rather subjected to undue influence. Depending on how seriously one views the pressure, it is even possible that the pressure could have been so strong as to deprive the victims of the ability to consent (cf the discussion of *Smith v Smith* 1948 (4) SA 61 (N) at 5.3.1 above).

48 Cf 4.2.1 i and 5.3.1 above.

49 *Memorandum on Defective Consent And Consequential Matters* (Scot Law Com Memo No 42, 1978) vol 2, 124 et sq.

50 Cf the reference to *Mahmud v Mahmud* 1994 SLT 599 at 4.2.1.i above.

51 Cf *Sutherland v Fletcher* 1977 SLT (Land Ct) 5, 13 August 1976. Here it was stated that a wife, "a fairly excitable woman", who signed a document after being visited by two men "in the half-darkness of a winter's morning and confused by the lack of her reading glasses", "undoubtedly felt that she was under some compulsion to sign it ...". Compulsion, or a "degree of duress", was regarded as present "even if she freely appreciated the contents of the document" (at 7). If fear could be regarded as reasonable under these circumstances, it would seem that little support for the values of fortitude and constancy underlying the *vir constans* requirement has remained (cf, in the context of South African law, *Block v Drogon, Dreier & Co* 1910 WLD 330, and in the context of English law, *Scott v Sebright* (1886) 12 PD 21 at 24; further cf Burrows, *The Law of Restitution*, 163).

52 Cf *Hislop v Dickson Motors (Forres) Ltd* 1978 SLT 73 at 75; *Hunter v Bradford Property Trust Ltd* 1977 SLT 33.

Roman law that the conduct causing *metus* had to be *contra bonos mores*. But how does one determine that a threat is illegal or unwarrantable? Threats of personal physical harm clearly meet this requirement and do not present problems. If threats of diligence were used to obtain more than was due, recovery would usually also be possible. In some other cases it was more difficult to determine what constitutes an "illegal or unwarrantable" threat. However, it is clear from the works of the Institutional writers as well as Scottish case law that threats of economic harm could be sufficient for the provision of relief on grounds of force and fear.[53] As Professor McBryde acknowledges "there does not appear to be a difficulty in the recognition by Scots law of economic threats as a form of force and fear or extortion".[54] Professor Andrew Thompson has also submitted that

> ... there is sufficient authority for Scottish practitioners to argue that economic duress is a valid segment or sub-category of the general concept of duress already recognised in Scots law ... The English precedents could then be employed as a persuasive authority dealing with various fact situations in which the doctrine may (or may not) apply.[55]

Scots law can indeed benefit from referring to English case law dealing with economic threats. But certain considerations should be kept in mind. The first is that the position in English law used to be quite different from that in Scots law: in English law the traditional examples of duress were threats to the person, and threats to seize or withhold goods; only more recent developments in the case law suggest that "economic duress" could also be a ground for relief.[56] The approach to duress seems to have been to add categories in broadening the scope of duress. In Scots law the position was, and still is, different. The essential test for force and fear was that the fear should be caused by conduct or threats which are illegal and unwarrantable. Within this broad framework it was possible for the courts to decide specific cases.

Another consideration is that while it may be of value to refer to English examples, it may be less valuable to use the label "economic duress". The use of such a label presupposes that it makes sense to categorise threats according to their effect on certain interests such as personal physical integrity, reputation or dignity, and economic worth. The label of "economic duress" would then (broadly speaking) cover cases of duress affecting economic interests. However, the label does not indicate what amounts to the duress—it only indicates what interest the duress affects. Again it should be noted that Scottish courts view the test of "illegal and unwarrantable threats" generally, and do not need to distinguish between various forms of force and fear in terms of their effect on certain interests.[57]

---

53 Cf Stair, *Institutions*, 1.9.8 (based on D 4.2.9); Bankton, *Institute*, 1.10.51; *Wiseman v Logie* (1700) Mor 16505; *Gow v Henry* (1899) 2 F 48; *Education Authority of Dumfriesshire v Wright* 1926 SLT 217; *Sutherland v Montrose Fishing Co Ltd* (1921) Sh Ct Rep 239; cf also *Mcafee v Gray or Mcafee* (Outer House) 6 July 1990; *Memorandum on Defective Consent And Consequential Matters* (Scot Law Com Memo No 42, 1978) vol 2, 115.

54 *The Law of Contract in Scotland*, 252 et sqq.

55 1977 SLT 85 at 88.

56 Cf *Occidental Worldwide Investment Corporation v Skibs A/S Avanti (The Siboen and The Sibotre)* [1976] 1 Lloyd's Rep 293; *North Ocean Shipping Co Ltd v Hyundai Construction Co Ltd (The Atlantic Baron)* [1979] QB 705; *Pao On v Lau Yiu Long* [1980] AC 614; *Universe Tankships of Monrovia v International Transport Workers Federation and Laughton (The Universe Sentinel)* [1981] ICR 129, reversed [1983] AC 366; Guest (ed), *Chitty on Contracts*, vol 1, 404 et sqq.

57 Viewed in this light, the Law Commission's description of the type of threats beyond those of physical violence which should be relevant as a ground of annulment is problematic. According to the Commission, "[o]ur view is that where an obligation has been concluded through the use by one party against the other of threats of harm to the person, or of serious harm to any lawful

A third consideration to be kept in mind is that there is an inherent danger that various sets of rules may develop to cover various cases of force and fear when in principle there is no reason to do so. This seems to be a trap into which the South African courts have walked. In *Hendricks v Barnett*[58] it was decided that in cases of duress of goods the pursuer would have to prove he made an unequivocal protest.[59] There seems to be no sound reason why this requirement should be set in addition to the general one that the threats have to be "illegal and unwarrantable". Once it has been established that this general requirement has been satisfied, relief should be provided. It is submitted that in determining what constitutes an "illegal or unawarrantable" threat, German law provides particularly clear criteria. "Economic duress" is not recognised as a specific category of duress or *Drohung*: the essential feature of *Drohung* is proof of an illegal threat, and the illegality of the threat can lie in the threatened conduct, the desired outcome, or simply the relationship between threatened conduct and desired outcome.[60] These criteria are quite abstract, but, it is submitted, the courts should have as much freedom as possible to determine the content of "illegal and unwarrantable threats" within the context of changing social values.

6.2.2 *The effect of force and fear*

In modern Scots law, the effect of force and fear is mainly that of a factor which affects the validity of contracts. In the chapter on the modern law it was indicated that it is not clear how force and fear performs this function. Here the two most important questions are whether a compelled act retains its validity until it is reduced, and whether, once reduction has been granted, the basis of recovery of compelled transfers is contractual or based on unjustified enrichment.

i. Voidness and voidability

The question whether a compelled act retains its validity until it is reduced, or whether it gives rise to voidness or voidability, only needs to be dealt with briefly. An analysis of the case law in the chapter on modern law already has shown that even though the authorities generally treat contracts concluded under force and fear as void, such an approach is problematic. It was shown that voidness is not compatible with case law which recognises the possibility of ratification or homologation of extorted deeds,[61] that it goes against the grain of acquisition by third parties,[62] and that it denies the victim the choice (however remote the possibility that he would want to exercise it) to uphold the extorted act. Modern commentators then also find an approach based on voidability more appropriate. Professor McBryde, for example, has stated that it "would bring more logical consistency to the law", if the House

---

personal or economic interest of that other, then the obligation so extorted should be annullable" (Memorandum on Defective Consent And Consequential Matters (Scot Law Com Memo No 42, 1978) vol 2, 126). The problem here is that the focus is on the interests of the threatened party, and not on the nature of the threat. Inasmuch as these issues are simply two sides of the same coin, the difference is academic, although it would certainly lead to greater clarity to refer to an illegal threat, rather than a threat of harm to a lawful interest. But the test is unsatisfactory if these issues are not treated as two sides of the same coin, so that an illegal threat to an "unlawful interest" would be regarded as admissible.

58 1975 (1) SA 765 (N) at 768H–769A.

59 Cf De Wet and Van Wyk, *Kontraktereg en Handelsreg*, 45; 5.3.1 above.

60 Cf 5.4.1 above.

61 Cf 4.2.2.i above.

62 Cf 4.2.2.i above.

of Lords were to treat some contracts induced by force and fear as voidable.[63] This view is endorsed—not only for the reasons mentioned above, but also because the consequence of voidability is more in line with the historical development of force and fear or *vis et metus* in the *ius commune*. Initially in Roman law it was not asked whether the contracts were void or voidable: the *actio quod metus causa* was available, and the victim of fear could claim against anyone who obtained something "*metus causa*", i.e. "*as the consequence of fear*". But in the *ius commune*, which, like canon law and some Institutional writings (most notably that of Bankton), recognised the distinction between *vis absoluta* and *vis compulsiva*, it was perceived that *vis absoluta* should give rise to voidness, and *vis compulsiva* to voidability.[64] It is only Stair's support for voidness which provided the impetus for the later popular acceptance of the view that force and fear leads to voidness. However, these remarks were not made in the context of contract or unjustified enrichment, but in the context of delict. Later Scots law did not follow Stair's view that force and fear should only be regarded as a delict, and generally deals with it in the form of *vis compulsiva*. It is therefore submitted that the balance of evidence favours voidability rather than voidness. From a comparative perspective this view is preferable, and its acceptance will bring Scots law in line with the position in comparable jurisdictions.

ii. Restitutio in integrum

In Scots law the remedies in cases of voidness differ from those in cases of voidability. The remedies in cases of voidness are based on unjustified enrichment: if there never was a contractual basis for the transfer, no contractual remedy can be provided, and actions based on unjustified enrichment should then be used for recovery.[65] However, if it is accepted that compulsion does not give rise to voidness but to voidability, it can be argued that the fact that a transfer was initially made on a contractual basis indicates that contractual remedies should be provided, rather than remedies based on unjustified enrichment. There is support for the proposition that this is in fact the position in Scots law. In this regard it has been stated that *restitutio in integrum* is not only a condition for reduction of a voidable agreement,[66] but also a remedy on rescission, and that "it seems to be regarded invariably as a contractual remedy".[67] This, by and large, is also the position in South African law. The classical position there is formulated as follows by Professor Wouter De Vos. According to him, *restitutio in integrum* is "... the action with which a person asks that a voidable contract be set aside, and with which he claims the return of that which he had given or its value, while he also restores from his side. It is a separate legal remedy, with its own *raison d'être*, and is not an enrichment action".[68]

However, Professor Danie Visser has recently challenged this view, and argued that *restitutio in integrum* should rather be regarded as an enrichment remedy. In the context of Scots law, Stewart, like Visser, also regards *restitutio in integrum* as a

63 McBryde, *Void, Voidable, Illegal and Unenforceable Contracts in Scots Law*, 36. Cf also Memorandum on Defective Consent And Consequential Matters (Scot Law Com Memo No 42, 1978) vol 2, 2 et sqq; McKendrick, "Economic Duress—A Reply" 1985 SLT (News) 277; contra Thompson, "Economic Duress" 1985 SLT (News) 85.

64 Cf Zimmermann, *The Law of Obligations*, 655, 660; 5.2.2 above.

65 Cf also this section below.

66 Cf Gloag, *The Law of Contract*, 533 et sqq; McBryde, *The Law of Contract in Scotland*, 626; Woolman, *An Introduction to the Scots Law of Contract*, 83.

67 Whitty, "*The Taxonomy of Unjustified Enrichment in Scots Law*", essay prepared for Seminar on the Law of Unjustified Enrichment, 23 October 1993, 17 n 65.

68 De Vos, *Verrykingsaanspreeklikheid in die Suid-Afrikaanse reg*, 158 (own translation).

"restitutionary remedy for unjust enrichment", but still acknowledges that *restitutio in integrum* "... is now subsumed within the procedures and requirements for avoiding contracts. That is the path Scots law has taken and it is so far ingrained that it cannot be unravelled and neither is it particularly desirable to do so. It can be left with the law of contract but should be recognised as supporting the vitiation aspect of 'unjust' enrichment".[69]

These views need to be evaluated. At least two considerations are relevant in determining whether a claim is contractual or based on unjustified enrichment. The first is the measure of recovery. If the measure of a claim based on unjustified enrichment is different from that of a contractual claim, then a basis for differentiation is at hand. For example, De Vos argues that *restitutio in integrum* is not an enrichment remedy since it could be used to obtain payment of interest *ex tunc*, and since loss of enrichment cannot be pleaded as a defence. To this Visser countered that in the South African law of unjustified enrichment the measure of recovery is not fixed, and that these differences do therefore not necessarily mean that *restitutio in integrum* is not a remedy of unjustified enrichment. It seems that in the context of Scots law the measure of recovery does not provide much guidance either. Differences in the measure of recovery within the law of unjustified enrichment indicate that it would probably not be possible to say that the measure of recovery with *restitutio in integrum* provides any indication of whether a claim of unjustified enrichment lies or not.[70]

The second criterion is more theoretical in nature. If a contract is void and ownership passed, recovery is based on unjustified enrichment. A contract never existed, and contractual remedies are therefore inappropriate. But if the contract is voidable, a contractual basis for the transfer exists until reduction. This would indicate that, as in the case of breach of contract,[71] the basis of relief is contractual. This is the position in South African law, which, as we have seen, regards *restitutio in integrum* as a contractual remedy.[72] However, if it is accepted that reduction works retrospectively (*ex tunc*), the situation is practically the same as when the contract was void from the beginning. Enrichment remedies are then appropriate. However, sight should not be lost of the rule that *restitutio in integrum* is a condition for avoiding a contract. In German law, for example, *restitutio in integrum, eo nomine*, has disappeared but in its place there are remedies of unjustified enrichment, in particular the *condictio indebiti*[73] and the mechanism of the *Saldotheorie*, which entails that if two parties have enrichment claims against each other arising from void mutual agreements, the enrichment debtor's counterclaim has to be diminished to the extent that he cannot retransfer what he has obtained.[74] It therefore indicates

69 Stewart, *The Law of Restitution in Scotland*, 214.

70 Cf Whitty, "*The Taxonomy of Unjustified Enrichment in Scots Law*", essay prepared for Seminar on the Law of Unjustified Enrichment, 23 October 1993, 16 et sq.

71 Cf Visser, "Rethinking Unjustified Enrichment: A Perspective of the Competition between Contractual and Enrichment Remedies" 1992 *AJ* 203. On the rather unusual application of the *condictio causa data causa non secuta* in Scots law in cases of rescission for breach of contract, cf *Cantiere San Rocco v Clyde Shipbuilding and Engineering Co* 1922 SC 723; Evans-Jones, "Unjust Enrichment, Contract and the Third Reception of Roman law in Scotland" (1993) 109 *LQR* 663; McQueen, "Unjustified enrichment and breach of contract" 1994 *JR* 137 at 142 et sqq.

72 Cf 5.3.2.i above.

73 Cf Visser, "Rethinking Unjustified Enrichment: A Perspective of the Competition between Contractual and Enrichment remedies" 1992 *AJ* 203 at 216 n 65.

74 Cf RGZ 54, 137; RGZ 163, 360 et sq; BGHZ 1, 75(81); BGHZ 53, 145; BGHZ 57, 147 et sq; V Beuthien, "Das Rätsel Saldotheorie" 1979 *Jura* 532; Lieb, *Münchener Kommentar* § 818 n 86 fn 192; Koppensteiner and Kramer, *Ungerechtfertigte Bereicherung*, 137; Visser, "Rethinking Unjustified

how the law of unjustified enrichment should deal with voidable transactions, such as contracts induced by compulsion. It should be noted, though, that the theory has been criticised for failing to address openly the questions it is supposed to answer. German law, like Scots law, needs to develop a theory which clearly states who carries the risk of accidental loss of enrichment where a transfer has been made pursuant to an invalid reciprocal agreement, and also how the risks are to be allocated where one or both of the parties are in some way responsible for the loss of enrichment. In this regard it is submitted that in dealing with compulsion as a source of voidability, an approach should be adopted which generally favours the victim, and places the risk on the wrongdoer.[75]

In conclusion, some words need to be said about the relationship between *restitutio in integrum* (whether based on contract or unjustified enrichment) and delictual remedies. It will be recalled that *restitutio in integrum* was provided in a mainly delictual environment in Roman law, and that Stair and Bankton treated it similarly. Stair in fact specifically recognised that the delictual remedy of reparation, could entail "restitution of the same thing".[76] However, this analysis is problematic. As already pointed out in the chapter on Roman law, delictual remedies are unsuitable for claiming from bona fide third parties,[77] and Stair's analysis fails to explain why third parties could be *delictually* liable without fault. The value of a delictual remedy is rather that it can be raised against the extorter who did not himself receive the extorted object.[78] Such a claim does not provide "restitution of the same thing" if it is in the hands of third parties, but compensates one through holding the wrongdoer liable to pay damages. Of course, nothing prevents a legal system from allowing "restitution of the same thing", as Stair put it, on the grounds of unjustified enrichment as well as delict, but then the remedies would overlap, which necessitates ensuring that the pursuer does not obtain restitution twice. Finally, if *restitutio in integrum* is regarded as based on unjustified enrichment, rather than delict, it must be ensured that the wrongdoer is not able to claim loss of enrichment or "change of position". Otherwise the victim would only be able to recover to the extent of the recipient's actual enrichment at the time the claim is instituted. This problem can be overcome by denying loss of enrichment if the defender, at the time of receiving the transfer, knew that he was not entitled to retain it.[79]

6.3 OTHER FORMS OF COMPULSION

6.3.1 *Introduction*

When force and fear is relied upon in order to obtain the reduction of a contract, it plays the role of a "cause of action". In other words, it is a substantial condition,

---

Enrichment: A Perspective of the Competition between Contractual and Enrichment remedies" 1992 *AJ* 203, 215; Zimmermann and du Plessis, "Basic Features of the German Law of Unjustified Enrichment" 1994 *Restitution Law Review* 22 at 40 et sqq.

75 Cf also in the context of English law, Burrows, *The Law of Restitution*, 168.

76 Stair, *Institutions*, 1.9.4.

77 Cf 2.2.2.iii above.

78 Cf 4.4 above.

79 Cf § 819 BGB. In South African law, which regards *restitutio in integrum* as a contractual remedy, this problem does not arise. Loss of enrichment cannot be pleaded as a defence against a claim of *restitutio in integrum*. If the pursuer can provide *restitutio*, then the defender is liable for the full amount of what he has received, subject to some limited exceptions (cf De Vos, *Verrykingsaanspr eeklikheid in die Suid-Afrikaanse reg*, 158).

which, if met, gives the victim an enforceable claim.[80] A transfer made in purported fulfilment of such a contract is not supported by valid obligation and has to be returned.[81] But a transfer obtained under force and fear of course need not necessarily be made within a contractual context. Where such a transfer is not owed in any event, it is not clear whether force and fear still fulfils the function of "cause of action". It can be argued that such transfers should be recoverable in any event, and that force and fear is not then a "cause of action", but (merely) a factor which could influence the recoverability of the transfer which is not due. The same can be said of undue transfers obtained through other, "milder" forms of compulsion which do not amount to force and fear. These forms of compulsion may be too weak to act as grounds for reduction, but still retain some relevance in determining whether recovery, based on the unjustified enrichment of the recipient, should be awarded. In this section, the focus will be on the content of these "other forms of compulsion", which, as has been indicated in the chapter on the modern law, essentially covers threats not to perform an existing duty to return goods or to provide services, and (possibly) ultra vires demands for the payment of tax. Attention will be paid to their relationship with cases which fall under the law of force and fear, and the question whether compulsion should be regarded as the basis of recovery or "cause of action" in these cases.

6.3.2 *Threats not to perform a duty*

On a very broad level, a distinction can be drawn between force and fear in the form of either a threat to do something one is not supposed to do, or a threat not to do something one is supposed to. Examples of the former are threats of personal physical harm such as assault, of destruction of property, and of wrongful dismissal. Here a duty not to act in a certain way arises from, for example criminal law, the law of delict or the law of contract. Less prominent are the examples of the latter category, namely threats not to do something one is supposed to, such as to release goods. Curiously, it has not yet been held that a threat not to provide a service also falls under the law of force and fear.[82] In principle, there seems to be no reason why this should not be the case: in both instances the victim is induced by an illegal threat to withhold a benefit to which the victim is entitled—it is only the nature of the benefit which differs, and this in itself does not seem to be a convincing ground for treating these cases differently. These remarks on the relevance of threats to withhold the provision of services can be illustrated by the following examples, based on the facts of *British Oxygen Company, Limited v South West Scotland Electricity Board*.[83] Assume, for argument's

80 Cf, generally, Walker, *The Law of Civil Remedies in Scotland*, 878; J Burke (ed), *Stroud's Judicial Dictionary of Words and Phrases* 3rd ed (1952), vol 1, s v "cause of action"; J B Saunders (ed), *Words and Phrases Legally Defined* (1969), vol 1, s v "cause of action". On its various technical meanings—cf H C Black (ed), *Black's Law Dictionary* 4th ed (1963), s v "cause of action".

81 Cf 4.2.2.iii above; SME, vol 15 (1997), 438 et sq.

82 On the claim allowed in the restricted category of cases where excessive payments were demanded under "monopolistic" situations, especially by a public authority, cf 4.3.1 above. In principle there is no reason why public authorities should be regarded as the sole vestige of such power (cf, in the context of English law, Tettenborn, *The Law of Restitution in England and Ireland*, 235 et sqq; for an exposition of the traditional ground of distinction in English law between public and private demands, cf J Beatson, "Restitution of Taxes, Levies and Other Imposts: Defining the Extent of the Woolwich Principle" (1993) 109 *LQR* 401 at 407).

83 1958 SC 53; 1959 SC (HL) 17.

sake, that the South of Scotland Electricity Board threatened that it would immediately cut off the British Oxygen Company's electricity supply unless it entered into a new agreement to pay an increased rate, although the existing agreement was still in force. Future payments of the increased rates would then be made in terms of this new underlying agreement. These facts are quite similar to the facts of *Sutherland v Montrose Fishing Co. Ltd*,[84] and the consequences should therefore be quite similar: a claim for reduction of the contract based on force and fear, and possible claims for the recovery of the excessive payments. However, where the compelled act is not the concluding of a contract, but making a transfer, the situation changes. In *British Oxygen Company, Limited v South West Scotland Electricity Board*[85] the threats were not aimed at the conclusion of a new contract (as in the hypothetical example above and the *Sutherland* case),[86] but at the fulfilment of a supposed obligation to pay the excessive charges. The question as to whether these charges were excessive could be answered quite independently of any reference to compulsion—it was a question of statutory interpretation. This is quite unlike the facts of the *Sutherland* case,[87] where the liability for payment of the increased wages depended on proof that the agreement was concluded under force and fear. In these two situations compulsion plays different roles: it either affects the validity of an obligation (it would then have to amount to force and fear) or it affects the recoverability of transfer made as an act of fulfilment. The consequences of it performing the former function have been dealt with above in the discussion of the effect of force and fear. The latter function, however, still has to be explored and evaluated. One approach to this problem would be to argue that proof of compulsion is still the basis for recovery in these cases, irrespective of the fact that no obligation to pay existed. Support for this view can be found in some speeches in the *British Oxygen* case,[88] as well as some recent interpretations thereof.[89] This approach draws its inspiration from the railway cases of English law.[90] It will be recalled that these cases dealt with claims against railway companies or corporations which exacted charges contrary to certain statutory rules and apparently in circumstances where a failure to pay the charge would lead to a refusal of the railway corporation to carry the goods.[91] The traditional view of these cases is that the right of recovery was based on compulsion.[92] However, in recent times, some English lawyers have begun to doubt the desirability of such an approach. They prefer to base the right of recovery on the inequality of the parties,[93] or on the "want of

84 (1921) 37 Sh Ct Rep 239.

85 1958 SC 53; 1959 SC (HL) 17.

86 (1921) 37 Sh Ct Rep 239.

87 (1921) 37 Sh Ct Rep 239.

88 1959 SC (HL) 17 at 38 (per Viscount Kilmuir LC) and at 48 (per Lord Merriman).

89 Cf *Woolwich Equitable Building Society v Inland Revenue Commissioners* [1992] 3 WLR 367 at 406 (per Lord Jauncey of Tullichettle); Beatson, "Restitution of Taxes, Levies and Other Imposts: Defining the Extent of the Woolwich Principle" (1993) 109 *LQR* 401 at 407.

90 1958 SC 53 at 80 (per Lord Patrick), 1959 SC (HL) 17 at 38 et sq (per Viscount Kilmuir LC), and at 47 (per Lord Merriman). On these cases in general, 4.3.1 above.

91 Cf 4.3.1 above.

92 Cf *Great Western Railway Co v Sutton* (1868–1869) LR 4 HL 226 at 249 (per Wills J); cf generally Goff and Jones, *The Law of Restitution*, 248 et sqq; Burrows, *Essays on the Law of Restitution*, 172.

93 Beatson, "Restitution of Taxes, Levies and Other Imposts: Defining the Extent of the Woolwich Principle" (1993) 109 *LQR* 401 at 406; Tettenborn, *The Law of Restitution in England and Ireland*, 238.

lawful authority".[94] These authors of course view the cases from the perspective of English law, with its theory of "unjust factors" which are required to obtain recovery. However, this is not necessarily the case from the perspective of Scots law. If someone who retains the property of another without legal basis is in any event obliged to return it, an approach which regards "compulsion" as an unjust factor permitting recovery is unnecessary. In more concrete terms, it is not essential to justify the recovery of an undue transfer by relying on the presence of compulsion or inequality if the mere fact that the payment is excessive (i.e. undue) in any event already means that it is recoverable because it is retained without legal ground.

The question is of course whether Scots law follows this approach. In particular, it needs to be determined to what extent it is (still)[95] required to regard an undue compelled transfer as one made with an immoral or unlawful purpose, or whether the mere fact that it is not due is not sufficient to lead to it being retained without legal ground. It should be obvious that these questions cannot be answered in isolation. They can only be dealt with adequately in the context of a detailed examination of the essential features of the Scots law of unjustified enrichment in general. Due to the range of issues involved, this will be done in a separate chapter. To conclude this chapter, one last example of a form of compulsion which does not amount to force and fear will be examined. This is the by now familiar case where a person is subjected to an ultra vires demand for the payment of tax.

6.3.3 *Ultra vires demands for the payment of tax*

The use of a threat of legal proceedings to compel a person into submitting to a claim is not in itself objectionable. Even if the claim is unfounded, the general position is that there would be no relief if the person who was faced with the claim decided to settle or enter into an agreement of compromise.[96] However, he could also pay with no intention to settle, but simply because he was unable to refuse to pay in the short term.[97] This seems to be particularly true of unlawful claims for payment of tax. These claims are to a certain extent accompanied by compulsion in the form of implied threats of penalties, litigation and even bad publicity—all considerations which may induce submission to the demand in the short term.[98] In the chapter on modern Scots law it was indicated that the relevance of compulsion in the case of the undue payment of tax has not yet been determined. It was concluded that there arguably is scope for the application of the *condictio indebiti*, but that as long as error as to liability is regarded as an essential feature of this remedy,[99] such a claim would not lie. If the *condictio indebiti* is then inappropriate, what enrichment remedy remains? It was shown that from a historical and comparative perspective it is possible to work with an analysis based on an implied agreement to repay the debt if it is not due,

---

94 Birks, *An Introduction to the Law of Restitution*, 297. Since the decision in *Woolwich Equitable Building Society v Inland Revenue Commissioners* [1992] 3 WLR 367 it has been said that the traditional approach is presumably no longer of practical importance since payment made under such compulsion would in any event be recoverable on the ground that they involve an ultra vires demand by a public authority (cf Burrows, *Essays on the Law of Restitution*, 345 et sqq).

95 Cf 3.3.2.ii above.

96 Cf 4.3.1.ii above; *MacIntyre v Murray and Muir* (1915) 31 Sh Ct Rep 49.

97 Cf Visser, *Die rol van dwaling by die condictio indebiti*, 312.

98 Cf the judgment of Nolan J in *Woolwich Equitable Building Society v Inland Revenue Commissioners* [1989] 1 WLR 137 at 142 et sq.

99 Cf *Morgan Guaranty Trust Company of New York v Lothian Regional Council* 1995 SCLR 225.

but that such an approach has its defects.[100] Again, this can only be answered in the context of an analysis of the structure of the Scots law of unjustified enrichment in general. In essence, if Scots law, like English law, requires proof of an unjust factor, then such a factor will have to be identified. Alternatively, if proof of such a factor is not required, the question remains as to what the appropriate remedy would be, and of what relevance compulsion would be in determining whether such a remedy should be awarded.

Before this analysis is embarked upon on the next chapter, it would be useful, at least by way of introduction, to illustrate the different approaches to the recovery of unlawfully demanded tax payments by reference to the landmark decision of the House of Lords in the English case of *Woolwich Building Society (formerly Woolwich Equitable Building Society) v Inland Revenue Commissioners*.[101] Here it had to be decided under what circumstances tax paid in response to an ultra vires demand from a public authority would have to be repaid.[102] On the basis of its construction of certain financial regulations, the Revenue demanded payment from Woolwich of tax on dividends and interest which the building society had to pay to its members. Woolwich, on its reading of the regulations, did not regard itself liable to pay the tax, but nevertheless paid because it feared adverse publicity and penalties which might be imposed if it were wrong in its construction of the law. Each of Woolwich's payments contained the reservation "without prejudice to any right to recover". Later Woolwich was successful in proving that it was not liable to pay the tax. The Revenue repaid the payments, as well as interest upon them from the date of the first judgment that Woolwich was not liable to make the payments. Woolwich sought to recover the £6,730,000 interest which would have accrued for the period from the date of making the first payment to the Revenue until the date of the first judgment. In order to determine whether Woolwich could reclaim this interest, the House of Lords therefore had to determine if the rights giving rise to the obligations to repay arose on the dates of making the payments, or on the date of the first judgment.

In the speech of Lord Goff of Chievely it stated that the Revenue's position appeared "as a matter of common justice, to be unsustainable". If Woolwich were to be unsuccessful, the Revenue would have the benefit of a "massive interest-free loan as the fruit of its unlawful action".[103] The problem was that, in English law, Woolwich did not seem to have a remedy to reclaim the interest.[104] On the facts, no agreement between Woolwich and the Revenue that the payments would be repaid existed, and neither was there a statutory provision allowing for recovery. According to the English Common Law, the fact that a transfer was not due was not in itself sufficient to render it recoverable. The difficulty, though, was to determine what "unjust factor", such as a mistake of fact or compulsion, could be relied upon by the claimant to warrant restitution.[105] On the facts there was no

---

100 Cf *Commissioner for Inland Revenue v First National Industrial Bank Ltd* 1990 (3) SA 641 (A) at 646; R Evans-Jones, "Some reflections on the condictio indebiti in a mixed legal system" (1994) 111 *SALJ* 759.

101 [1992] 3 WLR (HL(E)) 366; [1993] 1 AC 70 (CA).

102 On what follows, cf also Du Plessis and Wicke, "Woolwich Equitable v IRC and the Condictio Indebiti in Scots Law" 1993 SLT (News) 303.

103 [1992] 3 WLR (HL(E)) 366 at 391B; [1993] 1 AC 70 (CA).

104 Cf generally, Beatson, "Restitution of taxes, levies and other imposts: defining the extent of the Woolwich principle" (1993) 109 *LQR* 401.

105 Cf McKendrick, "Restitution of unlawfully demanded tax" 1993 *LMCLQ* 88 at 93.

mistake of fact,[106] nor was it found that the payment was made under sufficient compulsion to allow for recovery.[107] In the words of Lord Goff "... since the possibility of distraint by the revenue was very remote, the concept of compulsion would have to be stretched to the utmost to embrace the circumstances of such a case as this".[108] This prompted the court to recognise that the law of restitution had to be reformulated so as to recognise a new unjust factor—a prima facie right to recovery based solely on the payment of money pursuant to an ultra vires demand by a public authority.[109] But, from a Scottish perspective, following this approach was not inevitable. As Lord Goff points out, instead of recognising the action for money had and received, the English Common Law "might have developed so as to recognise a *condictio indebiti*—an action for the recovery of money on the ground that it was not due".[110] This statement is of significance for the Scots law of unjustified enrichment, which recognises the *condictio indebiti*. Although the House of Lords was not called upon to consider the applicability of this remedy, it is significant that there is recognition for the centrality of the notion that the transfer had to be undue. The question is of course whether this view of the *condictio indebiti* accords with modern Scots law. If it does not, and error is rather the essential feature, and one of a number of "unjust factors" which act as grounds for recovery, it will have to be determined what the appropriate "unjust factor" is on which to ground a claim. If it does, it will still be necessary to develop rules which determine under which circumstances transfers that are not due can be recovered with the *condictio indebiti*. It is with an examination of these, and related questions that the final chapter is concerned.

---

106 If there was a mistake of law the payment would not be recoverable. Cf *Kiriri Cotton Co Ltd v Dewani* [1960] AC 192 (PC).

107 Lord Goff identified some categories of cases where money paid under compulsion could be recovered, explicitly mentioning that, "bearing in mind the development of the concept of economic duress", these categories cannot be regarded as closed. The first category he identified are those cases where money was paid as a result of actual or threatened duress to the person, or actual threatened seizure of a person's goods. These could all be regarded as force and fear cases in Scots law. Second, he stated that it would also be possible to recover money paid *colore officii*, i.e. paid to a person in a public or quasi-public position to obtain the performance by him of a duty which he is bound to perform for nothing or less than the sum demanded by him, to the extent that he is not entitled to it. Finally, he held that money paid to a person for the performance of a statutory duty, which he is bound to perform for a sum less than that charged by him, would also be recoverable to the extent of the overcharge ([1992] 3 WLR (HL(E)) 366 at 384; [1993] 1 AC 70 (CA) at 164F et sqq).

108 [1992] 3 WLR 366 (HL(E)), 392D; [1993] 1 AC 70 (CA) at 173D–E.

109 [1992] 3 WLR 366 (HL(E)), 396C. It should be noted that not all comment on this approach was favourable. It has been said that the approach is potentially hazardous, and that "in less skilled hands it could result in restitution based simply on the finding of injustice" (G Virgo, "Restitution of overpaid tax—justice at the expense of certainty" (1993) 52 *CLJ* 31 at 33 et sq). Uncertainty also surrounds the relationship of this rule with the mistake of law rule (cf T Hill, "Restitution from Public Authorities and the Treasury's Position: Woolwich Equitable Building Society v IRC", (1993) 56 *ModernLR* 856 at 858 et sqq), and its relationship to case where there was submission to an honest claim (cf McKendrick, "Restitution of unlawfully demanded tax" 1993 *LMCLQ* 88 at 98). It is also not clear what is to be understood under a public authority, and what exactly could be recovered.

110 [1992] 3 WLR (HL(E)) 366 at 391D. As is the position in South African law—cf 5.3.3. ii above.

6.4 CONCLUSIONS

1. Force and fear can have far-reaching effects on the validity of compelled acts. Unfortunately, although the modern Scots law of force and fear is rich in principle, it has not yet utilised these principles to their full potential. In this regard the following submissions are made.

1.1 The law of force and fear is characterised by terminological uncertainty. In this regard it is submitted that although the use of the term "force and fear" has been subjected to some criticism, its retention is desirable. It indicates that the claim is not based solely on fear, but fear instilled in a certain way, mostly by threats of harm. No discernible advantages can be gained from use of the terms "force or fear" or "extortion".

1.2 The requirement that the victim's will has to be overpowered or overborne in order to establish a case of force and fear gives rise to confusion between cases of *vis absoluta* and *vis compulsiva*. Since this distinction has important practical implications, especially as regards the protection of third parties, such confusion should be avoided. It is submitted that there are only a limited number of cases where the will of the victim truly is overborne: these include the situation of physically grabbing a person's hand to make a signature or inducing a state of fear which actually creates temporary insanity. In other cases where a person acts out of fear, his will is still exercised ("voluntas coacta tamen voluntas est"), but is "deflected". The question is then rather whether wrongful methods were used to induce the fear, and whether a causal connection existed between the act under fear and the application of these methods. Through inquiring whether the victim displayed constancy while being subjected to these methods, conclusions can be drawn as to whether such a causal connection exists.

1.3 Not enough attention has been paid to the question as to what amounts to an illegal threat of harm. Threats of personal physical harm are clearly regarded as unacceptable, but the same cannot be said of all threats of economic harm. Although it obviously includes unwarrantable threats of harm to property, and (possibly) the withholding or detention of goods, it is submitted that there is scope for the broadening of force and fear to include threats of other forms of harm, such as the refusal to comply with a duty to provide a service. In forming the legal contours within which these developments will take place, the courts will have to be guided by changes in social values, and especially contemporary views on what amounts to acceptable commercial practice.

1.4 Although there are indications in the case law that force and fear renders contracts and acts of fulfilment void, the preferable consequence is voidability. Once a contract has been avoided, the acts of fulfilment obtained through compulsion should be recoverable on the ground of the unjustified enrichment of the recipient. The regulatory device of requiring *restitutio in integrum* when a contract is avoided should be replaced by a mechanism which more clearly states who should bear the risk of loss of enrichment. It is submitted that in cases of force and fear the knowledge of the wrongdoer that he is not entitled to retain a transfer should provide a strong indication that he should bear the risk of loss of enrichment.

2. While it is obvious that compulsion in the form of force and fear acts as a "cause of action" when it is used to obtain the reduction of a contract, and therefore indicates that the retention of transfers made pursuant to such a contract is unjustified, its relevance is less clear in cases where a transfer which in any event is not owed is obtained by force and fear.
3. Similar problems arise in cases where transfers which are not owed are obtained by other "milder" forms of compulsion, i.e. compulsion which falls short of the standard required by the law of force and fear. Examples within the context of the law of unjustified enrichment are cases where a public authority obtains an "excessive" (undue) transfer by implied threats not to provide a service, or (possibly) the case where a person faces an illegal demand to pay tax, accompanied by implied threats to impose penalties if the transfer is not made. It is submitted that the role of compulsion in these cases can be viewed in two ways. On the one hand, it can be argued that because such a transfer is in any event not owed or due, it should be recoverable in principle. The compulsion is then not a "cause of action", but (merely) a factor which could influence the recoverability of the transfer with a claim based on unjustified enrichment. However, it can also be argued that the compulsion is in fact central to the claim, and that it acts as a "cause of action" or "unjust factor" which has to be proved in order to succeed with a claim based on unjustified enrichment. It is submitted that the question as to which of these approaches is preferable should not be answered in isolation, but rather against the background of an examination of the Scots law of unjustified enrichment in general.

Chapter 7

Compulsion and the taxonomy of the Scots law of unjustified enrichment

7.1 OVERVIEW OF THE DEBATE

After centuries of neglect, the Scots law of unjustified enrichment is currently the focus of considerable attention.[1] The first academic treatise which solely deals with this area of law was published in 1993[2] and an extraordinary number of academic articles have also appeared. The Scottish Law Commission has compiled extensive reports on the recovery of benefits conferred under error of law,[3] the judicial abolition of the error of law rule and its aftermath,[4] and the recovery of ultra vires public authority receipts and disbursements.[5] It further has arranged various seminars involving academics, practitioners and members of the judiciary. Significantly, this fresh examination of the law of unjustified enrichment has not been restricted to one or two specific topics (although much attention has been paid to the error of law rule and the recovery of money paid by and to public authorities). Fundamental research is being done on, amongst others, the taxonomy of the law of unjustified enrichment and its relationship with other branches of the law. That such research is well overdue does not require any argument and it is with some understatement that Lord Cullen in *Morgan Guaranty Trust Company of New York v Lothian Regional Council*[6] remarked that "the taxonomy of the quasi-contractual remedies which are afforded by the law of Scotland is not in a wholly satisfactory state".[7] Naturally, any developments such as a new taxonomy would have to take account of the role of compulsion in the law of unjustified enrichment. In the previous chapter it was shown that a number of problems surround the treatment of compulsion in this area

1 For an overview, cf Whitty, "Some Trends and Issues in Scots Enrichment Law" 1994 *JR* 127; Whitty, "The Civilian Tradition and Debates on Scots Law" 1996 *TSAR* 227 at 237; Whitty, "Die Reform des schottischen Bereicherungsrechts" 1995 *ZEuP* 216. As Stewart puts it, restitution was the "Cinderella obligation" (*The Law of Restitution in Scotland*, 4).

2 Stewart, *The Law of Restitution in Scotland.*

3 Scot Law Com D P No 95, 1993. The discussion paper was prompted by a request from the Lord Chancellor to the (English) Law Commission to examine the law relating to payments made but not lawfully due and in particular the common law rule that payments made under mistake of law are not recoverable. The need was then felt to embark on a similar exercise in Scotland, since there were good reasons to harmonise the position in these two jurisdictions.

4 Scottish Law Com D P No 99, 1996.

5 Scottish Law Com D P No 100, 1996.

6 1995 SCLR 225.

7 1995 SCLR 225 at 246F. Also see Whitty, "Some Trends and Issues in Scots Enrichment Law" 1994 *JR* 127; Recovery of Benefits Conferred under Error of Law (Scot Law Com D P No 95, 1993) vol 1, 99; Stewart, *The Law of Restitution in Scotland, Supplement*, 1.

of law. It will then mainly be with a view towards the solution of these problems that the modern taxonomies of the Scots law of unjustified enrichment will be examined here. Particular attention will be paid to the question whether compulsion should be regarded as an unjust factor, or whether compelled transfers should rather be dealt with in terms of a framework which bases relief on the principle of retention without legal ground.

7.2 THE MAIN TAXONOMIES

7.2.1 *The general description of the subject matter*[8]

The subject matter is brought home under the headings of "the law of restitution",[9] "quasi-contract",[10] "obligations arising from unjust enrichment",[11] or simply "unjustified enrichment".[12] The tendency seems to be to move away from the misleading description of "quasi-contract", and the confusing description of "restitution".[13] The Justinianic notion of "quasi-contract" (which was already rejected by Stair)[14] is misleading,[15] partially because it suggests that the obligation somehow arises from a type of implied contract or agreement that the enriched would return the enrichment. In many factual situations, for example insanity or minority, the use of the notion of a "quasi-contract" amounts to a fiction.[16] "Restitution", again, is confusing because it bears a variety of meanings. It acts as an umbrella term for all the remedies based on unjustified enrichment,[17] but it is also used to describe the vindicatory (real) remedy which an owner can use to reclaim his property,[18] and which "really has nothing to do with restitution for unjust enrichment".[19] It is also

8 Cf Birks, "Six Questions in Search of a Subject—Unjust Enrichment in a Crisis of Identity" 1985 *JR* 227 at 230–233.

9 Used in Stewart, *The Law of Restitution in Scotland.*

10 Gloag, *The Law of Contract*, 319; The ninth edition of W M Gloag and R C Henderson, *Introduction to the Law of Scotland* (1987) referred to "quasi-contract" (159). The tenth edition, which will be referred to in the rest of this chapter, and which was revised by The Lord President, Lord Rodger of Earlsferry, refers to "Unjustified Enrichment" (470).

11 Walker, *The Law of Contracts and Related Obligations in Scotland*, 585. According to Stewart, "unjust" is increasingly becoming associated with an event oriented approach and "unjustified" with a view of restitution based on the lack of legal cause (*The Law of Restitution in Scotland, Supplement*, 10).

12 Gloag and Henderson, *The Law of Scotland*, 470.

13 See the commentary of W D H Sellar in 1995 SCLR at 250D–E; cf also Evans-Jones, "Unjust Enrichment, Contract and the Third Reception of Roman law in Scotland" (1993) 109 *LQR* 663 at 678.

14 Cf Stair, *Institutions* 1.3.2; 1.7. He does, however, recognise the Roman roots of restitution: "... the Roman law ... holdeth these obligations [of restitution] not to be *ex contractu, sed quasi ex contractu*"; cf also SME vol 15 (1993), para 11.

15 For criticism see Birks, "Six Questions in Search of a Subject—Unjust Enrichment in a Crisis of Identity" 1985 *JR* 227 at 231; Birks, "Restitution: A View of Scots Law" (1985) 38 *CLP* 57 at 65.

16 In English law, use of the notion of an "implied contract" as the basis for quasi-contractual claims has been criticised severely—see *United Australia Ltd v Barclays Bank Ltd* [1941] AC 1 at 28–29; Goff and Jones, *The Law of Restitution*, 5 et sqq.

17 In Scot Law Com D P No 95, 1993, vol 1 at 100 it is described as "the English usage".

18 See Stair, *Institutions* 1.7; Gloag and Henderson, *The Law of Scotland*, 470.

19 Stewart, *The Law of Restitution in Scotland*, 96. "Restitution" in Scots law is therefore different from "restitution in English law, inasmuch as all restitutionary claims in the latter system are "united" by the principle of unjust enrichment (see Goff and Jones, *The Law of Restitution*, 15).

used in the context of delict.[20] Furthermore, *within* the law of unjustified enrichment the term "restitution" bears different meanings, but a surprising lack of consensus exists as to what these meanings are.[21] This is regrettable, since "restitution", together with "repetition" and "recompense", form the three Rs, which are the basic divisions in the modern Scots law of unjustified enrichment.[22] In order to understand this grouping properly, it is essential to trace its historical roots. These roots lie in the Institutional writings.

7.2.2 *The taxonomies of the Institutional writers*[23]

i. *Stair*

The authors of the *Practicks* provide very little on what nowadays would be termed remedies of "restitution" based on unjustified enrichment.[24] The first Scottish author who systematically dealt with this topic was Stair. A salient feature of his treatment of the law of obligations is the fundamental distinction he draws between "restitution" on the one hand, and "recompense or remuneration" on the other.[25] Using these headings in a division of obligations seems rather unusual, since the impression is created that the obligations are grouped according to the nature of relief they give rise to (e.g. the return of property, or money, or compensating expenses), and not the events which give rise to them.[26] However, closer inspection reveals that the heads of restitution and recompense are not only concerned with the nature of the relief,[27] but to a certain extent obscure underlying "reasons" for relief. Just as the heading of "reparation" in fact deals with obligations arising from "delinquence" or

20 For an example of the use of the term "restitution" in the context of reparation (the remedy in cases of delinquence or delict), cf Stair, *Institutions* 1.9.4; 1.7.1.

21 Cf Whitty, "Some Trends and Issues in Scots Enrichment Law" 1994 *JR* 127 at 131.

22 Cf Recovery of Benefits Conferred under Error of Law (Scot Law Com D P No 95, 1993) vol 1, 99 et sqq; Whitty, "Die Reform des schottischen Bereicherungsrechts", 1995 *ZEuP* 216 at 218 et sqq.

23 Cf, generally, Whitty, "The Taxonomy of Unjustified Enrichment in Scots Law", unpublished paper delivered at a seminar held by the Scottish Law Commission on 23 October 1993, Annexure "A".

24 See Balfour, *Practicks*, 45; Hope, *Practicks*, VI.38.26 et sqq, which in fact deal with *restitutio in integrum*.

25 Stair, *Institutions* 1.7 and 1.8. According to Stair, the obligations of restitution and recompense (together with conjugal obligations, obligations between parents and children, obligations between tutors and the obligation of reparation) are "obediential" or based on the will of God, as opposed to "conventional" or based on the will of man (*Institutions* 1.3.2–4). For a discussion cf MacQueen and Sellar, "Unjust Enrichment in Scots Law", in Schrage (ed), *Unjust Enrichment*, 289 at 290 sqq; A H Campbell, *The Structure of Stair's Institutions* (1954), 15 et sqq.

26 As in the case of conjugal and the other "obediental" obligations (cf Birks, "Restitution: A View of Scots law" (1985) 38 *CLP* 57 at 59). He prefers to view "restitution" as a response, comparable to compensation or punishment. Use of these headings is not in harmony with Stair's own criticism of the Roman distinction between obligations *ex contractu*, *quasi ex contractu*, *ex maleficio* and *quasi ex maleficio* on the ground that it "insinuates no reason of the cause or rise of these distinct obligations, as is required in a good and distinct division ..." (*Institutions* 1.3.2). On the decline of the category of "quasi-contract", see Zimmermann, *The Law of Obligations*, 20 et sq, 434.

27 In fact, in certain cases the same type of relief could be provided under different headings. Stair acknowledges that the obligation of "restitution" is not only confined to the separate title he created for it (Stair, *Institutions* 1.7), but can also arise by "voluntary engagement", or by "delinquence" (Stair, *Institutions* 1.7.1, 1.9.4). Similarly, "reparation" is not only provided on the basis of "delinquence", but also on the basis of contract. The contract is then the "original cause of the obligation" (Stair, *Institutions* 1.9.3).

delict,[28] the heading of "recompense", on a very broad level, deals with the obligation "to do one good deed for another"[29] while the heading of restitution deals with the obligation "... whereby that which is another's coming in our power, without his purpose to gift it to us, and yet without our fault, ought to be restored ...".[30]

It is then specifically those cases where a person retains or holds something in his power without a cause or legal basis which are of importance.[31] According to Stair there is the duty of restitution of

> ... things *quae cadunt in non causam*, which coming warrantably in our hands, and without any paction of restitution, yet if the cause cease by which they become ours, there superveneth the obligation of restitution of them, whence are the condictions in law, *ob non causam* and *causa data causa non secuta*"[32] ... But there is not the same ground for things given for an unjust cause, as *ob turpem causam*; in which the will of the owner, and his purpose to transfer the property is effectual, though his motive was not good. But positive law doth sometimes obviate the inconveniency by such donations, and makes them void, and either to return, or become caduciary and escheat. But in things received *ex turpi causa*, if both parties be in *culpa*, *potior est conditio possidentis*; so there is no restitution.[33]

Second, the duty of restitution "... extendeth to *indebitum solutum*, when any party through error delivereth or payeth that, which he supposeth is due or belongeth to another."[34] Stair's views on *indebitum solutum* and transfers *ob turpem causam* have been dealt with previously.[35] For present purposes it is only of interest to note that these transfers are regarded as examples of where something is retained without his intention to make a gift—in the case of *indebitum solutum* because an undue transfer was made in error as to liability, and in the case of the transfer *ob turpem causam*, because the transfer was made with an immoral purpose. As far as the

---

28 Stair, *Institutions* 1.9.3 ("But here are only understood obligations, which originally arise from *delinquence*, as the first cause thereof").

29 Stair, *Institutions* 1.8.1. Stair's treatment of recompense is rather cryptic. The impression is gained that the heading of the title could in fact have been "reciprocation", for it is the absence of reciprocation (e.g.in the form of "gratitude" or compensation for the *negotiorum gestor* or payment to the joint debtor who discharges the debt) which gives rise to it. A significant feature of recompense is that it is aimed at ensuring that something is given for another, and not at the return of the same thing. The latter is the domain of restitution.

30 Stair, *Institutions* 1.7.1.

31 It should be noted, though, that the obligation of restitution does not only encompass remedies which nowadays would be regarded as based on unjustified enrichment. In his title on restitution, Stair (from a modern perspective at least) conflates restitution as a proprietary remedy with restitution as a remedy based on unjustified enrichment—the title simply does not quadrate as neatly with unjustified enrichment as the title on reparation does with delict. On Stair's division cf Reid, "Unjustified Enrichment and Property" 1994 *JR* 167 at 169 and Whitty, "The Taxonomy of Unjustified Enrichment in Scots law", paper prepared for a seminar of the Scottish Law Commission, held on 23 October 1993, 70; MacQueen and Sellar, "Unjust Enrichment in Scots Law", in Schrage (ed), *Unjust Enrichment*, 289 at 294; D R MacDonald, "Restitution and Property Law" 1988 SLT 81 et sqq. See A H Campbell, *The Structure of Stair's Institutions*, 21–30 for indications that the structure derives from Pufendorf's *De Jure Naturae et Gentium libri octo* 4.13. These indications are vague. Grotius' *De Jure Belli ac Pacis* 2.10 certainly is no antecedent. it is only concerned with the remedies of the owner to recover his property; not with unjustified enrichment (see *De Jure Belli ac Pacis* 2.10.12).

32 Stair, *Institutions* 1.7.7.

33 Stair, *Institutions* 1.7.8.

34 Stair, *Institutions* 1.7.9.

35 Cf 3.3.2.i, ii(a) above.

expressions "condictions in law, *ob non causam* and *causa data causa non secuta*" are concerned, there was no *condictio ob non causam* in Roman law. Presumably Stair had the *condictio sine causa* in mind. Thus, in those cases where someone has something in his hands *sine causa*, without the intention of the transferor that it should be a gift, or without an underlying agreement that it should be returned, and without the fault of the recipient, an obligation of restitution arises.[36] The fact that Stair connects the *condictio ob non causam* with the *condictio causa data causa non secuta*, and also distinguishes it from *indebitum solutum*, indicates that he did not contemplate a Scottish equivalent of the Roman *condictio sine causa generalis*. The latter *condictio* in effect encompassed all the *condictiones* and had no independent relevance.[37] It rather seems as if he thought about the (residual) *condictio sine causa specialis*, which only applied in those cases of *sine causa* retention where none of the established *condictiones* were available.[38] Unfortunately, Stair is rather cryptic about the factual situations where this *condictio sine causa specialis* would apply. The crucial point is that the mere absence of a *causa*, or legal ground for what has been obtained, makes this *condictio* available.

In conclusion, it should be mentioned that in his treatment of the obligation of restitution, Stair is only concerned with the return of property and money.[39] It is also possible that a person could obtain something *sine causa* and not be able to provide restitution, but could still be bound by an obligation of recompense. The different fields of application of these obligations can be illustrated by reference to the case where something is acquired bona fide from someone who was not owner.[40] If the acquisition is still with the bona fide purchaser, he has to provide restitution without being entitled to the purchase price. However, if he sells the acquisition again at a profit, is enriched by retaining its fruits, or disposes of it after acquiring it gratuitously, he must provide recompense.[41] The distinction between these remedies could be of practical significance. In the case of "restitution", the measure includes fruits which are not consumed bona fide,[42] but excludes "lost" or erased enrichment.[43] In the case of recompense, the measure is determined by the extent to which a person has been "enriched" ("in quantum locupletior

36 Stair, *Institutions* 1.7.1 read with Stair, *Institutions* 1.7.9.

37 Cf Zimmermann, *The Law of Obligations*, 857, 871 et sq.

38 Cf also Stair, *Institutions*, 4.21.4, where the actions are listed seperately ("actions for restitution of things *quae cadunt in non causam*, or *ob turpem causam*, or if *indebite soluta*, or *causa data causa non secuta*").

39 Cf Stair, *Institutions* 1.7.1, 1.7.7, 1.7.9, where there are references to "things", "goods", delivery and payment. The expression "repetition" covered both "things" (cf Stair, *Institutions* 1.7.2) and money (cf Stair, *Institutions* 4.40.28).

40 Stair, *Institutions* 1.7.11.

41 Stair, *Institutions* 1.7.11. In the *ius commune* a *condictio sine causa*, based on acquisition *ex causa lucrativa*, apparently fulfilled a similar role. See De Vos, *Verrykingsaanspreeklikheid in die Suid-Afrikaanse reg*, 79–83; C G van der Merwe, *Sakereg*, 2nd ed (1989), 358. There was some debate as to the exact sphere of applicability of this *condictio*: see Voet, *Commentarius ad Pandectas*, 6.1.10, 6.1.11, where the reference is made in the context of a discussion of vindication; and W Schorer, *Aantekeningen over de Inleidinge tot de Hollandsche Rechtsgeleerdheid van Hugo de Groot* (Middelburg-Amsterdam, 1797); Ulricus Huber, *Heedendaegse Rechtsgeleertheyt soo elders, als in Frieslandt gebruikelyk* (Amsterdam, 1742), 3.35.16, tr P Gane, *The Jurisprudence of my time* (1939), vol 1, 570, where the reference is made in the context of the *condictio indebiti*. It should be apparent, though, that a *condictio indebiti* could not be used, since there was no undue transfer.

42 Stair, *Institutions* 1.7.10.

43 Stair, *Institutions* 1.7.11.

factus sit")[44] by, for example, the labour,[45] expenses,[46] property,[47] or payments of another.[48]

ii. Bankton

Unsurprisingly for someone who regards Stair's general method "most just and natural, and therefore a good model",[49] Bankton adopts Stair's general distinction between natural (obediential) and conventional obligations,[50] as well his specific distinction (within the subcategory of natural obligations) between restitution and recompense.[51] Unlike the natural obligations which arise from the relation and connection of the parties (whether familial or otherwise), the natural obligations of "restitution" and "recompense" depend on

> ... other accidental circumstances; as, where one man's goods happen, without his consent to come into another's possession, which subjects the possessor to Restitution;[52] or where one is benefited by the means of another, without intent of gifting, whence proceeds the obligation of Recompence ...[53]

Bankton's reference to restitution of another's property which comes into our possession "without his consent" is not entirely consistent with Stair's reference to restitution of another's property which is not intended as a gift. Although the two descriptions deal with essentially the same subject matter,[54] a transfer which is not intended as a gift is not necessarily the same is a transfer made without the consent of the transferor. For example, the non-gratuitous payment made in contemplation of marriage is not intended as a gift, but can come into our possession *with* the consent of the owner.[55]

As far as the list of examples of cases where "restitution" will be granted is concerned, Bankton, like Stair, conflates proprietary and enrichment-based

---

44 Stair, *Institutions* 1.8.6. Cf also Stair, *Institutions* 1.7.11, 1.8.3.

45 Stair, *Institutions* 1.8.4, 1.8.6.

46 Stair, *Institutions* 1.8.4, 1.8.6.

47 See the discussion above regarding things acquired bona fide from someone who was not owner (Stair, *Institutions* 1.7.11).

48 Where a debtor pays a debt for which he and his co-debtors are liable *in solidum*, his co-debtors are under an obligation of recompense (Stair, *Institutions* 1.8.2, 1.8.9).

49 Bankton, *Institute*, preface vii.

50 Bankton, *Institute*, 1.4.34. The category is in accordance with Stair's distinction between "obediential" obligations and "conventional" obligations (*Institutions* 1.3.2–4). Bankton also draws a general distinction between obligations which are "natural only" and obligations which are "civil", i.e. "such as may be made effectual by legal compulsion" (Bankton, *Institute*, 1.4.12 et sqq). The use of the word "natural" in both divisions is confusing, especially in the light of the fact that Bankton acknowledges that there are some "natural" obligations which are "effectual and secured by civil action" (Bankton, *Institute*, 1.4.34). Stair avoids this confusion by referring to "obediential" rather than "natural" obligations" (see Stair, *Institutions* 1.3.2–4 as opposed to *Institutions* 1.3.5).

51 Bankton, *Institute* 1.4.34, 1.8.1, 1.11.1.

52 Also see Bankton, *Institute* 1.8.1. Incidentally, *restitutio in integrum* relating to minors is dealt with separately (see *Institute* 1.7.74 et sqq).

53 Bankton, *Institute* 1.8 (introductory paragraph). The examples of cases where recompense would be due are similar to those provided by Stair (cf Bankton, *Institute* 1.9.24, 29, 41–45, and Stair, *Institutions*, 1.8.3–5, 7 et sqq).

54 Compare Stair, *Institutions* 1.7.9 with Bankton, *Institute* 1.8.2–24.

55 It could perhaps be argued that Bankton intended "consent" to mean "ultimate consent", i.e. not at the time of transfer, but thereafter. This is not stated clearly, and the interpretation seems rather strained—particularly in regard to the moment when such "consent" should be determined.

remedies, and also deals with the familiar examples of the latter category, namely cases where "the cause of the delivery ceases" (the terrain of the *condictio causa data causa non secuta*),[56] where things are given for an unlawful cause,[57] and where a person through error, "delivers or makes payment of what was not due, but which he believed to be due" (the *condictio indebiti* then applies).[58] As far as the nature of the relief which "restitution" gives rise to is concerned, there are references to the return of "goods",[59] and "things",[60] but also to "price"[61] and undue "payments".[62] Bankton also distinguishes between restitution of "things unduly received" and "sums unduly received".[63] This indicates that the duty of restitution could relate to corporeals as well as money. However, under certain circumstances a person who bona fide receives money "is not liable in restitution to the owner, because the currency of money ... must not be obstructed".[64] Like Stair, Bankton acknowledges that the obligation of restitution can terminate through loss of enrichment.[65]

iii. Erskine

Whereas Stair's approach to the general divisions of law is novel, Erskine follows the *Institutes* of Justinian[66] more closely by adopting the distinction between persons, things (or rights) and actions.[67] However, within the subdivision of moveable rights or obligations, Erskine deviates from the Roman approach. He recognises the deficiency of the Roman division between obligations arising from contract, delict, "something resembling a contract" and "something resembling a delict",[68] and prefers Stair's distinction between obediential or natural obligations on the one hand, and conventional obligations on the other.[69] According to Erskine, natural obligations also include "... those obligations which arise from the natural duty of restitution. In consequence of this, whatever comes into our power or possession which belongs to another, without an intention in the owner of making a present of it, ought to be restored to him".[70] This confirms Stair's view that it is the absence of the intention to make a gift, rather than the absence of consent, which determines whether an obligation of restitution arises.

Some of the examples of cases where the duty of restitution arises are quite familiar, namely where things "are given in the special view of a certain event ...

56 Bankton, *Institute* 1.8.21.
57 Bankton, *Institute* 1.8.22.
58 Bankton, *Institute* 1.8.23 et sqq. Also see Bankton, *Institute* 1.8.31 et sqq.
59 Bankton, *Institute* 1.8 (introductory paragraph), 1.8.1, 1.8.5–1.8.8.
60 Bankton, *Institute* 1.8 (introductory paragraph), 1.8.4, 1.8.9–1.8.11, 1.8.21, 1.8.22.
61 Where a person acquires something bona fide from a person who was not owner and then sells it for more than the price he paid for it, the difference or profit ("the overplus of the price") then has to be restored to the owner (Bankton, *Institute* 1.8.11).
62 Bankton, *Institute* 1.8.23. Also see Bankton, *Institute* 1.8.24–1.8.27.
63 Bankton, *Institute* 1.8.29. Also see Bankton, *Institute* 1.8.19.
64 Bankton, *Institute* 1.8.34.
65 Bankton, *Institute* 1.8.11. See Stair, *Institutions* 1.7.11.
66 Erskine strongly emphasises the importance of Roman law: "... great weight is to be laid on the Roman law in all cases not fixed by statute or custom, and in which the genius of our law will suffer us to apply it; and as we have few statutes in the matter of contracts, transactions, *restitutions*, servitudes, tutories and obligations, the knowledge of it must be singularly useful in determining controversies arising from those heads of the law" (own emphasis; Erskine, *Institute* 1.1.41).
67 Erskine, *Institute* 1.2.1, 3.1.1.
68 On the basis that "there are many instances of obligations, even proper, which are grounded neither in contract nor delinquency, nor any facts resembling either of them" (Erskine, *Institute* 3.1.9).
69 Erskine, *Institute* 3.1.10.
70 Erskine, *Institute* 3.1.10.

[which does] not afterwards exist", and where things are given *ob turpem causam*.[71] But, as indicated earlier on, Erskine rather curiously deals with the obligations arising from *indebiti solutio* in a different title from the *condictiones* mentioned above. In Book 3, title 3, which mainly deals with contractual obligations, he states that obligations are not only formed by proper contracts, but by *quasi contracts*: "These are constituted, not by explicit consent, as proper contracts are, but *ex re*; that is, merely by one of the parties doing such deeds as in their nature infer an obligation upon him in favour of the other party, or upon that other party, though he be perhaps ignorant of it, in favour of the first."[72]

Erskine regards *indebiti solutio* as one of the examples of cases where a quasi-contractual obligation will arise. Erskine's decision to deal with *indebiti solutio*, or "the payment to one of a debt not truly due to him"[73] (the Roman *condictio indebiti*) under the heading "quasi-contract", rather than restitution, warrants further attention. It will be recalled that Stair intentionally avoided the use of the category "quasi-contract". Instead, he grouped together "quasi-contractual" remedies under the headings of "restitution" and "recompense". In this way the *condictio indebiti* came to be regarded as a remedy for obtaining restitution, and was no longer described as being based on a "quasi-contract". However, even though he retained Stair's categories of "restitution" and "recompense", Erskine decided to re-introduce the heading of "quasi-contract" along lines strongly resembling the title on "quasi-contract" in the Institutes of Justinian: both Erskine and Justinian's titles deal with (inter alia) *negotiorum gestio*, the *actio communi dividundo*, and *indebiti solutio*.[74] This of course gives rise to uncertainty as to the exact relationship between "restitution" and "quasi-contract" as categories within the law of obligations. Could an obligation of restitution no longer arise from *indebiti solutio*?[75] It seems as if it still could: what Erskine essentially did was to retain Stair's classification of obligations arising from "restitution" and "recompense", and then to group together certain cases where these obligations would arise on the historical ground that they are based on a "quasi-contract". Whether this is necessarily useful is questionable: Stair clearly envisaged a completely new categorisation when he drew a distinction between remedies of restitution and recompense. To revert partly to the past by describing some of these remedies as "quasi-contractual" whilst retaining "restitution" and "recompense" as separate categories only gives rise to confusion.

In conclusion it should be mentioned that Erskine's requirement that there is no "purpose of donation" in cases of recompense, is very similar to his requirement that there is no "intention in the owner of making a present" in cases of restitution. In fact, it now becomes clear that "recompense" is not so much based on the substantive consideration of "reciprocation"—of doing one good deed for another, as Stair would put it—than on the fact that someone has been "enriched" and is obliged to "indemnify" the expenses of another. Recompense now moves much closer to being complementary to restitution, rather than being a completely separate source of obligations. Both remedies are concerned with providing relief where one

71 Erskine, *Institute* 3.1.10.

72 Erskine, *Institute* 3.3.51.

73 Erskine, *Institute* 3.3.54.

74 Compare Erskine, *Institute* 3.3.51 et sqq with *Institute* 3.27.1 (*negotiorum gestio*), 3.27.2 (*actio tutelae*) 3.27.3 (*actio communi dividundo*), 3.27.6–7 (*condictio* where a person pays another in error what he does not owe him).

75 Cf his treatment of *negotiorum gestio* and *the lex Rhodia de jactu*, which is regarded as giving rise to the obligation of recompense (Erskine, *Institute* 3.1.11), but is still dealt with under the heading of "quasi-contractual obligations" (Erskine, *Institute* 3.3.51–53, 55 et sq).

person has obtained something from another without the intention of making a gift, but while the former remedy is aimed at restoring that which has been obtained, the latter remedy is aimed at providing something in its place.

iv. Hume[76]

Unlike Erskine and Stair, Hume rejects the classical distinction between "persons", "things" and "actions", in favour of a division between "rights" and "actions".[77] However, within the subdivision of personal rights or obligations, he has no qualms about adopting the classical distinction between obligations which arise from contract, delict, quasi contract and quasi-delict.[78] According to him, the obligations *quasi ex contractu* are, inter alia, deduced from the most "remarkable maxim" that "no one shall be allowed to turn another's loss into his profit".[79] Such a person is then liable to provide restitution. A notable feature of Hume's treatment of restitution is that he draws a more clear distinction between personal rights and real rights. He grounds the duty to provide restitution on the general principle of Pomponius that no-one should enrich himself at the expense of another[80] and then provides a detailed assessment of the limits of this maxim,[81] and a list of cases where it applies. These, inter alia, include recovery of payments to legatees prior to dissolution of debts to creditors, payments of loans made to minors without authority, payments made in the improvement of another's property, and the *condictio indebiti*.[82] Although he mentions that an executor cannot have "repetition" of a sum when he pays a creditor the full debt in the belief that the executory funds are equal to all the claims upon them, the term "repetition" is not treated as a separate subdivision, such as restitution or recompense. "Repetition" seems to be a label which describes the claim for recovery or "restitution" of money paid in error.[83] It is apparently not a label which exclusively deals with claims for recovery of money either, for Hume also refers to the restitution of money.[84] None of the *condictiones*, such as the *condictio causa data causa non secuta, condictio ob turpem vel iniustam causam* or the *condictio sine causa* are discussed. Hume does recognise the obligation of recompense,[85] but gives a rather restricted interpretation of the subject matter, which lacks the broad sweep of Stair's "doing one good deed for another". However, it does seek to establish

---

76 Although Hume strictly speaking is not an Institutional writer (see *Fortington v Lord Kinnaird* 1942 SC 239), his views on unjustified enrichment are of such importance that they cannot be ignored in the present context.

77 Hume, *Lectures*, vol 1, 9.

78 Hume, *Lectures*, vol 1, 10, vol 2, 3.

79 Hume, *Lectures*, vol 3, 165. See D 12.6.14.

80 Cf generally, Hume, *Lectures*, vol 1, 10 et sqq, vol 2, 2 et sqq, vol 3, 201 et sqq. No more mention is made of things recovered from robbers, the enemy, things straying and the like. These matters belong to the title on right of property (Hume, *Lectures*, vol 3, 201 et sqq, 228 et sqq). However, the distinction is not entirely consistent. For example, Hume deals with the right to claim division of common property under the heading of obligations *quasi ex contractu* (see *Lectures*, vol 3, 403 et sqq). This is a right of an owner to claim his property, rather than a right based on the enrichment of another. It can be said, though, that the chapter on quasi-contract is predominantly based on enrichment. This represents a deviation from the practice of the Institutional writers to conflate proprietary and enrichment-based remedies.

81 Hume, *Lectures*, vol 3, 165–168.

82 Hume, *Lectures*, vol 3, 168–175.

83 Hume, *Lectures*, vol 3, 172–175, also see vol 3, 402, referring to Bell, *Commentaries*, vol 1, par 649.

84 Hume, *Lectures*, vol 3, 172.

85 Hume, *Lectures*, vol 3, 177. It encompasses *negotiorum gestio* and the *Lex Rhodia de jactu*.

a more substantive basis for recompense, rather than the mere fact that someone must indemnify another, as Erskine seems to require.

v. Bell

Unfortunately, Bell did not build upon Hume's pioneering work. Instead of continuing to provide a more clear basis of differentiation between proprietary and enrichment remedies, Bell rather opted for a terse exposition of some basic principles. It will be recalled that Stair criticised the Roman distinction between contract, delict, quasi-contract and quasi-delict on the ground that it "insinuates no reason of the cause or rise of these distinct obligations".[86] Bell, too, does not follow this division: according to him "... it seems to be simpler to consider all such grounds of action on account of *rights invaded*, under the heads of Restitution, Recompense and Reparation".[87] Bell's exposition of the examples of restitution is quite conventional: it contains the same conflation of proprietary and enrichment remedies one finds in Stair, with vindicatory claims aimed at recovery of things stolen[88] standing alongside enrichment claims, such as the *condictio causa data causa non secuta*[89] and, of course, the *condictio indebiti*,[90] which is dealt with in a separate paragraph. Unlike Erskine, Bell makes no mention of the *condictio ob turpem vel iniustam causam*. The same conventionality characterises his treatment of recompense: like Erskine and Bankton, he also mentions the requirements of "gain" or enrichment through the lawful act of another, "done without any intention of donation".[91] He lists the customary examples[92] and states that the nature of the remedy is determined by the "extent" of the acquisition",[93] the "benefit derived"[94] or the "expenditures" made.[95] However, this conventionality was not to last. Posthumous editions of Bell's *Principles* (i.e. from the fifth edition onwards), supplement the traditional two Rs of restitution and recompense with a third R—that of "repetition". The word "repetition" is not new, as is apparent from its intermittent appearance in the works of Institutional writers. However, what was new was its application as the "label" for a remedy distinct from, rather than subsumed under restitution. While Bell still dealt with erroneous payments under the heading of "restitution", the label of "repetition" was now used to describe cases falling under the following general rule:

> Whatever has been delivered or paid on an erroneous conception of duty or obligation, may be recovered on the ground of equity; provided the person reclaiming has no reason, or natural right, implied donation, or compromise, to rely on the acquisition as his own. The action by which, in the Roman law, this was effected was called Condictio Indebiti; and the term has been adopted by us.[96]

---

86 Stair, *Institutions* 1.3.2.

87 Bell, *Principles* 525, (own emphasis).

88 Bell, *Principles*, 527. He does, however, pay special attention to position of money (Bell, *Principles*, 528).

89 Bell, *Principles*, 530.

90 Bell, *Principles*, 531–536.

91 Bell, *Principles*, 538. For criticism, cf *Edinburgh and District Tramways Co Ltd v Courtney* 1909 SC 99 at 105; *Varney (Scotland) Ltd v Lanark Town Council* 1974 SC 245.

92 These are bona fide building on another's land (Bell, *Principles*, 538), *negotiorum gestio* (Bell, *Principles*, 540), and the *Lex Rhodia de Jactu* (Bell, *Principles*, 541). Bell does, however, recognise a rather cryptic category of "remuneration for services" (Bell, *Principles*, 539).

93 Bell, *Principles*, 538.

94 Bell, *Principles*, 539.

95 Bell, *Principles*, 540.

96 Bell, *Principles*, 531.

Thus, it is only during the second half of the nineteenth century that the third "R" "officially" joined restitution and recompense. It also joined it as an editorial heading (drawn up by Patrick Shaw), and was never personally used by Bell.[97] In essence, it covered the field of the *condictio indebiti*, and could be used for the recovery of both property and money. This ought to be obvious from the references to both the terms "delivered" and "paid".

vi. Conclusions

In the nineteenth century, with the explicit recognition of "repetition" within the traditional terrain of "restitution", the three Rs started to emerge as the dominant classificatory framework of the Scots law of unjustified enrichment. This is somewhat surprising, since this ground of distinction is as unsatisfactory as the Roman distinction between the quasi-contracts it succeeded to displace. However, before examining its progress in the twentieth century, it would be useful to pause and consider the way in which restitution and recompense were generally treated by the institutional writers. The following conclusions can be drawn:

1. The obligation of restitution generally arose when someone's property or money came into the power or possession of another without the intention that it should be a gift. More specifically, it could be used to recover things which came into someone's hands without a legal basis. It then covered the terrain of the *condictio indebiti*, the *condictio causa data causa non secuta* and the *condictio sine causa*. The obligation of restitution did not only arise in cases which would nowadays be regarded as instances of unjustified enrichment, but was also a remedy of property law. The distinction between personal rights and real rights was undeveloped.
2. Recompense was generally aimed at redressing another's gain, benefit, or enrichment—most notably through bona fide building on another's land, *negotiorum gestio* and the *Lex Rhodia de Jactu*. Stair still based the obligation for recompense on a lack of reciprocation, but the remedy simply came to be regarded as one aimed at obtaining some sort of indemnity or compensation due to another's gain or benefit.
3. It is only in the nineteenth century that "repetition" came to be regarded as a distinct category of quasi-contractual obligations. It was mainly associated with the payment of money in error as to liability.

7.2.3 *The modern taxonomies*

It has been said that more was written on the law of unjustified enrichment in Scotland in the last ten years than in the previous three hundred.[98] A salient feature of these modern writings is the diversity of approaches to a taxonomy of the subject. In fact, it seems as if it would be quite a while before some form of consensus is reached as to what constitutes the most desirable arrangement of categories within the law of unjustified enrichment: *quot homines, tot senties*. At present, the following approaches can be identified.

---

97 It is therefore not correct to refer to *Bell's* "division of the subject into the heads of restitution, repetition, recompense and negotiorum gestio" (cf SME vol 15 (1993), para 13; MacQueen and Sellar, "Unjust Enrichment in Scots Law", in Schrage (ed), *Unjust Enrichment*, 289 at 300). Further particulars are contained in a draft seminar paper prepared in 1996 by Professor Robin Evans-Jones and Mr Philip Hellwege.

98 SME vol 15 (1993), para 10.

First, there is the traditional taxonomy, based on a division between the three Rs of restitution, repetition and recompense. The label "restitution" (viewed narrowly) covers cases involving the recovery of moveable property, "repetition" the recovery of money, and "recompense" certain other cases of unjustified enrichment, most notably through expenditures, services, or use of property of another.[99] Second, it has been argued that the traditional approach is in principle acceptable, although it needs to be developed further "in the best eclectic Scottish tradition", particularly through the recognition of a general enrichment action within the law of recompense.[100] Third, there have been more serious challenges to the traditional approach in favour a major realignment of claims. However, here the basis of realignment differs substantially. On the one hand, support has been expressed for adopting the "unjust factors" approach of English law,[101] and on the other hand, the modern civilian approach, which focuses on the absence of a legal ground for the enrichment, has been proposed as the most suitable basis for further development.[102] A modification of the modern civilian approach, which in certain respects resembles the "unjust factors" approach, has also been proposed.[103] Finally, there has been support for a drastic break with the past through codification.[104] In the following section a brief overview of these approaches will be provided with a view towards setting the stage for a proper assessment of their treatment of compulsion in the section following thereafter. The starting point will be the traditional approach.

i. The traditional approach: the three Rs of restitution, repetition and recompense[105]

As indicated above, the fifth edition of Bell's influential *Principles of Scots law*,[106] which was revised by Patrick Shaw, adds the heading of "repetition" to the existing headings of "restitution" and "recompense". This division forms the basis of the modern presentation of the Scots law of unjustified enrichment. In Gloag and Henderson's early twentieth-century *Introduction to the Law of Scotland* a clear distinction is drawn

---

99 Cf *Morgan Guaranty Trust Company of New York v Lothian Regional Council* 1995 SCLR 225; Gloag and Henderson, *The Law of Scotland*, 470 et sqq and the general discussion at 7.2.3.i below. Cf also Walker, *The Law of Contracts and Related Obligations in Scotland*, 585 et sqq; G Gretton, "Unjust Enrichment in Scotland" 1992 *Scottish Business Law* 108.

100 Cf SME vol 15 (1993), para 10 et sqq, especially para 86; MacQueen and Sellar, "Unjust Enrichment in Scots Law" in Schrage (ed), *Unjust Enrichment*, 289 et sqq.

101 Cf the discussion of the views of Professor P B H Birks and Mr W J Stewart at 7.2.3.ii below.

102 Cf the discussion of the views of Prof R Evans-Jones at 7.2.3.iii below. For general comparisons between Common Law and Civil Law approaches, cf J P Dawson, *Unjust Enrichment: A Comparative Analysis* (1951); Zweigert and Kötz, tr Weir, *An Introduction to Comparative Law*, chs 45 and 46; Englard, "Restitution of benefits confered without obligation" in *International Encyclopaedia of Comparative Law*, vol X, ch 5, 3 et sqq; Zimmermann, *The Law of Obligations*, 887 et sqq; B Dickson, "Unjust Enrichment Claims: A Comparative Overview" (1995) 54(1) *CLJ* 100 (especially sources quoted at note 1); W J Swadling, "Restitution and Unjust Enrichment" in Hartkamp et al (eds), *Towards a European Civil Code*, 267 et sqq; P Gallo, "Unjust Enrichment: A Comparative Analysis" (1992) 40 *American Journal of Comparative Law* 431.

103 Cf the discussion of the provisional views of the Scottish Law Commission and Mr N R Whitty at 7.2.3.iv below.

104 Cf Judicial Abolition of the Error of Law Rule and its Aftermath (Scot Law Com D P No 99, 1996) Appendix, which contains draft rules on unjustified enrichment and a commentary. The paper was prepared by Dr E M Clive for a seminar held on 22 October 1994.

105 See, generally, Recovery of Benefits Conferred under Error of Law (Scot Law Com D P No 95, 1993) vol 1, 99 sqq; Birks, "Six Questions in Search of a Subject—Unjust Enrichment in a Crisis of Identity" 1985 *JR* 227 at 233 et sqq.

106 Cf 7.2.2.v above.

between the "quasi-contractual" obligation of restitution, which relates to the giving up of goods, the plea of repetition, which is used for the recovery of money paid, and recompense.[107] This type of analysis of the relationship between, particularly, restitution and repetition, has proved to be influential, and is widely recognised by modern writers[108] and the judiciary.[109] As far as recompense is concerned, the view has been expressed that it only covers those cases where the defendant's benefit derives from a service,[110] but the preferable approach is that its scope is broader and includes claims based on unjustified enrichment through the receipt of money and goods.[111] For present purposes it is not necessary to examine recompense in further detail.[112] The crucial question is rather what is to be understood under the subject matter of restitution and repetition, and more specifically, its relationship to the law of the *condictiones*.

In *Watson v Shankland*,[113] Lord President Inglis stated that the *condictio causa data causa non secuta*, the *condictio sine causa* and the *condictio indebiti* are "represented by the action of restitution and the action of repetition". This statement has been approved in the landmark decisions of *Cantiere San Rocco v Clyde Shipbuilding and Engineering Co*[114] and *Morgan Guaranty Trust Company of New York v Lothian Regional Council*.[115] In academic writings the balance of opinion is also in favour of the view that these *condictiones* underlie actions for both restitution and

107 W M Gloag and R C Henderson, *Introduction to the Law of Scotland*, 1st ed (1927), 67 et sq, 116; 2nd ed (1933), 122 et sq. In the second edition of Gloag's *Law of Contract* of 1929 the distinction is less clear: he refers to (a) the obligation of restitution, (b) the obligation to repay money paid by mistake (*indebiti solutio*), and (c) the law of recompense (319). Although Gloag nowhere explicitly states that an action of repetition only lies to recover payments of money, he only refers to it in this context (*The Law of Contract*, 60, 62).

108 Cf the 10th edition of Gloag and Henderson, *The Law of Scotland* (1995), 470 et sq, 478; Walker, *Principles of Scottish Private law*, vol 2, 505 et sqq; SME vol 15 (1993), para 14 et sq, 44; Recovery of Benefits Conferred under Error of Law (Scot Law Com D P No 95, 1993) vol 1, 99 et sqq; Judicial Abolition of the Error of Law Rule and its Aftermath (Scot Law Com D P No 99, 1996), 77. Cf, however, Evans-Jones, "From 'undue transfer' to 'retention without a legal basis' (the *condictio indebiti* and *condictio ob turpem vel iniustam causam*)" in Evans-Jones (ed), *The Civil Law Tradition in Scotland*, 213 at 217 et sqq, and Walker, *The Law of Contact and Related Obligations in Scotland*, 586, in favour of the view that repetition is concerned with claims for the recovery of money as well as property.

109 Cf, most recently, *Morgan Guaranty Trust Company of New York v Lothian Regional Council* 1995 SCLR 225 at 229B.

110 Birks, "Six Questions in Search of a Subject—Unjust Enrichment in a Crisis of Identity" 1985 *JR* 227 at 234.

111 Cf Recovery of Benefits Conferred under Error of Law (Scot Law Com D P No 95, 1993) vol 1, 104 et sqq; Judicial Abolition of the Error of Law Rule and its Aftermath (Scot Law Com D P No 99, 1996) 78; SME vol 15 (1993), para 82; MacQueen and Sellar, "Unjust Enrichment in Scots Law", in Schrage (ed), *Unjust Enrichment*, 289 at 296. Gloag and Henderson, *The Law of Scotland*, rather cryptically refer to "other actings" of the pursuer (470, 480).

112 In particular, it is not necessary to deal with the debate as to whether the division of the three Rs is "benefit" based, as Birks suggests ("Six Questions in Search of a Subject—Unjust Enrichment in a Crisis of Identity" 1985 *JR* 227 at 234; Birks, "Restitution: A View of the Scots Law" (1985) 38 *CLP* 57 at 61 et sqq), or "*quantum*" based (Recovery of Benefits Conferred under Error of Law (Scot Law Com D P No 95, 1993) vol 1, 105 et sqq; Judicial Abolition of the Error of Law Rule and its Aftermath (Scot Law Com D P No 99, 1996) 78). This debate is more relevant to recompense than restitution or repetition (Judicial Abolition of the Error of Law Rule and its Aftermath (Scot Law Com D P No 99, 1996) 77 et sqq).

113 (1871) 10 M 142 at 152.

114 1923 SC (HL) 105 at 124.

115 1995 SCLR 225 at 228G–229B.

repetition.[116] However, since the reported cases by and large deal with claims for the recovery of money payments,[117] the *condictiones* could for all practical intents and purposes be regarded as falling under the action of repetition.[118]

Unfortunately, it is not only the relationship between repetition, restitution and the *condictiones* which is disputed, but also the question which of the *condictiones* are at all recognised in modern Scots law. Traditionally, the case law has been concerned mainly with the *condictio causa data causa non secuta* and the *condictio indebiti*. The notion of *sine causa* retention is recognised,[119] but the *condictio sine causa* only features peripherally.[120] The *condictio ob turpem vel iniustam causam* is virtually obsolete, although references occur to its traditional companions, namely the rules which restrict recovery when both parties are tainted by turpitude. However, some new, or non-traditional approaches have adopted substantially different approaches to the applicability of these *condictiones*. In the following exposition of these approaches, particular attention will be paid to their treatment of the *condictiones*.

ii. The "unjust factors" approach

In the foreword to his *An Introduction to the Law of Restitution*, Professor Birks states that his book "... is pre-occupied with the task of finding the simplest structure on which the material in Goff and Jones can hang".[121] Goff and Jones is a standard textbook on the English law of restitution, and the structure of Birks's book strongly reflects English law. However, it is clear that he believes that this structure should not only be applied in English law alone. In two articles on the Scots law of unjustified enrichment, he shows how this structure could also be made useful for Scots law.[122] This lead was taken by William J Stewart in his *The Law of Restitution in Scotland*, the first book solely to deal with the Scots law of unjustified enrichment.[123] The reasons why Stewart followed the scheme of Birks are that it was also proposed for Scots law, and it is "convincingly logical".[124] It is then claimed that the scheme can cover adequately both the Scots law relating to "quasi-contract", "restitution" (in the broad

116 Cf, e.g., Gloag and Henderson, *The Law of Scotland*, 470 et sqq, 478 et sqq; SME vol 15 (1993), para 15, 46; Gloag, *The Law of Contract*, 57 et sq; Smith, *A Short Commentary on the law of Scotland*, 627; *Encyclopaedia of the Laws of Scotland*, vol 12, s v "Repetition".

117 Cf McBryde, *The Law of Contract in Scotland*, 204.

118 It has been argued that repetition relates to both property and money, and is best understood as that part of the law of unjustified enrichment which concerns the recovery of property or money with one of the recognised *condictiones* (Evans-Jones, "From 'undue transfer' to 'retention without a legal basis' (the *condictio indebiti* and *condictio ob turpem vel iniustam causam*)" in Evans-Jones (ed), *The Civil Law Tradition in Scotland*, 213 at 215–218). However, while Institutional authority in support of this argument is strong (cf Bell, *Principles*, 531), there is case law where in a *condictio indebiti* type of situation, restitution, and not repetition, was awarded (*Pride v St Anne's Bleaching Company* (1878) 16 S 1376; cf also generally *Savage v McAllister* (1952) 68 Sh Ct Rep 11; *Grieve v Morrison* 1993 SLT 852 at 855B).

119 Recovery of Benefits Conferred under Error of Law (Scot Law Com D P No 95, 1993) vol 1, 100.

120 Cf 7.3.2.iii below.

121 Birks, *An Introduction to the Law of Restitution*, 3.

122 Birks, "Six Questions in Search of a Subject—Unjust Enrichment in a Crisis of Identity", 1985 *JR* 227; Birks, "Restitution: A View of Scots Law" (1985) 38 *CLP* 57.

123 According to Stewart he was determined to follow Birks's lead "and untangle our native law and state it in a way full enough to reveal its theoretical and principled structure and in such a way that the practitioner can see the difficulties and complexities involved in such litigation" (*The Law of Restitution in Scotland*, vii).

124 *The Law of Restitution in Scotland*, 20.

sense) or unjust enrichment on the one hand, and the English law of restitution on the other. However, it should be noted that Birks does not profess that this scheme represents the current position in any of these systems: rather, it is offered as a model within which these systems could develop.

A central idea of the scheme of Birks is that the causative event of unjust enrichment at the cost of another triggers the response of restitution, i.e. causing one person to give back something to another.[125] The scheme then draws the primary distinction between two types of enrichment of a defendant, namely by subtraction from the plaintiff, i.e. when the defendant's gain represents a loss to the plaintiff, and by doing wrong to the plaintiff.[126] These are prima facie causes of action which are then "perfected" or completed by the addition of an unjust factor.[127] Under this approach, proof of such an unjust factor, as disclosed by the case law, is essential for a claim of restitution—as one commentator put it, "it is not simply a case of stating that the defendant has no legitimate reason to retain the enrichment".[128] In the case of subtraction, a number of these unjust factors, namely ignorance, mistake, inequality or compulsion are grouped together under the main heading "non-voluntariness", and under the subheading "vitiation".[129] This means that these factors share the general characteristic that the plaintiff did not mean the defendant to be enriched, and the more specific characteristic that the plaintiff did not exercise his judgment properly, or at all, in the enrichment of the defendant.[130] In addition to "non-voluntariness", the prima facie cause of action of subtraction can also be "perfected" by (amongst other) the unjust factor that a "policy motivation" requires restitution to be made.[131] However, this type of differentiation is not possible in cases of enrichment by wrongdoing: there the word "unjust" is "used in a technical and restricted sense to denote factors which are legally calling for an enrichment to be disgorged.[132] As one commentator pointed out, "the 'unjust factor' here is not to be found within the law of restitution itself. It will instead consist of a breach of duty laid down in some other part of the law".[133]

For present purposes, "non-voluntariness" is of particular importance. According to Birks, it is "the field marked out by Lord Mansfield in *Moses v Macferlan*,[134] based on the non-contractual heads of the Roman action of debt, the *condictio*, which

---

125 Birks, *The Law of Restitution*, 10 et sqq, 16.

126 Birks, *The Law of Restitution*, 23 et sq, 40 et sqq, 313 et sqq; 24; Birks, "Restitution: A View of the Scots Law" (1985) 38 *CLP* 57 at 65. Cf Burrows, *The Law of Restitution*, 16 et sqq.

127 Birks, "Restitution: A View of the Scots Law" (1985) 38 *CLP* 57 at 65.

128 Swadling, "Restitution and Unjust Enrichment" in Hartkamp et al (eds), *Towards a European Civil Code*, 267 at 268. It should be noted though that it is not necessary to refer to the unjust factor on the level of generality contained in the taxonomies in the modern texts on the law of Restitution (cf S Hedley, "Unjust Enrichment" (1995) 54 *CLJ* 578 at 582 et sqq).

129 Birks, *The Law of Restitution*, 100 et sqq, 140 et sqq.

130 Cf Birks, *The Law of Restitution*, 140. Another subheading under "non-voluntariness" is "qualification". Here the specific characteristic is not a problem with the plaintiff exercising his judgment. He does so in full, but recovery is allowed if he intended to give something on a basis which has failed to come about (cf Birks, *The Law of Restitution*, 101, 219 et sqq; Birks, "Restitution: A View of the Scots Law" (1985) 38 *CLP* 57 at 66).

131 Cf Birks, *The Law of Restitution*, 265 et sqq, 294 et sqq; Birks, "Restitution: A View of the Scots Law" (1985) 38 *CLP* 57 at 65 et sq.

132 Cf Birks, *The Law of Restitution*, 313 et sqq; Birks, "Restitution: A View of the Scots Law" 1985 (38) *CLP* 57 at 66.

133 Swadling, "Restitution and Unjust Enrichment", in Hartkamp et al (eds), *Towards a European Civil Code*, 267 at 270.

134 (1760) 2 Burr 1005.

itself directly dominates the equivalent Scots law".[135] It is then not surprising that for purposes of his analysis of Scots law, Birks attempts to correlate certain of the *condictiones* with unjust factors dealing with "non-voluntariness". Thus, the *condictio indebiti* is then supposed to be "a restitutionary claim on the ground of mistake", while the *condictio ob turpem (vel iniustam) causam* is supposed to be applied in cases of compulsion.[136] Given the English origins of the model, it is not surprising that the mere fact that a transfer was not due, and is therefore retained *sine causa*, does not in principle render it recoverable: an unjust factor is still required. The "unjust factors" approach therefore stands in stark contrast to the modern civilian approach, which regards these concepts as of central importance.

Before turning to an examination of the modern civilian approach, a few comments need to be made on the "unjust factors" approach. First, it is notable that, as a matter of policy, English law does not have a uniform tradition of favouring the recipient by requiring that the plaintiff has to prove the existence of an unjust factor. As Birks also acknowledges, in equity it is presumed that

> ... unless the subject-matter is land or the parties are in a relationship giving rise to a counter-presumption of advancement ... any transfer without consideration was not intended to benefit the recipient. Hence in equity restitution is effected unless the recipient can rebut the presumption of resulting trust.[137]

Second, there are indications in modern law that cracks are appearing in the unjust factors facade: it has to do with the notion of "absence of consideration" (which more than superficially resembles the expression "absence of legal ground" or "*sine causa*") as an unjust factor. The case of *Westdeutsche Landesbank Girozentrale v Islington London Borough Council* serves as an example.[138] Here the Court of Appeals held that payments under a void "swaps" contract were recoverable on the ground that they were made for no consideration. This has lead one commentator to state that

> ... the case has done more than simply add a new "unjust factor" to the existing list. If correct, it may well be that the English approach to the whole restitutionary enquiry stands in need of reappraisal, for it is reminiscent of the strategy prevailing in civil law jurisdictions and in Canada where the focus is on the absence of some 'juristic cause' for the enrichment rather than the enumeration of some specific factor calling for restitution.[139]

The point can be illustrated by way of a simple example of when an undue payment is made under mistake. If the fact that the payment is not due can be equated to an absence of consideration, and it is recoverable on this ground alone, then the presence of mistake is of secondary importance or even irrelevant. Unsurprisingly, this view has been criticised, especially in regard to the authority on which it rests. The judgment draws support from *Woolwich Building Society (formerly Woolwich Equitable*

135 Birks, "Restitution: A View of the Scots Law" (1985) 38 *CLP* 57 at 67.

136 Cf Birks, "Restitution: A View of the Scots Law" (1985) 38 CLP 57 at 70. But cf Stewart *The Law of Restitution in Scotland*, 141.

137 Birks, "Restitution: A View of the Scots Law" (1985) *CLP* 57 at 61; cf also Birks, *The Law of Restitution*, 9, 60 et sqq, 156 et sqq.

138 (1993) 91 LGR 323; 2 Bank LR 159; [1993] RLR § 135; [1994] CLC 96; [1994] 1 WLR 938; [1994] 4 All ER 890; [1996] 2 All ER 961 [HL].

139 W J Swadling, "Restitution for no consideration" 1994 *RLR* 73. Cf also M McInnes, "Bases for Restitution: A Call for Clarity with Unjust Factors" 1996 *Journal of Contract Law* 73 at 83.

Building Society) v Inland Revenue Commissioners,[140] where the existing framework of unjust factors proved itself incapable of accommodating a claim for recovery of a sum paid pursuant to an ultra vires demand by a public authority. In *Woolwich* it was then held that such payment is recoverable as of right, a proposition for which authority could be found in a constitutional principle contained in the Bill of Rights of 1689.[141] The criticism against the approach of the Court of Appeals in *Westdeutsche* is that it interpreted *Woolwich* wrongly by deciding that the unjust factor was not absence of consideration but rather this *sui generis* principle. When the decision of the Court of Appeals in *Westdeutsche* was taken on appeal to the House of Lords, Lord Goff of Chieveley took the opportunity to plaster the cracks caused by the court *a quo*'s interpretation of *Woolwich*. His Lordship then intimated that it was the failure, rather than the absence of consideration, which was the unjust factor allowing recovery of the payments made pursuant to the *ultra vires* swap agreement. However, these remarks are in fact *obiter*, since the narrow parameters of the appeal did not require of the court to decide this point.[142] From the aforegoing it should be obvious that in certain cases concerning ultra vires payments the insistence on proof of an unjust factor presents considerable difficulties. The temptation simply to regard the ground for the claim as the absence of consideration, or a legal basis, is then particularly strong.

Third, and this point relates to the former, the "unjust factors" approach is characterised by a certain lack of elegance.[143] Here the open-endedness of the system, constantly attempting to keep up with legal developments by the reinterpreting and identifying of unjust factors, rather than accommodating recovery within existing categories, is particularly unsatisfactory in that it seriously undermines legal certainty.[144] Other problems are the lack of economy brought about by duplication within the legal system, As Professor Zimmermann puts it:

> Mistake, in certain circumstances, invalidates the contract. Mistake also provides the basis for a claim for restitution. What is the relationship between these two enquiries? Why deal with one and the same issue in two different contexts? Why develop two different sets of rules in order to determine the sphere of operative mistakes? It is difficult to see why the law of unjustified enrichment should be saddled with the task of sorting out the fate of the contractual relationship between recipient and transferor.[145]

He then concludes:

---

140 [1992] 3 WLR 367; [1993] 1 AC 70 (CA and HL). Cf W J Swadling, "Restitution for no consideration" 1994 *RLR* 73 at 75.

141 Cf 6.3.3 above; W J Swadling, "Restitution for no consideration" 1994 *RLR* 73 at 75.

142 *Westdeutsche Landesbank Girozentrale v Islington LBC* [1996] 2 All ER 961 [HL] 967 et sq. The point on appeal was essentially whether compound, rather than simple interest should have been awarded.

143 Cf Zimmermann, "Unjustified Enrichment: The Modern Civilian Approach" (1995) 15 *OJLS* 403 at 416.

144 Although there is supposed to be a *numerus clausus* of restitutionary causes of action (cf Swadling, "Restitution and Unjust Enrichment" in Hartkamp et al (eds), *Towards a European Civil Code*, 267 at 268) there is support for the proposition that the categories of unjust enrichment are not in fact closed (cf *Cash & Carry v Gallaher* [1994] 4 All ER 714, 720). Cf also Evans-Jones, "From 'undue transfer' to 'retention without a legal basis' (the *condictio indebiti* and *condictio ob turpem vel iniustam causam*)" in Evans-Jones (ed), *The Civil Law Tradition in Scotland*, 213 at 247.

145 Zimmermann, "Unjustified Enrichment: The Modern Civilian Approach" (1995) 15 *OJLS* 403 at 416.

> All in all therefore, it is hardly conceivable that a legal system engaged with the task of rationally reorganizing its law of unjustified enrichment should take its lead from English jurisprudence. Scots law ... has all the less reason to do so, since the Institutional writers have implanted in it the germ of the modern civilian enrichment-by-transfer claim: the *condictio indebiti*.[146]

iii. The modern civilian approach

In many modern civilian systems, the law of unjustified enrichment still strongly reflects its Roman origins, most notably through the recognition of contemporary versions of the *condictiones*, the *actio de in rem verso*, certain claims based on *negotiorum gestio* or Pomponius' famous enrichment principle that "no person should be enriched to the detriment of another".[147] Through this Roman influence, and particularly that of the law of the *condictiones*, many of these systems share a key feature, namely the grouping together of cases of unjustified enrichment brought about by a transfer.[148] Particularly where such a transfer is made to discharge an obligation (a *datio solvendi causa*), the absence of such an obligation, or legal ground, renders its retention unjustified. Unlike English law, it is not required that an unjust factor perfects subtraction (by way of transfer). For example, in a number of modern civilian systems, error as to liability is no longer a requirement for reclaiming an undue transfer.[149] This does not mean that the potentially irresponsible behaviour which the error requirement is supposed to prevent, namely making an undue transfer only to reclaim it later, is necessarily allowed. Where a transfer is made in the knowledge that it is undue, recovery could be barred—generally if the impression is created that the recipient is entitled to keep it.[150] If one moves on from transfers *solvendi causa* to other forms of transfer, it is clear that these are also not based on unjust factors. In German law, for example, use is still made of the Roman categories of transfers *ob rem* (i.e. made with a view towards obtaining counterperformance) and transfers *ob turpem vel iniustam causam*. However, the relevance of these distinctions has diminished

---

146 Zimmermann, "Unjustified Enrichment: The Modern Civilian Approach" (1995) 15 *OJLS* 403 at 416.

147 Pomp D 12.6.4. On the modern civilian approach in general, cf inter alia Zimmermann, "Unjustified Enrichment: The Modern Civilian Approach" (1995) 15 *OJLS* 403; Englard, "Restitution of Benefits Conferred Without Obligation" in *International Encyclopaedia of Comparative Law*, vol X, ch 5; Zimmermann, *The Law of Obligations*, 863 et sqq, 870 et sqq, 883 et sqq, 887 et sqq, 895 et sqq; Zweigert and Kötz, tr Weir, *An Introduction to Comparative Law*, 576 et sqq, 600 et sqq, 606 et sqq. On German law in particular, cf R Zimmermann and J E du Plessis, "Basic Features of the German law of Unjustified Enrichment" 1994 *RLR* 14.

148 Zimmermann, "Unjustified Enrichment: The Modern Civilian Approach" (1995) 15 *OJLS* 403 at 404 et sqq, 411. For present purposes it is not necessary to examine the cases of enrichment which have not been brought about by a transfer. Here it is more difficult to determine whether the enrichment has been at the expense of another. The general requirement is still that such enrichment has to be disgorged if obtained without legal ground. Cf, generally the Zimmermann article cited above at 417 et sqq; P Gallo, "Unjust Enrichment: A Comparative Analysis" 1992 (40) *American Journal of Comparative Law* 431 at 448 et sqq.

149 Cf Art 6:203 of the new Dutch Civil Code; § 812 BGB, read with § 814 BGB (cf 5.4.2.i above). Italian law does not favour the general application of an error requirement to all claims for the recovery of undue transfers, while French law only requires it in exceptional cases (cf Zimmermann, "Unjustified Enrichment: The Modern Civilian Approach" (1995) 15 *OJLS* 403 at 410 et sq; Gallo, "Unjust Enrichment: A Comparative Analysis" 1992 (40) *American Journal of Comparative Law* 431 at 442 et sqq; P Gallo, "Remedies for Unjust Enrichment in the History of Italian law and in the Codice Civil" in Schrage (ed), *Unjust Enrichment*, 275 at 279 et sq).

150 Cf the discussion of German law at 5.4.2 i. above; Zimmermann, "Unjustified Enrichment: The Modern Civilian Approach" (1995) 15 *OJLS* 403 at 407, 410.

considerably: due to the ascendancy of the principle that bare or mere agreements are enforceable, their fields of application are now largely occupied by the *condictio indebiti*. Transfers which were previously made to obtain a counterperformance, whether it materialised or not, are now regarded as being made to discharge an obligation.[151] Somewhat uncertain is the relevance of the *condictio sine causa specialis*. By and large it seems to have been absorbed in general enrichment actions.[152] It should therefore be obvious that the modern civilian approach stands in clear contrast to the "unjust factors" approach which Birks and Stewart proposed for Scots law. In essence, even though the outcomes may be the same, there is a marked difference in perspective: the Common Law approach sketched above looks at enrichment from the standpoint of the plaintiff and asks whether an unjust factor exists which entitles him to recovery; the modern Civil Law, which mainly acknowledges a general enrichment action, again focuses on the position of the recipient, and asks whether there is any reason why he should retain something which he obtained without legal ground.[153]

In Scotland, Professor Evans-Jones has proposed an approach which in many respects ties in closely with the modern civilian approach. Central to his approach is the conviction that Scots law possesses a strong civilian heritage, particularly in the form of the Institutional writings, and that it needs to draw on this heritage to mould its future development. A key feature of this heritage is the fact that Stair has unified the *condictiones*, as received in Scots law, under the principle that they deal with retention without a legal basis or retention *sine causa*.[154] The law of repetition is then regarded as that part of the law of unjustified enrichment which concerns the recovery of property or money with one of the recognised *condictiones*.[155] He has further identified a number of factual situations where transfers are retained without a legal basis, and therefore give rise to a claim for repetition under one of the *condictiones*.[156] First, a claim under the *condictio indebiti* arises if a transferor intends to discharge a legal duty, but fails to do so. Such a transfer is made *solvendi causa*.[157] The failure of the purpose of the transfer could be the result of an error, but

151 On the relevance of the *condictiones* in the modern German law of unjustified enrichment, cf Zimmermann and du Plessis, "Basic Features of the German law of Unjustified Enrichment" 1994 *RLR* 14 at 18 et sqq. On the position in Roman-Dutch law, cf 5.2.3 above.

152 Cf, in the context of German law, Zimmermann and du Plessis, "Basic Features of the German law of Unjustified Enrichment" 1994 *RLR* 14 at 18 sq. On the need for such a qualifier, cf Stewart, *The Law of Restitution in Scotland—A Supplement*, 40.

153 Cf B Dickson, "Unjust Enrichment Claims: A Comparative Overview" (1995) 54(1) *CLJ* 100 at 115; Swadling, "Restitution and Unjust Enrichment" in Hartkamp et al (eds), *Towards a European Civil Code*, 267 at 282.

154 Evans-Jones, "From 'undue transfer' to 'retention without a legal basis' (the *condictio indebiti* and *condictio ob turpem vel iniustam causam*)" in Evans-Jones (ed), *The Civil Law Tradition in Scotland*, 213 at 241. Cf Stair, *Institutions* 1.7.7.

155 Evans-Jones, "From 'undue transfer' to 'retention without a legal basis' (the *condictio indebiti* and *condictio ob turpem vel iniustam causam*)" in Evans-Jones (ed), *The Civil Law Tradition in Scotland*, 213 at 215 et sqq, 218.

156 Evans-Jones, "From 'undue transfer' to 'retention without a legal basis' (the *condictio indebiti* and *condictio ob turpem vel iniustam causam*)" in Evans-Jones (ed), *The Civil Law Tradition in Scotland*, 213 at 218. A transfer is defined as a passage of wealth which the pursuer consciously intended to confer on the defender for a particular purpose (219).

157 Evans-Jones, "From 'undue transfer' to 'retention without a legal basis' (the *condictio indebiti* and *condictio ob turpem vel iniustam causam*)" in Evans-Jones (ed), *The Civil Law Tradition in Scotland*, 213 at 218 et sqq. However, he does admit that it is not generally recognised in modern Scots law that a failure to discharge a duty underlies the *condictio indebiti* (222, 233). It is also argued that claims should arise under the *condictio indebiti* if the transferor intended to create an obligation. Such a transfer is made *obligandi causa*. Here the purpose of the transfer fails if the legal duty is

need not necessarily be so. As pointed out above, Scots law has traditionally also recognised an approach which does not require proof of error, but rather excludes liability in certain cases where the transferor knew[158] that no debt was due.[159] Evans-Jones then argues that the latter approach is preferable, and in conformance with the dominant understanding of the civilian tradition.[160] Second, save when certain exclusionary rules apply, transfers with an illegal or immoral purpose are also regarded as recoverable under the *condictio indebiti*. It will be recalled that the *condictio ob turpem vel iniustam causam* only plays a minor role in modern civilian systems, and that it has virtually disappeared from Scots law. According to Evans-Jones, the explanation for its fate in Scots law is then that it has been absorbed by the *condictio indebiti*,[161] due to the fact that such transfers can also be regarded as being made in order to fulfil an obligation (i.e. *solvendi causa*). This purpose then fails because the underlying agreement, containing the obligation, is void as a *pactum illicitum*. However, this does not mean that the pursuer will necessarily escape the operation of the *in pari delicto* rule, which bars recovery where both parties are in *culpa*. This rule is regarded as applicable to the whole of the law of repetition (understood in the sense of the law of the *condictiones*).[162] He further takes issue with the view that the *condictio ob turpem vel iniustam causam* should be revived to enable recovery of transfers made under compulsion. This view will be considered when compulsion is dealt with below.[163] Finally, in accordance with the modern civilian approach a distinction is drawn between transfers made for a purpose which succeeds temporarily and then fails (the *condictio ob causam finitam*), transfers made for a future purpose (normally outwith contract) which fails (the *condictio causa data causa non secuta*),[164] and a residual category of causes of action (the *condictio sine causa*).[165] It is then recognised that the scope of the latter *condictio* is determined by the scope of the *condictio indebiti*. For example, in Italian law the general enrichment action is strictly subsidiary to the remedy of

---

not created (235). In modern Scots law, such claims have been dealt with within the category of recompense. It is further argued that the *condictio indebiti* should also be available when a transfer is made pursuant to an underlying agreement of gift (*donandi causa*) and the purpose of the transfer then fails, e.g. because of an error as to the identity of the recipient.

158 As to the relationship between the error and knowledge approaches, cf Du Plessis and Wicke, "Woolwich Equitable v IRC and the condictio indebiti in Scots law" 1993 SLT (News) 303.

159 Cf 3.3.2.i., 4.3.1.i. above.

160 Cf Evans-Jones and Hellwege, "Swaps, Error of Law and Unjustified Enrichment" (1995) 1 *SLPQ* 1 at 8; Evans-Jones, "From 'undue transfer' to 'retention without a legal basis' (the *condictio indebiti* and *condictio ob turpem vel iniustam causam*)" in Evans-Jones (ed), *The Civil Law Tradition in Scotland*, 213 at 240.

161 Evans-Jones, "From 'undue transfer' to 'retention without a legal basis' (the *condictio indebiti* and *condictio ob turpem vel iniustam causam*)" in Evans-Jones (ed), *The Civil Law Tradition in Scotland*, 213 at 244.

162 Evans-Jones, "From 'undue transfer' to 'retention without a legal basis' (the *condictio indebiti* and *condictio ob turpem vel iniustam causam*)" in Evans-Jones (ed), *The Civil Law Tradition in Scotland*, 213 at 245.

163 Cf 7.3.2.ii below.

164 Cf Evans-Jones, "Unjust Enrichment, Contract and the Third Reception of Roman law in Scotland" (1993) 109 *LQR* 663 for an analysis of the misguided application of the *condictio causa data causa non secuta* to the frustration of a contract.

165 Evans-Jones, "From 'undue transfer' to 'retention without a legal basis' (the *condictio indebiti* and *condictio ob turpem vel iniustam causam*)" in Evans-Jones (ed), *The Civil Law Tradition in Scotland*, 213 at 218; Recovery of Benefits Conferred under Error of Law (Scot Law Com D P No 95, 1993) vol 1, 100.

"pagemento dell'indebito", which is the ground for recovery of all undue payments or transfers of property or money.[166]

Thus far, the courts have not openly endorsed the exposition of the modern civilian approach as set out above. In the recent case of *Morgan Guaranty Trust Company of New York v Lothian Regional Council*[167] it has been held that proof of error is essential for a claim with the *condictio indebiti*. The mere fact that a transfer was not due was not regarded as a sufficient ground for recovery, and nor was knowledge that no debt was due regarded as a bar to recovery. This approach could be interpreted in two ways. First, it could be said that the approach of the court was not really that far removed from the modern civilian approach. It recognised that the purpose of the error requirement is in fact only to show the absence of an intention to make a donation; something which the knowledge bar could have performed equally well. The important feature is that the court unequivocally endorsed the centrality of the notion of the undue transfer. This can be built upon further, and in any event places Scots law in an entirely different position from systems which follow an "unjust factors" approach. An alternative approach would be to regard the decision in *Morgan Guaranty* as being in line with a traditional affirmation in Scots law of a modification of the civilian approach: while it recognises civilian concepts such as (*sine causa*) "retention without a legal ground" or transfer of an *indebitum*, these are not regarded as sufficient, since recovery depends on proof of additional "grounds for recovery" such as error or compulsion. This alternative approach which, for want of a better term, will be described as the modified civilian approach, has recently been expanded upon by the Scottish Law Commission, and in particular one of its Law Commissioners, Mr Niall R Whitty.

iv. The modified civilian approach

In 1993 the Scottish Law Commission released a Discussion Paper titled Recovery of Benefits Conferred under Error of Law (Scot Law Com D P No 95). In essence, it recommended the statutory abolition of the Common Law rule whereby money paid in error of law as to the payer's liability to the payee is not recoverable.[168] However, this step proved to be unnecessary. In 1995, the Court of Session held in *Morgan Guaranty Trust Company of New York v Lothian Regional Council* that this rule in fact did not form part of Scots law.[169] The implications of this decision were then analysed in the subsequent Discussion Papers No 99 on the "Judicial Abolition of the Error of Law Rule and its Aftermath", and No 100 on the "Recovery of Ultra Vires Public Authority Receipts and Disbursements". Although the titles of these Discussion Papers suggest a fairly narrow scope of inquiry, they in fact contain detailed analyses of key features of the Scots law of unjustified enrichment, such as the characteristics of the remedies and the taxonomy of the subject matter. For present purposes it is the general analysis of the modern law through the identification of certain "grounds for recovery", as well as its proposals for law reform which merit attention.

---

166 Cf arts 2033—2040 of the Italian Civil Code; P Gallo, "Remedies for Unjust Enrichment in the History of Italian Law and in the Codice Civil" in Schrage (ed), *Unjust Enrichment*, 275 at 279.

167 1995 SCLR 225.

168 Recovery of Benefits Conferred under Error of Law (Scot Law Com D P No 95, 1993), vol 1, 73, 190.

169 1995 SCLR 225.

The starting point is its analysis of the three Rs. Discussion Paper No 95 correctly points out that the type of benefit received[170] does not form the basis of the distinction between the three Rs, since there are certain cases where recompense is used when the benefit received was property or money.[171] It then suggests that a quantum-based theory, which looks at the type of redress or remedy sought, is preferable. In terms of such an analysis, repetition relates to claims for money plus interest, restitution to specific property with its fruits and accessions or their value, and recompense to a sum representing the extent of the defender's enrichment.[172] These divisions of course do not say much about why, or on what grounds, the three Rs are awarded. Further detail is provided in an analysis of repetition. The following main requirements for repetition of money paid by a pursuer (P) to a defender (D) are listed:

> "(1) P must have paid money to D.
> (2) Except possibly in certain compulsion cases, the payment must have been undue (indebitum).
> (3) The orthodox view is that P must found on one or other of a number of specific grounds of repetition which, in the case of money paid for an existing cause (causa praeterita), include inter alia error or improper compulsion.
> (4) There must be no equitable or other defence precluding decree of repetition".[173]

For the moment, requirements (1) and (4) need not be considered. Of material concern is the treatment of requirements (2) and (3). The argument is essentially that repetition is not merely available if a payment is not due, but that the pursuer must prove some specific basis or ground for recovery. The paragraph quoted above does not specifically deal with the *condictiones*, and only refers to some of the grounds of repetition, but the Discussion Papers, read with certain writings of Whitty, reveal that the *condictiones* are related to certain grounds for recovery.

First, the *condictio indebiti* is regarded as the remedy whereby undue[174] payments or transfers made in error as to liability are recovered.[175] The ground for recovery

---

170 According to Birks if money was received there would be a claim for repetition, whereas restitution (in the narrowest sense) related to property and recompense to services or the product of services (see "Six Questions in Search of a Subject—Unjust Enrichment in a crisis of identity" 1985 *JR* 227 at 235).

171 Cf Recovery of Benefits Conferred under Error of Law (Scot Law Com D P No 95, 1993) vol 1, 105 et sq; Judicial Abolition of the Error of Law Rule and its Aftermath (Scot Law Com D P No 99, 1996), 77 et sq; Whitty, "Some Trends and Issues in Scots Enrichment Law" 1994 *JR* 127 at 129.

172 Cf Recovery of Benefits Conferred under Error of Law (Scot Law Com D P No 95, 1993) vol 1, 105 et sq; Judicial Abolition of the Error of Law Rule and its Aftermath (Scot Law Com D P No 99, 1996), 78 et sq; Whitty, "Some Trends and Issues in Scots Enrichment Law" 1994 *JR* 127 at 129.

173 Cf Judicial Abolition of the Error of Law Rule and its Aftermath (Scot Law Com D P No 99, 1996), 84 sq; cf Whitty, "Some Trends and Issues in Scots Enrichment Law" 1994 *JR* 127 at 129.

174 It is not always clear whether the requirement of an undue payment is insisted upon in the context of the *condictio indebiti*: certain references create the impression that error in itself is sufficient to found a claim of repetition under the *condictio indebiti* (cf Judicial Abolition of the Error of Law Rule and its Aftermath (Scot Law Com D P No 99, 1996) 73, 88, and 100; but cf also Judicial Abolition of the Error of Law Rule and its Aftermath (Scot Law Com D P No 99, 1996), 84 et sqq; Recovery of Benefits Conferred under Error of Law (Scot Law Com D P No 95, 1993), vol 2, 42).

175 Cf Recovery of Benefits Conferred under Error of Law (Scot Law Com D P No 95, 1993), vol 2, 40 et sq, 42 et sqq, 115; Judicial Abolition of the Error of Law Rule and its Aftermath (Scot Law Com D P No 99, 1996), 87 et sq; Recovery of Ultra Vires Public Authority Receipts and Disbursements (Scot Law Com D P No 100, 1996), 23, 129.

is then error. Second, there are indications that the *condictio ob turpem vel iniustam causam* is regarded as an appropriate remedy for the recovery of certain transfers made under compulsion,[176] as well as other transfers tainted by illegality.[177] This view of compulsion as a ground for recovery will be dealt with in detail below.[178] Third, Whitty also refers to the failure of an assumption as to the future to materialise (the terrain of the *condictio causa data causa non secuta*), and the failure of an extant state of affairs to continue (covered by the *condictio ob causam finitam*).[179] Finally, there is recognition of a residual category of cases where repetition would be allowed, but not on any of the grounds referred to above. This is the terrain of the *condictio sine causa specialis*, which in modern Scots law is covered by innominate actions of repetition and restitution.[180]

However, the fact that the modern law can be presented in the way set out above does not mean that this is regarded as a suitable taxonomy. Of particular concern is the constant uncertainty whether new grounds should be recognised. As Discussion Paper No 100 correctly points out, it is questionable "... whether development by way of the ever increasing recognition and extension of specific grounds of recovery is the hall-mark of a mature system of restitution of undue payments and transfers or of unjustified enrichment generally".[181]

The Discussion Paper then suggests that a new type of approach could be followed, which is based on broader grounds of recovery. This approach could be set out in a discussion paper, containing a "non-binding" statement (or "restatement") of the existing Scots law on unjustified enrichment.[182] An indication is then also given of the type of broader grounds of recovery which would be suitable for Scots law. In Discussion Paper No 95 it is provisionally proposed that the German Wilburg-von Caemmerer taxonomy was more likely than any other so far seen to serve as a useful model for Scots law.[183] This essentially civilian model draws a fundamental distinction between enrichment obtained by way of a transfer,[184] and enrichment obtained in another way.[185] The claim based on enrichment by way of a transfer (the

176 Cf Recovery of Benefits Conferred under Error of Law (Scot Law Com D P No 95, 1993), vol 2, 201 et sqq. The transfer need not necessarily be undue. Cf requirement (2) above.

177 Cf Judicial Abolition of the Error of Law Rule and its Aftermath (Scot Law Com D P No 99, 1996), 100; Whitty, "Some Trends and Issues in Scots Enrichment Law" 1994 *JR* 127, 130.

178 Cf 7.3.1.ii(b) below.

179 Whitty, "Some Trends and Issues in Scots Enrichment Law" 1994 *JR* 127 at 130.

180 Recovery of Benefits Conferred under Error of Law (Scot Law Com D P No 95, 1993) vol 1, 101; Judicial Abolition of the Error of Law Rule and its Aftermath (Scot Law Com D P No 99, 1996), 86.

181 Recovery of Ultra Vires Public Authority Receipts and Disbursements (Scot Law Com D P No 100, 1996), 129 et sq, Whitty, "Some Trends and Issues in Scots Enrichment Law" 1994 *JR* 127 at 135.

182 Judicial Abolition of the Error of Law Rule and its Aftermath (Scot Law Com D P No 99, 1996), 108 et sqq.

183 Recovery of Benefits Conferred under Error of Law (Scot Law Com D P No 95, 1993), vol 1, 119 et sqq; Whitty, "The civilian tradition and debates on Scots law" 1996 *TSAR* 227 at 237.

184 Cf 5.4.2 above.

185 The notion of enrichment "in another way" ("oder in sonstiger Weise") broadly covers three situations, namely that of unauthorised encroachment in another's entitlements or property rights (the terrain of the *Eingriffskondiktion*); unauthorised expenditure on the property of another in the belief that it is one's own (the *Verwendungskondiktion* then applies), and payment of another's debt (recovery is then achieved with the *Rückgriffskondiktion*). Cf Recovery of Benefits Conferred under Error of Law (Scot Law Com D P No 95, 1993) vol 1, 121 et sqq; Zimmermann and du Plessis, "Basic Features of the German Law of Unjustified Enrichment" 1994 *RLR* 14 at 24 et sqq; 5.4.2.i above.

Leistungskondiktion) encompasses the law of the *condictiones*.[186] However, its internal categorisation departs radically from the "grounds for recovery" approach, since, according to the prevailing view, it flows from the application of the general test of *sine causa* retention based on the failure of the purpose of the transfer.[187] From the more recent Discussion Papers it can be discerned that there is growing support for developing Scots law closer towards the modern civilian approach.[188]

v. The "unjustified unless" approach

The proposed "restatement" would not be the first attempt to provide a structured and comprehensive model for the Scots law of unjustified enrichment. An appendix to Discussion Paper No 99 already contains certain "tentative and exploratory"[189] draft rules on unjustified enrichment and a commentary prepared by a Law Commissioner, Dr E M Clive. This code is born from pessimism about the possibility of identifying sensible divisions of the existing law and of using such divisions to devise a framework for future development. According to Clive, "there is probably no satisfactory basis for the tripartite division" (i.e. between the three Rs).[190] His proposal, while quite understandable from a purely civilian perspective, is radical from the perspective of the existing Scots law: in principle all enrichments at the expense of another are regarded as unjustified and should be redressed.[191] It is only if the enrichment is justified, whether by a legal cause or by public policy, that this is not necessary. Enrichment at the expense of another is therefore "unjustified unless" justified.[192] One of the advantages of this approach is that it does not require defining certain grounds for recovery such as error and compulsion, and thus avoids an "unprincipled proliferation of specific grounds".[193]

The Draft Rules further contain detailed provisions on the subjects of "enrichment", "at the expense of another person", "indirect enrichment", and the measure of recovery, but for present purposes a detailed analysis of these provisions is not called for, nor can justice be done to their depth and complexity. Only certain basic observations will be made. First, the Draft Rules clearly constitute a clean break with the traditional approach. There is no attempt to salvage something of

186 Cf 5.4.2.i above.

187 Cf 5.4.2.i above.

188 Cf Recovery of Ultra Vires Public Authority Receipts and Disbursements (Scot Law Com D P No 100, 1996), 17, where it is stated that "we think that broader grounds of recovery should be developed which, according to some commentators, represent the natural development of our civilian common law (cf also 13, where reference is made to the views of Evans-Jones, Zimmermann, Clive and Whitty, and Judicial Abolition of the Error of Law Rule and its Aftermath (Scot Law Com D P No 99, 1996), 102 et sqq, which contains an exposition of the modern civilian approach).

189 Judicial Abolition of the Error of Law Rule and its Aftermath (Scot Law Com D P No 99, 1996), Appendix, 14.

190 Judicial Abolition of the Error of Law Rule and its Aftermath (Scot Law Com D P No 99, 1996), Appendix, 17. The draft rules in 3–13 will be referred to as "Draft Rule", followed by the number.

191 Draft Rules 1 and 4; Judicial Abolition of the Error of Law Rule and its Aftermath (Scot Law Com D P No 99, 1996), Appendix, 44.

192 Of course, there are certain exceptional cases when an enrichment would still not be justified, such as certain cases of unenforceability (a type of *in pari delicto* rule then applies), or where gifts are made in error or are subject to a condition. Cf Draft Rule 7; Judicial Abolition of the Error of Law Rule and its Aftermath (Scot Law Com D P No 99, 1996), Appendix, 57 et sqq.

193 Judicial Abolition of the Error of Law Rule and its Aftermath (Scot Law Com D P No 99, 1996), Appendix, 44 et sqq.

the three Rs by using them as general classificatory tools.[194] There is also no attempt to recognise certain unjust factors which would entitle the pursuer to relief. The whole point of departure here is civilian: the focus is on the defender's enrichment at the expense of the pursuer. Reasons should be provided why he is entitled to keep it, and not the other way round. However, the Draft Rules go even further than certain modern civilian models, which at least recognise basic categories of events which give rise to enrichment, such as a transfer to pay a debt, a transfer to elicit a counterperformance, or encroachment. This brings one to the second comment, namely how successfully it could be applied in practice. For a system such as Scots law, which is unfamiliar with the level of abstraction contained in many Continental civilian codes, the adjustment to the Draft Rules could prove quite difficult. On the other hand, certain provisions are so detailed and specific that they can only really be understood with the benefit of expert knowledge of the existing law. It seems as if this could detract from the usefulness of the Draft Rules as a framework for the future development of the law.[195] However, it would be unfortunate if the advances made in freeing Scots law from the disadvantages of a system based on narrow grounds of recovery would be lost. It may then well be that a future restatement could draw inspiration from these draft rules.

7.3 THE PLACE OF COMPULSION IN THE TAXONOMIES OF THE SCOTS LAW OF UNJUSTIFIED ENRICHMENT

The focus now has to shift from the general to the particular. In the previous chapter it was shown that compulsion, whether through force and fear or in related form, can influence the availability of remedies of repetition or restitution, or (to put it in more civilian terms) remedies based on unjustified enrichment. It was constantly pointed out that questions relating to these remedies cannot be answered in isolation from certain basic features of the Scots law of unjustified enrichment—most notably the basis of recovery. In the overview contained in the previous section it was shown that a variety of approaches exist as to the ideal taxonomy for Scots law, and that at present none have gained common acceptance. In this final section these different approaches will be evaluated in terms of their ability to accommodate problems in the law of unjustified enrichment associated with the phenomenon of compulsion.

7.3.1 *Compulsion as an unjust factor or ground of repetition*

i. The "unjust factors" approach

It will be recalled that compulsion can play the role of unjust factor which perfects a case of subtraction and gives rise to a claim of restitution.[196] The "unjustness" of

194 This stands in clear contrast to the view expressed in SME vol 15 (1993), para 86, that "unjust enrichment should be regarded as one of the success stories of Scots law", and that restitution and repetition should be treated as a unity, covering the return of both goods and money, on the analogy of the *condictiones*", while recompense should be regarded as the general enrichment action.

195 In Judicial Abolition of the Error of Law Rule and its Aftermath (Scot Law Com D P No 99, 1996), it is said that "at the seminar on 22 October 1994, there was little overt support from the floor for codification of Scots enrichment law and some opposition" (at 3).

196 Although compulsion could cause enrichment by subtraction in circumstances in which the subtraction is also a wrong, this is of little practical significance. Birks mentions the example where the defendant imprisons the plaintiff until he pays the defendant £1000. He then states

compulsion then lies in the fact that the victim's judgment was not properly exercised, and more specifically, in the fact that it could not be exercised freely for fear of some evil consequence.[197] In more technical terms his judgment is vitiated by compulsion. For purposes of presenting English case law, Birks has grouped certain categories of compulsion together. He then suggested that these categories, in more or less unaltered form, can be used in Scots law. The categories are: (1) coercion, i.e. duress or actual undue influence; (2) compulsion by legal process; (3) moral compulsion, i.e. arising from the needs of others; and (4) circumstantial compulsion.[198] From a Scottish perspective, such a proposal is unusual.[199] Thus far, in the context of Scots law, the expression "compulsion" has been used in a fairly narrow sense to describe certain cases of the unlawful application of harm or threats of harm which induce another person to do something, such as sign an agreement or make a payment.[200] Essentially, it covers force and fear and similar, though milder cases. On the assumption, for the moment, that compulsion should be regarded as an unjust factor in Scots law, it needs to be examined whether these categories can and should be grouped together as cases of "compulsion" in Scots law. These categories, excluding duress (which generally covers similar terrain as force and fear) will now be examined in turn.

(a) Undue influence

In the English Common Law, relief used to be provided on the basis of duress only if there was improper pressure which involved an element of violence to the person.[201] The need existed for a remedy to cover cases which were sufficiently serious to justify the provision of relief, but which were not able to meet this stringent standard of

---

that "[i]n this case the award of restitution is explicable either as a non-voluntary subtraction . . . , to which the quality of the wrong as such is irrelevant, or as restitution for the wrong itself. We can only tell that it is the latter if the judge distinguishes between the two possibilities and chooses the latter expressly or if he allows the claim to behave in a way incompatible with the other analysis, as by allowing recovery of a greater sum than P lost by the subtraction or by allowing the claim to survive some defence or restriction which would apply to it on the other analysis." He then adds that the conditions for making this choice in this category of case are rarely satisfied. Rather, restitution for wrongs would be provided in the category of cases in which there was no subtraction, and the only nexus or link between the plaintiff and the defendant's enrichment is the defendant's wrong to the plaintiff (cf Birks, "Restitution: A View of the Scots Law" (1985) 38 *CLP* 57 at 74). For an analysis of the limited role "wrongs" play within the context of the Scots law of unjustified enrichment, cf J Blackie, "Enrichment and Wrongs in Scots law" 1992 *AJ* 23.

197 Birks, *An Introduction to the Law of Restitution*, 141, 173; "Restitution: A View of the Scots Law" (1985) 38 *CLP* 57 at 65 et sq.

198 Birks, "Restitution: A View of the Scots Law" (1985) 38 *CLP* 57 at 66. This differs just slightly from his model for English law, in that the latter model contains five elements, since it does not group duress and actual undue influence together under the heading coercion, but deals with them separately.

199 Even Stewart, who supports the "unjust factors" approach in general, observes that this division of compulsion "is based upon English authorities and need not be adopted for Scotland." Unfortunately it is not quite clear what Stewart understands under "compulsion" in Scots law. He refers to two articles of Thompson and McKendrick (Thompson, "Economic Duress" 1985 SLT (News) 85 and McKendrick, "Economic Duress—A Reply" 1985 SLT (News) 277, dealt with at 6.2.1.iii above), and states that they have "addressed this general question in the context of Scots law." These articles essentially deal with the general problem of what constitutes duress, which creates the impression that Stewart thinks of compulsion in terms of "duress" or force and fear. But then he proceeds to discuss compulsion in the form of moral compulsion and legal compulsion, which was not touched on in any of the articles. This seems to indicate that he views compulsion in a broader light than force and fear.

200 Cf ch 1 above.

201 Cf *Cumming v Ince* (1847) 11 QB 112 at 120.

duress. This relief was provided by the Courts of Equity, which administered the doctrine of undue influence and applied it chiefly "to cases where some fiduciary relationship existed between the parties but was not in any way limited to them".[202] In this way a promise to pay money could be set aside if it was obtained by a threat to prosecute the promisor for a criminal offence.[203] When Equity and Common Law were merged by the Judicature Act of 1873, the courts had to deal with these cases of coercion in the light of their combined effect, and it is therefore not surprising that when the courts began to recognise that relief could also be provided on grounds of "economic duress", the distinction between duress and undue influence became blurred.[204] However, in Scots law, the situation was quite different. The doctrine of undue influence was clearly acknowledged in *Gray v Binny* in 1879.[205] At that time, the rules regarding force and fear were sufficiently broad in scope to cover cases of coercion not involving an element of violence to the person.[206] The doctrine of undue influence therefore only really played an independent role where there was no coercion, but advantage was taken of a special relationship between the parties involving natural affection or trust,[207] or advantage was taken of someone's weakness or facility.[208] Unfettered by a doctrine of duress which was historically only applicable to cases involving an element of violence to the person, Scots law is therefore able to assume a position closer to Continental European law, which draws a clear distinction between duress and abuse of a necessitous condition:[209] force and fear can then be equated to duress, while undue influence, facility and circumvention, and probably certain cases of "extortion"[210] or unconscionability could be equated to abuse of a necessitous condition.[211] If it is accepted that force and fear is a discrete category, while undue influence can be brought home under the heading "abuse of a necessitous condition" there is also obviously no need to draw the somewhat amorphous distinction between actual and relational undue influence.[212]

---

202 Guest (ed), *Chitty on Contracts*, vol 1, 402.

203 Cf Treitel, *The Law of Contract*, 377.

204 Guest (ed), *Chitty on Contracts*, vol 1, 402 et sq.

205 (1879) 7 R 332. Cf McBryde, *The Law of Contract in Scotland*, 245. Just more than a decade earlier Lord President Inglis still confined the grounds for reduction of deeds to incapacity, force and fear, fraud and essential error (*Tennent v Tennent's Trs* (1868) 6 M 840 at 876).

206 Cf Memorandum on Defective Consent and Consequential Matters (Scot Law Com Memo No 42, 1978), vol 2, 119.

207 Cf McBryde, *The Law of Contract in Scotland*, 248. From Lord President Inglis's judgment, it seems as if this was in fact the role he intended it to play: He states that "[w]here a relation subsists which imports undue influence, together with confidence reposed, on the one side, and subjection to the influence and the giving of the confidence on the other, the Court will examine into the circumstances of any 'transaction of bounty' ... and will give relief if it appears to have been the result of influence abused or confidence betrayed" ((1879) 7 R 332 at 338 sq).

208 In the latter case the appropriate remedy would be facility and circumvention (cf McBryde, *The Law of Contract in Scotland*, 248).

209 Cf Zweigert and Kötz, tr Weir, *An Introduction to Comparative Law*, 456.

210 Cf the discussion of Erskine's views at 6.2.1.i above.

211 In fact, the Scottish Law Commission has proposed a reclassification of cases of defective consent or vitiation of consent along similar lines. According to the Scottish Law Commission, it could have been unnecessary to adopt the doctrine of undue influence: "[i]t would have been possible to extend further the concept of extortion in Scots law and also, perhaps, if the introduction of a new category was expedient, to consider continental doctrines regarding exploitation of a necessitous condition" (108 et sq).

212 For example, it would not be necessary to determine whether a case like *Re Craig* [1971] Ch 95 was one of relational or actual undue influence (cf Birks, *An Introduction to the Law of Restitution*, 184 et sq).

(b) "Legal compulsion"

In the English Common Law, payment of another's debt is traditionally frowned upon.[213] It is only in certain exceptional cases, such as "legal compulsion", that someone who pays the debt of another will succeed in legally discharging the debt, and in obtaining a right of recoupment from the debtor.[214] The principle has been formulated as follows:

> Where the plaintiff has been compelled by law to pay, or being compellable by law, has paid money which the defendant was ultimately liable to pay, so that the latter obtains the benefit of the payment by the discharge of his liability; under such circumstances the defendant is held indebted to the plaintiff in the amount.[215]

According to Birks, "legal compulsion" could then also be introduced into Scots law as a subcategory of compulsion.[216] However, such a view ignores the fact that Scots law has traditionally adopted a more generous, civilian approach to payment of another's debt, which entails a greater willingness to allow the person who paid such a debt a claim of recovery.[217] In Scots law it is therefore unnecessary to deal with the somewhat strained approach that a debtor who pays under these circumstances is acting under compulsion.[218] It is then submitted that it is more sensible to deal with cases of "legal compulsion" through an extension of civilian principles, than by analysing it in terms of compulsion.[219] In any event, in the light of the fact that debts are freely assignable in English law, little has remained of the rationale of the "legal compulsion" exception.[220]

---

213 Cf Goff and Jones, *The Law of Restitution*, 17 et sq; Zimmermann, "Unjustified Enrichment: The Modern Civilian Approach" (1995) 15 *OJLS* 403 at 424.

214 Cf Goff and Jones, *The Law of Restitution*, 17 et sq, 343 et sqq.

215 Cf *Moule v Garrett* LR 7 Ex 101, 104; *Brook's Wharf and Bull Wharf, Limited v Goodman Brothers* [1937] 1 KB 534. In the latter case, the plaintiffs, who were bonded warehousemen, paid a certain amount to the Customs in lieu of duties on packages of squirrel skins imported from Russia by the defendants, a firm of furriers. According to the Customs Consolidation Act of 1876, s 85 these warehousemen had to pay the duty on the goods deposited in their warehouse, even though the defendants as the importers were primarily liable for the duties. The packages were stolen and the defendants refused to compensate the plaintiffs for paying these duties. It was then held that the defendants were in fact liable to do so.

216 Birks, "Restitution: A View of Scots law" (1985) 38 *CLP* 57 at 66.

217 Cf Whitty, "Die Reform des schottischen Bereicherungsrechts" 1995 *ZEuP* 216 at 231; Zimmermann, "Unjustified Enrichment: The Modern Civilian Approach" (1995) 15 *OJLS* 403 at 424. It is therefore not difficult to explain why relief was awarded in the type of situation covered by *Brook's Wharf and Bull Wharf Ltd v Goodman Brothers* [1937] 1 KB 534 (cf n 215 above; Birks, "Restitution: A View of the Scots Law" (1985) 38 *CLP* 57 at 70).

218 Co-obligants are generally liable pro rata, and not for the full amount. Where liability is joint and several, the creditor may sue any of the debtors, but such a debtor or debtors would have the right of relief, which falls under the law of recompense. Cf McBryde, *The Law of Contract in Scotland*, 358; Walker, *The Law of Contracts and Related Obligations in Scotland*, 439; *Coats v Union Bank of Scotland* 1929 SC (HL) 114. According to Stair the obligation of relief is derived from the obligation of recompence. In the absence of contractual or legal provisions to the contrary, the obligation of relief arises when one of the debtors who are jointly and severally liable pays more than his share. The person who paid is not presumed to have done it *animo donandi* (*Institutions* 1.8.9).

219 In German law the cases of legal "compulsion" described above would be covered by specific statutory provisions (in the case of common debts it would be §§ 421 et sqq BGB), or a type of *Rückgriffskondiktion*, which is the enrichment remedy used in German law to recover payments whereby another is released from his debt (cf 5.4.2.i above). This is a more precise and clear category than that of "lawful compulsion not in conformance with social morality".

220 Cf Goff and Jones, *The Law of Restitution*, 18.

(c) "Moral compulsion"

In the English Common Law it is not generally accepted that an obligation could arise from the situation where work or labour is done, or money is expended by one person to preserve or benefit the property of another.[221] As Bowen LJ put it in *Falcke v Scottish Imperial Insurance Co*,[222] "liabilities are not to be forced on people behind their backs any more than you can confer a benefit upon a man against his will". However, through use of the notions "moral compulsion", Birks has attempted to justify some obligation towards the person who preserved or benefited the property of another.[223] The argument is apparently that because such a person feels himself to be morally compelled or bound to assist another, there should be restitution. In Scots law, which recognises claims based on *negotiorum gestio*, such an analysis is not required. *Negotiorum gestio* entails the voluntary management by one person of the affairs of another without the consent or even knowledge of the other.[224] The basis of the claim is clearly not compulsion, and an essential feature is in fact the voluntary conduct of the gestor.[225] Birks, rather paradoxically, acknowledges this difference in approach. He states that "[c]ivilian systems recognise the regime of *negotiorum gestio*, not to relieve plaintiffs who have intervened in another's affairs by reason of moral compulsion, but rather to promote the policy that the affairs of the absent should not be allowed to go to rack and ruin".[226] Why he then proposes that the category "moral compulsion" should be used in Scots law, which recognises *negotiorum gestio*, is not clear. Scots law does not have to regard the good Samaritan as someone acting under compulsion in order to provide him with a remedy.

(d) "Circumstantial compulsion"

The last category which Birks discusses, is circumstantial compulsion. If a person is "acutely anxious for his own welfare or that of his family or property", and someone who is not responsible for the circumstances giving rise to this anxiety then obtains something as a consequence thereof, it could be argued that the recipient should be under an obligation of restitution.[227] Examples of such situations are where a Jewish person gave someone diamonds in order to obtain a false passport, enabling him to escape persecution in France during the Nazi era, or where an extortionate amount was claimed for salvage.[228] Whether similar claims would be allowed in Scots law is not clear. The general notion of "extortion" could conceivably encompass such claims, but it would then be extortion in the sense Erskine used

221 Cf *Falcke v Scottish Imperial Insurance Co* (1886) 34 Ch 234 at 248; Goff and Jones, *The Law of Restitution*, 25, 176, 363 et sqq, 384; Zimmermann, *The Law of Obligations*, 448. On exceptional cases, cf Goff and Jones, *The Law of Restitution*, 369 et sqq.

222 (1886) 34 Ch 234 at 248.

223 Cf Birks, *An Introduction to the Law of Restitution*, 193 et sqq, 304 et sqq; Goff and Jones, *The Law of Restitution* refer to "necessity" (363 et sqq).

224 Cf SME vol 15 (1993), 65.

225 According to Stair the conduct should be "without our command or commission" (*Institutions* 1.8.3). Bell states that it should be "spontaneously undertaken" (*Principles*, par 540). More recently, Walker called it a "voluntary intervention of a person" (*The Law of Contracts and Related Obligations in Scotland*, 590).

226 *Introduction to the Law of Restitution*, 308.

227 Cf *Introduction to the Law of Restitution*, 203.

228 Birks refers to *Liebman v Rosenthal* (1945) 26 A Div 1062, 59 NYS 2d 148; *The Medina* (1876) 1 PD 272; 2 PD 5; *The Port Caledonia and The Anna* [1903] P 184. The latter two cases should apparently be distinguished from the case where someone conducts a salvage operation out of moral compulsion. It would then not be the party in distress, but the party helping him, who would be acting out of compulsion (cf Birks, *Introduction to the Law of Restitution*, 304 et sqq).

it, namely "oppression" or the "catching of an advantage",[229] which, as a Scottish Law Commission Memorandum has acknowledged, "corresponds to Continental developments of a doctrine of 'exploitation of state of necessity'".[230] As indicated previously, these cases are traditionally distinct from force and fear and related cases of compulsion.[231]

From the above overview it should then be clear that, due to a variety of policy and doctrinal considerations, it is questionable to use the label of "compulsion" in Scots law to cover not only force and fear, but also undue influence, payment of another's debt, *negotiorum gestio* and some forms of extortion through abuse of another's anxiety. For purposes of application of the model to Scots law, these examples of "compulsion" could conceivably be broken up into separate unjust factors or be brought home under different categories, e.g. "policy motivated restitution", but this would only provide further proof in support of the general criticism raised above, namely the constant lack of certainty surrounding the content and number of unjust factors. However, these are not the only problems surrounding the proposed recognition of compulsion as an unjust factor in Scots law. Even if "compulsion" is only defined in terms of the restricted sense of coercion, the attempts to relate the model to the existing law are problematic. According to Birks,

> There are three places where one can expect to find information in relation to coercion, namely in relation to the formation of contracts, amongst civil wrongs, and in the context of unjust enrichment. Very little is said in Scots law in this third context though much of what is collected in relation to contracts can in fact be carried over, since factors which go to the reduction of a contract do in general also call for restitution of enrichment. In the treatments of unjust enrichment (restitution/recompense) this matter ought to be brought to bear on the modern descendant of the *condictio ob turpem causam* but the books concentrate heavily on the *condictio indebiti* and *condictio causa data causa non secuta*, and are unnecessarily coy about expanding the discussion of *ob turpem causam*. Erskine, however, gives a lead: "If, for instance, one accused of a crime should give money to another so that he does not bear false witness against him, he may recover the sum so given by a *condictio ob turpem causam*."[232]

The reference to the material in the law of contract raises the spectre dealt with above,[233] namely a duplication of investigations into what constitutes compulsion for purposes of the law of contract, as well as for purposes of the law of unjustified enrichment. If one turns to the material contained in the law of unjustified enrichment,

---

229 Erskine, *Institute* 4.1.27. Cf McBryde, *The Law of Contract in Scotland*, 255 et sqq; Walker, *The Law of Contracts and Related Obligations in Scotland*, 311 et sqq.

230 Memorandum on Defective Consent and Consequential Matters (Scot Law Com Memo No 42, 1978), vol 2, 113. Cf also Zweigert and Kötz. tr Weir, *Introduction to Comparative Law*, 456 et sqq.

231 Cf 5.4.1 above. However, it has been argued that in Roman law cases of "collective persecution" (*Kollektivverfolgungen*) could be brought home under the *actio metus causa*. At a Studienstiftung seminar held in Regensburg in January 1997, Prof Berthold Kupisch of the University of Münster pointed out that relief was provided on grounds of *metus* when "men from Sulla" (*Sullani homines*), as a group, instilled a general situation of fear and certain people then benefited therefrom (cf *Cicero ad Quintum fratrem* 1.1.7.21; ch 2 n 7 above). Nowadays, such situations are rather dealt with in terms of specific legislation enabling restitution to victims of persecution. It seems that the notion that fear had to be instilled with the purpose of obtaining a transfer, whether obtained by the wrongdoer or a third party, is too firmly entrenched in Scots law to accommodate these situations.

232 Birks, "Restitution: A View of Scots law" (1985) 38 *CLP* 57 at 70; Erskine, *Institute* 3.1.10.

233 Cf 7.2.3.ii above.

and the *condictiones* in particular, it becomes apparent that Birks is essentially trying to relate different *condictiones* to different unjust factors. The *condictio indebiti* is then related to error (viewed broadly, in the sense of a mistake), and the *condictio ob turpem (vel iniustam) causam* to compulsion. Such a representation of course has to surmount a considerable problem, namely the strong tradition that an undue transfer is an essential requirement of the *condictio indebiti*. According to Birks, "if one works within the category of *indebitum*, which is not a category of mistake but more narrowly of liability-mistake (i.e 'not due' supposed to be due)", one would restrict the application of the *condictio indebiti* too narrowly. In this regard, Birks refers to the case of *The Fraternity of Masters and Seamen of Dundee v Cockerill*.[234] This case is significant for the Scots law of unjustified enrichment, and needs to be examined in some detail.

In essence, the pursuers wrongly believed a lost seaman to be dead and then paid his widow an annuity legally due to her, as well as a further payment to supplement it. The annuity was obviously paid in error as to liability and held to be recoverable under the *condictio indebiti*. However, this was not the case with the additional, *ex gratia* payment. Birks then argues that it is unacceptable to confine the *condictio indebiti* to recovery of an "*indebitum*", and thus to liability mistakes. The problem with Birks's analysis, though, is that it fails to take into account the different purposes of the payments, namely to comply with the provision of the policy, and to assist the widow in her need. That the judge in that case chose to regard the annuity payments as recoverable, but refused recovery of the additional sum, is not as arbitrary as Birks indicates. A gift made under an error of motive is not necessarily invalid.[235] It could of course be argued that this is wrong, and that it should still be recoverable, but even then it is not necessary to base recovery on mistake. The gift in question could be regarded as made under an implied assumption or condition that the money should be returned if not due,[236] or that the parties to the agreement of gift laboured under the essential common error that Mr Cockerill was dead.[237] It therefore does not seem as if *The Fraternity of Masters and Seamen of Dundee v Cockerill*[238] indicates that there is a need to expand error to mistake, and to dislodge the *condictio indebiti* from the undue transfer requirement.

If one turns to the view that the compulsion ought to be dealt with in terms of the modern descendant of the *condictio ob turpem causam*, two problems arise. The first is that turpitude and compulsion, particularly in the form of force and fear, are treated as quite distinct legal phenomena in Scots law.[239] That they can co-exist is apparent from the example Erskine provides, namely a payment not to bear false witness. But this does not lead to the conclusion that compulsion, especially if it is viewed broadly, necessarily involves turpitude. The second problem relates to the relationship between the *condictio ob turpem causam* and the *condictio indebiti*. Insofar

---

234 (1869) 8 M 278.

235 Cf also SME vol 15 (1993), 26, where it is stated that "[t]he reason for the decision may lie in the question of donation. It could be argued that the fraternity intended to make an unqualified gift of the *ex gratia* annual payment, taking on themselves the risk that the mate might reappear".

236 Cf, generally, McBryde, *The Law of Contract in Scotland*, 88 et sqq; Gloag and Henderson, *The Law of Scotland*, 85 et sqq.

237 Cf Gloag and Henderson, *The Law of Scotland*, 117; McBryde, *The Law of Contract in Scotland*, 184.

238 (1869) 8 M 278.

239 Cf 4.3.2 above.

as transfers tainted by turpitude are not due (a consequence of the invalidity of the underlying agreement), it is arguable that the modern descendant of the *condictio ob turpem causam* is in fact that the action of restitution or repetition under the *condictio indebiti*. Of course, if error is regarded as an essential feature of the *condictio indebiti*, it cannot fulfil this purpose: as in modern South African law, the *condictio indebiti* would then have to be interpreted broadly so as to allow recovery of undue transfers made under compulsion.[240]

ii. The modified civilian approach

According to the modified civilian approach, compulsion can act as a "ground of repetition" of payments.[241] Although this view is redolent of the "unjust factor" approach, the scope of "compulsion" and its relationship with the *condictiones* is not viewed similarly. First, it is recognised that repetition, and therefore also those cases of repetition based on compulsion, generally deal with claims for the recovery of payments that are not due.[242] It is only certain cases of compulsion which are "possibly" excluded.[243] And second, compulsion is defined relatively narrowly to encompass force and fear, as well as cases where the *condictiones* were awarded due to the actual or threatened harm to the person or property of the payer, or due to threats to withhold the provision of goods, services or other benefits which the person exercising the compulsion was bound by law to provide.[244] Some of it therefore falls under the traditional law of force and fear, while other cases are spread over the law of unjustified enrichment. The important feature of these cases is that the improper compulsion is supposed to act as a "ground of repetition".[245] It will now be examined whether compulsion does in fact play this role, or whether there are not alternative explanations for recovery. For purposes of such an inquiry it is necessary to distinguish between two possible ways in which compulsion could play such a role, namely as a factor influencing the validity of the underlying basis of a transfer (e.g. a contract), and a factor influencing the validity of the transfer itself. Use of the term "ground of repetition" tends to telescope these two possible effects of compulsion. The inquiry will adopt the broad distinction between those cases of compulsion which can be brought home under the "doctrine of force and fear", and those which fall under the law of the *condictiones*.

---

240 Cf 5.3.3.ii above.

241 Cf Judicial Abolition of the Error of Law Rule and its Aftermath (Scot Law Com D P No 99, 1996), 84 et sq; Whitty, "Some Trends and Issues in Scots Enrichment Law" 1994 *JR* 127 at 129.

242 Judicial Abolition of the Error of Law Rule and its Aftermath (Scot Law Com D P No 99, 1996), 84 et sq; Whitty, "Some Trends and Issues in Scots Enrichment Law" 1994 *JR* 127 at 129.

243 Judicial Abolition of the Error of Law Rule and its Aftermath (Scot Law Com D P No 99, 1996), 84 et sq. Reference is made to *Hislop v Dickson Motors (Forres) Ltd* 1978 SLT (Notes) 73 (OH), dealt with at 7.3.1.ii(a) below.

244 Recovery of Benefits Conferred under Error of Law (Scot Law Com D P No 95, 1993) vol 2, 201 et sq, 207, 222 (cf also Whitty, "The Taxonomy of Unjustified Enrichment in Scots Law", essay prepared for Seminar on the Law of Unjustified Enrichment, 23 October 1993, 31 et sqq). The Discussion Paper adds the proviso that these categories are "mentioned for ease of exposition and are not hard and fast categories which necessarily exhaust the whole field of repetition on grounds of compulsion." In particular, it is mentioned that it is not clear which (if any) of the above-mentioned categories of compulsion applied to cases where creditors have obtained bills from a bankrupt as a secret preference, and "have been held liable in repetition on the ground of extortion or concussion". It is argued above that compulsion was in fact not the ground of recovery in these cases (cf the discussion of *Arroll v Montgomery* (1826) 4 S 499 and *Macfarlane v Nicoll* (1964) 3 M 237 at 4.3.2 above).

245 Recovery of Benefits Conferred under Error of Law (Scot Law Com D P No 95, 1993), vol 2, 201.

(a) Compulsion as ground of repetition in cases of "force and fear"

In a certain sense, it is understandable that compulsion could be regarded as a "ground of repetition" when a contract has been reduced on grounds of force and fear, and recovery is sought of a transfer made pursuant to such a contract.[246] Without proof of compulsion in the form of force and fear, the agreement remains valid, and the transfer made pursuant to it would not be recoverable. Proof of compulsion is therefore essential for recovery. Whether the compulsion relates both to the formation of the contract and the transfer, or merely to the formation of the contract does not matter. From a practical perspective it would normally affect both, since it is hardly likely that the victim will perform freely after the force and fear which gave rise to the formation of the contract has abated. If he did not perform, it would be up to the wrongdoer to enforce payment, which would be met with an exception or claim of reduction.

However, where there is no proof that force and fear affected the validity of an underlying agreement, a different analysis has to be followed. Here two possibilities exist. If a debt was due, and payment was enforced by force and fear, it can still be argued that compulsion is the "ground of repetition". In this regard, Scottish Law Commission Discussion Paper No 99, 1996 refers to *Hislop v Dickson Motors (Forres) Pty Ltd*,[247] where the pursuer recovered a payment made to replace funds she allegedly stole from the defenders, and was therefore liable to repay them. But where no debt is due, and a transfer is obtained by compulsion, it becomes more difficult to establish whether compulsion is in fact the "ground of recovery". This type of problem particularly arises when an undue transfer is obtained by certain types of compulsion not traditionally regarded as serious enough to amount to force and fear. A number of these cases which usually have been dealt with in the context of the law of the *condictiones* will now be considered.

(b) Compulsion and the *condictiones*

According to Scottish Law Commission Discussion Paper No 95, 1993 "improper compulsion", due to the lack of the reasonable alternative not to pay,[248] was the basis of recovery in *British Oxygen Co Ltd v South West Scotland Electricity Board*.[249] It will be recalled that this case dealt with a claim for the recovery of overpayments of electricity charges apparently made under the implied compulsion that the supply would be cut off upon failure to pay. It is submitted that although certain dicta in the judgment support this interpretation, they have to be approached with caution.[250] Not only are they made in the context of the English "railway cases", which are more in harmony with the "unjust factors" approach, and foreign to traditional Scots law, but they are also of doubtful prominence. In this case, the "improper compulsion" was an automatic consequence of the lack of lawful authority for the charge, which rendered it not due. The compulsion simply flowed from the fact that the charges were not lawful, and to accord it the status of "ground of repetition" is

---

246 Cf *Sutherland v Montrose Fishing Co Ltd* (1921) 37 Sh Ct Rep 239, where proof of force and fear was essential to determine whether payment would be made in terms of a valid agreement to raise the wages. It is only by reference to force and fear that it could be determined that the agreement was invalid and that the transfers were recoverable. Cf also *Mcafee v Gray or Mcafee* Outer House, 6 July 1990.

247 1978 SLT (Notes) 73 (OH).

248 Recovery of Benefits Conferred under Error of Law (Scot Law Com D P No 95, 1993), vol 2, 211.

249 1958 SC 53; 1959 SC (HL) 17.

250 1958 SC 53 at 72, 79, 91 et sq.

therefore doubtful.[251] This is not to say that the compulsion was irrelevant: insofar as it negates the intention to settle a dispute, it is of some evidential value, but this is merely one aspect of the decision to make the transfer. As to the validity of the legal basis of the transfer, the compulsion has nothing to say. Unsurprisingly, even English commentators have focused on the inequality of the parties and the lack of lawful authority for the overcharge, rather than on the compulsion.[252] The explanation of lack of lawful authority is particularly notable, since, from a Scottish perspective, it is not that far removed from an approach which bases recovery on the fact that the transfer was not due.

The question now is what the appropriate remedy would be with which to recover such a transfer. A valid problem with the above decision, also pointed out in Scottish Law Commission Discussion Paper No 95, 1993 is the failure of the court to draw on the existing Scots law, and in particular the law of the *condictiones*. After a review of the relationship between the *condictiones* and compulsion, the Discussion Paper states that

> It could be argued that in the *British Oxygen Co* case, the defender electricity board obtained the overcharge *ob turpem vel iniustam causam* and as the pursuer company was not at fault (*in pari delicto* or *in turpitudine*) but the defender board was, the pursuer could recover his money.[253]

In essence, it is then suggested that a *condictio ob turpem vel iniustam causam* should be available if transfers are obtained under compulsion. This view is based on an overview of earlier Scottish authorities, as well as comparative legal material. These materials certainly suggest that when compulsion and illegality co-exist, recovery would be possible on the basis that a transfer was made *ob turpem causam*. Cases like *Rossie v Her Curators*[254] and *Mushet v Dog*[255] in any event dealt with a breach of a special position of trust, namely that of curator and tutor-at-law. To regard such payments as made *ob turpem causam* is therefore understandable. However, it does not seem as if they provide support for the proposition in modern Scots law that compulsion inherently involves turpitude and that compelled transfers should be regarded as transfers *ob turpem causam*.[256] The Discussion Paper refers to cases derived from Roman law, namely where payments are made to get back something deposited[257] or loaned,[258] or stolen.[259] These ways of obtaining a transfer may have been tainted by turpitude in Roman times, but it is doubtful whether modern Scots law shares the same notions of *infamia* or disrepute, and consequently would base the right to recovery thereon. If anything, the demise of the *condictio ob turpem vel iniustam causam* indicates the contrary. It is also not surprising that even modern South African law, which still recognises the *condictio ob turpem vel*

251 In this respect it resembles the cases dealing with unlawfully demanded tax: there the compulsion (possible implied threats of penalties or similar punishment) is also inherent in the demand, and of little independent relevance.

252 Cf 6.3.2 above.

253 Recovery of Benefits Conferred under Error of Law (Scot Law Com D P No 95, 1993), vol 2, 206.

254 (1642) Mor 9456.

255 (1639) Mor 9456.

256 Cf 4.3.2, 7.3.1.i(d) above (on the early law see 3.3.2.ii(b).

257 D 12.5.2.

258 C 4.7.7 (Diocletian and Maximian).

259 D 12.5.9.

iniustam causam, prefers to use the *condictio indebiti* to recover undue transfers made under compulsion.[260]

7.3.2 *Compulsion and the retention of transfers without legal ground: the modern civilian approach*

As indicated above, a key feature of the modern civilian approach is the grouping together of cases of unjustified enrichment brought about by a transfer.[261] The retention of such a transfer is then unjustified if it is not supported by a legal ground or *causa*. Depending on the facts of each case, there are a number of reasons why compelled transfers can be retained *sine causa*.

i. The retention of the undue transfer: the condictio indebiti

One of the situations under which a transfer is retained *sine causa* is if it was made in order to fulfil a debt, but failed to achieve this purpose because no debt was due. The label generally used to describe the remedy available in such circumstances is the *condictio indebiti*. This type of analysis works particularly well when dealing with transfers made in error—then it can be said that at the time of the transfer the transferor did in fact intend that a debt should be discharged. Was it not for the error as to liability, the transfer would not have been made. However, where such an analysis is applied to compelled undue transfers, it gives rise to somewhat strained results. The victim of compulsion, especially in serious cases,[262] does not intend to discharge a debt: usually he knows that no debt is due and this explains why he has to be compelled to make the transfer. It is therefore submitted that in these circumstances it is preferable to apply a more objective approach, which simply inquires whether the transfer is supported by a valid relationship of indebtedness between the parties.[263] The transfer cannot discharge a debt where no debt was due, and the transfer is then recoverable irrespective of whether the transferor intended to discharge an obligation or not. Such an approach implies a broader scope for the

---

260 Recovery of Benefits Conferred under Error of Law (Scot Law Com D P No 95, 1993), vol 2, 206 refers to Wessels, *The Law of Contract in South Africa*, vol 2 para 3767. Although Wessels indicates that the *condictio ob turpem vel iniustam causam* is available in cases of extortion in South African law, this statement is simply derived from the Roman authority above, and ignores the modern case law which points to the *condictio indebiti* (cf 5.3.3.ii above). On the positions in Roman-Dutch law, which still strongly drew on Roman law, cf 5.2.3.i above.

261 Cf 7.2.3.iii above.

262 In cases of serious compulsion, such as force and fear, where a person is subjected to threats of personal harm, the victim may intend to make a transfer, but it is questionable to state that he in fact intend that this transfer should discharge a debt. If anything, he is only making it to ensure that the compulsion comes to an end. It is only in milder cases of compulsion, e.g. through implied threats to impose penalties for late payment of tax, or to cut off the electricity supply, that it becomes more plausible to state that he intends to discharge a debt and to try and obtain some form of relief later on. Such a payment can conceivably be regarded as being made *solvendi causa*, although the distinction is somewhat subtle. The problem with regarding compelled transfers as transfers *solvendi causa* is reflected in Prof Detlef König's proposal for the re-codification of the German law of unjustified enrichment. He clearly distinguishes between a transfer made in order to fulfil an existing or future obligation (§ 1.1(1)), and a transfer not made in order to fulfil an obligation but on account of compulsion or threat (§ 1.3). For the text see Zimmermann, "Unjustified Enrichment: The Modern Civilian Approach" (1995) 15 *OJLS* 403 at 426.

263 Cf 5.4.2.i above on the position in German law. This relationship of indebtedness need not necessarily arise from an obligation; it could also be created by an understanding between the parties as to the basis on which the transfer is retained (e.g. in the case of the *datio ob rem*).

condictio indebiti—in essence it becomes the remedy for the recovery of any undue transfer.

However, this does not imply that relief would always be provided. It is obviously important to ensure that the recipient who believes he is entitled to retain the transfer should not be unduly prejudiced—a consideration which concededly does not weigh heavily in cases of compulsion. An important mechanism which serves to protect the recipient is the rule that transfers made in the knowledge that they are not due are not recoverable.[264] The rationale of this rule, as indicated above, is to prevent a voluntary *venire contra factum proprium*, or act contrary to good faith,[265] e.g. when a person in fact intends to relinquish his claim,[266] or to donate[267] or to make a compromise. It should therefore not exclude recovery of the compelled undue transfer.[268] Even in systems which still link the *condictio indebiti* to transfers made in error, rather than in the absence of knowledge that they are not due, compulsion is recognised as a factor which either overrides the error requirement,[269] or acts as an additional ground for its availability.[270]

So far then as to the position of undue transfers. Due transfers also present difficulties. It can be argued that these cases in any event do not fall within the domain of the law of unjustified enrichment: the argument is essentially that if a

264 On this rule, cf 3.3.2.i, 4.3.1.i, 7.2.3.iii above. In Scots law repetition will of course also not be awarded if equitable considerations so require, and here compulsion can be a factor indicating that recovery should not be barred (cf *Unigate Foods Ltd v Scottish Milk Marketing Board* 1975 SC (HL) 75, 90; Gloag and Henderson, *The Law of Scotland*, 477). The measure of recovery would then also be higher: "In such a situation bona fide consumption by the recipient would provide no answer to a demand for repayment" (*Unigate Foods Ltd v Scottish Milk Marketing Board* 1975 SC (HL) 75, 90). Presumably, this also holds true in the case of a claim for the recovery of an undue transfer under the *condictio indebiti*. Cf *Dickson v Halbert* (1854) 16 D 586, 597 where reference is made to the exclusion of *voluntary* payments on equitable grounds; Gloag and Henderson, *The Law of Scotland*, 477. It should be noted, though, that in *Unigate Foods Ltd v Scottish Milk Marketing Board* 1975 SC (HL) 75 Lord President Emslie also stated that, "[i]n my opinion, while I do not quarrel with the general proposition that repetition based on the *condictio indebiti* is an equitable remedy there is very real difficulty in fitting this case comfortably into the class concerned with repetition of money paid under a mistake in fact by the payer" (89).

265 Cf 5.4.2.i above on the position in German law.

266 Cf *Dalmellington Iron Company v The Glasgow and South-Western Railway Company* (1889) 16 R 523 at 534 ("There is high authority for the proposition that a payment made in the knowledge that it is not due cannot be recovered. It seems to depend on the principle that such a payment imports a waiver of all objections, and an admission that the debt is justly due").

267 On the significance of this requirement, cf *Morgan Guaranty Trust Company of New York v Lothian Regional Council* 1995 SCLR 225 at 239. In the *ius commune*, the rule "cuius per errorem dati repetitio est, eius consulto dat donatio est", contained in D 50.17.53, traditionally proved to be the strongest justification for the error requirement (cf Visser *Die Rol van Dwaling by die Condictio Indebiti*, 299 et sqq).

268 Visser points out that the doctrine only applies where it is intended that the recipient should retain the transfer, which is not the case when a transfer is made under compulsion (*Die Rol van Dwaling by die Condictio Indebiti*, 303 et sq).

269 Cf *Dalmellington Iron Company v The Glasgow and South-Western Railway Company* (1889) 16 R 523 at 534 where reference is made to a *voluntary* waiver and admission; cf also ch 5 n 172 above on the position in French law.

270 Cf Englard, "Restitution of benefits conferred without obligation" in *International Encyclopaedia of Comparative law*, vol X, ch 5, 8, 23 et sqq; 5.3.3 above on the position in South African law. It should be noted though that support has been expressed for the notion that in South African law the compelled undue payment made under protest should rather be recovered with a *condictio sine causa (specialis)* (cf De Vos, *Verrykingsaanspreeklikheid in die Suid-Afrikaanse Reg*, 172). De Vos does not elaborate on this statement.

due transfer is obtained by compulsion, and then succeeds in validly discharging a debt due by the victim,[271] the law of unjustified enrichment should not come into play since there is no enrichment. The payment simply took the place of the debt in the creditor's estate. However, it could also be argued that the effect of the compulsion is to render the payment ineffective in discharging the debt. The recipient is then still enriched: he (factually) receives a transfer, but the debt is still due to him. Such a transfer which failed to fulfil an obligation should then still be recoverable with the *condictio indebiti*.[272] However, the difficulty with such an argument is not only that it terminologically seems rather fanciful that due payments should be recoverable with the *condictio indebiti*, but also that it can now be reasoned, per analogiam, that due payments in error should also be recoverable with the *condictio indebiti*. This is doubtful.[273] Furthermore, if a payment is merely the factual event of a transfer of money, it is difficult to isolate it from the debt: discharge of the obligation then follows as a matter of fact, together with the transfer of ownership.

It now becomes attractive to search for alternative remedies to the *condictio indebiti*. Within the modern civilian approach, two remedies present themselves. First, it can be argued that compelled transfers are obtained in such an unacceptable way that their receipt is automatically tainted by turpitude, and that they are recoverable on that basis alone, even if they are due. An alternative solution is to regard such cases as *sui generis* examples of *sine causa* retention, recoverable with a *condictio sine causa specialis*. These two options will now be explored.

ii. The retention of transfers tainted by turpitude: the condictio ob turpem vel iniustam causam

The focus above was on the recoverability of transfers based on the fact that they were not due. Another reason why a transfer could be retained *sine causa* is that its retention is immoral or unlawful. It will be recalled that in Roman law, Roman-Dutch law and during the Institutional era, certain cases of compulsion which did not fall under the law of *vis et metus* or force and fear, were regarded as cases involving transfers that were retained immorally or unlawfully. However, as indicated above, in the modern civilian approach it is unnecessary to make use of this mechanism if the transfer is not due in any event: it simply is a matter of applying the *condictio indebiti*. Whether or not the transfer was compelled is only of limited relevance, namely to

---

271 According to Peiris, "although a remedy may be available in appropriate circumstances under the *actio iniuriarum* or under the criminal law, there is no warrant for the grant of restitution in the absence of pecuniary damage sustained by the plaintiff" (*Some Aspects of the Law of Unjust Enrichment in South Africa and Ceylon*, 153). Presumably, Peiris regards the compelled payment as a valid act of performance of the obligation. The reduction of the plaintiff's patrimony by the payment, together with the increase in his patrimony by the extinction of the debt then leads to a nil balance. Cf also *B & H Engineering v First National Bank of South Africa Ltd* 1995 (2) SA 279 (A), where the *condictio sine causa* was not awarded, due to the fact that payment by way of a cheque extinguished a due debt, even though the cheque was countermanded.

272 Cf the Sri Lankan case of *Attorney General v Saibo* (1923) 25 CNLR 321, which supports the proposition that a *condictio indebiti* can be used to reclaim a payment made in consequence of an unlawful threat, even though the payment was due (cf Peiris, *Some Aspects of the Law of Unjust Enrichment in South Africa and Ceylon*, 153).

273 For example, the fact that a payment of an existing debt was made in error does not render it undue under modern South African law (cf Visser, *Die Grondslag van die Condictio Indebiti*, 228; Eiselen, *Unjustified Enrichment—A Casebook*, 142, and cases quoted there). Cf also *The Fraternity of Masters and Seamen of Dundee v Cockerill* (1869) 8 M 278 (inasmuch as a valid agreement of donation supported the *ex gratia* payment).

act as a factor which indicates why the rule that recovery is barred if both parties are tainted by turpitude should be applied.[274]

However, as indicated above, it is problematic to award the *condictio indebiti* to recover a compelled *due* payment. Here it becomes more attractive to award a *condictio ob turpem vel iniustam causam* on the basis that the means used in obtaining an act of fulfilment are so reprehensible that recovery should still be awarded. The law of unjustified enrichment then in effect becomes a measure aimed at ensuring that lawful means, rather than the taking of the law into one's own hands, are used to obtain acts of fulfilment. In a modern day context particular care then has to be exercised not to apply a standard of illegality which may have been required in the past to supplement the lack of insufficiently developed alternative remedies,[275] or which reflected different social views as to what conduct involves turpitude.[276] In certain serious cases of compulsion, such as threatening to assault a debtor if he does not pay, there may be scope for the application of such an analysis. But this is not the case when dealing with less serious cases of compulsion. Suppose, for example, that a depositary refuses to return a deposit unless the depositor pays him a debt which is due. The compulsion will then be wrongful in the absence of some right of security, but to regard the payment as a transfer *ob turpem vel iniustam causam* seems somewhat strained. An alternative approach is simply to state that an act of fulfilment obtained in such a way is not valid, and gives rise to *sine causa* retention. The appropriate remedy will then be the *condictio sine causa (specialis)*.[277]

iii. The *condictio sine causa (specialis)*

In essence the scope of the *condictio sine causa (specialis)* depends largely on the scope of the *condictio indebiti*. If the scope of the *condictio indebiti* is narrow (as in modern Scots law), and it applies to transfers made *solvendi causa* but in error as to liability, the *condictio sine causa (specialis)* can be used to obtain recovery of certain undue transfers falling outside the scope of the *condictio indebiti*.[278] In the context of modern Scots law it has been suggested that in certain cases where a public body demanded payment of taxes or other levies under an ultra vires enactment, and there was no mistake about liability, an action of repetition under the *condictio sine causa*, and not the *condictio indebiti*, would lie.[279] Conversely, the field of application of the *condictio sine causa (specialis)* is limited if, as the modern civilian approach requires, the scope of the *condictio indebiti* is viewed broadly. A *condictio indebiti* which is applicable to

274 Cf 5.4.2.i(b), 7.2.3.iii above.

275 Cf 2.3.3, 3.3.2.ii(b) above on the traditionally limited scope of the *metus* remedies and the *condictio indebiti*.

276 Cf 2.3.1 and 2.3.2 above on Roman conceptions of *infamia*.

277 The term *specialis* is put in brackets, since in the context of modern law it is somewhat superfluous.

278 In Scots law the *condictio sine causa (specialis)* covers cases where a transfer to which the pursuer is entitled was made to the defender without legal justification, and none of the other *condictiones* apply. Cf Gloag and Henderson, *The Law of Scotland*, 474 et sqq, 479. Specific reference is made to the South African case of *Govender v Standard Bank of South Africa Ltd* 1984 (4) SA 392 (C), where the necessity of the *condictio sine causa specialis* in South African law is explained. Cf also *B & H Engineering v First National Bank of South Africa Ltd* 1995 (2) SA 279 (A). According to the SME vol 15 (1993), 16, the *condictio sine causa* "can be treated as having been subsumed within the *condictio indebiti*".

279 Cf Gloag and Henderson, *The Law of Scotland*, 476, inter alia referring to *Woolwich Equitable Building Society v Inland Revenue Commissioners* [1993] 1 AC 70 (CA and HL); *British Oxygen Co Ltd v South of Scotland Electricity Board* 1959 SC (HL) 17. However, as indicated above, in terms of the modern civilian approach these cases would be dealt with under the *condictio indebiti*.

all undue transfers[280] renders the *condictio sine causa (specialis)* superfluous for the recovery of compelled undue transfers. However, as indicated above, in the case of the compelled due transfer the *condictio indebiti* does not lie. It is submitted that insofar as such a transfer does not discharge an obligation, and is retained *sine causa*, the *condictio sine causa (specialis)* is a suitable remedy for recovery. It is not hampered by the difficulties associated with applying the *condictio ob turpem vel iniustam causam*, which covers only cases of compulsion involving turpitude. Thus, despite its limited recognition in modern Scots law, the *condictio sine causa (specialis)* is essential to supplement the *condictio indebiti* by allowing recovery in residual cases of *sine causa* retention. To treat it as subsumed within the *condictio indebiti*,[281] would deprive Scots law of a valuable residual category, even when the scope of the *condictio indebiti* is viewed broadly, as the modern civilian approach suggests.

iv. Future development

The overview above shows that the various approaches to the Scots law of unjustified enrichment differ substantially in their treatment of the recoverability of compelled transfers. The key question is whether compulsion should be regarded as an independent unjust factor or ground for recovery, or whether it is a factor which either indicates that transfers are retained without legal ground (e.g. when it acts as a ground for reduction of contracts), or merely influences the recoverability of transfers which are in any event retained without legal ground. From the overview it is further apparent that although none of the approaches are free from limitations, the modern civilian approach generally succeeds in addressing the main problems faced when dealing with compelled transfers. Unlike the "unjust factors" approach, it does not attempt to unify what, from the perspective of Scots law, is an unrelated variety of cases involving some or other element of compulsion. By distinguishing between due and undue transfer, it makes it unnecessary to become entangled in the considerable definitional difficulties faced when trying to base recovery on mild forms of compulsion, such as implied threats to impose penalties. It also avoids awkward problems which arise when compulsion and turpitude are identified too closely, resulting in what from a modern perspective amounts to peculiar applications of the *condictio ob turpem vel iniustam causam*.

The problem, of course, is that although strong Institutional foundations have been laid for the application of the modern civilian approach in Scots law, its present character is more that of an ideal towards which the modern law can develop than a reflection of it. The current approach is epitomised by the milestone judgment in *Morgan Guaranty Trust Company of New York v Lothian Regional Council*:[282] while the court was willing to refuse recognition of an aberration like the error of law rule, it was not prepared to go as far as jettisoning the error requirement of the *condictio indebiti* in favour of a broader approach, whereby undue transfers would be recoverable in principle. In a system which honours the principle of *stare decisis*,[283] such caution is inevitable, but unfortunate insofar as it indicates limited scope for judicial development of the law. Given the current dissatisfaction with the traditional approach, characterised by the unnecessary splitting up of the *condictiones*

---

280 Cf Evans-Jones, "From 'undue transfer' to 'retention without a legal basis' (the *condictio indebiti* and *condictio ob turpem vel iniustam causam*)" in Evans-Jones (ed), *The Civil Law Tradition in Scotland*, 213 et sqq; Du Plessis and Wicke, "Woolwich Equitable v IRC and the condictio indebiti in Scots law" 1993 SLT (News) 303.

281 As is suggested in SME vol 15 (1993), 16.

282 1995 SCLR 225.

283 Cf, generally, Gloag and Henderson, *The Law of Scotland*, 16 et sqq.

under the heads of "restitution" and "repetition", the considerable uncertainty surrounding the nature and limits of recompense, and the ad hoc recognition of new cases of unjustified enrichment,[284] it is apparent that if the courts do not adopt a bolder stance towards law reform the only alternative is some form of legislative intervention. It is submitted that irrespective of the method of reform, the process could benefit from a facilitative framework, such as a "restatement", which indicates how the contours of the existing law could be reformed.[285] Such a restatement could then provide the opportunity to synthesise repetition and restitution, realign the *condictiones* on more rational and practical grounds, and provide greater clarity as to the content of recompense. But even such a framework may prove to be incapable of satisfactorily taking into account new developments of the law. Ultimately, it may well be that only the recognition of a general enrichment action could allow the courts sufficient flexibility to accommodate these new cases, and devise a taxonomy most suited to the needs of modern Scots law. The German experience has shown that such an action can be the catalyst for a whole new division of the law, while the South African example shows that it is inadequate only to deal with new cases on an ad hoc basis by reference to the principles common to a general enrichment action, without actually recognising such an action. Perhaps Scots law is not so far from this goal as it may seem: the fact that it is possible to group certain cases of *sine causa* retention of a transfer together under a residual *condictio sine causa (specialis)*, combined with the ability of recompense also to cover certain residual cases of unjustified enrichment, indicates that there is scope for such a development.[286] However, the recognition of such an action does not imply that

---

284 Recovery of Ultra Vires Public Authority Receipts and Disbursements (Scot Law Com D P No 100, 1996), 129 et sq (also see 17, 256); Whitty, "Some Trends and Issues in Scots Enrichment Law" 1994 *JR* 127 at 135.

285 This has in fact been proposed in Judicial Abolition of the Error of Law Rule and its Aftermath (Scot Law Com D P No 99, 1996) and Recovery of Ultra Vires Public Authority Receipts and Disbursements (Scot Law Com D P No 100, 1996).

286 It is doubtful, though, whether it is desirable to regard recompense as *the* general enrichment action of Scots law. As indicated in Judicial Abolition of the Error of Law Rule and its Aftermath (Scot Law Com D P No 99, 1996), it would be pointless to formulate strict rules governing the scope of the nominate *condictiones* if an action of recompense based on the general principle of unjustified enrichment is available in any event. In the concluding remarks to his work on the South African law of unjustified enrichment, Prof de Vos warns against retaining the existing nominate heads of unjustified enrichment whilst only acknowledging a subsidiary category of cases where liability could be established based on a general enrichment action. According to him,

> "This position is unsatisfactory insofar as one then still has to deal with an unnecessary multiplicity of actions, and with unnecessary casuistry which at times demands a meticulous, literal approach. It is also unsatisfactory because the various enrichment actions are at different stages of development. In the case of the old enrichment actions we have to deal with incomplete enrichment actions which still have to reach maturity, and there we move along the rigid grooves of age-old doctrine. The general enrichment action, on the other hand, is a fully modern and developed enrichment action. One then reaches the illogical and inelegant position that the impoverished person who has transferred ownership of something will have to claim with one of the old actions, while he would have to claim with the general enrichment action if he performed a *factum* under exactly the same circumstances! The bona fide possessor acts against the owner with an old action, and the bona fide occupier with a general action ... How can this state of affairs be justified? Such a position cannot be regarded as a satisfactory end result, only as a temporary resting-point. Our law must develop further. The development which I am proposing is that the general action should lose its subsidiary character and

the existing nominate heads of the *condictiones* have to be discarded: within the broader context of the modern civilian approach they can still be used to describe typical factual situations which are manifestations of the general enrichment action. In this regard it is submitted that by analysing the *condictiones* in terms of their treatment of compulsion, valuable conclusions can be reached as to their proper fields of application.

7.4 CONCLUSIONS

1. The taxonomy of the modern Scots law of unjustified enrichment is not in a satisfactory state. In essence, it is based on the distinction between the three Rs of "restitution", "repetition" and "recompense". The term "restitution" is particularly problematic, in that it is used in a variety of meanings which creates considerable uncertainty. To understand why Scots law has adopted these divisions, it is essential to look at their historical background.
2. The historical roots of the division between the three Rs lie in the works of the Institutional writers. Their views can be summarised as follows:
   2.1. The obligation of restitution generally arose when someone's property or money came into the power or possession of another without the intention that it should be a gift. More specifically, it included the recovery of things which came into someone's hands without a legal basis—*quae cadunt in non causam*. It then covered the terrain of the *condictio indebiti*, the *condictio causa data causa non secuta* and the *condictio sine causa*. The obligation of restitution did not only arise in cases which would nowadays be regarded as instances of unjustified enrichment, but was also a remedy of property law. The distinction between personal rights and real rights was undeveloped.
   2.2. Recompense was generally aimed at redressing another's gain, benefit, or enrichment—most notably through bona fide building on another's land, *negotiorum gestio* and the *Lex Rhodia de Jactu*. Stair still based the obligation for recompense on a lack of reciprocation, but the remedy simply came to be regarded as one aimed at obtaining some sort of indemnity or compensation due to another's gain or benefit.
   2.3. It is only in the nineteenth century that "repetition" came to be regarded as a distinct category of quasi-contractual obligations. It was mainly associated with the payment of money in error as to liability.
3. In the modern Scots law of unjustified enrichment, the three Rs are the dominant mode of classification: if the claim relates to moveables, it is termed restitution, if it relates to money and interest, it is termed repetition, while recompense mostly covers cases involving expenditure, services or the use of the property of another. The *condictiones indebiti*, *causa data causa non secuta* and *sine causa* are then "represented" by actions for restitution and repetition.

---

that its field of application should be broadened so that it can be applied in all cases of unjustified enrichment. To put it differently, the classical enrichment actions have to be superseded, and requirement (4) [that the case should not fall under one of the classical enrichment actions] must disappear" (own translation, *Verrykingsaanspreeklikheid in die Suid-Afrikaanse reg*, 371 et sq).

A significant number of commentators have expressed dissatisfaction with the traditional approach. Their views can be summarised as follows:

3.1 In terms of the "unjust factors" approach, which has been developed in the context of the English Common Law, enrichment at the expense of another gives rise to a response of restitution if there is a factor which renders the enrichment "unjust". Compulsion, which has been described as arising when a person cannot exercise his will freely for fear of some evil consequence, is regarded as such an unjust factor. Compulsion has been subdivided into (1) coercion, i.e. duress or actual undue influence; (2) compulsion by legal process; (3) moral compulsion; and (4) circumstantial compulsion. It is submitted that this approach is unsuitable for Scots law. First, there is no need to unify these categories under the heading of "compulsion" in Scots law. Second, while coercion in the form of duress could conceivably be regarded as an unjust factor in the limited sense that it acts as a ground for reduction, it is not at all clear that it performs such a function in all cases where someone is enriched through retention of a coerced transfer. Attempts to correlate the *condictio ob turpem vel iniustam causam* with compulsion as an "unjust factor" are particularly unconvincing, in that they fail to take into account changing views of turpitude, and the fact that the application of this *condictio* in cases of compulsion is mainly due to a historically narrow field of application of the remedies based on force and fear. Third, there are also more general objections against the application of the unjust factors approach. The most notable are the challenge to its integrity through the emergence of "absence of consideration" as an unjust factor, its open-endedness, lack of economy and inelegance.

3.2 The roots of the modified civilian approach, by contrast, are fixed more firmly in Scots law, most notably through recognition of the centrality of the civilian notion of the undue transfer in the context of the law of repetition. However, its portrayal of compulsion (and error) as "grounds of recovery", which represents a modification of the civilian approach, is problematic. In certain cases, some form of compulsion may have been present when a transfer was made, but this does not mean that compulsion should be regarded as the "ground for recovery". It should be noted, though, that proponents of the modified civilian approach have expressed doubts as to whether development by way of the ever-increasing recognition and extension of specific "grounds of recovery" is the hallmark of a mature system of unjustified enrichment. Proposals have then been made that Scots law should adopt the general civilian distinction between enrichment by way of transfer and enrichment in another way.

3.3 To the modern civilian approach, which draws most of its strength from the Institutional writings, the notion of the retention of enrichment without a legal ground is central. In contrast to the unjust factors approach, which looks at enrichment from the point of view of the pursuer, and asks whether an unjust factor exists which entitles him to recovery, the civilian approach focuses on the position of the recipient and asks whether there is any reason to return something he retained without legal ground. If a transfer is not due, it is recoverable because it is not supported by a relationship of indebtedness. This type of case can be brought home under the heading of the *condictio indebiti*. The only relevance of compulsion in this context is that it indicates that certain rules which bar recovery of undue transfers, namely the knowledge rule and the rule that the transferor who is also tainted by turpitude is barred from recovery, should be relaxed. If a compelled transfer is due, there are two possible solutions. Insofar as a due transfer validly discharges a debt, there is no enrichment. This apparently would be the case if milder forms of compulsion are employed. However, if the compulsion is so serious that the transfer cannot be regarded as validly discharging a debt, it can be said that there is enrichment and that the transfer is held *sine causa*. Inasmuch as the method employed involved turpitude, the claim could be brought home under the *condictio ob turpem vel iniustam causam*. However, it is preferable simply to award a *condictio sine causa specialis* in all cases where an act of fulfilment is obtained so improperly that it cannot validly fulfil an obligation.

4. Although none of the approaches referred to above are free from limitations, it is submitted that within the context of the Scots law of unjustified enrichment the modern civilian approach generally succeeds in providing the most satisfactory framework for the treatment of compelled transfers.

Bibliography

Ankum, H and Pool, E, "*Rem in bonis meis esse* and *rem in bonis meam esse*—Traces of the Development of Roman Double Ownership", in P Birks (ed), *New Perspectives in the Roman law of Property—Essays for Barry Nicholas* (1989) 5

Ankum, J A, "Eine neue Interpretation von Ulpian Dig 4295–6 über die Abhilfen gegen *metus*", in *Festschrift für Heinz Hübner* (1984) 3

Balfour, Sir James, *The Practicks of Sir James Balfour of Pittendreich*, P G B McNeil (ed) (1962)

Bankton, Andrew McDouall, Lord, *An Institute of the Laws of Scotland* (1751)

Barton, J (ed), *Towards a General Law of Contract* (1990)

Baur, F, *Lehrbuch des Sachenrechts*, 16th ed (1992)

Bell, G J, *Commentaries on the Law of Scotland and on the Principles of Mercantile Jurisprudence*, J M'Laren (ed), 7th ed (1870)

Bell, G J, *Principles of the Law of Scotland*, 4th ed (1839)

Berger, A, *Encyclopedic Dictionary of Roman Law* (1953)

Beatson, J, *The Use and Abuse of Unjust Enrichment* (1991)

Beseler, G, *Beiträge zur Kritik der römischen Rechtsquellen*, vol 1 (1910)

Birks, P, "Restitution: A View of the Scots law" (1985) 38 *CLP* 57

Birks, P, "Six Questions in search of a subject—Unjust Enrichment in a Crisis of Identity" 1985 *JR* 227

Birks, P, *An Introduction to the Law of Restitution* (1985, rev ed 1989)

Brox, H, *Allgemeiner Teil des Bürgerlichen Gesetzbuchs*, 20th ed (1996)

Buckland, W W, *A Text-book of Roman Law from Augustus to Justinian*, 3rd ed, rev by P Stein (1975)

Burrows, A (ed), *Essays on the Law of Restitution* (1991)

Burrows, A, *The Law of Restitution* (1993)

Canaris, C-W, *Lehrbuch des Schuldrechts*, vol 2(2), 13th ed (1994); for vol 1, see Larenz, *Lehrbuch des Schuldrechts*, vol 1

Carey Miller, D L, *The Acquisition and Protection of Ownership* (1986)

Carey Miller, D L, *Corporeal Moveables in Scots law* (1991)

Craig, Sir Thomas, *The Jus Feudale by Sir Thomas Craig of Riccarton*, vol 1, tr J A Clyde (1934); Latin 1st ed (1655)

Daube, D, "Turpitude in Digest 1255" in Bagnall, R S and Harris, W V (eds), *Studies in Roman Law in Memory of A Arthur Schiller* (1986) 33

Dawson, J P, "Economic Duress and the Fair Exchange in French and German Law" (1937) 11 *TulaneLR* 345

De Vos, W, *Verrykingsaanspreeklikheid in die Suid-Afrikaanse reg*, 3rd ed (1987)

De Wet, J C and Van Wyk, A H, *De Wet en Yeats—Die Suid-Afrikaanse Kontraktereg en Handelsreg*, 4th ed (1978)

De Wet, J C, *Die Ou Skrywers in Perspektief* (1988)

Du Plessis, J E and Wicke, H, "Woolwich Equitable v IRC and the condictio indebiti in Scots law", 1993 SLT (News) 303

Ebert, U, "*Vi metusve causa*" (1969) 86 *ZSS (RA)* 403
Englard, I, "Restitution of Benefits conferred without obligation" in *International Encyclopedia of Comparative Law*, vol X, ch 5 (1991)
Encyclopaedia of the Laws of Scotland, vol 6 (1928), vol 12 (1931)
Erskine, J, *An Institute of the Law of Scotland in Four Books In the order of Sir George Mackenzie's Institutions of that Law*, J B Nicolson (ed) 8th ed (1871)
Evans-Jones, R, "Identifying the Enriched" 1992 SLT 25
Evans-Jones, R, "Unjust enrichment, Contract and the Third Reception of Roman law in Scotland (1993) 109 *LQR* 663
Evans-Jones, R, "Some reflections on the condictio indebiti in a mixed legal system" (1994) 111 *SALJ* 759
Evans-Jones, R, "From 'undue transfer' to 'retention without a legal basis' (the *condictio indebiti* and the *condictio ob turpem vel iniustam causam*)", in R Evans-Jones (ed), *The Civil Law Tradition in Scotland* (1995) 213
Evans-Jones, R and MacCormack, G D, "*Iusta causa traditionis*" in P Birks (ed), *New Perspectives in the Roman law of Property—Essays for Barry Nicholas* (1989), 99
Evans-Jones, R and McKenzie, D, "Towards a profile of the condictio ob turpem vel iniustam causam in Scots law" 1994 *JR* 60
Evans-Jones, R and Hellwege, P, "Swaps, Error of Law and Unjustified Enrichment" (1995) 1 *SLPQ* 1
Feenstra, R and Zimmermann, R (eds), *Das römisch-holländische Recht—Fortschritte des Zivilrechts im 17 und 18 Jahrhundert* (1992)
Giesen, D, *BGB Allgemeiner Teil: Rechtsgeschäftslehre* (1991)
Glegg, A T, *A Practical Treatise on the Law of Reparation in Scotland* (1892)
Gloag, W M, *The Law of Contract: A Treatise on the Principles of Contract in the Law of Scotland*, 2nd ed (1929)
Glück, C F, *Ausführliche Erläuterung der Pandekten*, vols 1–34 (from 1832)
Goff, R and Jones, G, *The Law of Restitution*, 4th ed (1993)
Gordley, J, "Natural Law Origins of the Common Law of Contract" in Barton (ed), *Towards a General Law of Contract* 367
Gordon, W M, "The Importance of the *iusta causa* of *traditio*", in P Birks (ed), *New Perspectives in the Roman law of Property—Essays for Barry Nicholas* (1989), 123
Groenewegen van der Made, S, *Tractatus de legibus abrogatis et inusitatis in Hollandia vicinisque regionibus* (1669)
Grotius, H, *De Jure Belli ac Pacis*, tr F W Kelsey (1925)
Grotius, H, *Inleidinge tot de Hollandsche Rechts-geleerdheid*, F Dovring, H F W D Fischer and E M Meijers eds (1952)
Guest, A G (ed), *Chitty on Contracts*, vol 1, 26th ed (1989)
Guthrie Smith, J, *The Law of Damages: the Reparation of Injuries as Administered in Scotland* (1864)
Hartkamp, A S, *Der Zwang im römischen Privatrecht* (1971)
Hartkamp, A S et al (eds), *Towards a European Civil Code* (1994)
Honoré, A M, "*Condictio* and payment" 1958 *AJ* 135
Honoré, A M, "Degrees of Invalidity" (1958) 75 *SALJ* 32
Honoré, T, "A Theory of Coercion" (1990) 10 *OJLS* 94
Honsell, H, *Die Rückabwicklung sittenwidriger oder verbotener Geschäfte* (1974)
Honsell, H; Mayer-Maly, T and Selb, W, *Römisches Recht*, based on the work of P Jörs, W Kunkel and L Wenger, 4th ed (1987)
Hope of Craighall, Sir Thomas, *Hope's Major Practicks*, J A Clyde (ed) (1937)
Huber, U, *Heedensdaegse Rechtsgeleertheyt* 4th ed (1742)

Hume, D, *Baron David Hume's Lectures 1786–1822*, G C H Paton (ed) (from 1939 onwards)
Hume, D, *Commentaries on the Law of Scotland*, vol 1 (1844, repr 1986)
Hutchison, D et al, *Wille's Principles of South African Law*, 8th ed (1991)
Innes, C (ed), *Liber Officialis Sancti Andree* (1845)
Introduction to Scottish Legal History, An, various authors, with an introduction by Lord Normand, Stair Society vol 20 (1958)
Introductory Survey of the Sources and Literature of Scots Law, An, various authors, with an introduction by The Rt Hon Lord Macmillan, Stair Society vol 1 (1936)
Jauernig, O (ed), *Bürgerliches Gesetzbuch*, 7th ed (1994)
Jolowicz, H F, *Historical Introduction to the Study of Roman Law*, 2nd ed (1952)
Joubert, D J, *General Principles of the Law of Contract* (1987)
Judicial Abolition of the Error of Law Rule and its Aftermath (Scot Law Com D P No 99, 1996), with Appendix (Draft Rules on Unjustified Enrichment and Commentary)
Kahn, E; Lewis, C and Visser, C, *Contract and Mercantile Law: A Source Book* 2nd ed, vol 1 (1988)
Kames, Henry Home, Lord, *Principles of Equity* (1825)
Kaser, M, "Das Geld im römischen Sachenrecht" (1961) 29 *Tijdschrift voor Rechtsgeschiedenis* 220
Kaser, M, "Rechtswidrigkeit und Sittenwidrigkeit im klassischen römischen Recht" 60 (1940) *ZSS (RA)* 95
Kaser, M, "Zur in integrum restitutio, besonders wegen metus und dolus" (1977) 94 *ZSS (RA)* 101
Kaser, M, *Das römische Privatrecht, Erster Abschnitt* 2nd ed (1971) cited as Kaser, *Das römische Privatrecht I*
Kaser, M, *Das römische Privatrecht, Zweiter Abschnitt* 2nd ed (1975) cited as Kaser, *Das römische Privatrecht II*
Kaser, M, *Das römische Zivilprozessrecht* (1966)
König, D, *Ungerechtfertigte Bereicherung—Tatbestände und Ordnungsprobleme in rechtsvergleichender Sicht* (1985)
Koppensteiner, H-G; Kramer, E, *Ungerechtfertigte Bereicherung*, 2nd ed (1988)
Kramer, E in *Münchener Kommentar* Band 1, 3rd ed (1993)
Kunkel, W, *Römisches Privatrecht*, based on the work of P Jörs, 3rd ed (1949, reprinted 1978)
Kupisch, B, *In integrum restitutio und vindicatio utilis bei Eigentumsübertragungen im klassischen römischen Recht* (1974)
Lambiris, M A, *Orders of Specific Performance and Restitutio in Integrum in South African Law* (1989)
Larenz, K, *Lehrbuch des Schuldrechts*, vol 1, 13th ed (1993) also see Canaris, C-W, *Lehrbuch des Schuldrechts*, vol 2(2)
Laws of Scotland, The: Stair Memorial Encyclopaedia, vol 15—Obligations (1997); vol 18—Property (1993)
Lee, R W, *The Elements of Roman Law with a Translation of the Institutes of Justinian*, 4th ed (1956)
Levy, E, "Zur nachklassischen in integrum restitutio" (1951) 68 *ZSS (RA)* 360
Levy, E, *Privatstrafe und Schadensersatz im klassischen römischen Recht* (1915)
Lieb, M in *Münchener Kommentar*, 2nd ed (1986)
Liebs, D, "The History of the Roman *Condictio* up to Justinian", in N MacCormick and P Birks (eds), *The Legal Mind—Essays for Tony Honoré* (1986), 163
Lotz, J G, "Enrichment" in W A Joubert (ed) *The Law of South Africa*, vol 9 (1979)
Lubbe, G F and Murray, C M, *Farlam and Hathaway—Contract*, 3rd ed (1988)

Mackenzie of Rosehaugh, Sir George, *The Laws and Customes of Scotland in Matters Criminal* (1688)

Mackenzie, Sir George, *Institutions of the Law of Scotland* (1684)

Maier, G H, *Prätorische Bereicherungsklagen* (1932)

McBryde, W W, *The Law of Contract in Scotland* (1987)

McBryde, W W, *Void, Voidable, Illegal and Unenforceable Contracts in Scots Law* (unpublished doctoral thesis, Glasgow, 1976)

McKendrick, E, "Economic Duress—A Reply" 1985 SLT (News) 277

McKendrick, E, "Restitution of unlawfully demanded tax" 1993 *LMCLQ* 88

MacQueen, H, and Sellar, W D H, "Unjust Enrichment in Scots Law" in E J H Schrage (ed), *Unjust Enrichment: the Comparative Legal History of the Law of Restitution* (1995), 289

Medicus, D, *Allgemeiner Teil des BGB*, 6th ed (1994)

Medicus, D, *Bürgerliches Recht*, 17th ed (1991)

Medicus, D, *Schuldrecht I (Allgemeiner Teil)*, 8th ed (1995) and *Schuldrecht II (Besonderer Teil)*, 7th ed (1995)

Memorandum on Defective Consent and Consequential Matters (Scot Law Com Memo No 42, 1978), 2 vols

Mugdan, B (ed), *Die gesammten Materialien zum Bürgerlichen Gesetzbuch für das deutsche Reich* (1899, reprinted 1979)

Nicholas, B, *An Introduction to Roman Law* (1969)

Olivier, P J J, "Onregmatige Vreesaanjaging" (1965) 28 *THRHR* 187

Palandt—Bürgerliches Gesetzbuch, 56th ed (1997)

Palmer, G E, *The Law of Restitution* (1978)

Peiris, G L, *Some Aspects of the Law of Unjust Enrichment in South Africa and Ceylon* (1972)

Philips, M, "Are coerced agreements involuntary?" 1984 *Law and Philosophy* 133

Pothier, R J, *Traité des obligations*, tr W D Evans (1806)

Recovery of Benefits Conferred under Error of law (Scot Law Com D P No 95, 1993), 2 vols

Recovery of Ultra Vires Public Authority Receipts and Disbursements (Scot Law Com D P No 100, 1996)

Regiam Majestatem and Quoniam Attachiamenta, Lord Cooper, ed and tr (1947)

Reid, K G C, "Unjustified Enrichment and Property Law" 1994 *JR* 167

Reuter, D and Martinek, M, *Ungerechtfertigte Bereicherung* (1983)

Scholtens, J E, "Justa causa traditionis and contracts induced by fraud" (1957) 74 *SALJ* 280

Schulz, F, "Die Lehre vom erzwungenen Rechtsgeschäft im antiken römischen Recht", 1922 (43) *ZSS (RA)* 171

Schulz, F, *Classical Roman Law* (1951, reprinted in 1961)

Schwarz, F, *Die Grundlage der Condictio im Klassischen Römischen Recht* (1952)

Scottish National Dictionary, W Grant (ed) (1976)

Shaw, P, *A Treatise on the Law of Obligations and Contracts* (1847)

Simpson, P J D, *Die Rückabwicklung von sitten- und rechtswidrigen Rechtsgeschäften im heutigen deutschen und schottischen Recht*, unpublished LL M Dissertation, University of Regensburg (1995)

Smith, T B, Professor Sir *A Short Commentary on the Law of Scotland* (1962)

Spotiswoode, Sir R, *Practicks of the laws of Scotland, observed and collected by Sir Robert Spotiswoode*, Spotiswood, J (ed) (1706)

Stair, James Dalrymple, 1st Viscount, *Institutions of the Law of Scotland*, D M Walker (ed), 16th ed (1981) cited as Stair, *Inst*

Stein, P, *Legal Evolution* (1980)

Stewart, W J, *The Law of Restitution in Scotland* (1992); *Supplement* (1995)

Tayler, W J, *Treatise on the Differences between the Laws of England and Scotland relating to Contracts* (1849)

Tettenborn, A, *The Law of Restitution in England and Ireland*, 2nd ed (1996)

Thomas, J A C, *Textbook of Roman Law* (1976)

Thompson, A, "Economic Duress" 1985 SLT (News) 85

Trayner, J, *Latin Maxims and Phrases* (1894)

Treitel, G H, *The Law of Contract*, 9th ed (1995)

Trotter, W F, *The Law of Contract in Scotland* (1913)

Van der Keessel, D G, *Praelectiones iuris hodierni ad Hugonis Grotii introductionem ad iurisprudentiam Hollandicam*, P van Warmelo et al tr and ed (1967)

Van der Linden, J, *Rechtsgeleerd, Practicaal en Koopmans Handboek* (1806)

Van der Merwe, N J and Olivier, P J J, *Die Onregmatige daad in die Suid-Afrikaanse reg*, 6th ed (1989)

Van der Merwe, S W J et al, *Contract—General Principles* (1993)

Van der Merwe, S W J and Van Huyssteen, L F, "The force of agreements: valid, void, voidable, unenforceable" (1995) 58 *THRHR* 549

Van Huyssteen, L F, *Onbehoorlike Beïnvloeding en Misbruik van Omstandighede in die Suid-Afrikaanse Verbintenisreg* (1980)

Van Leeuwen, S, *Censura Forensis Theoretico-Practica*, 4th ed (1741) tr S H Barber and W A Macfadyen (1902)

Vinnius, A, *In Quatuor Libros Institutionum Imperialium Commentarius Academicus & Forensis* (1665)

Visser, D P, "Die Grondslag van die condictio indebiti" (1988) 51 *THRHR* 492

Visser, D P, "Rethinking Unjustified Enrichment: A Perspective of the Competition between Contractual and Enrichment Remedies" 1992 *AJ* 203

Visser, D P, *Die rol van dwaling by die condictio indebiti*, unpublished Dr iur thesis, University of Leyden (1985)

Voet, J, *Commentarius ad Pandectas* (Paris edition, 1829), tr P Gane as *The Selective Voet being the Commentary on the Pandects by Johannes Voet and the Supplement to that work by Johannes van der Linden* (1955)

Von Jhering, R, *Geist des römischen Rechts auf den verschiedenen Stufen seiner Entwicklung* (1888)

Von Lübtow, U, *Beiträge zur Lehre von der Condictio nach römischem und geltendem Recht* (1952)

Von Lübtow, U, *Der Ediktstitel "Quod metus causa gestum erit"* (1932)

Von Savigny, F C, *System des heutigen Römischen Rechts* (from 1840 onwards)

Walker, D M, *Principles of Scottish Private law*, vol 2, 4th ed (1988)

Walker, D M, *A Legal History of Scotland*, vol 1 (1988), vol 2 (1990)

Walker, D M, *The Law of Civil Remedies in Scotland* (1974)

Walker, D M, *The Law of Contracts and Related Obligations in Scotland*, 3rd ed (1995)

Walker, D M, *The Law of Delict in Scotland*, 2nd ed (1981)

Walker, D M, *The Scottish Jurists* (1985)

Walker, D M, *The Scottish Legal System*, 6th ed (1992)

Walker, D M (ed), *Stair Tercentenary Studies* (1981)

Wertheimer, A, *Coercion* (1987)

Wessels, J W, *The Law of Contract in South Africa*, A A Roberts, E L Jansen and J J Trengove (eds), 2nd ed (1951)

Whitty, N R, "The Taxonomy of Unjustified Enrichment in Scots Law", essay prepared for a seminar on the law of unjustified enrichment held in Edinburgh on 23 October 1993

Whitty, N R, "Some Trends and Issues in Scots Enrichment law" 1994 *JR* 127
Whitty, N R, "The civilian tradition and debates on Scots law" 1996 *TSAR* 227, 1996 *TSAR* 442
Whitty, N R, "Die Reform des schottischen Bereicherungsrechts" 1995 *ZEuP* 216
Wilson, W A et al (eds), *The Law of Scotland*, by W M Gloag and R Candlish Henderson, 10th ed (1995)
Woolman, S, *An Introduction to the Scots Law of Contract*, 2nd ed (1994)
Zimmermann, R, *The Law of Obligations, Roman Foundations of the Civilian Tradition* (1990)
Zimmermann, R, "Unjustified Enrichment: The Modern Civilian Approach" (1995) 15 *OJLS* 403
Zimmermann, R and du Plessis, J, "Basic Features of the German Law of Unjustified Enrichment" 1994 *RLR* 14
Zweigert, K and Kötz, H, *Introduction to Comparative Law*, 2nd ed, tr T Weir (1992)

Index

THE STAIR SOCIETY

The Stair Society

Instituted in 1934 to encourage the study and advance the knowledge of the History of Scots Law

THE STAIR SOCIETY was founded in 1934 to encourage the study and advance the knowledge of the history of Scots Law by the publication of original documents and by the reprinting and editing of works of sufficient rarity or importance. Since 1934 it has produced some 50 volumes, aiming to publish a volume each year (although this is not guaranteed). At its Annual Meeting each November a distinguished Lecturer is invited to give an address, which is followed by lunch for members and their guests. The Society also funds a postgraduate scholarship in furtherance of its objectives. In making knowledge of the past readily accessible and fulfilling its objectives, the Society depends on the support of Scottish lawyers, both advocates and solicitors, and on legal historians throughout the world, as well as upon libraries and institutions.

Constitution

The Society was formed on 17th November, 1934

1. The Society shall be called "The Stair Society".
2. The object of the Society shall be to encourage the study and advance the knowledge of the history of Scots Law especially by the publication of original documents, and by the reprinting and editing of works of sufficient rarity or importance.
3. Membership of the Society shall be constituted by payment of the annual subscription, and shall cease if this be in arrear for one year.
4. The amount of the annual subscription shall be fixed by the Council from time to time, and shall be payable in advance on 1 January in each year.
5. The management of the affairs and funds of the Society shall be vested in a Council consisting of the President, Vice-President, a Chairman, a Vice-Chairman and not more than ten ordinary elected members. The Council shall have power to form Sub-Committees from amongst its own members for such purposes as it shall determine.
6. The President, Vice-President, Chairman and Vice-Chairman shall be elected annually at the Annual General Meeting, to hold office for the following calendar year, and shall be eligible for re-election.
7. At every Annual General Meeting of the Society, the Society shall elect ordinary members to fill any vacancies within Council that may have occurred, or that may be due to occur at the end of the year, members so elected to hold office from the ensuing 1st of January. The ordinary members of Council shall hold office for no more than five years. Two ordinary members of Council shall retire each year as at 31 December, and shall not be eligible for re-election for one year. The two members to retire annually shall be those who have the longest continuous period of service, and, as among those of equal service, shall be selected by agreement or by lot.
8. In addition to the elected members, the Council shall have power to co-opt as additional members of Council any member of the Society who, in their opinion, may be fitted to render special service in promoting the work of the Society. Such co-opted members shall hold office for such period, not exceeding

five years, as the Council may in each case determine. At no time shall the co-opted members of Council exceed three in number.

9. The Society at the Annual General Meeting shall appoint a Literary Director or Directors, a Secretary and a Treasurer, and such other officers as may from time to time be deemed necessary, who shall be subject to the direction of the Council in the performance of their duties, and who shall receive such remuneration as the Council may determine. Those so appointed shall not be members of Council, but may be invited to attend any meeting of Council.

10. Any casual vacancies in the offices of President, Vice-President, Chairman, Vice-Chairman or elected members of the Council, or among the officers of the Society, may be filled up by the Council, appointments so made to be for the period till 31 December following the next Annual General Meeting.

11. In any year in which a volume is published each member who has paid his subscription for that year shall be entitled to receive one copy.

12. The Annual General Meeting shall be held between 1 November and 31 March at such time and place as may be fixed by the Council. If the Meeting is not held until after 31 December in any year, office-bearers and members of Council then due to retire shall remain in office until the Meeting is held. The Council may also at any time call a Special General Meeting of the Society, and shall do so on a requisition from not less than ten members, which shall specify the object for which the Meeting is to be called. Seven days' notice shall be given of all General Meetings.

13. The Constitution of the Society as contained in these Rules may be amended at any General Meeting on twenty-one days' notice of the proposed amendments being given to the Secretary and included in the Agenda circulated for the Meeting.

Publications of the Stair Society

50 THE BUSINESS OF THE COLLEGE OF JUSTICE IN 1600. By Dr Winifred Coutts. 2003.

49 MISCELLANY IV. By various authors. Edited by H L MacQueen with a Preface by Lord Hope of Craighead. 2002.

48 Not yet published.

47 THE ABERDEEN SHERIFF AND COMMISSARY COURT STYLEBOOK 1722. Edited by Professors M C Meston and A D M Forte. 2000.

46 THE MINUTE BOOK of THE FACULTY OF ADVOCATES, Volume 3, 1751–1783 edited with commentary by Angus Stewart, QC, Keeper of the Advocates Library with an introduction by The Hon Lord Davidson. 1999.

45 MEDIEVAL PAPAL REPRESENTATIVES IN SCOTLAND: LEGATES-NUNCIOS AND JUDGES-DELEGATE 1125–1286 by Paul C Ferguson, PhD. 1997.

44 QUONIAM ATTACHIAMENTA edited and translated with an Introduction by T David Fergus. 1996.

43 BANKTON'S INSTITUTE. An Institute of the Laws of Scotland in Civil Rights with Observations upon the Agreement or Diversity between them and the Laws of England in Four Books. Volume Three. 1995.

42 BANKTON'S INSTITUTE. An Institute of the Laws of Scotland in Civil Rights with Observations upon the Agreement or Diversity between them and the Laws of England in Four Books. Volume Two. 1994.

41 BANKTON'S INSTITUTE. An Institute of the Laws of Scotland in Civil Rights with Observations upon the Agreement or Diversity between them and the Laws of England in Four Books. Volume One. 1993.

40 SELKIRK PROTOCOL BOOKS 1511–1547. The Protocol Books of John Chepman 1511–1536 and 1545–1547, Sir John Chepman 1536–1543, John and Ninian Brydin and Other Notaries 1526–1536 and John Brydin 1530–1537, transcribed and edited by Teresa Maley and Walter Elliot with an Introduction by Peter Symms. 1993.

39 MISCELLANY III. By various authors. Edited by Professor W M Gordon with a Preface by Professor Emeritus Gordon Donaldson. 1992.

38 THE COURT OF THE BARONY AND REGALITY OF FALKIRK AND CALLENDAR. Volume 1. 1638–1656. Doreen M Hunter, MA. 1991.

37 THE SCOTTISH WHIGS AND THE REFORM OF THE COURT OF SESSION 1785–1830. Nicholas Phillipson. 1991.

36 FORMULARY OF OLD SCOTS LEGAL DOCUMENTS, Peter Gouldesbrough. 1985.

35 MISCELLANY II. Edited by W D H Sellar with a Preface by the Rt Hon Lord Avonside. 1984.

34 THE COURT OF THE OFFICIAL IN PRE-REFORMATION SCOTLAND. By Simon D Ollivant, PhD. 1982.

33 THE STAIR TERCENTENARY STUDIES by various authors. 1982.

32 FACULTY OF ADVOCATES MINUTE BOOK, Volume 2, 1713–1750. Edited by John M Pinkerton. 1982.

31 PERPETUITIES IN SCOTS LAW by Robert Burgess, LL.B, PhD. 1979.

30 THE SYNOD RECORDS OF LOTHIAN AND TWEEDDALE 1589–1590. Edited with an Introduction by Dr James Kirk of the Department of Scottish History, Glasgow University. 1977.

29 THE MINUTE BOOK OF THE FACULTY OF ADVOCATES 1661–1712. Edited by John M Pinkerton, Clerk of Faculty, Volume 1. 1976.

28 SELECTED JUSTICIARY CASES, 1624–1650 edited with an introduction by J Irvine Smith, MA, LL.B. Advocate, Sheriff of Lanarkshire at Glasgow. Volume III. 1974.

27 SELECTED JUSTICIARY CASES, 1624–1650 edited with an Introduction by J Irvine Smith, MA, LL.B, Advocate, Sheriff of Lanarkshire at Glasgow. Volume II. 1972.

26 MISCELLANY I by various authors with a Preface by The Right Honourable Lord Clyde, LL.B, Lord Justice-General and Lord President of the Court of Session. 1971.

25 THE JUSTICIARY RECORDS OF ARGYLL AND THE ISLES, 1705–1742 edited by John Imrie. Volume II. 1969

24 WILLIAM HAY'S LECTURES ON MARRIAGE transcribed, translated and edited by The Right Rev Monsignor John C Barry, MA (Cantab), DCL (Rome), Rector of St Andrew's College, Drygrange, Melrose; Consultor to the Pontifical Commission for the Revision of the Code of Canon Law. 1967.

23 THE ORIGINS AND DEVELOPMENT OF THE JURY IN SCOTLAND by Ian D Willock, MA, LL.B, Advocate and Professor of Jurisprudence in the University of St Andrews. 1966.

22 THE PRACTICKS OF SIR JAMES BALFOUR OF PITTENDREICH edited by Peter G B McNeill, MA, LL.B. PhD, Advocate. Volume II. 1963.

21 THE PRACTICKS OF SIR JAMES BALFOUR OF PITTENDREICH edited by Peter G B McNeill, MA, LL.B. PhD, Advocate. Volume I. 1962.

20 AN INTRODUCTION TO SCOTTISH LEGAL HISTORY by various authors with an Introduction by The Right Honourable Lord Normand, PC, LL.D, Lord of Appeal in Ordinary, 1947–1953. 1958.

19 BARON DAVID HUME'S LECTURES, 1786–1822 edited and annotated by G Campbell H Paton, MA, LL.B, Advocate and Lecturer in the History of Scots Law in the University of Glasgow. Volume VI. 1958.

18 BARON DAVID HUME'S LECTURES, 1786–1822, Edited and annotated by G Campbell H Paton, MA, LL.B, Advocate and Lecturer in the History of Scots Law in the University of Glasgow. Volume V. 1957.

17 BARON DAVID HUME'S LECTURES, 1786–1822 edited and annotated by G Campbell H Paton, MA, LL.B, Advocate and Lecturer in the History of Scots Law in the University of Glasgow, Volume IV. 1955.

16 SELECTED JUSTICIARY CASES, 1624–1650 edited and annotated by Stair A Gillon, BA, LL.B, Advocate. 1953.

15 BARON DAVID HUME'S LECTURES, 1786–1922 edited and annotated by G Campbell H Paton, MA, LL.D, Advocate and Lecturer in the History of Scots Law in the University of Glasgow. Volume III. 1952.

14 ACTA DOMINORUM CONCILII ET SESSIONIS, 1532–1533 edited by Ian H Shearer, MA, LL.B, Advocate. 1951.

13 BARON DAVID HUME'S LECTURES, 1786–1822 edited and annotated by G Campbell H Paton, M.A., LL.B., Solicitor. Volume II. 1949.

12 THE JUSTICIARY RECORDS OF ARGYLL AND THE ISLES, 1664–1705 transcribed and edited, with an Introduction by John Cameron MA, LL.D, Ph.D. 1949.

11 REGIAM MAJESTATEM AND QUONIAM ATTACHIAMENTA, based on the text of Sir John Skene edited and translated with Introduction and Notes by The Right Honourable Lord Cooper, LL.D. 1947.

10 THE REGISTER OF BRIEVES, 1286–1386, as contained in the Ayr MS, the Bute MS and the Quoniam Attachiamenta edited by The Rt Hon Lord Cooper, LL.D, Lord Justice-Clerk. THOMAS THOMSON'S MEMORIAL ON OLD EXTENT edited by J D Mackie, CBE, MC, MA, Professor of Scottish History and Literature in the University of Glasgow. 1946.

9 ST ANDREWS FORMULARE, 1514–1546 Edited by Gordon Donaldson, MA, Ph.D, with Prefatory Note by David Baird Smith, CBE, LL.D. Vol II. 1944.

8 ACTA DOMINORUM CONCILII, 26 March 1501 – 17 January 1502–1503, Transcribed by J A Crawford, MA, LL.B, Advocate. Edited with an Introduction by The Right Honourable James Avon Clyde, LL.D., formerly

Lord Justice-General of Scotland and Lord President of the Court of Session. 1943.

7 ST ANDREWS FORMULARE, 1514–1546. Text transcribed and edited by Gordon Donaldson, MA, Ph.D and C Macrae, MA, D.Phil. Vol I. 1942.

6 LORD HERMAND'S CONSISTORIAL DECISIONS, 1684–1777 edited by F P Walton, KC (Quebec), LL.D, Honourable Fellow, Lincoln College, Oxford, formerly Director, Royal School of Law, Cairo with biographical sketch of Lord Hermand by James Fergusson. With portrait. 1940.

5 BARON DAVID HUME'S LECTURES, 1786–1822, edited and annotated by G Campbell H Paton, MA, LL.B, Solicitor and Assistant to Professor of Law in the University of Glasgow. Volume I with portrait.

4 HOPE'S MAJOR PRACTICKS, 1608–1633 edited by The Right Honourable James Avon Clyde, LL.D, formerly Lord Justice-General of Scotland and Lord President of the Court of Session. Volume II. 1938

3 HOPE'S MAJOR PRACTICKS, 1608–1633 edited by The Right Honourable James Avon Clyde, LL.D., formerly Lord Justice-General of Scotland and Lord President of the Court of Session. Volume I with portrait. 1937.

2 ACTA CURIAE ADMIRALLATUS SCOTIAE, 6 September 1557 – 11 March 1561–1562. Edited by Thomas Callendar Wade, MA, LL.B, Solicitor, Falkirk. 1937.

1a An Index to Volume No. 1, compiled by James Cowie Brown, MA, LL.B, Ph.D. 1939.

1 AN INTRODUCTORY SURVEY OF THE SOURCES AND LITERATURE OF SCOTS LAW. By various authors, with an introduction by The Right Honourable Lord Macmillan, PC, LL.D, Lord of Appeal in Ordinary. 1936.

SUPPLEMENTARY SERIES

Sup Vol 3 GUIDE TO THE NATIONAL ARCHIVES OF SCOTLAND, Scottish Record Office, Joint Publication with The Stair Society. 1996.

Sup Vol 2 THE CIVIL LAW TRADITION IN SCOTLAND edited by Robin Evans-Jones. 1995.

Sup Vol 1 THE COLLEGE OF JUSTICE. Essays by R K Hannay. Introduction by Hector L MacQueen. 1991.

JOINT PUBLICATION WITH THE SALTIRE SOCIETY

Saltire Society THE SCOTTISH LEGAL TRADITION (New Enlarged Edition) by Michael C Meston, W David H Sellar and Lord Cooper. Foreword by Lord Mackay of Clashfern. 1991.